Refuge in the Land of Liberty

Return to the Land of Liberty

# Refuge in the Land of Liberty

**France and its Refugees, from the Revolution to the End of Asylum, 1787–1939**

Greg Burgess

First published 2008 by
PALGRAVE MACMILLAN
Houndmills, Basingstoke, Hampshire RG21 6XS and
175 Fifth Avenue, New York, N.Y. 10010
Companies and representatives throughout the world

PALGRAVE MACMILLAN is the global academic imprint of the Palgrave
Macmillan division of St. Martin's Press, LLC and of Palgrave Macmillan Ltd.
Macmillan® is a registered trademark in the United States, United Kingdom
and other countries. Palgrave is a registered trademark in the European
Union and other countries.

ISBN-13: 978–0–230–50775–3   hardback
ISBN-10: 0–230–50775–1   hardback

This book is printed on paper suitable for recycling and made from fully
managed and sustained forest sources. Logging, pulping and manufacturing
processes are expected to conform to the environmental regulations of the
country of origin.

A catalogue record for this book is available from the British Library.

Library of Congress Cataloging-in-Publication Data

Burgess, Greg, 1957–
    Refuge in the land of liberty: France and its refugees, from the
    Revolution to the end of asylum, 1787–1939/Greg Burgess.
        p. cm.
    Includes bibliographical references and index.
    ISBN 0-230-50775-1 (alk. paper)
    1. Refugees—France—History. 2. Political refugees—France—History.
    3. Asylum, Right of—France—History. I. Title.

JV7982.B87 2008
305.9'06914094409034—dc22                                    2007048954

10   9   8   7   6   5   4   3   2   1
17   16   15   14   13   12   11   10   09   08

Printed and bound in Great Britain by
CPI Antony Rowe, Chippenham and Eastbourne

# Contents

France, departments and prefectures, after the First World War, showing neighbouring provinces

*Note*: The two Savoy departments (Savoie and Haute-Savoie) and the Alpes-Maritimes were incorporated into France in 1860. The two Alsace departments (Bas-Rhin and Haut-Rhin) and the Lorraine department (Moselle) were German possessions between 1871 and 1918.

Un jour, à son tour, pris par le piège des choses,
Tremblant du résultat dont il construit les causes,
Il fuira, demandant un asile, un appui,
Un abri. « Non! diront ses amis d'aujourd'hui,
Non! Va-t'en!–C'est pourquoi je tiens ma porte ouverte. »
Victor Hugo, *L'Année terrible*, XVI, 'juin 1871'

# Introduction

# Refugees and Asylum

Enlightenment jurisprudence described the natural right of an individual to find refuge in a foreign state, and the obligation of that state to grant refuge. In 1646, Hugo Grotius wrote: 'A permanent residence ought not be denied to foreigners who, expelled from their homes, are seeking a refuge'.[1] In 1758, Emmanuel de Vattel, declared this a part of natural law:

> Banishment and exile do not take away from a man his human personality, nor consequently his right to live somewhere or other. He holds this right from nature, or rather from the Author of nature, who has intended the earth to be man's dwelling-place.[2]

Christian Wolff followed Vattel's teaching in his 1764 treatise on the laws of nations:

> By nature the right belongs to an exile to dwell anywhere in the world. For exiles do not cease to be men because they are driven into exile ... Therefore, since by nature all things are common ... by nature the right belongs to an exile to live anywhere in the world.[3]

Two principles persist to this day. One is that refugees do not cease to have rights when uprooted or banished from their place of origin. Indeed, the highest right would seem to take precedence: that one's human rights are recognised and respected. The other is that a state provides asylum for uprooted refugees, in recognition of their rights.

These are high ideals indeed, and they have come under enormous stress in recent times because they challenge principles of state sovereignty. A state makes laws and exercises power over its territory and its people, and no foreigner is entitled to reside in its territory unless authorised. This gives rise to two opposing views of asylum: a refugee-centred notion, which recognises a refugees' right of asylum, and a state-centred notion, by which the state determines to whom asylum is granted.[4]

1

Today, refugees are a major challenge for European states and the Western world. 'The wish to bar the door is strong', Jeremy Harding wrote of Europe's responses to refugees in the year 2000.[5] With the end of the cold war, former post-Second World War certainties evaporated. A geographical division of wealth replaced the ideological divide that had separated Europe until 1990. The states of the European Union no longer seemed willing to provide sanctuary to those who sought it. And things have not improved since. Potential immigrants and potential refugees face ever-tightening restrictions on entry, and therefore take even more desperate measures to try to penetrate closed borders.

International refugee law attempts to mediate the tensions between refugee-centred asylum and state-centred asylum. It seeks to define and impose criteria to identify refugee rights and spell out state obligations. But because states and not individuals are the objects of international law, it serves state concerns over the control of refugee movements. It also disguises a central tension. The need to define principles and to impose objective criteria derives from the abstraction and vagueness of the principles that underlie refugee protection, yet this very vagueness refuses definition. The right of a refugee to asylum is an abstraction of the principles of refugee protection. Yet international refugee law might indeed even react against the possibility that the principles of asylum signify abstract values, that they might offer some undetermined form of 'protecting power', as Atle Grahl-Madsen has aptly described the values inherent in asylum, that overshadow a state's jurisdiction.[6]

Before developments in international law during the second half of the twentieth century introduced moderating elements in the admission and protection of refugees, asylum was a relationship between the refugee and the state, moderated at the state's discretion. Asylum was defined and redefined by responses to various refugee movements and the contingent circumstances that constrained the state's capacity to act. The protection offered, the form it took, and the recognised rights of refugees – in short, the practice of asylum – were shaped by social, cultural, political, and economic factors. But asylum was also defined by principles. The word itself was attributed values that placed certain rights in the person of the refugee and imposed certain obligations on the protecting state. This right of asylum for refugees often conflicted with what the sovereign state was prepared to concede.

This conflict is the subject of this book. It examines how the refugees' right of asylum and the concerns of the sovereign state came together and diverged, and how the notion of asylum, in both principle and practice, changed in response to distinct waves of refugees over the course of the nineteenth and early twentieth centuries.

It concerns the refugee in the history of France since the great revolution of 1789. The revolution brought Enlightenment principles of natural rights into state governance, and declared them as the rights of man in August 1789. Among these was the right to resist oppression, from which France assumed an obligation to protect the defenders of liberty from their oppressors. The admission of refugees and their asylum in France was therefore one legacy of the revolution to which subsequent regimes were beholden. The French experience nevertheless shows that this legacy was reinterpreted under different political and social conditions. Asylum itself, the state's obligations, and the rights of refugees, were therefore reinterpreted as many and various refugee groups imposed an obligation that new regimes faced up to reluctantly.[7]

Although international refugee law holds to the state-centred conception of asylum, the notion of the right of asylum as a human right of refugees has continued to shape refugee discourses. It interposes some sense of a 'protecting power' between the state and the refugee. Historically, the notion was argued whenever there were demands for refugee protection. It informed the principles underpinning the relationship of refugees with their protecting state: the respect for the individual's human dignity; recognition of certain civil rights that followed the grant of asylum, to residence, welfare, and work; and protection from the sources of a refugee's oppression or persecution, by refusing extradition or forced repatriation.

The relationship between the refugee and the state was therefore prone to many influences. Refugees imposed a burden, sometimes a heavy one, and therefore the state had to properly balance issues of resource distribution, internal order, and national security. The nature and the background of different refugee groups often evoked different responses: sympathy for some was often witnessed at the same time as antipathy to others. International political circumstances and popular sentiments at home also shaped responses.

The purpose of this book therefore is to study how the views of asylum changed over time. What factors shaped asylum in both its principle and practice? What were the changing meanings ascribed to it and how were these argued and justified? What impact did they have on the state? And on the refugees themselves? This is therefore as much a history of France since the 1789 revolution, as it is a history of the refugees who found asylum there.

It is important not to be led astray by the understanding we have today of the terms 'refugee' and 'asylum', which are rooted in doctrines of human rights, humanitarian law, and legal discourses. They must instead be placed within their historical contexts. These terms were largely unfixed, and acquired their meanings as debates shifted over time and through different historical moments.

Other countries, notably the United States and Great Britain, can make claims to being a 'land of liberty' with their long histories of free migration and their liberal reception of refugees. France has a unique historical tradition as the *pays de la liberté*, however. It has claimed itself to be the *terre d'asile*, the land of asylum for those in flight from oppression. Its geographical position has made it a destination for those fleeing conflict or repression in eastern, central and southern Europe, and in more recent times from the Middle East and North and West Africa.[8] The revolution and the Napoleonic Empire took France's principles of the rights of man and resistance to oppression into the monarchies of Europe, and won to its side many friends of liberty who were exposed to reprisals when autocracy was restored in 1815. These principles lay dormant, erupting again in the national and social revolutions of 1830 and 1848. France was again the natural asylum for defeated revolutionary exiles.[9] The enduring legacy of these revolutionary principles, found in the persistence in memory of the phrase 'the right of asylum' (*le droit d'asile*) is therefore a historical problem. Did the meaning of the phrase remain constant as the principles of asylum were reformulated in response to changing circumstances? Why was it used and why was it important?

The admission of refugees after each major rupture in European affairs profoundly influenced political debate in France. Policy responses often conflicted with the principles ascribed to asylum and France's sense of its responsibilities for refugee protection. As a result, there is such a rich abundance of sources that respond to and question France's protection obligations and the direction of policy, and, indeed, illustrate the experience of refugees that is not replicated in the United States and Great Britain, where refugees were subsumed within the long historical streams of free migration. These issues largely passed undocumented there until the early twentieth century, when immigration restrictions were introduced.

Histories of refugees in France are most frequently retold in the histories of immigration and migrant communities. Forced and unforced migrations merge in stories of the settlement of foreigners and their place within French communities. The particular nature of the refugee experience is a source of a national consciousness among the different national communities, whose greater self-consciousness was stirred by the remembering of immigration history around the time of the bicentenary of the revolution in 1989. This was the time when historians themselves recovered this largely forgotten past.[10] As a consequence, a discrete history of refugees comes up against the broader issues of migration, the nation, and the alienation of the foreigner.[11]

A history of asylum is also a history of France's responses to those who went into exile there. The temptation of exploring the lives in exile of the various refugee communities who found asylum in France is very strong indeed, but there are infuriatingly too few glimpses in the archival and documentary sources into their daily lives, their encounters with their protecting state and with the French people whose communities they shared. When we find these glimpses, the picture is much clearer and adds much to our understanding of refugees and asylum. But this work is not intended to be a history of the national groups who have made up France's large refugee communities. A number of national groups nevertheless had a distinct impact on French responses, and therefore played a significant role in shaping policy and practice. The national groups discussed in this book therefore are those who best illustrate how the principles and practices of asylum were defined and revised.

The book is divided into four parts, which trace the important transitions in the history of refugees and asylum. The first part covers the period from the liberal revolutions of the late-eighteenth century to the Restoration. It concerns the transition of asylum from monarchy to revolutionary politics, and stabilisation during the Restoration. The second part examines changes during the July Monarchy, when France faced large numbers of exiles from nationalist revolutions across Europe while asserting a neutral position in international affairs and a conservative political order at home. The third part, from the Second Republic to the First World War is quite distinct from the other parts. It traces the shifting currents of asylum, the changing nature of refugees, and the growing question of immigration for the French nation during a period of stabilisation, and the consolidation of republican institutions – noting, of course, the rupture of the Second Empire and the great traumas of the Franco-Prussian War and the Paris Commune. Refugees drift into the background, either converging with the industrial migrations of the late-nineteenth century, or dwelling in the shadows among anarchist terrorists or communist revolutionaries. There were consequently important conceptual shifts as the nation, nationality, the foreigner, and the nature of the political 'crime', were more precisely defined. The fourth part concerns the most problematic period, refugees in interwar France to the outbreak of the Second World War. The social, political, and economic stress of these years had the most profound impact on what the French people were prepared to tolerate and what their government would permit.

Parts of chapter 9 were first published as 'France and the German Refugee Crisis of 1933', in *French History*, 16, no. 2 (2002): 203–29. Financial assistance from the Australian Academy of the Humanities allowed me to complete my archival research in France and I am grateful for its support.

I owe a great deal to Peter McPhee of the University of Melbourne for his support and encouragement from the moment I first raised this topic with him. My thanks also to Chips Sowerwine and Steven Welch of the Department of History at the University of Melbourne for nurturing my research since my first tentative questions about the history of France and of Europe's refugees. The work presented here is the culmination of studies long encouraged by them both. This work would not have been possible without having to hand the tremendous research collection on French history at the Baillieu Library of the University of Melbourne. I thank Jean-Luc Mayard,

Mike Rapport, John Merriman, and Anna Maria Rao for their advice and suggestions as this work progressed. Barrie Rose, Adrian Jones, and Vesna Drapac, and my former colleagues at the University of Melbourne and the University of Tasmania, have provided friendship, support, and good counsel throughout, for which I am extremely thankful.

# Part I  Asylum and the French Revolution

Even beyond France the first anniversary of the fall of the Bastille was a moment of joyous celebration. Of the 18 toasts drunk by some 652 'Friends of Liberty' gathered at the Crown and Anchor in London on 14 July 1790, the first were to the 'majesty' of the French people, its nation, law and king, 'the glorious French revolution', the 'triumph of liberty', and the 'trophies' of the ruins of the Bastille, a stone of which was displayed before them. They also swore the very oath that day sworn at the Federation Festival on the Champs de Mars in Paris by the representatives of the French people. Then they drank more toasts: to the equal enjoyment of the liberty of conscience for all humanity, and to the 'sacred rights of man' and the countries that defend them. Then they vowed that the hearts of Englishmen would never let liberty be defeated.[1]

In Amsterdam, Dutch Patriots had perhaps more reason than most to rejoice at France's resistance to oppression and its Declaration of the Rights of Man. These democratic republicans had been driven underground since the Prussian invasion of the United Provinces of the Netherlands in 1787 to put down their rebellion and secure the rule of the Stadtholder Prince William V of Orange. Unlike the English 'Friends of Liberty', they could not celebrate so openly and joyously, but they still anticipated the Federation Festival in Paris as a great spectacle that would enliven the hopes of all peoples and be a great affront to liberty's enemies. So they gathered secretly in the countryside with a small number of Frenchmen, and swore, 'on the same day, at the same hour, midday, 14 July, under the same sky', their love of freedom and their admiration for the free constitution proclaimed in France.[2]

The subjects of other monarchies therefore claimed the rights of man as their own. One of the many slogans displayed on the grand confederation arch in Paris, between the Seine River and the Champs de Mars, was theirs: 'the rights of many have been misunderstood over the centuries; they have been reclaimed for all humanity'.[3]

While sympathetic observers abroad imagined the meanings the festival had for them, many of the oppressed subjects of Europe who had turned to France to find freedom in exile witnessed the event. They claimed a role in the festival for themselves when Jean-Baptiste Cloots, a Prussian subject from the Rhineland, led a delegation of foreigners to the National Assembly on 19 June 1790 to ask that they might serve as the representatives of humanity. 'This is not only a French festival', he declared, 'it is also a festival for humankind. The trumpet that sounds the revolution of one great people resounds in the four corners of earth'. If they had a central place on the Champs de Mars, he told the Assembly, they would send a message to the oppressed elsewhere that sovereignty resides in all people.[4]

A mix of nationalities such as Cloots' delegation—men from Avignon, Liège, Savoy, Brabant, Genoa, Sicily, Poland, England, Prussia, Holland, Austria, Geneva, and Turkey—who had come to the Assembly in their national dress, had not been seen before. They were greeted with mockery, insensitivity, incomprehension, but also sheer wonder.[5] Counter-revolutionary historians later disparaged their reception, attributing it partly to the ine- briation of the deputies and partly to misplaced pride in their achievements (the delegation was received on a Saturday evening in the session that immediately followed the banning of the nobility).[6] Some deputies wondered if they could be trusted. These 'self-declared ambassadors', one complained, were an affront to French liberty and the king; they were 'ambassadors of tyrants' and a 'mob of Europeans' (*la racaille de l'Europe*).[7] Later, historians such as Jules Michelet held them in awe for their demeanour and grandeur. One is left to wonder how and to what extent their declarations of fidelity to the French people moved the Assembly.[8]

The National Assembly certainly saw no harm in granting Cloots' request, and believed that there might be some value in the propaganda of sharing the festival with foreigners sympathetic to France's liberty. The request was therefore approved on condition that they return to their homelands after- wards to tell their compatriots what they witnessed.[9] At this moment, Georges Lefebvre observes, the National Assembly recognised the universal appeal of the revolution. Foreigners had assumed the role of publicists, although the Assembly was not yet sure precisely what part they could play.[10]

Cloots was allowed to set up a marquee on the Champs de Mars from which as many as 1000 foreigners could witness the Festival.[11] But they do not seem to have been noticed. Cloots himself described the scene with typical self-promotion: 'the triumphal arc, the bridge across the river, the Romanesque palace', and himself 'at the head of the foreigners, at the tribune of the palace, acting as ambassador for humankind [as] the ministers of tyrants looked at us with a jealous, uneasy eye.'[12] But none of the lengthy accounts of the festival in the many Parisian journals mentions them.

Devised by General Lafayette as a demonstration of the confederation of the former provinces into a united nation under a new constitution, the

Federation Festival brought to Paris delegates of the National Guards from the 83 new administrative departments. It would indeed be surprising that this festival of the nation should be recalled for the part a small group of foreigners played in it.[13] They were undistinguished among the thousands of confederates and the 300,000 Parisian spectators. Yet the promise of the universal significance of the revolution and its Declaration of the Rights of Man also turned the festival into a highly symbolic event that elevated it above its national purpose.[14] The foreigners in Paris at this time, of whom Cloots was the most articulate, had claimed this universal significance for themselves. Political refugees who had fled repression for the pursuit of liberty in their own lands, from the Swiss Cantons of Berne, Fribourg and Geneva, and from the United Provinces of the Netherlands, placed their political aspirations alongside the French revolutionaries. The French had won their liberty, while they had been defeated in their own struggles for it. They had come to France for the protection it offered and found themselves caught up in revolutionary upheaval. Other refugee groups soon joined them during the course of 1790, from the prince-bishopric of Liège and from the short-lived republic in Belgium. They also found protection in France and the opportunity to express their own revolutionary ideals.[15] Cloots' delegation of 19 June 1790 was the first notable intervention of foreigners in revolution-ary politics; others followed, as foreigners joined the political clubs and were radicalised through the shifting currents of the revolution. Revolutionary politics shaped their political aspirations, but above all the refugees engaged in revolution to further their ambitions of national liberation.

Historians often overlook the particular characteristics of the political refugees and their distinct place among foreigners drawn to the excitement and the hopes unleashed by the French Revolution. Histories of refugees consequently merge into the histories of foreigners. Moreover, recent impor-tant studies of nationality and citizenship in revolutionary France, which have assessed the development of principles of inclusion into nationhood and, along with them, divisive tendencies of exclusion and the alienation of those of distinct nationalities, reveal that the integrative force of the revo-lutionary project came at the cost of the universal promise so alluring for foreign revolutionaries. These histories therefore demonstrate that there were two possible ways of viewing foreigners: as an enemy or potential enemy, or as friends of France and adherents to the revolution. But the point of division between the two was seldom clear.[16]

Georges Lefebvre certainly identifies the distinct place of political refugees within the revolution. They were distinguished, he writes, by the bitterness of exile and their desire for revenge against the ruling powers in their home-lands, which made them useful publicists for the French revolutionary cause.[17] Indeed, Lefebvre does not go far enough. Their bitterness in exile and desire for revenge also made them eager participants in revolutionary politics, a role that Jacques Godechot does not ascribe to them until war took the revolution into their homelands.[18] They bound their aspirations to France from the earliest times, becoming much more than the publicists Lefebvre describes. They were willing actors in a European revolutionary project, and the French willingly nurtured their aspirations. As a consequence, political refugees had a distinct relationship with France.

Yet, like other foreigners, the political refugees walked a very narrow path between the revolution's national objectives and its universal promises: they could be perceived as enemies as they were by origin subject of the European monarchies prepared to put down the revolution by force. Foreigners attracted to France during the cosmopolitan fervour of the revolution's early years were caught up in its shifting political currents; they were victims of the failure of the revolution to realise its ideological promise as its gradual radicalisation necessitated exclusive conceptions of nationality and citizenship for reasons of internal security and the fight against counter-revolution.[19] Foreigners, Michael Rapport shows, were perceived either as remnants of the old regime (soldiers in the King's service, clergy, financiers to the court, and so on) or as potential enemy subjects. In both cases they were highly suspect and forced to negotiate each turn of events as best they could so as not to lose favour in the eyes of the new regime.[20] Refugees from liberal revolutions abroad were better able to ride these shifting currents and withstand anti-foreign reactions during the darkest days of the Republic, the Terror, and the war. The political refugees embodied the true universality of the rights of man, but they also embodied the xenophobic limits of revolution as the Jacobin republic took defensive and paranoid turns against the threat of its enemies.

Central to this distinction between foreigners generally and the specific place of refugees was the doctrine of asylum. It inferred a distinct relationship between the refugees and the state. But, as the course of the revolution shifted, so did French responses to the refugees and their expectations of them. How then was asylum formulated, and how did it change over the course of the revolution, from monarchy to Republic?

Although article 120 of the 1793 constitution, by which the 'French people offered asylum to those banished for the cause of liberty', has defined asylum in historical memory as a republican doctrine and a special legacy of the revolution, it is also cited as the limit of revolutionary idealism. Even before the people voted on it, the revolution had moved in a new direction, becoming a war for survival against foreign enemies and terror against enemies within.[21] Its promise of asylum, Gérard Noiriel argues, emphasised the 'phantasmagorical' character of high revolutionary ideals of cosmopolitanism and universal liberty, which the sudden shifts of revolutionary politics could not sustain.[22]

The shifting meaning of asylum during the revolutionary years shows, to the contrary, that despite coming under severe stress asylum nevertheless preserved some of these high revolutionary ideals by holding firmly to its protecting principles. It sustained these into the Restoration, when asylum was again reformulated in entirely new ways.

# 1
# Exiles and Patriots

The Dutch Patriots who had taken refuge in northern France in 1787 experienced the most dramatic shifts in asylum. Originally received and assisted by the monarchy, the terms of their asylum were renegotiated under the revolutionary government of the National Assembly. At the same time, the revolution exposed serious fractures among the Dutch, rupturing relations between their elites, and breaking the bonds of trust and deference to their protector, Louis XVI.

From the start an unstable compound of old Dutch aristocratic and new popular elements, as Robert Palmer recounts, the Dutch Patriot movement was aroused by revolutionary insurgencies in America and Ireland. The American War of Independence against the British above all gave the lead to the more democratically minded Dutch. They opposed the House of Orange's deference to British economic and naval power and the Stadtholder, William V's, support for the British against the American revolutionaries. Patriot opinion turned against Orangist power in the provincial assemblies, above all in Amsterdam and Utrecht. The more radical democrats called for the Patriots to arm themselves and rebel as the Americans had. They therefore took up arms and organised themselves into Free Corps; they put on uniforms and drilled, preparing for conflict. Mobilisation thus strengthened the democratic wing of the Patriot movement, drawing to it the educated, professionals, and religious minorities. The democrats asserted liberty as an inalienable right of all citizens, and, in order to secure their liberty, the citizens had to strike at their system of government and replace it with a republican commonwealth, with the stadtholder subordinate to the representatives of the people. France supported their anti-British position, backed the Patriots against William V, and financed arms for the Free Corps. Conflict broke out in 1787 when William turned to Britain to secure his position. William's wife won the support of her brother, the King of Prussia. The Duke of Brunswick led 20,000 troops into Utrecht and Amsterdam, and the Free Corps and citizen-soldiers melted away, scarcely firing a shot in resistance.[1]

11

Theirs was no organised exodus from the Netherlands, writes Simon Schama. They fled across the nearest frontier, into Germany and Belgium, and then into northern France. The Patriots led a popular movement into exile, a cross-section of Dutch bourgeois society: the Patriot leaders, to be sure, and the rank-and-file Patriots, Free Corps offices, predicants, journalists, university students, shopkeepers, and 'renegade aristocrats'. It was a migration also of families. Some 40,000 left the United Provinces; of them about 5000 are thought to have arrived in northern France. The insurrection's leaders first formed themselves into an Assembly of Patriots in Bruxelles to give the emigration a semblance of authority and order, and to promote and defend Patriot interests to Louis XVI.[2] It was also an attempt to reform themselves into something akin to their former provincial assemblies so as to maintain their social order and political structures.[3] A commission of the assembly determined who among the Dutch exiles was truly a Patriot for having stood against William V and the Prussians, and therefore who was entitled to the financial aid that Louis XVI had promised when they had settled in northern France. The commission registered their social status or military rank, noted their reasons for emigration, and even commented on their political character; this information was then used by the French to determine the amount of assistance to be paid and how it would be distributed. The commission, in short, decided which individuals would receive French aid, leaving room therefore for factional disputes among pretenders to leadership and over the legitimacy of the authority they claimed for themselves.

By March 1788, the Dutch exiles had been dispersed into depots (*dépôts*) in the townships of St. Omer, Gravelines, Dunkerque, and Béthune. These were communities where refugees lived among the local population, but were distinguished as depots because of the special arrangements for their accommodation. They were placed in barracks, hotels, and other public buildings under the supervision of the regional commissaire, and placed under special police orders. Aid, called variously *secours* (an initial act-of-grace payment) and *subsides* (regular and on-going financial allowances), totalling 60,000 livres a year, was distributed among them to meet their daily living expenses.[4] Military officers, numbering 134 individuals, were absorbed into the King's army at a further cost of 152,000 livres.[5]

The records of the aid and assistance they received give only a narrow view of their exile; they suggest at best a financial relationship between them and their French hosts, based on dependence and welfare. The king alone, acting through his ministers and officials, determined who was entitled to asylum and aid to meet their subsistence needs.[6] Their asylum was therefore gained in deference to the monarch, who bestowed benefits directly onto them. The administration of the depots was put in the charge of the district commissaire, Collignon (no first name is noted in the public welfare records), who was responsible for the distribution of aid, order, and policing. For the refugees, therefore, Collignon had the most important influence on their asylum, as he was responsible for maintaining the refugee registers and therefore determining who would receive aid.

A more complete picture of their exile is found in the private archives of the Patriot journalist Dumont-Pigalle, an associate of Johan Valckenaer, one of the competing leadership aspirants.[7] This remarkable collection of papers shows how the Patriots' asylum was organised and administered, and how the community itself responded to the conditions of exile. Most revealing are the factional rivalries and the consequences this had for the Patriots' relationship with the French monarch.

Collignon, commissaire of the refugee depots, had direct control over the refugees' daily lives and was responsible for maintaining order and peace in the depots. To this end he set down police orders on their behaviour and conduct. There were two classes of refugees in these depots, those sheltered in military barracks or encamped in tents, and those lodged in boarding houses. Both caused problems of discipline and sanitation. Gathered into confined spaces among the French townsfolk, their good conduct was imperative; fines or the loss of their allowances were punishments for disruptive behaviour. Good conduct included good sanitary habits. One police order authorised by Collignon forbade the dumping of excrement in public places, and another compelled the surrender of dogs so they would not foul the barracks. Other orders show a general distrust of their behaviour. Noisy gatherings were banned; a 10:30 p.m. curfew was imposed, with fines for singing or dancing at a later hour. Entry to the room of another after curfew was prohibited; so too was remaining overnight in another's room. Any Dutch refugee arriving from another town had to produce a Certificate of Good Conduct and Habits (*certificat de bonne vie et mœurs*), signed by a magistrate before departure, in order to secure public lodgings.

These orders were to ensure that the Dutch lived well and harmoniously with each other, and maintained good relations with the French residents of the depot townships. They also reveal the unwelcome tendency of the Dutch to engage in acts of retribution against their compatriots and to enforce their own code of justice. Any complaints that the refugees might have, the police orders insisted, were to be heard by the French authorities: 'no refugee' they stated, 'has the right to render justice himself'. The orders imposed on them a regime that left no illusions that French law did not apply to them, and that they would be deprived of the benefits of their asylum if they failed to recognise this.[8]

These orders regulated their daily lives. The king himself decreed the terms of their asylum. *Secours* and *subsides* were intended only for those refugees genuinely in need of financial assistance; even so, the refugees had to demonstrate by their contribution to the kingdom, through service, industry, or labour, that they were truly worthy of the king's beneficence. They were therefore all expected to pursue useful occupations. The 'superior class' of capitalists, bourgeoisie, and military officers were encouraged to enter industry, commerce, or the king's service. This was also the class of the 'the most distinguished and most revolutionary' of the Dutch, the Patriot leaders, who had been awarded state pensions on agreement between the finance and foreign ministries, quite distinct from the king's *subsides*.[9] Artisans and the lower-status workers (*ouvriers et gens d'un état inférieur*) were encouraged to establish businesses if so skilled or otherwise to work at a craft, in agriculture, as seamen or soldiers, or at whatever else they could find. All were required to declare to the commissaire Collignon what enterprises, occupations, or labour they intended to pursue; those who did not were struck off the refugee registers.[10] Certain reservations were again expressed about Dutch behaviour. Their industry was welcomed, but drunkardness and laziness, and the disorders these created, marred their public reputation. Bankrupts were refused aid, suggesting that some had run up debts without any means or intention of repaying. Calumnies against and injuries to their compatriots were also punished.

In order to enforce the king's intentions, a census was made of all Dutch refugees leasing rooms or houses in the many towns across northern France in which they resided—St. Omer, Gravelines, Dunkerque, to be sure, but also the smaller towns of Bergues, Cassel, Beaubourg, and places thereabouts.[11] A new register of the Dutch refugees was subsequently compiled to review the distribution of aid. These were more than the lists of names, status or rank, and reasons for emigration that were compiled previously. They were personal testaments made by individual refugees themselves, which had two purposes. They declared, of course, identity, rank, or social position before exile, and therefore supported their claims for financial aid, but they were also personal petitions to the king requesting his aid. Moreover, they could be personal pleas for additional assistance, such as for passports or a special grant to meet the cost of travel within France or of repatriation. One Dutchman 'of the superior class', M. van Nievett, although 'honoured to give his thanks for the king's beneficence' of 110 livres a month, was nevertheless in need, and petitioned the king himself for a passport and an advance of four months' *subsides* to meet his travel expenses so that he could return to the Netherlands.[12]

Petitions such as this formed the essential character of asylum under the monarchy. As asylum was a personal relationship between the king and the refugee, the refugee petitioned for his aid and in so doing submitted to his will. Deference to the king's grace by service, industry, or labour, therefore determined the refugee's status in exile. The king's assistance was repaid in one notable example by the establishment of Dutch fisheries in Gravelines and Dunkerque.[13] Ordinarily, useful activity and good conduct sufficed as deference; the refugees benefited in turn from the quiet enjoyment of their asylum.

The numbers of the refugees, their geographical dispersion, and the administration of public funds allocated for their assistance, however, all worked against a direct relationship between the refugees and the king. There were distinct levels of intervention that troubled this relationship: the self-declared representatives of the Dutch refugee community, the ministers to whom they appealed, and the commissaire of the refugee depots. Collignon greatly antagonised the Dutch leaders as he stood between them and their people, and they came into conflict during 1789 over the compilation of these new registers, when accusations were made that his maladministration had caused genuine poverty among the refugees.

By this time, many new refugees had arrived from Bruxelles, but the public funds allocated for the provision of aid had not risen. The final day on which Dutch refugees would be allowed to enter the depots and receive aid was originally set down as 1 April 1788, but the steady rise in their numbers afterwards saw this extended to 1 January 1789. New admissions were paid provisional aid while awaiting inclusion on the new refugee lists, but as January 1789 passed, new aid allocations were not forthcoming. By then, some 2000 Dutch patriot refugees received French aid, amounting to total expenditure for the year, from the already strained national budget, of 829,000 livres.[14]

The date after which new admissions would not be accepted, 1 January 1789, seemed of no purpose other than to put a cap on expenditure for refugee assistance. It certainly did not stop the flow of new Dutch Patriot exiles into France. As new sentences of banishment and confiscation of property were passed on Patriots in Utrecht and Friesland, many more were forced to find refuge in Bruxelles. They were subsequently driven out of Bruxelles when the political and religious reforms of the Austrian emperor Joseph II produced a wave of religious hostility towards Protestants. So they joined their compatriots in northern France. In August 1789, they requested asylum and additional financial aid from the French government but no more was forthcoming.[15] The new registers worried many that the latest refugee arrivals would be left entirely without aid. Indeed, the new arrivals suffered from both sides, from the lack of French assistance, and from the unwillingness of their compatriots to help. The disruption of public administration caused by the events of 1789 also seems to have caused considerable fluctuations in the total monthly distribution and further anxieties among the Dutch about their immediate well-being. Aid distribution varied considerably, from 44,568 livres in February and 59,339 livres in June, to 23,942 livres in July and only 14,875 livres in September.[16]

These changes in fortune alienated a section of the Dutch refugees from the French monarchy. In an exchange of correspondence with government ministers during September and October, three of their number, Geelvinck, Gevers, and Huber, a separate faction from the recognised leadership group who claimed to act as elected representatives of an assembly of Dutch citizens resident in France, protested the inadequacies of aid and the inequities of its distribution. Through Necker, the Minister for Finance, they petitioned the king as 'a friend of justice and humanity, who, by his beneficence, would correct the misfortunes of their circumstances'.[17] They brought to the king's attention the insufficiency of the 829,000 livres that had been allocated for their aid and stressed the poverty that the inequities of its distribution had produced. Only by correcting these inequities, they pleaded, could he improve their circumstances. They offered their services in this task, as, they claimed, they could best identify those who no longer merited his aid, those who received more than they needed, and those who were left without as a consequence. But to do so they would need to have the government's refugee registers handed over to them.[18]

There is no response to this request on record. Dutch frustrations were less constrained in later correspondence. On 17 October, Huber charged that Collignon's maintenance of the register was the cause of their poverty, and declared that the assembly of Dutch refugees had no trust in him. Instead, the assembly was working to correct the errors of his mismanagement. He also blamed the king's ministers for poorly instructing Collignon in the merits of the claims of individuals to asylum and assistance. Huber most of all revealed the depth of frustration among the Dutch at their powerlessness to administer their own affairs, which prevented them from doing anything to improve their own welfare, and indeed prevented them from seeking retribution for the injustices of their compatriots against others. He denounced some of the Dutch for having misinformed Collignon as 'singularly occupied with their own exclusive advantage ... who, stripped of all human sentiment, would watch indifferently as their brothers perish in misery ... and take from them their last piece of bread'.[19]

Simon Schama relates this exchange of correspondence to the factional rivalries at the upper levels of the Dutch émigré community. More than personal animosity and historical vendetta, he writes, factions were divided over who should rightfully represent the exiles to the French monarch. The faction of Johan Valckenaer, who had settled in Paris and gained access to Necker and his government, vied with the faction of van Beijma, through whom aid for the Dutch was channelled, and whom the French government blamed for the financial maladministration.[20] Both believed they acted legitimately on behalf of their compatriots, but French recognition of one or the other as the rightful leader brought influence over the distribution of the king's aid, political representation at the court, and the command of the loyalty of the refugees themselves. Conflicts over how they should conduct themselves in exile, Schama continues, became more critical during 1789 as the revolution unfolded around them.[21] Many of the Dutch took the side of the revolutionaries, partly because of their own spirit of revolution, partly because of the grievance they still bore towards the king and his ministers for refusing to come to their aid during their insurrection of 1787.[22]

By the end of 1789, their factional rupture had opened serious divisions between the Dutch refugees and the French government. Bearing openly their grievance at France's failure to aid their failed rebellion, Dutch embitterment easily turned to impertinence, breaking the bond of trust and supplication to Louis XVI. This could only reshape the political alignments of the Dutch Patriots and their relations with the French government.

Whatever the ruptures within the Dutch Patriot community, the outcome was a severe rebuke from the king himself. These self-declared leaders of the Dutch Patriots in exile could not represent their people to their protector, nor did the king recognise their self-proclaimed assembly as a discrete political organisation authorised to act on behalf of their compatriots. The Dutch could not be considered as anything other than 'simple individuals, living in the Kingdom under the protection of [the king's] laws'. Louis' rebuke offers a clear declaration of the purpose of asylum under the monarchy and the terms on which it was extended. The refugees were accorded protection and financial assistance by 'the king's grace'. He could grant and withdraw both asylum and financial aid 'at his pleasure, and need not account for his decisions'.[23] Louis had extended them the benefits of his grace and he therefore expected in turn their respect for his wishes, compliance to the law, and submission to his will.

This proclamation of monarchical asylum was made in December 1789, at precisely the moment when it was most under challenge. Among the many shifts in power away from the crown over the course of that year was the power to hold exiles from other countries in deference to his acts of grace. Through his Controller-General of Finance, Lambert, Louis rebuked the Dutch for their insistence that they be handed the refugee registers so that they might take charge of the distribution of aid. This would have amounted to recognising their claims of political authority and the legitimacy of their acting as a representative body of the Dutch refugees. Asylum was accorded to individuals who could live freely in the realm under French law, not to a constituent group bound by their own laws and loyalties. If there were disputes and complaints, they could be made by individual petition, which would be examined and resolved by reason and justice.[24]

Dutch grievances were therefore compounded by this rebuke, and some were prepared to voice them more freely. One of Huber's colleagues, van Hoey, suspected the hand of the king's untrustworthy ministers—an insinuation against Valckenaer for his influence on Necker. He asked how could the king, 'so gentile, so just, so beneficent', be responsible for this rebuke? Van Hoey wrote stridently that the king owed the Dutch much more than asylum and assistance, since, by failing to come to their aid against the Prussians in 1787, he was responsible for their misfortunes. His ministers treated the Dutch instead as a 'group of beggars, to whom they throw a few crumbs of bread and call it charity'.[25]

Monarchical asylum consequently ceased with this breach between the Dutch, the king, and his ministers. Poverty and the imbalance of aid distribution persisted. In a gesture motivated either by exasperation at these examples of impertinence or, as is more likely, by the need to relieve the pressures within the depots that had built up with the most recent arrivals from Bruxelles, Lambert offered an advance of four months' allowance to pay the passage of any refugee who wished to return to the United Provinces or settle elsewhere in France.[26] The impact this had is uncertain. The Patriot movement itself turned away from the king and his court and towards the National Assembly to petition for Dutch interests. Deference was then made to the French nation and its 'august representatives'.[27]

## A revolutionary contract

As the French and their European sympathisers celebrated liberty from oppression during the Federation Festival in July 1790, troops of the Austrian empire entered the small prince-bishopric of Liège to put down its popular government. In need of an ally and protector, the Liégeois turned to France. On 18 September 1790, their representatives were invited before the National Assembly to plead for its assistance. They and the French were now united in the same struggle for liberty, the delegation told the deputies. Even the French could look upon their long tradition of liberty with admiration and sympathy; their shared aspirations for liberty gave their peoples a spiritual and political bond. How then could the representatives of the French suffer the terror under which the people of Liège now lived, the delegation asked; how could the French stand by while the people of Liège suffered the destruction of their towns and fields?[28] More pragmatically, there was an outstanding debt that that Liégeois now called in. The French kingdom still owed 1,500,000 livres from the purchase of arms during the Seven Years' War; under the new regime this had become a kind of contract struck between the peoples of Liège and France, through the proximity and similarities of their two revolutions.[29]

The third group of revolutionaries who found protection in France were from the short-lived Belgium Republic in the Austrian Netherlands. Emperor Joseph II had alienated the first and second estates in Bruxelles when his religious, administrative, and legal reforms stripped them of their autonomy and their privileges. An independent republic emerged briefly after their insurrection of 1789, but the competing interests of conservatives, whose intent was to preserve their privileges, and the increasingly assertive democratic reformers, fractured the estates.[30] The Belgian democrats, like the Liégeois, imagined their rebellion as another moment in the one democratic revolution of the late eighteenth century. Like the French, they were fighting for their sovereignty and reclaiming their rights from a despotic monarch; they too found a natural exile in revolutionary France.[31]

The revolts in Liège and Bruxelles had quite separate causes and consequences, but both proved Austria the enemy of liberty. The revolt in Liège, Philippe Raxhon writes, had its origins in profound structural changes in its key industries of coal and wool production and metallurgy, which affected all workers and artisans, one-third of whom were dependent on charity. Revolution in August 1789, Raxhon remarks, had more to do with the restoration of the democratic character of past institutions than their destruction as the first step towards renewal.[32] The revolution's popular roots made it especially radical. The Marquisat of Franchimont, with a large working population, provided the most radical political currents within the prince-bishopric and later in exile. The radical elements readily threw in their hand with the French revolutionaries, settling in Paris to participate more directly in the exhilaration of its political fervour.[33] Chronically factionalised, the Republic of Belgium had ceased to function as a viable state when Austrian troops entered Bruxelles on 24 November 1790.[34] Two distinct groups, united by their resistance to Austrian occupation but divided by their revolutionary objectives, went into exile. Traditionalists, the faction of H. van der Noot, who fought for the restoration of old regime traditions and privileges, fled north to Holland. The democrats, influenced by ideas of the French Enlightenment and pursuing popular sovereignty, fled into northern France, assembling around the faction of Jan-Frans Vonck in Douai and Lille.[35]

By the end of 1790, therefore, there were three important refugee groups in France. Each pursued separate objectives, but each cultivated individuals and factions within the National Assembly and sought out sympathisers in the vibrant political culture of this most cosmopolitan phase of the revolution. They turned to the French for support, and the French were eager to provide it. The refugees from Liège, a small province which had dared to stand against the might of imperial Austria, had become dependent on another great power to regain their freedom; they willingly placed their political aspirations in French hands, therefore.[36] For the time being, Belgian democrats were quiet in exile, and scarcely enter the documentary record. The French Revolution, however, had radicalised the Dutch. The atmosphere of fraternal goodwill, Simon Schama writes, had transformed these 'sad fugitives of abortive uprisings' into 'heroes of the new order of international liberty'.[37] Like the Liégeois, they presented themselves to the National Assembly to plead their case for assistance, and, by doing so, they renegotiated their asylum with the new regime.

But unlike the Liégeois, they did not present their case from the tribune of the Assembly. Instead, they prepared a long and detailed memorandum on the origins, history, and aspiration of the Dutch Patriot movement that placed their fortunes in the hands of the French. Presented on 19 November 1790, the Patriots claimed an equal role in the liberal revolutions of the late eighteenth century, and described their revolution as a precursor to the French Revolution. Like the Liégeois before them, the Dutch insisted that they and the French were also engaged in the one struggle for liberty.[38]

Three separate drafts of this memorandum are retained in the Dumont-Pigalle archive, which attest to the care taken with its wording and the impression that it would have on the deputies. It retold the history of the Patriot movement in a new language that assumed for itself France's revolutionary ideology. Each draft suggests different emphases, with inclusions and deletions, but they were consistent in their aim of recasting the Patriot movement as an insurrection to reclaim the universal rights of man. Prince William V of Orange had consequently proved himself at one with the imperial tyrants of Europe by turning to the Prussians to suppress the Dutch spirit of liberty. Because the Dutch and the French were engaged in a single quest for liberty, the Dutch people had a natural home in France. Moreover, the memorandum strenuously argued that the French owed them asylum in repayment for the king's betrayal in 1787. The network of alliances between France, the Netherlands, and Britain had stayed his hand, and still tied the hands of the National Assembly from intervening on their behalf for the restoration of their liberty.[39]

Although the language of the memorandum remade the Dutch Patriot movement as a precursor of the French Revolution, it had one very pragmatic objective: it was quite simply a petition to secure the continuation of financial aid into 1791. In this it was successful, persuading the National Assembly to assume the protection obligations that the king had thus far borne.[40] Despite the urgency of the financial crisis then confronting France, the Assembly agreed to maintain funding at the same level as prescribed for the previous year, a total of 829,000 livres.[41]

As the refugees identified themselves in revolutionary ideology, French revolutionaries found renewed purpose in the promise of asylum. France would stand firm against its enemies, the émigré princes and their alliance with foreign monarchies, the Marquis de Condorcet declared to the National Assembly in December 1791. France would meet them in war if that were what they chose; it would uphold the spirit of liberty against their tyranny. Asylum for their victims was a great expression of the spirit that they would defeat. 'The asylum that we open to foreigners will not be closed to the inhabitants of those countries the princes force to attack us', Condorcet declared; 'they will find a sure refuge among us ... No danger will let France forget that its soil belongs entirely to liberty, and that equality is a universal law'.[42]

As war loomed, such declarations set the ideological foundations on which it would be fought. At the same time, however, the laws that assured equality and liberty had to respond to the threats of France's enemies. Condorcet's declaration was made during a debate on the need for surveillance measures and restrictions on suspect foreigners.[43] Conditions were placed on liberty in order to protect its spirit. These were urgent and necessary, forced upon France against its will. 'France will take up arms with regret', Condorcet continued, 'but with ardour, for its security and its internal peace, and it will be gladly put down again when it has nothing more to fear'.[44]

After France's declaration of war in April 1792, security concerns brought into question the reliability of foreigners and political refugees. Contrary to Condorcet's proclamation of 'sure refuge', doubts fell on to the Austrian subjects from the Lowlands, and on to the Dutch Patriots, whose homelands were allied with Britain and Prussia. In September 1792, when the National Assembly's finance committee addressed the question of ongoing aid for the Dutch refugees, the impact of the 1790 Dutch Patriots' memorandum was clear. Their declaration of fidelity to revolutionary principles was viewed with approval, and the Assembly gladly assumed the role of their protectors and benefactors. The Dutch Patriots, the Assembly was told, had a right to asylum and the aid that came with it, which was their rightful due because of their attachment to France, their service to it, and the past promises France had made to them but failed to honour. It was a 'precious alliance France had contracted with the Dutch Republic ... which will not be empty today'.[45]

The finance committee gave these sentiments practical form, drafting legislation on the administration of refugees. It presented to the Assembly a decree on aid entitlements and its distribution in order to regulate expenditure on the Dutch refugees and prescribe their rights and entitlements while they lived on French soil. In a total of 69 articles, the decree prescribed all aspects of their legal status as beneficiaries of asylum, including the status of their wives and children; it specified at length on what grounds widows and children of deceased refugees could continue to receive financial allowances. The decree even went so far as to propose a central administrative bureau to administer the legislation. It codified the existing arrangements for the declarations of rank and status (which could be made in Dutch if the refugee could not understand French) and the means by which aid would be distributed across the depots and townships in the north where they resided.[46] The decree was deferred, however, when the Assembly rose in August 1792 to make way for the National Convention.

The Dutch Patriot emigration is best remembered for the leaders and their factions who frequented the political circles of Paris and forged relations with important ministers for their own ends.[47] The important question of aid and its distribution was an issue around which power relations and factional rivalries were played out. These were the wealthy exiles who lived by independent means in Paris, or had received pensions from secret funds of the Foreign Ministry. They numbered about 200 in all, a figure that included their wives and children.[48] They were not a part of the communities of the northern townships, who were by contrast middle and lower bourgeoisie, artisans and workers, but they were eager to act on their behalf and claim authority as their representatives. The vast majority of the refugees, it is certain, lived in these northern towns, quite separate from revolutionary politics, making a living from their craft and labour. The Dutch themselves reported about 2000 beneficiaries of financial aid (a figure included in an early draft of the 1790 memorandum to the National Assembly but curiously deleted from the final draft).[49]

The records of aid distribution do not provide a figure for the total number of assisted Dutch refugees, but they do show that in 1793 there were 198 refugees from Liège and its surrounds, and 95 refugees from Bruxelles who received financial allowances.[50] These numbers do not give any sense of the true size of the refugee population; they were certainly much larger than these low numbers might suggest. France's political refugees were able to field no fewer than 54 companies of volunteers prepared to fight alongside the French armies in defence of the revolution.[51]

Nevertheless, specific ideological and political questions remained concerning the Dutch refugees when the National Convention considered the draft decree of September 1792. They had been settled in France much longer than the Belgians and the Liégeois; indeed, their asylum had been granted under the monarchy, which left doubts about their loyalty to and status in the new republic. An unnamed representative of the Convention visited the depots in northern France and reported that their continued support was as much an ideological problem as it was a financial problem. The ideological question of asylum gave no simple answer: whether the refugees, 'received and assisted by a Monarchy', could be viewed in the same way by a popular sovereign government?[52] There were also many practical considerations about the ties the refugees had formed with France, which complicated their status and need for assistance. Three questions especially placed asylum beyond strictly political considerations, however. How long had the Dutch refugees lived in France and continued to receive assistance? What would be the status of the Dutch officers who had served the republic since the start of war if the conditions of asylum were changed? What would be the status of the families of deceased Dutch refugees who now depended on the government for their subsistence?[53] These were the same questions the draft decree of 1792 had addressed; asked again, they affirmed that asylum, as it related to the majority of the refugees, rested on practical and humanitarian considerations, which assured their continued asylum and the payment of assistance.[54]

## Asylum, *patriotisme*, and *civisme*

Among the elites of the refugee communities asylum related much more to their affinities with revolutionary politics. As they turned for support and aid to the National Assembly, monarchical asylum gave way to political asylum, in which these affinities were critical. Asylum subsequently became an engagement between two powers, the representatives of France and the representatives of the foreign exiles. Yet this was not always an engagement directed by France; the refugees themselves invoked it through their own political actions, their declarations of affinities with the French, and their invocations of the principles of liberty, equality, and the rights of man as the foundation principles of their own political aspirations.

The Liégeois and Dutch refugees had made this clear in their direct intercessions to the National Assembly. The Belgians did not make such a proclamation, but as the revolution unfolded, divisions emerged between moderates and radicals. Moderates, followers of the democrat leader Vonck, remained in Douai and Lille to avoid the political turmoil of Paris, and Vonck himself resisted the pressures of radicals to take their cause into France's revolutionary politics. The radical Belgians acted when Vonck would not, however. They established themselves in Paris and fostered relations with the Girondins to win their support for war against the Austrians, for Belgian liberation, and even for the annexation of Belgium into the French Republic.[55]

Political asylum more than nurtured political aspirations of these exile communities; it brought their aspirations into the very revolutionary project. War further radicalised asylum and the refugee communities. After France's declaration of war against Austria in April 1792, the front line of the revolution moved to the northern and eastern frontiers, and placed the Dutch, Belgians, and Liégeois between the French and their enemies. After France's victory at Valmy on 5 October 1792, they placed their fortunes in the hands of General Dumouriez and his Army of the North, anticipating his advance into Belgium and the Netherlands; they imagined their return at his side to liberate their homelands.[56]

War also radicalised political discourse within France about the status of foreigners. In the climate of extreme fear that followed the Brunswick Manifesto and the fall of the monarchy on 10 August 1792, asylum was highly politicised as the refugees, like all foreigners, were caught precariously between their affinities with revolutionary idealism and suspicion that any political gesture on their part could be interpreted as counter-revolutionary support for France's enemies. Public demonstration of their affinities with the French was essential proof of their fidelity to their revolution. The French demanded nothing less of them. Their future aid was conditional on their holding a Certificate of *Civisme* in accordance with laws of 19 June and 20 September 1792. The certificate was issued to all foreigners from an enemy country—which included the United Provinces, the Austrian Netherlands, and Liège—after satisfying a local surveillance committee that they were properly established in France and for whom six citizens attested to their civic sentiment, their *civisme*. The certificate served as an identity document and a testimonial of public reliability; it was evidence of fidelity to the ideals of the revolution, and, quite literally, made French 'patriots' of those foreigners who held them. Those who did not have a certificate risked condemnation as counter-revolutionaries, and therefore arrest and imprisonment.[57]

A reliable foreigner was a patriot to the French revolution; patriotism was therefore the mark of a foreign refugee. Asylum and assistance were determined by the refugee's 'patriotic' struggles, and implicitly their fidelity to ideals of the revolution. They were true patriots because they had absorbed these ideals and had applied them in their own countries; now in exile they committed their spirit of liberty to the republic.[58] This was the premise of a refugee's asylum. Their patriotic revolutionary struggles defined them and bound them to French revolutionaries, committing them in turn to the war that France took to the imperial tyrants of Europe.

As the war radicalised the French revolution, patriotism radicalised the refugees. In need of allies, the Liégeois leaders allied themselves with radical Belgian democrats who were increasingly dominated by the Society of the Friends of Liberty and Equality (*Société des amis de la liberté et de l'égalité*). They forged a common position, adopting the title of the Committee of United Belgians and Liégeois (*Comité belges et liégeois unis*). In the name of their peoples, they declared war on the Austrian emperor and the privileged orders. They adopted principles of popular sovereignty and anti-clericalism similar to the French Jacobins, and by agreeing to a constitution for a united Belgium, they tied their national aspirations to the French Revolution and the revolutionary wars more firmly. But they went further, declaring their desire to become French through the annexation of their united Belgium into the French Republic.[59]

After victory at Jemappes on 6 November 1792, the Belgian and Liégeois refugees took their part in the liberation of their homelands alongside the Army of the North. The French entered Bruxelles on 14 November, but the people did not follow; the mass of peasants and artisans were barely touched by their revolutionary propaganda. Nor did the privileged classes support them.[60] Barely had Belgium been liberated and the first steps taken to implement the constitution for a unified Belgian-Liège republic (a vote based on universal male suffrage was held for a national convention and for union with the French Republic), the Austrians had regrouped and drove the French back from Aix-La-Chapelle, and then from Liège itself. Bruxelles was again occupied, and, by 25 March 1793, the Austrians had recovered the territories they had only a few months earlier lost to the French. A second exile for the Belgians and Liégeois had begun.[61]

## Asylum and the Terror

Defeat at the hands of their enemies, Michael Rapport argues, poisoned the relationship between the French and foreigners. As fear of an invasion of northern France and an advance of the foreign armies on Paris became all too real during 1793, patriotism turned xenophobic as the French turned against suspect foreigners within. Thereafter, foreigners, refugees among them, walked a precarious path between radical patriotism and counter-revolutionary suspicion.[62] Historians also point to the changes in political discourse during 1793 that more readily identified affinities and alliances between foreigners and France's enemies as proof of the climate of terror then taking hold.[63] In the minds of many representatives of the National Convention, the intent of foreigners was no longer the promotion of revolution, but counter-revolution. Fears of infiltration and secret associations haunted the deputies, and, in the spring and summer of 1793 as the Austrians advanced into northern France, political refugees came under even greater suspicion.[64] Specific examples of the xenophobic turn in the currents of the revolution are found in the law on suspects of 1 August 1793, under which all subjects of enemy powers who had arrived in France since 1789 could be arrested, and the Germinal decrees of 15–16 April 1794 (named after the month of the revolutionary calendar in which they were adopted, 26–7 Germinal year II), which ordered the expulsion of the subjects of enemy powers from Paris, French port cities, and its frontier towns. Dutch, Belgian, and Liégeois refugees, subjects of foreign monarchies, could all be swept up in the application of these laws.

The status of foreigners at this critical stage of the revolution was therefore divided between revolutionary affinities and by crippling suspicions, which demanded fervent proclamations of patriotism so as not to be looked upon as an enemy alien or counter-revolutionary. Political discourse did not distinguish neatly between the French and foreigners; differences were identified rather between France and its enemies. Robespierre's report on revolutionary government of 25 December 1793 contrasted 'good citizens' (revolutionaries) with the enemies of the revolution (aristocrats and the foreign powers drawn into an alliance against France). War therefore demanded extraordinary measures to weed out 'conspirators', 'plotters', and 'intriguers', all friends of tyrants.[65] Article 120 of the new constitution drafted in April 1793 made refugees from other countries 'good citizens' because they had demonstrated their revolutionary patriotism in their own struggles for liberty and, more impressively, in their exile and the bonds they forged with the French. Here the Republic expressed its spirit of universal fraternity and the fundamental right to resist oppression by promising asylum 'to foreigners banished from their homeland for the cause of liberty'. Adopted along with a group of articles on France's foreign relations, article 120 expressed in practical terms the solemn declaration that 'the French people declare themselves the friend and natural ally of free peoples', and the enemies of tyrants and traitors who were at war with liberty.[66]

The 'good citizen', the revolutionary patriot, was defined against its opposite, the traitor and counter-revolutionary. The distinction was clear against the background of Robespierre's notion of 'Revolutionary government'— war against France's foreign enemies, and terror against the revolution's internal enemies. As the term 'patriot' was freely attributed to refugees whose asylum expressed the principles of equality, fraternity, and liberty, the term 'refugee' was henceforth applied without discrimination to any person in flight from France's enemies. This included families forced from their homes by the Austrian advance into northern France. On 4 March 1794 (14 Ventôse year II), the Convention approved 20,000,000 livres in aid for 'all patriot refugees in the invaded districts'.[67] Many families had been forced to abandon their properties and possessions to seek sanctuary in Douai, Quesnoy, and Valenciennes; the administrator of the department of the Nord described them as the 'best patriots' for having resisted 'the yoke of despotism'.[68] Conditions were grave; there was a real risk of starvation in Valenciennes. The promised aid was insufficient and there was an urgent need for more. Bread rather than money was distributed in Douai. Seminaries and the deserted houses of émigré nobles were requisitioned to shelter the refugees from the countryside.[69]

The terms 'refugee' and 'patriot' were common and interchangeable; both described the victims of France's enemies. Refugees from the Vendée were classified as patriots because they had refused to take up arms against the Republic. Expatriate French men and women returning from Britain were similarly regarded as patriots and refugees because they were victims of oppression in an enemy state. Corsicans fleeing the Paolists and expatriates from the slave rebellion in the Caribbean colonies were similarly classified as refugees and patriots.[70] Financial relief followed as a matter of course, to compensate for the loss of property, to reward their patriotism, and, as with all refugee aid, to ensure their immediate welfare needs.

The place of foreign refugees had been dramatically transformed, and the Republic had become enmeshed in a much greater refugee problem. The numbers of Belgians and Liégeois had increased substantially since the second Austrian occupation of 1793: estimates were as high as 6000–7000 Belgian and Liégeois. There were also some 600 Rhenish Germans scattered about northern and eastern France. These new refugees were put to work in the French military or civil administration.[71] On 29 November 1793 (9 Frimaire year II), the Convention approved provisional aid of 150,000 livres specifically for the assistance of foreign refugees. But this scarcely made an impact. On 26 July 1794 (8 Thermidor year II), the Committee of Public Safety set the rates of assistance at 212.90 livres for each man, 144.19 livres for each woman, and 77.90 livres for each child, which, in the Ardennes, the one department for which records of refugee aid at this time remain, was only enough to assist 13 single men and 11 families.[72] The prefect of the Ardennes complained that this fell far short of what was needed, and that refugees were therefore forced to eke out a living by whatever means they could.[73]

This larger problem of assistance spread the burden away from foreign refugees and diminished their claims to it. Petitions for the favour of the French and for recognition of their *civisme* were again important for preserving their relationship with the Republic and the good terms of their asylum. Most of the refugees from the Lowlands after the Austrian reoccupation settled in the border regions as before and remained remote from the strife of revolutionary politics, although from time to time they were buffeted by the shifting fortunes of the revolutionary war. In Paris itself, community assemblies were established to organise and administer the affairs of their refugee communities.

During the war emergency, therefore, foreign patriots and patriot refugees were brought into the service of the Republic. Laws and decrees of the Convention dealt with other foreigners, the suspect and the counter-revolutionaries. The law of suspects of 1 August 1793 allowed the imprisonment of any foreigner or refugee who had made no demonstration of patriotism and *civisme*, or who otherwise gave reason for suspicion. The Germinal decrees of year II (15–16 April 1794) banished subjects of enemy powers from the capital, from ports, and from frontier towns. The Republic was therefore able to deal with suspected enemies by imprisonment and banishment, while assisting at the same time foreign patriots who had demonstrated their republican fraternity and loyalty.

Demonstrations of patriotism and *civisme* were therefore critical. Assemblies of the refugee communities made this a priority so that they and their compatriots maintained the good will of the Republic. These assemblies therefore moderated the relationship between the refugees and the state. They were formed to organise community affairs and to represent community interests; they directed affairs among themselves, intervening between the individual refugees and the French authorities when it suited their interests. Their major role was the compilation of refugee lists, from which the distribution of aid would be determined. Aid distribution itself was administered by the little known Committee of Public Welfare (*Comité des Secours Publics*), which operated from the information the community assemblies provided. It followed that these assemblies could exclude individuals from their refugee lists and leave them prone to political suspicion and impoverishment. Many refugees were simply excluded because they were not known to the assemblies in Paris.[74]

Individual petitions for assistance to the Committee of Public Safety were also important for their declarations of patriotism and *civisme*. These reasserted asylum as a direct relationship between the state and individual refugees at the same time that the assemblies of the refugee communities assumed a leadership role on their behalf. These individual petitions were most often requests for assistance in extreme moments, and all attested to their good *civisme* and therefore submitted themselves to the good grace of the Committee members. A Franchimontois refugee who had found his way to Reims after the evacuation from the Belgian territories in 1793 complained that he had been omitted from the refugee list compiled by the Liégeois assembly in Paris although he had 'performed patriotic service' to the revolution in Belgium before evacuation.[75] A young woman who described herself as a 'Liégeois Patriot' and signed her petition as 'your co-citizenness' had fled to France with her two children but had made no claims for assistance until now. She was driven to request assistance only after the death of one child and becoming pregnant with her third; she requested the 218.19 livres to which she believed she was entitled.[76] The responses to these petitions are not documented.

Three Italians from Turin also petitioned the Committee of Public Safety. Self-declared 'Piedmontese patriots' who had tried to stir up an insurrection against the Sardinian 'tyranny', they had come to Paris for asylum and assistance, and placed themselves on 'the trust and protection that the Republic generously offers' to all who act as they had.[77] Their petition was not accepted without cautious inquiry; the citizens who had authorised their certificates of *civisme* were asked to explain their reasons.[78]

Individual petitions were generally considered sympathetically because they presented personal accounts of distress, testimonies of patriotism, and declarations of affinity to the Republic. Collective petitions on the other hand could turn opinion against the refugees. The Belgian assembly collectively petitioned the National Convention on 14 February 1794 (26 Pluviôse year II) for additional assistance because the 150,000 livres in aid previously allocated was insufficient even to repay the debts that many of them had incurred in their second flight from the Austrians. Not even their further declarations of patriotism and Republican loyalty moved the Committee of Public Safety, however. The petition was taken instead as a rebuke, revealing the Belgians' ingratitude, and their unwillingness to make the same sacrifices for the Republic that other patriots were making. Instead of finding sympathy, they were denounced for having provided refugee lists compromised by false information, as a consequence of which French aid was paid to men who worked for their own state and not for the Republic, and to men who had no need for it. More surprising was the accusation that the Belgians claimed this additional assistance after wasting their resources in debauchery and libertinage, proved by the cases of venereal disease among them.[79]

The assemblies were tolerated however because they served the useful purpose of regulating the behaviour of their refugee communities and constraining their political demeanour. As it was imperative the refugees demonstrate their patriotism and service to the Republic to win and retain Jacobin favour, moderates were silenced and radical factions came to the fore. The Committee of Public Safety used their fears to its own advantage. The assemblies of the Belgians and the Liégeois functioned independently as the administrative body of their respective communities, but it was clear their first loyalty was to the French Republic. They were particularly suited to providing attestations of a refugee's background and qualifications for employment or service, for the Certificates of *Civisme*, and for financial aid. Yet alert to the implications that their decisions and even the demeanour of the individuals they represented might have on French opinion, they restrained their debates and activities to what the Committee of Public Safety expected of them. The Belgian assembly paid much attention to questions that the Committee posed about the *civisme* and patriotism of various individuals, for example. In one instance, the assembly offered its assistance to investigate allegations that a Belgian refugee had provided arms to the enemy during the French occupation. Within a few days it had found that the accused was the mayor of Liège at the time and therefore denounced him to the Liégeois assembly. The arrest of a Belgian refugee at Lille in December 1793 prompted the assembly to denounce her excess of revolutionary patriotism; it then placed her under its own surveillance.[80] Demonstrations of loyalty were also made by the denunciation of certain individuals for turning against the Republic.[81] In other instances, the assemblies supplied information to the Committee of Public Safety about the mistreatment of their compatriots at home under Austrian occupation.[82] Denunciation of their common enemies therefore best demonstrated their revolutionary patriotism.

The broad sweep of xenophobia could readily identify enemies or potential enemies, but there were real problems of the enforcement of the laws, leading to highly pragmatic outcomes. The law on suspects of 1 August 1793 led to a great number of arrests, but many foreigners were quickly released and leniency was shown to enemy subjects who did not pose a serious threat. Common sense and a judgement of the personal attributes, character, and social position of individuals determined police responses, especially when foreign workers inhabited the poorer districts of Paris where the police feared to go.[83] Similar pragmatism is evident in the enforcement of the Germinal decrees of 15–16 April 1794. Although foreigners were required to leave the cities and ports, Michael Rapport illustrates how exemptions were allowed for the economically useful: sail-makers, merchants, and others were requisitioned for the service of the Republic, as were foreigners employed in arms manufacture. Many gained exemption from the decrees because, although foreign subjects, they had nevertheless demonstrated their patriotism by other means. Foreign women married to French citizens, for example, were not considered enemy aliens.[84] Some circumstances were more difficult to prove, however. Those who had no reason previously to question their French identity, although born of foreign parents or who had previously lived in a foreign country, suddenly had to defend their loyalties. Those with most to fear were not the enemy aliens whom the decrees intended to expel, but the infirm, aged, orphans, and those of foreign birth or born to a foreign parent who had nevertheless been resident in France for many years. Testimonies of *civisme*, proof of loyalty in their past actions, and attestations to their renunciation of their foreign heritage, or, more simply, appeals to the Committee of Public Safety's compassion, were usually sufficient to gain exemption.[85] The machinery of terror, Rapport concludes, equated foreigners with a danger out of all proportion to their numbers.[86] But it nevertheless spread fear among the foreign populace that through no fault of their own they might fall foul of law.

Among those unsettled by the Germinal decrees were the foreign refugees. They asked whether the Dutch, Belgians, Liégeois, and Rhinelanders, all subjects of France's enemies, face banishment although hitherto they had been assured asylum.[87] Despite earlier ideological declarations that France held to its breast foreign refugees who had suffered for their pursuit of liberty, the Convention could not immediately answer this question, and therefore commissioned a report into their standing under the decrees. This suggests two things: the decrees had been adopted in the heat of the war emergency with little thought about their impact, and that the pressure on the Convention was so intense that it was unsure even of its own laws. The status of political refugees under the decree, it was shown, was perfectly clear; the question should not have been a matter of contention. They had all been incorporated into the Republic by the Convention's own decree of 14 April 1793, which followed the loss of occupied territories. The inhabitants of these lands would not be abandoned to the 'tyrants with whom France was at war', and their rights in France would not be extinguished.[88]

The fact that the Convention was unsure of the status of foreign refugees from the Lowlands and the Rhineland under the anti-foreign measures of the Germinal decrees might have been the result of a mistake or an oversight, or it might simply be a reflection of confusion arising from the war emergency. It might also suggest that there was a current of thought among the revolutionaries that their high ideals might have reached their limits during the war emergency, beyond which even the earlier ideological proclamations failed to move them.

## After Thermidor

Revolutionary patriotism served the national interests of the exiled communities as much as it served the interests of revolutionary government. The refugees' primary objective was to garner French support for their political struggles at home, an ambition that also served the Republic's war against its enemies. The French recruited them into their military cause, while victories against the Austrians in early 1793 seemed to realise the Belgian and Liégeois dream of returning to reclaim liberty for their peoples. They bided their time through a second exile, the Austrian reoccupation of their homelands, the reign of terror in France, and then through the fall of the Jacobins and the Thermidorean reaction of 1794–5. Their patience and service were rewarded when the French armies reoccupied the Austrian Lowlands and the Rhineland in the summer of 1794, and moved on to occupy the United Provinces in December. After the annexation of Belgium on 1 October 1795 (9 Vendémiaire year IV) and the United Provinces on 5 October 1795 (13 Vendémiaire year IV), the refugees were nominally made citizens of the Republic.

As Bonaparte took the revolution into Italy in 1796, he also built up the ranks of foreign patriots and new adherents to the Republic. By 1798, revolution seemed unbound, reaching into Germany, Ireland, and Sweden, which, in the view of one British diplomat, was plagued by Jacobins. Even the United States of America, Robert Palmer notes, had its Jacobin fears.[89] The Republic attracted new refugees displaced by abortive insurrections and reactionary oppression, such as Irish rebels after the failed uprising of 1798, and nascent nationalist movements, such as in Italy from April 1799.[90]

With the defeat of the Jacobins, France under the Directory was much less swayed by the aspirations and radical inclinations of foreign patriots. Its purpose was instead, Peter McPhee concludes, the consolidation of the bourgeois republic in order to protect it from both Jacobin popular democracy and royalist counter-revolution. Political culture was thereafter committed to the protection of private property, on which rights rested, and a *laissez-faire* economy. It was also a culture unable to strike a viable social basis of support; political clubs had been closed and the popular movement in Paris had been suppressed.[91]

When foreign patriots now turned to France, they found only grudging support. Italians received no encouragement for their campaigns of national unity, although they were partisans of France and were driven by French republican ideals.[92] Because their service was to France, their peoples would not follow. Alienated by occupation, military requisitions, and high prices and taxes, they rose in anti-French rebellions when, from April 1799, after Bonaparte's departure for Egypt, Austrian and Russian armies moved into the peninsula to recover the Italian republics for their former rulers.

One by one, from the Cisalpine, Piedmont, Tuscany, Naples, and the Roman provinces, Italian republicans fled the advance of their enemies. By the end of the year some 5200 Italian refugees had arrived in France, settling mainly in Briançon, Grenoble, Bourg, Marseille, and Paris.[93] Their enemies condemned them as Jacobins and anarchists who Italy was best rid of. They found protection among French Jacobins who took them in as republican allies. The Council of 500 proclaimed a motion that 'France still offers hospitable asylum'.[94] But the sentiment was no longer widely shared; the Italians instead exposed serious political fractures between rival Jacobin and anti-Jacobin factions.

In contrast to French reluctance to support the Italians' national aspirations, support for the United Irishmen was more forthcoming because it promised real strategic benefits. When, in 1796, an embassy of United Irishmen requested French military support for their planned insurrection against British occupation, they relied not on appeals to outmoded principle, but offered instead the more alluring if exaggerated prospect that an Irish rebellion would force Britain to abandon its war with France.[95] Having promised its backing for the rebellion when it broke out in 1798, France was duty bound to take in Irish fugitives from British repression.

France was not always a willing refuge, however. Certainly, there was sympathy for their plight, and there was the prospect of financial aid to see the Irish through their exile. But suspicion that the Irish refugees might give cover to British spies delayed the grant of passports and imposed strict conditions on relief. Moreover, Marianne Elliott observes, French responses to the Irish were characterised by administrative confusion that accompanied the arrival of Irish and Italian refugees at more or less the same time, and by resistance to the unrealistic demands of individual Irish rebels and the United Irish committee in Paris. The United Irish committee interceded between the government and the refugees for the distribution of aid, but found that aid was not so readily forthcoming as it had expected. Many Irishmen arrived with misconceptions about the aid they were due and misplaced optimism that their welfare and aspirations would be secure in France until a French invasion of Ireland could be organised. Far from finding themselves willingly accommodated, Elliot concludes, the Irish exiles found instead that they were reduced to 'begging dependence' on France. Public relief was not forthcoming; instead they were paid assistance from secret funds of the Foreign and Interior Ministries, which consigned many of them to the status of a military contingent at the service of French war aims.[96] From their number an Irish Legion was formed to fight with Bonaparte's armies against the British and their allies.[97]

Public allocations for the general welfare of the Irish refugees was 10,000 francs, drawn from a total of 894,000 francs set aside for all refugee aid during 1798–9. Some 80 francs a month were paid to each Irish refugee from 20 June 1800 (1 Messidor year VIII), barely enough to assist a small number of Irish seminary students who had been studying in Paris at the time of the 1798 rebellion. These figures are uncertain at best; there were large monthly variations, and no provision seems to have been made for aid beyond 1800. The most definite figures show that 5280 francs were allocated for the assistance of 21 Irish refugees for the months of June to August 1800 (Messidor, Thermidor, and Fructidor year VIII).[98]

This much is consistent between the reception of refugees during 1798–9 and earlier years. The shifting currents of revolutionary politics had again altered asylum and the nature of the refugees' relationship with the state, however. There were now questions about France's ability to provide financial relief and even about the merits of providing it at all. The Interior Minister Quinette de Rochemont asked in 1799 whether it was right to pay assistance to the Irish when there were many more Italians in need of assistance. More to the point, he asked why they should be supported from public funds when the value of Irish property in France would more than match the cost of the aid that they demanded and expected.[99]

The Italian patriots of the Directory period had much less room to manoeuvre. More than any other refugee community that found sanctuary in France during the revolutionary years, the Italians were alienated from their protectors. Certainly, as the historian of the exiled Italian patriots, Anna Maria Rao, well illustrates, they took with them into exile, grievances against the Directory for having prohibited them from forming national armies to defend their liberties, as well as internal conflicts that set moderates against extremists.[100] Radical Italians exposed raw fractures within the French revolutionary government; they found support among Jacobins, which only further alienated them from the anti-Jacobin factions of the Directory. The fate of Italy and the Italian republicans was therefore at the centre of new political turmoils during the short period of Jacobin ascendancy after 18 June 1799 (30 Prairial year VII). The Italians and their supporters turned against the Directory for its betrayal of the sister republics; the Italian cause was brought back into the reopened Jacobin Clubs, and the Council of 500 passed resolutions in favour of Italian unity and independence. More practically, the Council was also generous in the assistance it authorised: some 200,000 francs were sanctioned for refugees from the Cisalpine, and another 100,000 francs for Piedmontese and others.[101]

They later suffered for this favour of the Jacobins when the anti-Jacobin forces regrouped and took back control of the Republic. Italian patriots were then condemned as anarchists who had brought the threat of new political disturbances into Paris when France again faced a coalition of enemies at its borders. The need to 'disperse them ... and make them disappear' was quickly recognised.[102] They were no longer considered patriots because they were Jacobins; they were consequently considered less the victims of tyranny than dangerous men who were a threat to the Republic. Repressive measures were therefore essential. The Police Minister Fouché ordered the full enforcement of the laws on passports and the policing of foreigners against 'these dangerous migrants' who had been 'vomited into French cities'. The impact, Rao shows, fell on the refugees' personal well-being. Instead of finding Paris welcoming and hospitable, they found it a place of control and rejection, where their daily lives were filled with the worries of subsistence. These were not the great foreign patriots of the earlier years of revolution; they were treated like the poor and homeless. They were given charity when they needed it, but they were also subjected to surveillance and were forced to live separately and in isolation.[103]

The Italian refugees were therefore forced into quiescence before French authority, which would not allow them the role of patriots or radical republicans. They witnessed, Rao concludes, the last debates on the 'patrie en danger', which revived momentarily the earlier cosmopolitanism of the revolution, and the political turn that led Bonaparte to terminate the revolution with the coup of 9 November 1799 (18 Brumaire year VIII). Bonaparte's ascendancy revived their political aspirations; as he had brought them liberty in 1796, they held firm to the hope that he would again liberate the peninsula.[104] The Italians therefore had experienced a turn against refugees and the reframing of the terms of asylum. It was no longer grounded in revolutionary patriotism; reluctant toleration supplanted principle.

There were some 295 Neapolitan refugees in Paris in 1800, requiring a total monthly expenditure of 7335 francs in direct aid.[105] Most of the Italian refugees, however, lived in the provinces; many also moved between depart-ments looking for work. In Bourg-en-Bresse and Marseille, the refugee depot had been reconstituted in form if not in name for the distribution of aid and the administration of the refugees accommodated there. Many had been removed from Paris to Bourg-en-Bresse, which grew to accommodate the largest community of Italian refugees in France at that time. An aid distri-bution committee was organised under the prefecture of police to distribute financial assistance and a daily food ration. Similar committees were formed in Marseille, where there were about 500 Italian refugees, and in Toulon, where there were another 49 (along with some 362 refugees from Malta who had followed Bonaparte back from his campaigns in the eastern Mediterranean). French victory at Marengo on 14 June 1800 ensured that these were only temporary arrangements. The Italian sister republics had been reclaimed, and their refugees no longer had need of asylum; their repa-triation was subsequently ordered.[106]

The distribution committees with responsibilities for refugee relief in Bourg-en-Bresse and Marseille met an immediate need; the refugees' accom-modation, on the other hand, illustrates the development of an enduring administrative system for admission, transportation, shelter, and the provi-sion of welfare. All relief measures required planning and execution by the prefectures of police and departmental officials, and the deployment of resources through various levels of the public administration for the work of the distribution committees to be effective. Because administrative arrange-ments had become well developed, the order for the repatriation of the Italians could be carried out quickly and efficiently.

In contrast, the Italians who remained in Paris were more onerous for the government to deal with. Life in Paris was also more difficult for the refugees themselves; the high cost of living quickly consumed the aid they received, while their dispersal across the city made its distribution much less sure. They were more impecunious, therefore, yet they lived more freely. The government's order that they return to Italy had little impact and it could barely be enforced. When refugees in the southeast were being repatriated to Italy, therefore, those in Paris gained permission to remain.[107]

* * *

The relationship between the political refugees and the French state had followed the currents of revolutionary politics. The monarchy ensured the king's grace was conferred on them, but political asylum under revolution-ary government assumed ideological purpose rooted in the ideals of universal liberty. The shifting ground of revolutionary politics, however, compelled the refugees to tread a narrow path between ideals and reality, between the promise of universal liberty and the imperatives of revolutionary patriotism, between the revolution's cosmopolitanism and its national objectives.

Foreign exiles were therefore caught between the contradictions of the great revolutionary project.

There were nevertheless important continuities in this relationship that bridged these ruptures. Asylum was also a practical response to the needs of foreign refugees. Financial aid and the freedom to reside were consistent responses. The means of administration and organisation might have varied, but the refugees were willingly accommodated; their protection from the forces of oppression, and care for their material well-being, were not brought into question.

Nevertheless, monarchical asylum demanded their compliance to the king's will in order to receive these benefits. Republican *civisme*, although it also demanded their compliance, imposed much greater expectations on their behaviour and their political demeanour. The danger of being considered a counter-revolutionary—always a possibility since the refugees were subjects of France's enemies—radicalised them. They were not only willing revolutionaries, they became eager Jacobins, to maintain French favour while continuing to advance their national aspirations.

Still, the refugees radicalised by the shifting currents of revolutionary politics were a relatively small number of elites, who had taken their grievances and aspirations into exile, and who took advantage of the opportunities opened to them. Asylum for them rested on their political affinities with revolutionary government. Unknown numbers lived in quiet obscurity; for them asylum had the more practical purpose of affording protection, safe refuge, and the opportunity to make the best of their lot, which was repaid by their labour and their service to the Republic.

After Thermidor, radicalism was itself a danger. Asylum was compromised in the conservative, bourgeois republic of the Directory, as it turned away from radical republicanism. Refugees inspired by the Republic and its revolutionary ideals were marginalised. Since asylum was radicalised during the most radical phase of the revolution, its protective principles were subsequently compromised in the conservative reaction in these latter years in order to neutralise refugee radicalism.

# 2
# Asylum, Empire, and Restoration

The Napoleonic Empire and the Bourbon Restoration, both faced two problems of asylum: the inheritance of refugees, and along with them the ideals of political asylum forged in the cosmopolitan fervour of the revolution; and the asylum of new refugee communities produced by new political ruptures. In neither was there a return to monarchical asylum, although the nation was centred in the person of the emperor and the restored monarchy, just as in the old regime the nation had been centred in the king. These were very different regimes with very different responses to refugees. The empire had taken the French nation into Europe to spread its revolutionary ideals in foreign monarchies. In doing so, it attracted to it adherents and collaborators, willing participants in the French occupation of their countries and eager agents in the remaking their own nations. The Restoration wound back the empire to France's former frontiers; it was a conservative and pacific monarchy, whose political culture was organised around constitutionalism, the law, and new institutional structures. It inherited refugees from the empire, and it received new refugees from the unfolding of empire and the suppression of the forces the empire had ignited.

Refugees had earlier been incorporated into the Republic when the French armies advanced into the Austrian Lowlands and the United Provinces in 1794 and 1795. And when the French frontier was extended to the Rhine, the German Rhineland was also incorporated into the Republic. After Bonaparte had recaptured the Italian 'sister republics' in 1800, the Italian refugees largely shunned by the Directory could return with their national fervour and deep affinities with the French restored.

The Empire inherited refugees from two sources: repatriated colonists from the Caribbean who had lost their properties in the slave revolts; and refugees from the Mediterranean and the Middle East who had followed Bonaparte back to France in 1799. A bare minimum can be learned about the former from the records of their assistance during the Empire. In 1806, the Emperor personally authorised 480,000 francs to assist in their resettlement and to compensate them for their losses. By 1809, this had been reduced to 300,000 francs

36

annually. A total of 3562 colonists from St. Domingue and another 894 from St. Pierre et Miquelon were recorded to still be in receipt aid during 1812.[1]

Among the second category of refugees inherited by the Empire was a contingent of 362 Maltese settled in Toulon. They had become established there along with Italian republicans, but remained after the Italians were repatriated during 1800. Also returning with Bonaparte's expedition was a heterogeneous group of exiles from the Levant, conveniently categorised for French purposes as 'Egyptian refugees'. Compromised in one way or another by their service to the French in the Middle East, this mix of Muslims, Greek Orthodox, Copts, Malachite Catholics, traders and customs officials, poorer workers from villages in Palestine, Mamelouk soldiers who had joined the French army, black slaves, and Greek sailors, settled in Marseille with the benefit of aid that allowed them to live independently.[2]

Since they were drawn to side with France when the Republic took the revolution into foreign lands, these Levantine refugees assumed for themselves French conceptions of national identity, which allowed them to withstand their classification as 'Egyptians'; they also conformed to the imperative of political asylum by their reformation as a 'nation in embryo' while in exile. Their quest for national independence from Ottoman autarchy, however, seemed illusory once Bonaparte had withdrawn his army.[3] These 'Egyptians' consequently formed a new community of refugees; their numbers grew through new births and new arrivals to about 1000. In Marseille and Paris they formed new and visible Arab communities, and assumed new forms of settlement and socialisation. Along with this the nature of their asylum changed. The community in Marseille was officially designated a depot for 'Egyptian refugees'. They were allowed their own council to administer their affairs and to deal with disturbances, even to the extent of reporting troublesome refugees to the police. It was, however, a depot fractured by an economic divide, with the poorer members concentrated in one quarter and an elite in another.[4] This is consistent with how refugee depots and refugee self-administration had previously mediated the relationship of the refugees with the state. Also consistent with past refugee communities was the long reach of a few principle figures into the politics of the French nation and into its national culture. From Marseille, Ian Coller shows, a community of Arabs gradually stretched all the way to Paris, as individuals and elites moved to the capital and tentatively established themselves and their families.[5]

The striking difference between these refugee communities—repatriated colonists and Levantine exiles—was the permanence of their exile. This distinguished them from earlier refugee movements, who had aligned themselves with the revolutionary project for their own national ambitions. The advance of the French armies into their homelands had allowed their return and the fulfilment of their long-held republican aspirations. Neither the colonists nor the 'Egyptian refugees' could look ahead with any expectation of return, however. They had to remake themselves, starting with the small amount of assistance they received from the Emperor. The 'Egyptians' might have taken nationalist aspirations into exile with them, but as time passed they began to identify themselves more fully as French as they perceived France as a place of definite resettlement.[6]

But their exoticism, their clearly visible character as outsiders, was accentuated in the Arab 'villages' of Marseille. Many could not speak French and were even illiterate in their own language, and therefore had great difficulties integrating through work or service. They were also emblematic of Empire, both its achievements and its failures: the dress of the Mamelouks, Coller argues, was integral to the iconography of the Empire, evoking with it the menace of Islam and the power of the Emperor.[7] With Napoleon's return from Elba, the Arabs of Marseille incurred the wrath of legitimists; when news of disaster at Waterloo arrived, they were the first victims of the 'White Terror', massacred in their marginalised quarter of the city. The survivors thereafter retreated into the quiet corners of French society, or they left France altogether over the following years.[8]

## Asylum and the Restoration

The restoration of the Bourbon monarchy in 1814 brought forth entirely different questions about responses to refugees. Among the refugees were 'friends of France', drawn to it during the revolutionary wars or who had followed in the wake of the retreat of the Napoleonic armies. Important questions follow. How would the restored monarchy formulate asylum for revolutionaries, radical republicans, foreign nationalists and Bonapartists? And would this mean a return to monarchical asylum as seen before the revolution?

The history of these refugees during the Restoration, Emmanual Monasse finds, is unfortunately clouded by a distinct lack of sources.[9] Yet these questions can be addressed by considering the manner in which refugee admission was organised and administered during the Restoration. It is immediately apparent that asylum was not constrained by political affinities.

The process of admission is seen most clearly in the context of the fury of restoration and rebellion in the troubled Iberian countries after 1814. The conflicts between liberals and legitimists in Spain and Portugal forced refugees of all persuasions into France; they were all admitted without distinction. Spanish liberals and constitutionalists held to the gains of political and constitutional reform under French imperial occupation, while legitimists, after Ferdinand VII reclaimed the Spanish throne and reimposed his former absolutism, quite ruthlessly resisted their liberal challenge. The Spanish were by far the largest national refugee group to turn to France during the Restoration. The responses to them make it apparent that the Restoration monarchy did not return to earlier forms of monarchical asylum. Instead, asylum was reformulated within the state administration. Asylum was conferred and moderated by a bureaucratic apparatus that was as striking for the breadth of its authority as it was for the efficiency of its methods, which kept refugees at a safe distance from government, and therefore allowed sanctuary even to its enemies.

There were three distinct forced migrations from Spain. The *afrancesados*, Spaniards compromised by their collaboration with the French occupation, followed Joseph Bonaparte to France after his expulsion from Spain in 1814. Liberal victories against Ferdinand's reimposition of autocracy between 1820 and 1823 caused the second migration, of absolutists from Catalonia; they settled mainly in Montpellier.[10] At the same time, liberals who had previously taken flight from Ferdinand made their way back into Spain.[11] The third migration, the largest in number and the most important for its impact on France, followed French military intervention in 1823 to secure Ferdinand's hold on the throne. Two separate refugee streams followed: liberals in flight from absolutist repressions, who, it transpired, would spend most of the next 10 years in exile; and prisoners of war captured by the French expeditionary force. The expeditionary force, the '100,000 Sons of Saint Louis', as they were known, put down liberal resistance and captured a legion of foreign militia, mostly of Italians, the Légion Libérale Étrangère, who fought to overthrow Ferdinand. A total of 12,459 Spanish and Italian prisoners of war were taken from Barcelona in military custody so that they would not again threaten the Spanish throne, and so that their liberal views could not infiltrate France.[12] Now firmly in power, Ferdinand set about purifying the country of its anti-royalist sentiments.[13]

The prisoners were dispersed into depots across the southern and south-eastern departments. The largest, in the Cantal, held 2527 prisoners of war; another 1723 were held in the Gard.[14] The depots were little more than buildings transformed into prisons.[15] A total of 629 Spanish soldiers and non-commissioned officers, along with 23 women and 5 children, were detained in Sète (Hérault); 74 Piedmontese and Neapolitan officers were held in Montpellier.[16] The police in Marseille reported 551 Spanish, 96 Neapolitans, and 1257 Piedmontese in residence in 1824, the largest political migration, historians of the city note, it had yet experienced.[17]

The depots were dissolved in April 1824, in advance of an amnesty of 1 May that allowed for the return of Spanish prisoners. Some 442 political refugees, liberals least assured of their personal security in Spain because of their past anti-royalist agitation remained under the jurisdiction of the Interior Ministry.[18] Among them were a dozen Italians who enjoyed the protection of asylum and the benefits of financial aid in Montferrand. They were lodged in the town, lived among the local community and carried out their professions, but were nevertheless constrained from leaving the town without the authorisation of the prefect.[19]

The experience of these Italian refugees in Montferrand best illustrates the character of asylum during the Restoration. They were truly political agitators. They had been sentenced to death in Italy for their opposition to Austrian occupation and had fled to join the foreign legion in Spain to fight on the side of the liberal constitutionalists. Taken to France as prisoners of war, they remained as political refugees, were paid financial assistance for their personal welfare and gave no reason for adverse comments about their conduct.[20] Yet Italians captured among the foreign legion were seldom above suspicion. They were, after all, liberals who had taken up arms against the European monarchies and therefore a close watch was kept on their movements and associations so that the French authorities were forewarned of plots or sedition. Even after four years the interior minister still demanded to be personally informed of the movements of particular Italians who gave reason to doubt their political demeanour.[21] Suspicions persisted even into the 1830s. It was believed that the Italians in Montferrand had received visits from suspect political figures and were members of secret societies such as the *Charbonnerie*, and the *Aide-toi, le ciel t'aidera*.[22] Within the larger population of Marseille, Italian refugees had established friendships with other exiled Italians and with Frenchmen sympathetic to their revolutionary struggle.[23] This was reason enough to doubt they would remain quiescent and would not at some point in time, if allowed the freedom to plot and conspire, threaten the civil order and the security of the monarchy.

But they were not refused asylum despite these suspicions. Instead, their right to asylum and protection in France, recognised by their admission, the provision of a place of residence, and the grant of on-going financial aid, was not challenged so long as they presented no problems. Nevertheless, their political backgrounds justified measures of policing and surveillance to keep them in check. The form that asylum took during the Restoration, therefore, was developed along with more intrusive measures for the policing of foreigners and more effective methods of state administration.

The admission of political refugees from Spain after 1820, royalists and liberal constitutionalists alike, therefore, revealed an elaborate system for the provision of aid and dispersal into depots. Spread across France, refugee depots were places of aid as well as confinement and surveillance. At the end of the Restoration, some one thousand Spanish refugees were still accommodated in depots in Tours, Moulins, Poitiers, Blois, Bourges, Alençon, Le Mans, and Montferrand.[24] The provision of aid placed specific responsibilities on the prefects of police and his sub-prefects. The emphasis on competence, which John Merriman shows transformed both the personnel and the function of policing in Restoration France, can be seen in the expansion of the regional bureaucracy responsible for the administration and surveillance of refugees, and in the devolution of responsibilities to local officials.[25] These officials represented the state to the refugees; they implemented directives from their superiors as well as attended to the daily welfare of the refugees themselves. Asylum, the relationship of refugees with the state, was mediated through them.

The location of refugee depots changed as refugee numbers changed and as administrative priorities required. Conflict between competing factions among Spanish refugees was ample reason to shut down one depot and disperse the refugees to others. Many had taken their factional allegiances into France with them. Soldiers were therefore separated from their officers so that they would not succumb to their influence and become a dangerous force for the local French police to deal with.[26] Nevertheless, antagonism and rivalry could still break out into open hostilities, which could be quite brutal. The depot of Cahors was closed after the murder of one refugee, when royalist agents had infiltrated a group of Spanish liberals to subvert them and to revenge a past wrong.[27]

The network of depots also indicates a highly developed system of intervention and reception. A cordon along the Spanish border responded to both health and security concerns, but it also protected France from the dangers of liberal infiltration.[28] On arrival, each refugee was registered; military ranks or social positions were verified as best they could be before the proper entitlement to aid was authorised. Passports were authorised and issued, the refugees were allocated to a designated depot and transport arranged and paid for. These were all tasks that required much coordination and an exchange of papers and finances between the police, mayors, sub-prefects, prefects, and the Interior Ministry. Accommodation then had to be made ready, and the police instructed on the need for surveillance.[29]

The local officials in those departments along the Spanish border performed these tasks with a definite conception of the characteristics of political refugees and France's obligations towards them.[30] The priority accorded to the question of extradition required them to take particular care in examining the refugees' personal circumstances and political backgrounds. The officials had to decide who was a fugitive from the law extraditable under the terms of the Franco-Spanish extradition convention of 1765, and who was a refugee from political troubles and therefore entitled to asylum.[31] Only then could the refugees be moved on.

Administration was not without its problems, however. Registration errors were common. Misunderstandings of language caused Spanish names to be given French approximations; misspellings in turn sometimes changed their identity and made coordination between departments and the Interior Ministry all the more difficult.[32] Nevertheless, while delays and cumbersome organisational and accounting procedures were inevitable as the local officials awaited instructions, complied with registration requirements, and accounted for expenditure, admission, dispersal, and the provision of aid seem to have progressed smoothly.

The Spanish refugees therefore draw attention to the process of admission and accommodation, two of the key measures in the grant of asylum. The question posed by Italian refugees who came to France after the 1820–1 uprisings in Piedmont and Naples was one of policing. Their admission was authorised before arrival, when they were issued passports to enter France by the French legation in Turin. They were assured safe passage and protection after arrival, but on condition that they were removed from the frontier, resided in France discretely and caused no disruption, and submitted themselves to the authority of the police.[33] The surveillance of known leaders of the Italian liberals and revolutionaries was a matter of the strictest security, especially when Austria pressured the French for their extradition. But a strict watch was kept on Italians generally.[34] The mayor of Rive-de-Gier in the Loire complained that if the surveillance orders were to be properly carried out, the many Italian miners, stonemasons, and plasterers in the municipality would also have to be watched.[35] Two possibilities worried the authorities: of Italian revolutionaries disappearing among Italian workers, and the workers themselves being infected with their radical liberal politics.

The surveillance of Italian refugees after 1820 introduced a period of attention to the policing of foreigners not experienced since the dark years of the Republic. The many instances of travellers found without passports, or without proper authorisation noted on their passports, raised doubts about the enforcement of existing regulations controlling the movement of foreigners. Interior Ministry officials worried that lax policing in the provinces ran the grave risk of subversive infiltration. The enforcement of passport regulations was therefore another important step in the consolidation of public administration, policing, and the control of foreigners.

Since the old regime, passports had been a means of controlling the movements of citizens and foreigners alike. During the revolution passports also served a security purpose; they were used to identify travellers and verify the validity of a foreigner's residence and rightful entitlement to travel inside France.[36] During the Restoration, they were again used to regulate the internal travel of both foreigners and French subjects. Under the regulations in force from 1816, all foreigners had to have special authorisation from the Ministry of General Police before being allowed to travel or reside in France. Foreign travellers had to surrender their national passports to the departmental prefecture or the mayoral office of the commune in which they first arrived in France; this was dispatched to the Ministry of General Police, which then issued a visa permitting travel and residence for one year. The visa was sent on to the traveller's intended destination to ensure proper registration after arrival there. In the meantime, the prefect or mayor issued a provisional travel document noting the intended destination, the authorised route, and the dates of travel. Travellers arriving without a passport were placed under surveillance and could not leave their place of arrival until further orders were received.[37]

Travellers who failed to declare their presence could be arrested and expelled if they could not give an adequate reason. Suspect individuals could be refused a visa or have it revoked at a later time. Other violations of the regulations could include being in a place other than one authorised or arriving at a destination after a specified date. Both suggested travel elsewhere along the way, which in turn suggested the possibility of suspect if not unlawful behaviour. Hotel proprietors were an important link in the policing of travellers. In the Rhône during 1823, many arrests for passport violations followed their reports of suspicious foreigners. Interviews with these travellers revealed their illegal activities. Vagabondage, smuggling, and the trade in contraband were common offences; one Swiss woman was arrested for prostitution.[38]

The proper enforcement of the passport regulations required more interventionist policing. The path to sedition often followed travellers, the Director of Police in the Interior Ministry reminded the prefects. 'Travellers, under the pretext of commerce, make their way about France with, it seems, no other intent than to sow the seeds of sedition'.[39] Attention to foreign travellers was therefore a matter of urgency. Special instructions of March 1823 reminded the prefects of their responsibilities and set out the necessary compliance measures. 'The laws on passports must be enforced rigorously ... Keep a most careful watch on public carriages and any place frequented by travellers'. The instruction continued: 'stir the zeal of the sub-prefects, mayors and the gendarmerie, all agents responsible for the public peace' to arrest anyone who spoke of sedition or displayed criminal intent.[40] The years 1822–3 were therefore especially busy years for the surveillance of foreigners, which demonstrates in turn the lengthening reach of the police and public administration.[41]

Of particular concern were foreigners from countries where there had been recent political ruptures. The Spanish and Piedmontese were specifically identified as politically dangerous and therefore worthy of special surveillance. There were, however, relatively few incidents in which they were involved. Reports of vagabonds, merchants, and other travellers found without passports, or passports not properly authorised, far outnumbered reports of foreign revolutionaries or political refugees.[42] This could attest to the effectiveness of policing as much as to overstated security concerns centred on Spanish and Italian liberals.

The remaining problem of responses to refugees during the Restoration was that of the organisation of large numbers in need of humanitarian aid. The administration of the depots for the Spanish refugees was one aspect of this problem. But what were the appropriate financial arrangements that underpinned the admission of refugees to asylum? As the measures taken for Portuguese refugees who arrived in the port of Brest in April 1829 illustrate, there was no easy solution.

They numbered just under 700 when they disembarked in Brest, and as they were moved from the port, a sequence of administrative measures was set in train to place them in more suitable locations and to secure aid for their welfare. Like most of the Spanish and Italian refugees of the Restoration, they were also liberal constitutionalists, in flight from the violent repressions of Dom Miguel's absolutist reaction in Portugal during 1828.[43] The prefect of the department of the Finistère was charged with organising their removal into depots prepared specifically to receive them at Fougères in the department of Ille-et-Vilaine, and at Laval and Mayenne in the department of the Mayenne. Two detachments of refugees were sent separately from Brest, two days apart, so that they might be accommodated and provided for more easily on route. The sum of 30,000 francs was allocated to meet the cost of transport. The transfers were complete by 12 May, having proceeded orderly and without 'the slightest excitement', it was noted.[44] In all, 634 officers and soldiers were accommodated in these three depots, with monthly expenditure in relief and aid amounting to 30,720 francs even before the recovery of the debts incurred on their reception in Brest. The shortfall was met by a special grant of 9000 francs.[45]

Some 200 Portuguese were sent to Fougères and lodged in vacant military barracks at the expense of the War Ministry. Errors of planning, however, were probably unavoidable because of the haste with which the authorities cleared the refugees from Brest. Some 80 Portuguese were originally sent to Quimper, only to find that the barracks in which they were to be housed were already occupied by a French garrison; they were then sent on to Fougères.[46] Suggesting that these were the first dealings the prefect of the Ille-et-Villaine had with political refugees, the interior minister advised him of the measures he needed to take to ensure their proper care: 'they should not to be considered a military contingent, nor prisoners of war', he wrote. 'You will understand perfectly their position in respect to France, and you will act accordingly in your dealings with the principles among them'.[47]

The prefect of the Mayenne faced a common complaint of refugees, that their financial aid was not sufficient for their subsistence needs. He was sympathetic, but there was little he could do. 'For the most part', he advised the interior minister when requesting further aid, 'they are without means and live only on what has been provided to the end of the month'.[48] He also expressed grave concerns about the refugees' general well-being. Material conditions in the depots deteriorated as funds ran short, and the unwelcome consequences of accommodating them was all too apparent: the evident despair of the refugees themselves, and the continued drain on state outlays, which already amounted to 330,164 francs in the five months after their arrival.[49]

By then, 612 remained from the 634 refugees originally sent to the depots. Twenty-one had left for Brazil in the meantime. By September 1829, it was clear that the refugees were unable to provide for themselves and relied entirely on public assistance. Little work was available in these depot townships and only five of the refugees had found employment. They could not support themselves, and there was no remedy for their dire circumstances.

In October, therefore, on advice from the interior minister, King Charles X ordered the closure of the depots and the relocation of the refugees to towns where they would have a better opportunity to earn a living.[50]

They were relocated primarily to St Malo (Ille-et-Vilaine), in small detachments over eight consecutive days during October 1829.[51] As the refugees left the depots, the documentary record becomes less clear. Rennes and Brest were subsequently named as refugee depots, although the nature of the arrangements there is not explained. Refugees remained in other parts of the Ille-et-Villaine. They were free to move and settle elsewhere, but would have to forgo their financial aid if they did so.[52]

Most, indeed, went elsewhere; the majority reportedly went to Brazil.[53] The five refugees who had found work in Fougères remained behind with their employers when the depot was vacated, but the authority under which they were allowed to do so was doubtful. The minister's instructions were that all the refugees be removed, and the sub-prefect of Fougères ordered their immediate departure.[54] They took to the road, settling in village of Dol, outside St Malo, where they join up with others who had earlier left Fougères. But their fortunes turned from bad to worse. By January 1830, 39 Portuguese refugees had settled in Dol and were reportedly in the direst poverty because they had lost their financial assistance. Dol is a 'very poor village', its mayor warned the prefect of the Ille-et-Vilaine, 'and was unable to ensure these poor unfortunates an honest existence'. They had to be moved, he advised, to a town with a larger population where they would have better opportunities to improve their lot.[55] The Portuguese themselves resisted all moves to force them to leave, however, insisting that they had settled in the village and had developed personal relations they did not wish to abandon. Recognising their genuine humanitarian need, which a strict reading of earlier instructions would only worsen, the prefect secured from the Interior Ministry the reinstatement of their assistance so they could remain.[56]

\* \* \*

The formal organisation of refugee assistance drew together the various developments in the practice of asylum during the Restoration. These developments, which addressed problems of admission, policing, and organisation, reshaped asylum into an administrative function of the state. As this administrative system developed in response to refugees from the political ruptures in Spain, Italy, and Portugal, there was left in its wake a significant documentary trail from which it is possible to recover the changing character of asylum, and tantalising suggestions of the actual experiences of at least some the refugees. But it is a fragmentary trail. It is more complete on the question of organisation, which demanded cooperation and correspondence between various levels of the state bureaucracy, but it is less certain on admission and policing.

The documentary trail does, however, provide an answer to one key question of asylum under the Restoration. If the true value of asylum is the protection it offers to a regime's ideological opponents, then the Restoration was far more accommodating of refugees than was any stage of the revolutionary years. The main beneficiaries of asylum were liberal constitutionalists, opposed to the restoration of the European monarchies, against which many had taken up arms, and would do so again if circumstances allowed. Their admission to France might have been circumspect, and there was explicit emphasis on the surveillance of their movements and associations in order to police sedition. Yet they were assured asylum and for the most part were provided financial assistance for their material welfare.

This, then, was no return to monarchical asylum centred on the king's grace. Rather, the responses to problems of admission, policing, and organisation had centred asylum in the fabric of the state, its police and administrative apparatus. Provincial officials mediated the relationship of the refugees with France, and they were sensitive to the conditions that the refugees experienced in exile, above all their poor material circumstances. At the bureaucratic centre in the Interior Ministry, concern was more about the impact of refugee assistance on the state: the administrative burden of admission and organisation; the security burden of policing; and the burden of the cost of financial aid.

The costs could only be controlled by cutting back on the assistance paid directly to the refugees, irrespective of the impact this would have on their personal circumstances. In June 1830, therefore, the Interior Ministry decided to cease paying financial aid altogether from 1 August 1830. By then, however, the Restoration monarchy had been swept away in revolution.[57]

# Part II   Revolutionary Exiles and the July Monarchy, 1830–48

The French Revolution of July 1830 revived nationalist hopes across Europe as revolutionaries in Spain, Italy, Belgium, and Poland once more took up arms. With these hopes suppressed since the Congress of Vienna's restoration of the old regime, a new generation of revolutionaries now took inspiration from France. In the Italian duchies of Parma and Modena and in the northern Papal States, nationalists rose to oust the occupying Austrians; in Poland, nationalists went to war against Russian autarchy.[1]

For revolutionaries in France, the spirit of the July days advanced once more the cause of liberty first awakened in 1789; they would realise a new republic and throw off the tyranny that those usurpers of liberty, Britain, Austria, and Russia, had reimposed on them in 1814. The men who assumed power on 29 July 1830, however, imagined that anything less than the restoration of the Charter of 1814 would cast over France the dark shadow of the worst days of the Republic. They refused to speak of a new republic and passed the throne instead to the alternative royal line, Louis-Philippe, duc d'Orléans, the last rallying point, it is said, able to save French society from dissolution.[2]

Still, the July Monarchy embodied the uncertainties of the July revolution of 1830. General Lafayette, veteran now of three revolutions, the man who presented the new king to the people of Paris, proclaimed the regime to be the 'best of republics'. Louis-Philippe himself, the 'citizen king', declared that he would hold a 'popular throne surrounded by republican institutions'.[3] But he intended little more than the restoration of a free press and the liberal freedoms prescribed in the Charter. Popular sovereignty was limited to the high bourgeoisie, who alone could vote and sit in the parliament. Republicans and Bonapartists found no comfort in this. One king had replaced another when they had taken to the streets for a greater purpose. Disillusioned by the bourgeois betrayal of the their popular revolution, their agitation continued through the following years, questioning the July Monarchy's legitimacy and from time to time shaking its very confidence and authority. Only after this new regime had assumed some of the traits of autocracy, resistance to which had brought it to power, was it secure.[4]

The assertion of its legitimacy at home therefore shaped the July Monarchy's first years. A government of notables and high bourgeois, dominated at first by General Lafayette, then by the wealthy bankers Jacques Lafitte and Casimir Périer, and later by François Guizot and Adolphe Thiers, the new regime turned against the social revolution that had brought it to power. The change of monarchy did not amount to political revolution, official histories would say; instead, the events of July 1830 were described as a coup against Charles X to preserve liberty and restore the Charter.[5] The July Monarchy therefore resisted its own revolutionary origins in the face of the popular challenge to its legitimacy. The purpose of Orléanism was therefore the maintenance of civil order and the assertion of the rule of law against republican disorder. On these the regime's legitimacy rested. 'The government must be obeyed and served according to the spirit of its intentions', Casimir Périer, premier and interior minister, told the Chamber of Deputies on 18 March 1831. 'Respect for the law – that is the principle behind the July Revolution'.[6]

The July Monarchy also had to assure its legitimacy abroad. The revolution in France had turned the minds of the European monarchies back to 1789, and war seemed to threaten as insurrection rippled across Europe in its wake. Foreign monarchies viewed the overthrow of Charles X with alarm, and they had it within their powers to invoke the Concert of Europe's resolutions of 1815 to prevent France ever again destabilising Europe.[7] Anxious therefore not to be looked upon as a usurper, and eager to assure the foreign monarchies of his peaceful intentions, Louis-Philippe expressed his desire for peace. He had assumed the throne when it was offered to him, he assured them, to preserve the peace, to quell disorder, and to suppress republican anarchy that could embroil Europe if left unchecked.[8] France, therefore, would remain neutral and not intervene in insurrections abroad.

The opposition 'party of movement' found Louis-Philippe's timidity before the great powers reprehensible. Intervention in foreign insurrections was the revolution's inevitable outcome, republicans argued, but this was inconceivable for Louis-Philippe and the 'party of resistance' around him. Even the talk of war, they feared, exposed France to Austrian and Russian retaliation, and therefore the possibility of their occupation of Paris for a third time, and a third Bourbon restoration.[9]

The nationalist insurrections in Italy and Poland compounded the divisions and lingering resentments left from settlement of July 1830. They even alienated moderates from the new regime. Lafayette, whose political aspirations soon after the elevation of Louis-Philippe to the throne had settled somewhat uneasily between the two 'parties' of resistance and movement, believed that France still had an important role to play in the liberation of other peoples and therefore advocated military support for the revolts in Italy and Poland. Others berated the folly of war when France was so ill prepared for any foreign campaign.[10]

The great achievement of this moment, François Guizot, ideologue of Orléanism, recalled in his memoirs, was that, with so many reasons for war, Europe presented the rare spectacle of a passion for peace.[11] The consequences of this peace were grave for Spaniards, Italians, and Poles, however, as the authoritarian monarchies and foreign powers prosecuted dissenters. Many thousands went into exile, and although peace had flowed from French neutrality, France could not isolate itself from them. The revolutionary exiles from these insurrections were therefore a further challenge to the July Monarchy despite Casimir Périer's proclamation of October 1831, when defeated Polish nationalists began to arrive at the French frontier, that 'French generosity will always welcome the victims' of tyranny.[12] This was as it should be, Lafayette responded. The Poles were France's 'brothers in liberty ... disciples of '89, disciples of the right and sacred duty to resist oppression ... allies dedicated to the struggle against counter-revolution'.[13] Although France could not but welcome them as protector and benefactor, Périer's government could not accept such revolutionary sentiment.

It was certainly a 'noble and necessary prerogative' for independent states to offer the protection of their laws to foreigners, Guizot later recalled, but he worried that it also strained international relations. As a question of European law and domestic legislation, he continued, the 'right of asylum' (*droit d'asile*) was yet in its infancy. Internal security and external relations limited the realisation of the principles asylum embodied, but peace was maintained despite it: 'Our weak and incoherent ideas about its meaning not only aggravated the difficulties of keeping the peace after 1830, it vitiated against the peace, and prevented it from bearing its full fruits'.[14]

The phrase 'droit d'asile' entered into usage sometime between the French Revolution and the July Monarchy.[15] The use of 'droit', meaning both 'right' and 'law', to modify 'asile', reshaped asylum into a legal doctrine. But it was yet to take hold in custom and state practice and therefore its implications were uncertain. Its humanitarian purpose was clear, but the protection of revolutionaries at war with a foreign power had the potential to draw the protecting state into conflict with that power. Peace between these two powers, Guizot implies, could not be assured so long as the protecting doctrine of asylum was as uncertain as it was. Indeed, asylum vitiated against the peace because it offered exiles the freedom to pursue, unhindered by law, their revolutionary objectives.

The July Monarchy admitted refugees to asylum fully conscious that their political character ran contrary to its desire to maintain harmonious relations with the great powers. Its challenge then was to assure asylum while maintaining these harmonious relations. In both law and practice during the July Monarchy, therefore, asylum was defined and applied by constraints.

The legal and political implications of asylum were argued and contested within the parliament. Especially in its early years, the meaning of asylum was one issue of public policy that defined the very ideological tendency of the July Monarchy. The very nature of France's obligations to the refugees from foreign insurrections was questioned and debated in the Chamber of Deputies, raising principles of law and the administration of public policy, as well as legacies of French traditions.

# 3
# The Limits of Tolerance

Suspicion and distrust of certain groups of foreign refugees legitimised the imposition of constraints. Their role in civil disturbances was of special concern. In August 1831, 200 Italians led disturbances in Paris, when they expressed, according to the police report, the 'most contradictory opinions' against the government. Because a certain number of them posed such a danger to the civil order, the police recommended that they should be removed from the city altogether.[1] Elsewhere, troubles among Spanish refugees were particularly alarming. The prefect of police in Perpignan stressed the 'shameful role' they played, not for the first time, in local disturbances as they awaited a popular uprising. Their unrest attracted even more refugees, the prefect complained. 'We see [more] arrive every day at the frontier ... under the pretexts of persecutions they have suffered in their own country'. He advised that as a matter of urgency all foreigners should be removal from the city, and be allowed to live no closer than Montpellier.

These reports were sufficient for Casimir Périer to question the refugees' respect for the laws of the country that had so generously offered them asylum. Addressing the Chamber of Deputies, he twice read the concluding comment of the prefect in Perpignan: 'I regard it as essential and most proper that these effervescing germs (*germes d'effervescence*) be removed from the population of this department'.[2] These sorts of civil disturbances had become nothing less than contagion, and the cause, these hostile foreign refugees, had to be quarantined to quell dissent. Périer did not go so far as to adopt his suggestion, but it was nevertheless indicative of a policy of policing and containment that he and his government were beginning to implement, the central feature of which was the expansion of the network of depots where refugees were placed under police surveillance and the authority of the law.

The July Monarchy had inherited a large refugee population, and with it a highly developed system for their reception, accommodation, and assistance, including the use of depots to concentrate the refugees and moderate their activities. In September 1831, some 5000 refugees were provided financial assistance. Their numbers grew as defeated revolutionaries arrived from Italy, Spain, and Poland. Of the 1524 Italian refugees in France in 1831, 600 were accommodated in depots at Mâcon, Moulins, and Auxerre, 200 in Paris, 200 in Marseille, and 190 in Lyon, Dijon, and Clermont-Ferrand. Another 1800 Spanish offices and soldiers, engaged in the ongoing conflict with Ferdinand VII, had arrived during 1831. New depots, in the departments of the Cher, Lozère, Dordogne, Puy-de-Dôme, Vienne, and Haute-Vienne were needed to relieve the pressures on the depots in Tours, Moulins, Poitiers, Blois, Bourges, Alençon, Le Mans, and Montferrand.[3]

The locations of the depots often changed as administrative requirements and refugee numbers changed. As new refugees arrived and others left, returning to their homelands or migrating onwards, their numbers fluctuated. Many refugees frequently transferred between depots. It was imperative that they be kept at a distance from the frontier so that they could not compromise France's foreign relations by continuing their struggles within France or engage in cross-border militancy. Control over their activities was therefore reinforced by their confinement to the depots; they could not receive their financial allowances unless they remained there, and they were not free to travel without the interior minister's authorisation.[4]

The refugee depots expose contradictions in both the conception and practice of asylum, however. They were the practical expression of the protective principle of asylum, but they also confined and contained. Their purpose was twofold: the provision of assistance and special care, and the moderation and control of the refugees' behaviours and movements. The depots were a place of sanctuary, certainly, but the daily lives of the refugees within them were strictly policed. In at least one instance there was a ready comparison between the depot and a prison. Near Montferrand, 300 Spanish liberals were confined to a deserted military barracks. Local instructions specifically stated that they 'should not be considered prisoners' but should instead be shown special care: 'They have the right to all that a generous and hospitable nation is pleased to accord them'. Still, not all the refugees' behaviour could be controlled. Confined to the barracks and with nothing to do all day, they grew agitated and subsumed by their internal conflicts. The local community was exasperated when Spanish refugees were seen marauding through the fields and gardens wielding knives.[5] The idea of the refugee depot as a prison therefore could well have been reassuring to the inhabitants of the townships in which the depots were placed.

The rise in refugee numbers during 1831 placed increasing demands on France's resources. On three occasions the government requested special advances from the Chamber of Deputies to meet the cost of refugee assistance: for 600,000 francs on 30 September, 500,000 francs on 26 October, and a further 500,000 francs on 28 November, to make a total of 1,884,320 francs for 1831.[6] Each request was an opportunity for debate on France's protection obligations and the very meaning of asylum. As head of government in the Chamber, Périer used these debates to defend the limits he wanted to impose on France's obligations in order to contain the drain on resources and demand the respect of the refugees for their protectors and benefactors.[7] Events in Poland in late 1831 put further pressure on the July Monarchy. News of the fall of Warsaw to Nicholas I's Russian army arrived in November; stories of atrocities perpetrated against the Poles soon followed. Fears for these courageous Poles, who stood apart in the minds of many as the true inheritors of France's spirit of revolution, brought Paris once more to the verge of insurrection.

The Polish liberation struggle had brought the French together in a common cause and forged a certain unity out of the divisions of July 1830. Lafayette had formed a national committee, the Comité Polonais, to raise money to send to the Poles.[8] The French people could therefore make a personal gesture in their support when the government refused aid and military support. The public mood ebbed and flowed with the changing fortunes of the insurrection, from despair at Polish setbacks to delight and joy at Polish victories.[9] In March 1831, after the Poles were defeated at Grochow, students occupied the Place du Panthéon for several days. Demonstrating their sympathies for their Polish heroes, they wore red and white ribbons of the Polish national colours, and black armbands of mourning. They marched through the streets shouting 'vengeance for Poland, death to Russia!' as they made for the Chamber of Deputies.[10]

Popular sentiment seemed to be drawing France to war, but when news arrived of Polish victories in April 1831, the Parisian police reported a palpable relaxation of the public mood, which stayed fears of growing insurrectionary ferment.[11] But bitterness at Louis-Philippe's refusal to intervene on the side of the Poles continued to disturb the public mood. On news of the fall of Warsaw, there were four days of protests and riots. Business was suspended and shops closed. Italian refugees, already angered by the government's timid response to events in Italy, were among the most active. An angry crowd surged through the streets chanting their support for Poland, hurling insults at Louis-Philippe and Casimir Périer, and demanding vengeance against Russia. Ten thousand people occupied Place Louis XV, and a crowd besieged the Palais-Royal, Louis-Philippe's residence, and then moved on to try to invade the Chamber of Deputies.[12]

Sympathies for foreign revolutionaries flowed over into support for the refugees even before they had arrived in France. The money subscribed to the Comité Polonais was subsequently used to assist Polish refugees and to support them in their journey across central Europe.

As support for the Poles could be construed as open hostility to Russia, their asylum in France could be mistaken as an act that threatened the peace. This Périer could not countenance. It was not the government's intention, he asserted in the Chamber, that assistance for the Polish refugees bear any hint of support for their political cause; his opponents were mistaken if they thought otherwise. 'Some insist', he declared, 'that it is political to help the refugees. We don't think so. We insist that it is only humanitarian ... France undertakes only to help the person in adversity, and from that moment he contracts an obligation to recognise an act of charity (*bienfait*)'. France offered asylum as a humanitarian gesture, an act of *bienfaisance*. Nor, Périer continued, was asylum the recognition of a right: it 'cannot and ought not' have such an implication.[13]

*Bienfaisance* set definite parameters around the protection of refugees. It moved beyond the politics and principles asylum had acquired during the years of revolution, which recognised the legitimacy of insurrection and the natural right of protection for the pursuit of liberty. As a revolutionary principle, asylum had held the protecting state to more than protection; it implied above all political support for their insurrectionary struggles. *Bienfaisance*, on the other hand, implied that there were obligations on the refugees commensurate with the obligations asylum made on the French. These were assumed, Périer argued, when France extended protection and assistance to foreign refugees; refugees then assumed in return an obligation to respect French laws. If this was not asked of them, Périer maintained, France would be unguarded before their revolutionary sentiments and their political hostilities, and be greatly burdened by liabilities on the public purse. Refugees had no unquestioned right to receive asylum; the French people judged who was in need of protection and properly granted it to them. Périer likened asylum to 'hospitality', which expressed France's 'affinity' with refugees, as well as their deference to their protectors.[14]

Thus Périer, and shortly after him François Guizot, reframed the terms of asylum consistent with the conservative ideology and political neutrality of the July Monarchy. If circumspection and caution were required when refugees were admitted to France, Guizot stressed, it was because the government had to guard against foreigners whose different values and different ideals might adversely impact on events and on popular passions. The aim of government under the July Monarchy at such a time, he continued, was to set the precise limits of tolerance. It had to balance what it could tolerate with what it could not, so as to safeguard the 'national polity' and to ensure that 'the peace, prosperity, security, sound foreign relations, all the interests of the country, are not compromised by passing events and the emotions they might excite'.[15]

*Bienfaisance* and hospitality therefore expressed a restrictive notion of asylum. They were terms unencumbered by principles of rights or political ideals inherited from earlier times. *Bienfaisance* placed asylum within the state's authority, to give to those whom it found deserving. Hospitality held to the tradition of France as a country open to foreigners and welcoming to those in need of protection. Other linguistic innovations emphasised this. Refugees were often referred to as 'guests' enjoying the benefits of French hospitality. Or they were described as 'les malheureux'—those suffering misfortune—to express humanitarian sentiment and the righteousness of assistance.

Although these terms implied a new conception of asylum, its protecting principle was nevertheless extolled as an expression of French values and its national sentiment. Asylum and the burdens that flowed from it were sacrifices France willingly carried to alleviate a refugee's suffering, Guizot asserted: 'This is the glory of our homeland, our national disposition'.[16] The Orléanist deputy Parant went so far as to suggest that 'hospitality' was 'owed by the nation, as it would be by an individual, to whosoever demands asylum ... because France is the land of liberty'.[17] Félix Barthe, the justice minister, stated that there was no question about the grant of asylum to those proscribed in their homelands for political reasons. They would always find 'inviolable asylum' on French soil, he told the Chamber, and France would willingly extend financial assistance to those 'who are without fortune or industry and who do not have a means of existence'.[18]

Asylum therefore conveyed a mix of sentiments. Politically it had been redefined around limits of tolerance, yet profound sentiments of national character, values and principles persisted. At the same time, the notion of the refugee became uncertain. The defining characteristic was assuredly their exile from their homelands for political reasons, but as new notions of asylum were articulated, the foreigner was sometimes more the subject of debate than the refugee. National distinctions justified state intervention and police controls. Périer at one stage declared that France could not but assert its authority over foreign refugees because it was 'French' and not 'Belgian, Italian and Spanish'.[19] Guizot argued that refugees could not share the same freedoms as the French because as foreigners they did not share the same rights; nor could they give the same guarantees to the state as the French: their 'interests, their affairs, their entire existence' were not bound to the country in which they lived.[20] Refugees were first and foremost foreigners. They were described as 'réfugiés étrangers', or more commonly 'étrangers réfugiés', where 'refugees' (*réfugiés*) is the adjective describing the character of foreigners (*étrangers*). As refugees, they were foreigners, but of a particular kind. These appellations merged two distinct conceptions into a unique classification that became the central characteristic of refugee discourse under the July Monarchy: the refugee was neither a national nor a foreigner, but held a distinct status, morally, legally, and politically. The assertions of French hospitality and the inviolability of asylum recognised the moral claims of refugees to protection from those who would punish them for their political actions, and affirmed the obligations of the French to protect their lives and liberties. Yet these very moral claims were troubled by the tendency of policy towards police surveillance and control. Both refugee policy and refugee discourse were consequently riven by ambiguities and uncertainties.

A number of deputies challenged Périer for what they believed was his affront to the revolutionary ideals and the spirit of liberation France inspired in others. The constraints on the liberties of refugees, his demands that they defer to the French people, respect French laws, and suffer the loss of their freedoms, denied the very sentiments that these ideals extolled. Refugees, therefore, were the cause of passionate debate about the ideological foundations and the political tendencies of the July Monarchy. Lafayette, by the end of 1831 estranged from the regime he had helped install, insisted that revolution was at the heart of French national sentiment, which Louis-Philippe had betrayed when he turned his back on the revolutionaries of Poland and Italy and deferred instead to the European monarchies.[21] The affinities between foreign revolutionaries and the July Monarchy's revolutionary origins should have defined the new regime, Anne-Joseph Salverte, a deputy from Paris, asserted in response to Périer. The refugees and the French deputies in the Chamber had pursued the same ideals of liberty and resistance to oppression: 'the difference between them and us', he asserted, 'is the success we have had'.[22] By rejecting this affinity and by constraining the freedoms of the refugees, Salverte insisted, the new regime not only turned its back on its origins, it also rejected the very principle of liberation through revolution.[23] For Jacques-François Joly, a radical deputy from the Ariège, the refugees represented wrongs that France was obliged to make good: by its intercession in Spanish affairs in 1823 France had created a crisis that had forced many refugees into exile; it could not now demand their deference. On the terms that Périer had outlined, Joly contended, the very concept of asylum was belittled since it humiliated those who were in need of it: 'They only ask for bread, provided it's not the bread of humiliation and contempt'.[24]

The dissenting deputies were certainly few in number. They had themselves experienced periods of exile or imprisonment after the Restoration of 1814 and now sat on the extreme left of the Chamber. But they were a radical challenge that compelled Périer and his government to defend their position. The contested ideals of the nation and France's revolutionary heritage were important points of contention. Another was the very ideological premise of asylum. Against the doctrine of *bienfaisance* that Périer and Guizot had advocated, Jean-Pierre Pagès, another radical deputy from the Ariège, reasserted principles of natural rights. If asylum possessed humanitarian value, Pagès began, it was because its meaning lay not in notions of *bienfaisance* but in natural law and the universal rights of peoples that governed international relations, the *droit des gens*. To argue otherwise, as Périer had, Pagès continued, one distorted natural law and the foundations it gave to proper relations between peoples. *Bienfaisance* and hospitality insulted the refugees, Pagès argued, because they stripped them of their natural rights. The inherent and universal rights of individuals did not require them to defer to the state; the state had to defer to them: refugees did not seek charity but invoked a right that France was obliged to respect. Assistance on the conditions that Périer had demanded was not an act of humanity but a 'bitter' act of arbitrary government, to 'prove to Europe that unhappy patriots find neither sympathy nor pity in France'.[25]

Although many deputies did not oppose the government on the principles of asylum, they were nevertheless willing to voice their support for Pagès and his criticisms of the powers that Périer, as interior minister, was assuming for himself. He could determine the refugees' place of residence and order their banishment without judicial oversight; he could raise or lower their levels of assistance at his own discretion, and he had therefore the unregulated power to revoke it entirely and to leave them destitute while offering only, in Pagès' words, 'dishonour or death by starvation'. His critics argued that Périer had granted the police special powers of intervention and surveillance and had made himself arbiter and judge of the conditions under which the refugees were granted asylum, the benefits that would flow from asylum, and the penalties for breaching the conditions imposed on them.[26] All these powers, many deputies observed, recalled the arbitrary rule of despotism.

## The law of asylum

The Asiatic cholera struck Paris in March 1832, arriving from the east at much the same time as the Polish refugees. Over the next six months it would kill 18,402 Parisians, mostly working poor in the overcrowded quarters. The notables on the right bank looked on with dread. Political anxieties merged with anxieties of contagion; it seemed revolution had unleashed so many dangerous forces. On 3 April, Casimir Périer himself took ill, suffering intolerably before dying on 16 May.[27]

The appearance of the thousands of uprooted Polish nationalists and revolutionaries, when Périer was absent from the Chamber, changed the rhetoric on refugees. Circumspection and caution about how the government should deal with the Poles replaced Périer's earlier condemnation of refugee behaviour. The government's response to earlier criticism that Périer had begun to assume too much arbitrary power for himself was to pass a statute to bring the administrative measures of 1831 into law. The Law Relating to Foreign Refugees Residing in France (*Loi relative aux réfugiés étrangers qui résideront en France*) received royal assent on 21 April 1832. The law confirmed the interior minister's discretionary powers over the residence and entitlements of foreign refugees. He had the power to order the confinement of refugees to specific depots; he could provide financial assistance to them but also to take it away if they should infringe the conditions of their asylum—by deserting the depots or by posing a threat to the public peace—or order the ultimate sanction, their expulsion from the country.[28]

The purpose of the law was therefore to define the power of the state over foreign refugees. The debate on the law, however, pertained less to the rights and entitlements of refugees than to the status of foreigners. The rapporteur of the legislative commission that drafted the bill, Narcisse Parant, identified three questions that needed to be addressed: What were the responsibilities of a state towards foreigners? Did foreigners have the same status before the law as nationals? Were there precedents for the government's intentions to legislate to give foreigners a different status?[29] Quite simply, Parant concluded, the differences between the French and foreigners were substantial. Reciprocal obligations, not individual rights, defined their relative status. The French national held more than hereditary ties with the land (*pays*); the law held the national, or subject (*régnicole*), to obligations of work, service (*assistance personnel*) and taxes (*contributions en argent*); specific benefits flowed from them. Only the French could share affinities with the nation; foreigners could not, nor did they have the same obligations as a subject. Foreigners therefore simply had no claim to the same rights as those enjoyed by French nationals.[30] Justice Minister Barthe therefore insisted that existing laws on the status of foreigners were imprecise as they had been enacted by the Republic when the infiltration of enemy aliens was a real threat. A new law was necessary to clarify the status of foreigners and France's authority over them under the new regime.[31]

The proposed law, however, related specifically to refugees and not to foreigners, and this distinction was overlooked in Parant's exposition. Not only does this suggest an imprecise conceptual understanding of the refugee but also an imprecisely delineated boundary between foreigners and refugees. Earlier affirmations of French hospitality and the inviolability of asylum recognised the moral claims of refugees to protection, but the distinct status of refugees before the law was justified on the grounds that they were foreigners, or 'foreign refugees' (*réfugiés étrangers*).

Who, then, were the proper beneficiaries of asylum? This too was imprecisely defined. Other double-epithets appeared. They were 'political refugees' (*réfugiés politiques*), where the political reasons for their expatriation was invoked. At other times their nationalities identified them in public discourse: Italian and Spanish refugees (*réfugiés italien, réfugiés espagnol*), or Polish refugees (*réfugiés polonais*). The word 'refugee' was rarely self-defining. These terms all assumed a common understanding of the refugee's revolutionary background. Lafayette again fell back on to old revolutionary principles, calling them 'foreign patriots' (*patriotes étrangers*).[32] General Lamarque, hero of Napoléon's Grande Armée who had earlier called on France to go to the defence of the Poles, rejected the term 'foreign refugees' because it described the alienation of their natural rights and therefore took from them their unquestioned right of asylum.[33] Lamarque was indeed perceptive. The purpose of the law of April 1832 was precisely to alienate the political aspirations and nationalist causes of foreign revolutionaries from the July Monarchy by recasting them as foreigners against whom special measures should be taken. Claims that they might have to a natural right of asylum were thereby neutralised. But, again, who were the proper beneficiaries of asylum?

The April 1832 law related only to refugees who were paid financial assistance. Similar conditions were not placed on refugees who lived by their private means, the number of whom was not known but seemingly considerable. The law therefore created two classes of refugees, assisted and unassisted (*secourus et non-secourus*). No restrictions were placed on the residence and movements of the latter, apart from those commonly applied to all foreigners while travelling and residing in France. Parant explained that the existing laws were sufficient for the government to intervene against these unassisted refugees when necessary and oblige them to leave the country if they too troubled the public peace.[34]

This exposed one further anomaly in the July Monarchy's response to refugees. Why should there now be a new law relating to refugees if there were existing laws that were considered sufficient for the control of foreigners? One explanation was that the existing laws dated from the Directory and there were doubts about their validity. Parant cited specifically laws of 26 Vendémiaire year VI (17 October 1797) and 22 Messidor year VII (10 July 1799) which authorised the surveillance of foreigners and conferred on the government the power to revoke their passports and expel them from the country if they troubled the public order.[35] Yet these same laws were considered sufficiently valid to be all the authority the government required to deal with troublesome foreigners and unassisted refugees.[36]

The law of 1832 therefore gave statutory authority to the confinement of foreign revolutionaries admitted to asylum so that they would be kept under surveillance and could not form secret alliances with French republicans, could not conspire and imperil France's foreign relations, or could not otherwise trouble the peace and security of the country. The justification of the law, that it was proper and legally valid for the state to make special laws relating to foreigners, was full of contradictions and anomalies that derived from uncertainties about how the new paradigm of asylum should be implemented. This new paradigm, as explained by Périer in October 1831, centred on reciprocal obligations, which held the refugees in deference to the state, to respect its laws, and not to trouble the public peace. It was decided that this could best be enforced by their confinement and surveillance in designated depots. This made asylum an instrument of state, politically, administratively, and legally. Law and not rights mediated the relationship between the refugees and the French state, and policing placed the refugees under the power of the state.

The April law nevertheless failed to answer precisely who could be defined as a refugee. As far as he understood the sense of the term, the deputy Justin Laurence intervened, a 'refugee' was 'not someone who travels in another country, roaming freely and living off his personal resources' but 'someone who receives hospitality at the expense of those who give it'. Did this include, he then asked, 'even the rich man who does not properly seek an asylum among us, but rather a peaceful respite that is not offered in his own homeland?'[37] There was no convincing response. Barthe replied that the law applied to those who reside in France 'without passport, with no money provided by an ambassador' and 'without relations with an ambassador ... they were, more simply, those found to be in a state that all would call the state of being a refugee'.[38] He was quickly reminded, however, that most of the refugees in France at that time had been provided with passports, either by French ambassadors abroad or on their arrival.[39] The deputy Nicholas Fiot described refugees as 'men who had fought for their own institutions, for a homeland, for their freedom', while General Lamarque shunned such subtleties and defined refugees, as had Lafayette, as 'friends of liberty', a description which nevertheless seemed to exclude Spanish royalists, for example, who supported Ferdinand VII's restoration of absolutism in 1823 and were victims of retaliation from liberal constitutionalists.[40] Charles Dupin described refugees more astutely as 'those foreigners residing in France without the protection of their government'.[41]

There was in fact no agreed meaning, and the attempts to define who was a refugee left its meaning even more confused.[42] There was, however, a general consensus on broad principles, which suggests that all the deputies had a fair idea about who they believed were refugees deserving of protection. Political refugees were made in flight and alienation from their homelands because of political circumstances. But the new terms of asylum under the July Monarchy defined the refugee in material and administrative terms: they were those exiles from political events abroad who were paid financial assistance and were confined to refugee depots, and suffered limits on their freedom in order to receive it.

There was still resistance to the powers that the April law placed in the hands of the interior minister, however. Jean-Pierre Pagès, who had first challenged Périer in the debate on refugees in October 1831, again took to the tribune to protest. The law confirmed the minister's arbitrary powers over the refugees, he complained; asylum was granted at his discretion, on terms he himself set. Asylum was therefore a relationship between the refugee and the minister himself on unequal terms and without guarantees of protection. This was an unacceptable arbitrary and discretionary power held by one minister of state, and Pagès demanded that it be removed from the law. He proposed an approach to asylum that was more in keeping with his notions of natural rights: it was a relationship between the refugees and the French people and therefore should be moderated by their representatives. To circumscribe the minister's powers therefore, and to place asylum on what he claimed to be a fairer, more-just footing, Pagès, along with Joly, who had also protested against Périer in earlier debates, and another deputy from the left of the Chamber, Jean-Baptiste Teste of the Gard, moved an amendment that would have established a parliamentary commission to determine the rights and entitlements of refugees. The powers conferred by the law would then be subject to parliamentary scrutiny and judicial oversight, and the relationship between the refugees and the state would retain its integrity. The rights and freedoms of the refugees would be respected in turn, and the refugees themselves would be free of the constraints on their movements. In short, all of the indignities that Périer forced onto them the previous year would be rescinded.[43]

Although this amendment was voted down, other deputies were nevertheless concerned about the arbitrary powers the law placed in the hands of the interior minister. Odilon Barrot and Garnier-Pagès both rose to denounce the tendency towards policing and discretionary ministerial authority displayed in the law, which they both asserted was reminiscent of despotism. Sensitive to these accusations, particularly that of despotism, government ministers conceded that the powers conferred by the law were only required to deal with the temporary political and social turmoil then fracturing France, and accepted that these special measures might not be required once the emergency had passed. The government therefore agreed to an amendment that that law be adopted for one year only instead of the permanent statute it originally proposed. This placated the anxieties of the government's critics and steadied the nerves of those who feared that the refugees might bring with them the troubles that had shaken Europe since 1830.[44]

## Containment, care, and control

The law of April 1832 consolidated a policy that had gradually taken shape around three objectives, containment, care, and control: containment through confinement of the refugees to designated depots; care through the provision of financial aid, which was conditional upon their remaining within the bounds of their depots; and control through police surveillance and the regulation of movements and other constraints on freedoms and associations in order to preserve the public peace. This was a policy that responded to the social and political conditions then afflicting France. Popular protest, unrest, and a general sense of disquiet across the country was reason enough for the government to impose controls on such a large number of foreign revolutionaries, then well in excess of 5000 assisted refugees and an unknown number of unassisted refugees, who kept their political struggles alive in exile.

In October 1831, Périer had condemned the refugees from Spain as 'effervescing germs' because they attracted more of their 'desperate countrymen'; they were a contagion spreading all sorts of ills which spilled unrest in Spain over into France.[45] The Polish refugees of 1832, in contrast, evoked great sympathies among the French people for their brave stance to reclaim their freedom from Russian autarchy. Public disquiet about the July Monarchy's failure to intervene on their side, and lingering resentments stirred by the growing presence of the Polish refugees, made the government more circumspect in its public statements. It preferred instead to stress the need for administrative control to quell any disruption that might follow in the backwash of events rippling into France.

The anxieties of malady were altogether real when the cholera struck and new fears took hold. The convergence of infectious disease, revolution, and the presence of the foreign refugees proved the depth of the social and political malaise that disturbed the conservative order of the July Monarchy. The cholera compounded a sense of decay that had followed the July revolution. Civil unrest continued while the public administration struggled to cope with the arrival of large numbers of poor from the provinces who settled in the overcrowded and decrepit neighbourhoods of the capital.[46] Foreign refugees were yet one more factor with which the government and its administration had to contend.

The contagion of cholera took a number of forms, all obscure and fearful. Among them was the infection of fear itself. It infected the working districts with the fear that the bourgeoisie was trying to resolve Paris' social problems by killing them off; it infected the bourgeois quarters with the fear that they were no longer safe from the dangerous classes.[47] Revolution, civil turmoil, and disease were all reminders of decay and of malady haunting the capital.[48] They all followed in quick succession. Sickness lay at the heart of Paris and was attributed to revolution.[49] After all, the spread of the disease could be traced back to the uprising in Poland. Some could blame it on the Russian army and its oppression of the Poles, as rumour spread that the cholera had 'attached itself to their caravans and their armies ... spilling its poisons into the war'.[50] Others blamed it on an excess of political passions, which, Catherine Kudlick argues, had a particular resonance for supporters of the July Monarchy, a regime that personified the bourgeois ethos of moderation, restraint, and balance.[51]

While medical science could dispel the fear that the infection was brought into France by the heroes of the great Polish insurrection of 1831, the general malaise of the infected capital defied rational understanding. At any given moment during the first half of 1832, Louis Chevalier writes, political agitation was simply the sum of other forms of agitation in which it was difficult to determine what was the public element and what was the private. Since the lower classes readily misunderstood the cholera epidemic as a form of criminality the bourgeoisie had inflicted on them, it was also difficult to determine what was political and what was criminal.[52] Nor could the purpose of civil unrest be determined, which made it all the more fearful. Strategies of containment were necessary for the administration of disease, which was a police as much as a medical matter. A policy of vigilance would ensure that calm and order were preserved; sanitary regulations served both law and order and health concerns.[53]

Social chaos, fear and decay, and the association of epidemic disease with revolution all recalled the worst excesses of the Republic in 1793–4. The very fear of these excesses was reason enough for the Orléanist bourgeoisie to recoil from of the volatile public mood and the desire of many for a new republic. The need to control disruptive elements justified the rigid policy of the containment of refugees. This was an attack on one source of social infection just as the medical profession launched an attack on the pathological infection of epidemic disease, and as the regime itself attacked sources of political dissent to impose order and stability.

Yet refugee protection was burdened with ideological significance. The rights of the refugees, Pagès had argued, lay foremost in principles of natural rights. Shared revolutionary aspirations and political affinities gave further meaning to rights and the principles behind them. The new paradigm of asylum as containment, care and control, not only rejected ideas of rights and political affinities, it set down a conception of asylum that was free of their imputations while nevertheless responsive to the humanitarian needs of the refugees. In describing asylum under the July Monarchy as *bienfaisance*, then, Périer and Guizot fell back onto another distinct tradition.

### The social role of *bienfaisance*

One of the more important changes to the provision of charitable aid during the eighteenth century, as Catherine Duprat shows in her exceptional work on the history of philanthropy, was the organisation of *bienfaisance* for the purpose of social improvement. Philanthropists made substantial investments of knowledge and time as well as money to improve social conditions through the expansion of education, public hygiene, work and production, and social protection.[54] Contemporary discourses would use terms such as 'les malheureux' (the unfortunates) to describe those on the social margins, whose 'asylum' was any place where they found assistance, care, or shelter.[55] By the time of the July Monarchy, Duprat continues, charitable assistance (*secours*) had become associated with the need for watchfulness (*surveiller*). The purpose of *bienfaisance* was less the provision of food for the poor and education for children than it was instruction, moralising, and surveillance of the poor, adults and children alike. Aid was an obligation that served a greater social purpose, the protection of public order: the poor would benefit from the better habits religion and work would give them, and society would thereby gain the best guarantees of security.[56]

The social programme of *bienfaisance* therefore already had assumed the character of containment, care, and control that Périer and Guizot applied to the political refugees under France's protection. There were clear continuities with measures for the administration of the poor and insane in the last years of the old regime. Instructions of 1785 on the management of poor houses (*dépôts de mendicité*) by Jean Colombier and François Doublet, for example, authorised official intervention in the care and confinement of the insane for the protection of the public order as much as for the care and protection of the insane themselves. This was more than a matter of civil order and protection, Jan Goldstein finds; such official intervention also expressed sentiments of pity and hope for the weakest members of society. How much, then, might the recurring linguistic description of refugees as 'les malheureux' express similar sentiments of pity and hope, and therefore justify the provision of welfare for their material benefit? Measures for the preservation of the social order and the provision of care to those in need were assuredly indistinguishable. Just as Périer ordered the surveillance of the refugees to guard the public safety while providing them aid, so too under these instructions of 1785 the insane required above all attention and surveillance, to assuage public fear by preventing them from troubling society while at the same time providing humanitarian care consonant with 'visions of *bienfaisance*'.[57]

The social role of *bienfaisance* was also evident in the medical profession. The medical journal, *Annales d'hygiène publique et de medicine légale*, founded in 1829, announced that the cure of illness was not the medical profession's sole objective; it also had an important social function, to aid legislators with the framing of laws, magistrates with their application, and the public administration with the maintenance of public health and civil order.[58] Another social function of medicine was the development of institutions for care and protection. The conversion of beggar's prisons into asylums for the infirm, orphans, beggars, and the insane had already begun in 1818. The asylum thereafter was conceived both as a place of incarceration as well as a place of protection as physical boundaries were drawn between those being protected by the state and those being protected from the abnormal. Three objectives sat comfortably together there: containment through incarceration, care through assistance, and control through surveillance. These were readily observed in practice when the first asylum for the insane was established in Auxerre in 1838.[59]

As the protective boundaries separating the infirm, the poor, and the insane from the rest of society defined 'asylum' in definite material form, attention also turned to the domain outside them. Deteriorating urban conditions, poverty, and the consciousness of the 'dangerous classes' within the urban milieu could not be so contained behind material boundaries; nevertheless, similar notions of containment, care, and control could be readily adopted to draw imagined boundaries. Social surveys could be as much prescriptive of solutions as they were descriptive of the ills they contemplated. Those of Morogue and Gérando, published respectively in 1834 and 1839, Louis Chevalier shows, reveal vastly different anxieties about these imagined boundaries. Morogue believed exclusion of the 'undesirable classes' was the best form of containment and the protection of public order. Because the poor and beggars, both equally dangerous and equally distressed, mingled in one and same mode of life, he proposed containment at its most extreme, their actual removal from cities. Gérando, on the other hand, saw the city itself as an asylum, an enclosed domain whose internal structures provided all that was required for the containment, care, and control of the undesirable classes. The city was self-moderating, where the middle-class between the poor and the rich extended the resources of their more liberal and more enlightened *bienfaisance*, and ensured the protection of the weak.[60] Within this city-asylum, the imagined boundaries had some tangible form—the city walls, separation between the urban precincts, class divisions—which mediated the forms of containment, care, and control.

Paris was itself portrayed as an asylum. Henri Wallon, who would succeed to Guizot's chair of History at the Sorbonne, made this the subject of his 1837 thesis for the Faculty of Letters. Like the sacred places of antiquity which had protected fugitives from the 'violence of the law' and the 'vengeance of justice', the faubourgs of medieval Paris grew in the protective shadows of monasteries, churches and the houses of lords and princes who moderated the life of the community through their protection, charity, and the administration of law.[61] Wallon presented a history of the practices and customs of asylum reconstructed from ancient scriptures and literature, and from the laws of lost civilisations. Its interest rests in Wallon's defence, perhaps the final defence, of the Christian values of asylum, which had scarcely been a part of its conception since the Enlightenment. The moral purpose of asylum, Wallon wrote, as evident in the Christian era as in antiquity, was the protection of the weak and vulnerable from the violence of the state when it sought to impose its justice to an excessive degree. The beneficiary of asylum was invested with a religio-moral status against temporal and secular authority. Yet, as the state acquired power over the church and asserted its authority more ruthlessly, this moral status was replaced by the imperfect recognition of rights and the unrestricted assertion of state authority over the individual. Wallon concluded that a choice was presented to both the church and the state in the eighteenth century, between saving offenders in flight from the violence of justice and exposing the innocent to punishment. In his view, the church correctly retained the right of asylum while it was abolished in secular state practice. The right of asylum remained a religious principle scarcely recognised in the secular state, he concluded; the appeal to divine law was the one form of protection that remained if the laws of man were instruments of violence.[62] Wallon's defence of antique values was more than reactionary nostalgia in the face of modern forms of political administration; it was above all an expression of the need to reinvest asylum in its modern form with past ideals.

## The *Droit des Gens* and the public rights of the French

When he invoked the natural right of asylum, Jean-Pierre Pagès similarly expressed less nostalgia for past ideals than the need for contemporary practices to reflect past ideals better. He returned to Enlightenment notions of natural rights and the *droit des gens* to defend the refugees' right of asylum, which legal and administrative state interventions had abused. Specifically, he asserted principals of the *droit des gens* in his attack on Périer's negation of refugee rights and the constraints he placed on their freedoms if they were to enjoy French charity. 'It is not a gesture of charity (*bienfait*) that the refugees seek from the humanity of France', Pagès proclaimed; 'it is a right they invoke, and in the midst of events shaking Europe each day, it is short-sighted to strip away the first rule of the *droit des gens*'.[63] The *droit des gens* for Pagès was steeped more in customary traditions than the positive law of representative government. As the *droit des gens* concerned the relations between peoples, customs and natural rights should therefore determine state behaviour. Therefore, Pagès held, when an individual was in flight, political rights were lost but the *droit des gens* was acquired. Refugees stood beyond state laws and therefore held a special status:

> The citizen who establishes himself in a foreign country cannot be apprehended by the government he has fled as he is outside its territory; nor can he be harmed by the government that he has adopted since it has nothing to reproach him with. When a foreigner presents himself, he does not claim the right of asylum; it belongs to him, because the right belongs to him, because he acquired it the moment he touched the foreign country's soil.[64]

By asserting natural rights, Pagès highlighted how they had lost their meaning. Yet the *droit des gens* was adaptable to different contexts. Its use in the debates on refugees confused rather than clarified abstract conceptions of rights and legal norms. Guizot had spoken of the *droit des gens* on two occasions in 1831, not, like Pagès, to defend natural rights, but rather to legitimise the obligations and constraints France had imposed on its refugees. In the first instance the *droit des gens* expressed humane respect for their misfortunes; the second expressed a doctrine that gave France both the power and the right to intercept Spanish refugees as they crossed the border in order to preserve France's good relations with the Spanish government.[65]

These ambiguities suggest doctrines in transition. Pagès believed that the principles of natural rights inherent in the *droit des gens* transcended state law; Guizot used it to assert the rule of law. Both argued quite divergent conceptions of asylum and refugee rights in the same terminology. But the significance of Pagès' intervention in the debates on refugees in 1831 is the degree to which he held fast to Enlightenment ideals. His defence of natural rights and his more traditional understanding of the *droit des gens*, which seems not to have moved beyond Enlightenment jurisprudence while sovereign states and positive law had moved in new directions, was a rejection of the diminution of these values in his contemporary France. By invoking these traditions he attempted to reinvest asylum and the rights of refugees with principles that politics and the law seemed to have stripped away. His insistence on natural rights especially was a reminder of the revolutionary inheritance of the French. On these the Declaration of the Rights of Man and the Citizen had rested, as did, in Pagès' mind, the ideal of France as an asylum for all in flight from oppression. But the July Monarchy had turned its back on this inheritance.

How then had the July Monarchy received its inheritance of the Declaration of the Rights of Man and the Citizen, and indeed how did it understand notions of individual rights? Because its legitimacy rested on the restoration of the Charter of 1814, the July Monarchy admitted no other document on rights than its 'Public Rights of the French', which were affirmed in full when redrafted into the Charter of 1830. The demands made of foreign refugees after 1830 were more firmly rooted in the principles of reciprocal obligations found in the Declaration of the Rights and Duties of Man and the Citizen of 1795 than in the natural rights upheld in the 1789 Declaration. The 1795 document emphasised the duties that flowed from the recognition of an individual's rights; it expressed the doctrine of the 'rights of man in society', which refuted the precedence of natural rights while affirming the limitation of political and civil rights. The goal of society was not the conservation of natural rights but the rule of law.[66] This was the foundation of social organisation, as it was the 'general will, expressed by the majority of citizens or their representatives'.[67] Personal liberty was therefore derived not from nature but from the individual's obligation to respect the laws of the majority.[68] This required the individual to serve society, to live subject to its laws, and to respect those who were the agents of the law, otherwise moral claims to membership within society were lost and, indeed, the individual was at 'war' with it.[69]

The Civil Code of 1804 made a correlation between rights and law in 'good civil law' (*bonnes lois civiles*), which was the source of custom and the guarantee of public peace.[70] One preliminary study of 1801 reflected on the distinctions between rights (*droit*) and law (*loi*), and contrasted the ideals of universal and supreme reason found in the nature of things (*droit*) with the positive rules of society (*loi*). Rights were morally compelling, but on their own they were without constraint. The law therefore moderated rights: rights directed while law commanded.[71] The Civil Code was applicable to all persons resident on French territory, therefore holding foreigners to the same constraints as nationals, and recognising their equal civil rights while permitted to reside in France.[72]

The 'Public Rights of the French' prescribed in the Charter of 1830 were equality before the law and individual liberty.[73] The Charter consolidated the legal state by securing the rule of law and guaranteeing the authority of parliament as the expression of national sovereignty. This legal state appropriated rights and reformulated them in the laws, which were passed back to society. The proclaimed rights of the French necessarily introduced profound distinctions between the French and foreigners.

\* \* \*

In the new paradigm of asylum as *bienfaisance*, asylum emerged from the protecting impulses of public charity. It was secularised twice over, from the Christian ideals whose passing Wallon lamented, and from revolutionary ideals that had carried forward Enlightenment doctrines of natural rights. Pagès' defence of the right of asylum was a reaction against the suppression of natural rights by the constraints of state law. As had Wallon with his reflections on Christian asylum, Pagès contrasted modern political authority with past ideals in order to reinvigorate ideals of rights with their traditional value. That they should do so is evidence of the emergence of a new ideology of the state and its understanding of rights.

# 4
# The Practice of Asylum

In September 1831, when the prefect of the Pyrénées-Orientales was warning the government in Paris about the 'effervescing germs' causing so much unrest in Perpignan, Spanish refugees were the largest refugee group in France, with 2867 individuals formally registered for financial aid and confined to depots. Italian refugees, the second largest group, numbered 1524, while Portuguese refugees totalled 962.[1] Their numbers ebbed and flowed over the next years as amnesties permitted the return of all but those most compromised by their past political actions or allegiances. Theirs was a temporary asylum, therefore, and consequently had little lasting impact on public expenditure and the July Monarchy's conception of asylum.

The impact of refugees from Poland was much greater. Because they were heroes of Poland's long struggle to throw off foreign oppression, the 'Great Polish Migration' of the 1831 and 1832, as it became known, was an epic period of its national history. It was a migration of the Polish national spirit, which took its government, its military, and its culture into exile. This was a story of romantic heroism and despair, fashioned by the great ideal of national liberation, which also profoundly affected the French people and the French state.

News of the fall of Warsaw to the Russians on 15 September 1831 brought irresistible stories of carnage and despair.[2] Thousands of Polish revolutionary nationalists fled into Austria and Prussia before the advancing Russians and could not return to Poland without reprisal. They were divided between and surrounded by Russia's allies. In the north, the Prussian army interned them on the pretext of the cholera; in the Galician southwest, the Austrians encircled them. By doing so, the Prussians and Austrians not only demonstrated their loyalty to the victorious Russians by demobilising the Polish army, they also revealed their own concerns for the rebirth of militant Polish nationalism. The Poles themselves, meanwhile, were torn between the urge to return to fight on and the shame of abandoning their homeland. Some Poles, on their own initiative or from the efforts of French diplomats, managed to escape to France, but most were detained in makeshift camps as prisoners of war.[3]

When Nicholas I approved an amnesty on 23 October 1831, which allowed the common Polish soldiers to return, the Austrian government quickly moved to force their repatriation. As there were no guarantees for the Poles' security, the Austrians were over zealous in their desire to rid them from their territory, even under the threat of armed force. The amnesty and its enforcement aimed at nothing less than the decapitation of the Polish nationalist movement: officers and former government officials were barred return, while courts in Warsaw decreed the confiscation of the properties of some 2339 insurrectionists, of whom 1146 were also condemned to death.[4]

Reports soon circulated that the first returnees under the amnesty had been brutalised and condemned to forced labour in Russia.[5] The offer of the French to admit Polish refugees was assuredly welcomed, by the Poles themselves, but also by the Austrian government which wanted to be rid of them. The French embassy in Vienna thereupon negotiated a protocol with Prince Metternich about the status of the Polish refugees and set the terms of their departure from Austrian territory.[6]

Concerned about the reports of atrocities and unsettled by the insurrectionary mood on the streets of Paris, Casimir Périer provided 500,000 francs to the French embassies in Vienna, Berlin, and Dresden to finance the Poles' passage to France.[7] French officials registered the Poles and issued their passports, while the legation in Munich negotiated their safe crossing of the south German states. No hindrance stood in their way; the route to Avignon via Regensberg, Munich, and Basel was decided upon. Poles in Prussia, meanwhile, were to leave by ship from Danzig for Dieppe, Rouen, Le Havre, and Bordeaux.[8]

One popular story of the time told of the appearance of the first Polish refugee in Paris on 20 October 1831. A young man, clearly foreign, his arm in a sling and his clothes ragged, appeared in the Faubourg Montmartre crying 'Honour to Poland!' Hearing his words a crowd formed and quickly took up the chant: 'Brave Pole! Long Live Poland!'[9] Popular protest against the government's refusal to go to the aid of the Polish revolutionaries gave way to sympathy and honour for these heroes and martyrs of liberty.

France was their natural home in exile. Historical bonds united the two countries in revolutionary struggles. The Poles themselves believed that just as Kosciuszko's insurrection of 1794 had distracted the Russians and Austrians from war against the French Republic, the November 1830 insurrection had distracted Tsar Nicholas I from his plans to send an army to put down the July Monarchy. They were two of Europe's great Catholic nations, separated by Protestantism; they were nations joined in the noble pursuit of liberty, surrounded by monarchs who would put it down. Defeat in 1831 inspired among the Poles and their French supporters new dreams of a Polish legion fighting alongside the French, like Poniatowski and the Polish legion of Napoleon's Grande Armée.[10]

These popular sentiments complicated formal responses. Périer saw only political problems. The formation of a Polish legion within France was particularly difficult as it had a direct bearing on its relations with the European monarchies.[11] Périer's insistence that asylum in France had no political purpose alerted the Poles that they would not find the military support they sought, and assured the Russians of French neutrality.

In October 1831, the Polish army numbered some 28,000 officers and soldiers; by late November 1831, it is believed to have still been more than 20,000, of whom 5000 were officers. The Russian amnesty had made no substantial impact on their numbers therefore; many common soldiers found their way to France with their officers. About 10,000 Poles arrived, with some 2000 to 2500 common soldiers.[12]

These are the higher estimates. More conservative estimates put the Polish emigration to France at little more than 5000.[13] Official figures, however, show that by March 1832, 2828 Polish military and civilians were registered in specially constituted refugee depots in Avignon, Besançon, and Châteauroux, considerably fewer than the 6000 Poles who, by January 1833, had approached its embassies in Prussia and Austria for assistance in getting to France.[14] The official figures count only those granted financial assistance, however; the numbers of unassisted refugees were not counted. At the end of 1832, a total of 4239 Polish refugees had registered for financial aid and had been placed in the depots. The differences between these higher and lower numbers nevertheless suggest that many of the Poles either decided to brave the risks and return to Poland, settled on route, or emigrated abroad.[15]

As the Polish émigrés travelled across Bavaria, they were welcomed by a blossoming network of supporters who came out to greet them as they approached in turn Regensberg, Donauwörth, Günzburg, and then proceeded into Würtemberg and Baden. They were offered wagons and other aid to help them on their way.[16] The prefects of France's eastern departments were instructed to admit them freely, to give them aid and to provide lodgings, clothing, and other necessities. They were also instructed on quarantine measures to be taken in order to stop the spread of the cholera, but the public mood of goodwill and celebration that greeted the Poles rendered these useless. As they arrived in Strasbourg and Colmar, they were divided and moved on, officers and soldiers to Avignon (Vaucluse), and civilians to Châteauroux (Indre).[17]

The prefect of the Haut-Rhin in Colmar reflected the popular spirit as the first Poles arrived, instructing the mayors of his department to call upon the 'patriotism of the inhabitants to warmly welcome our old but unfortunate brothers at arms'.[18] The first column of Poles that passed through Dijon was greeted with a parade of the National Guard, complete with marching band. Local inhabitants had come out to escort them to the Town Hall where an assembly of local dignitaries formally welcomed them. During their brief respite, they were fêted with theatrical performances and public dinners, where they burst into Polish nationalist songs and, more to the concern of the commandant of the gendarmerie, French republican songs. For the Poles, the singing of their nationalist hymn, *La Varsovienne*, 'recalled the sadness of their memories'; for the French it recalled their sentimental ties and stirred enthusiasm for the Poles' liberation struggles to come. On their departure, the townsfolk accompanied them on horseback, while the country folk lined the road to Beaune. Two more columns were greeted in a similar manner over the following weeks.[19]

Even into the following years such demonstrations of popular support and sympathy welcomed the Poles wherever they settled. In the northern cities of Arras and Lille, there were festivals in their honour.[20] In Le Puy (Haute-Loire), the warmth of their reception relieved in some small way the discomfort of their material circumstances.[21] Theatre, songs, and poetry kept the Polish cause of liberty alive in the French imagination. They also attacked the July Monarchy for its desertion of Poland. They created heroes and martyrs out of the Polish revolutionaries, while recalling the historical ties between Poland and France that served the political interests of the exiled Poles and French republicans.[22] In December 1831, one theatre piece, *The Poles*, represented the true Polish patriots as veterans of the French Imperial Army, proud of the scars they gained defending France, not the ministers of government who had skulked off as the Russians marched on Warsaw:

Look at this chest! Ten scars disfigure it. I have shed my blood for France in ten battles! One hundred thousand Poles have fought for France like me. All have been loyal to her, even under the very walls of Paris when many of her own children had abandoned her ... For twenty years the French and Polish soldiers have been brothers, for twenty years they have shared everything: the same fortune, the same glory, the same dreams, the same death ... No. No. Such a brotherhood is not forgotten, and the Russians will never obliterate our memory. The French will feel our wounds in their hearts. Forward then! Raise the eagle and the Polish flag. If we must die, at least let us die free.[23]

These were the true Polish patriots, veterans of many past battles in the name of liberty, who now stood against the Tsar's army before the gates of Warsaw, whose liberty the French would soon restore. So many hoped.

These sympathies were not always benign; they carried with them the seeds of rebellion and disorder, which alarmed the public authorities in the departments as much as the government in Paris. Deep political and social fractures could be easily exposed. In Strasbourg in January 1832, a riot broke out at a local boarding house when it was rumoured the proprietor had refused accommodation to a Polish captain. The rumour—false, it was later admitted—exposed raw divisions between legitimists and republicans and demonstrated the volatility of the public mood.[24] In Metz during 1832, Polish refugees joined Bonapartists and republicans in rioting.[25] A night at the theatre in Avignon in August 1832 was disrupted when some men objected to a Pole's whistling during the performance. A skirmish ensued and a Pole was arrested for disorderly behaviour. This trigged a tense confrontation between his friends, who demanded his release, and the police. Some local inhabitants joined, shouting 'down with the *juste-milieu*', 'long live liberty', and 'long live the Poles'. The police eventually relented after several hours and released the prisoner before more serious trouble broke out.[26]

The potential for unrest existed wherever Polish refugees were lodged. In truth, however, the fear of unrest was more real than unrest itself. One month after the riot in Strasbourg, 100 Poles and many more Strasbourgeois gathered for a service at the cathedral to commemorate the anniversary of the Battle of Grochow. The event was noteworthy because it passed without incident.[27] But the potential unrest was reason enough to quickly place the refugees in depots and under police surveillance.

## The refugee depot

Within two months of the first arrivals, the depots in Avignon and Châteauroux were both overcrowded, with more than 1000 refugees each, while still more arrived.[28] Other depots were therefore prepared to relieve the pressures, at Le Puy (Haute-Loire) and Bourges (Cher), and, in December 1831, at Besançon (Doubs), which was to serve as a temporary depot for military refugees in transit between Strasbourg and Colmar and eventual placement in Avignon.[29]

Avignon and Besançon were both garrison cities where the Polish military refugees were placed under French military authority. They were subjected to military discipline and regulation; military registers (*contrôles*) were adapted to record each refugee arrival and departure, and to record the payments of their financial allowances. Military travel passes (*feuilles de route*) were also adapted to authorise and regulate the movement of refugees between depots. The War Ministry took responsibility for the initial costs of provisions, accommodation, and allowances until the parliament approved funding for the Interior Ministry to meet the cost of the refugees' ongoing aid.[30]

Once the decision to establish a new depot in Besançon was taken, the civil and military authorities of the city immediately set about getting it in order to receive the Poles. Barracks, made up mostly of tents, were prepared in the arena to place the lower ranks, while rooms in the city's hotels were set aside for the officers. The military intendant supervised the refugees' arrival and settlement. Their personal documents were surrendered so that they became entirely dependent on him for official authorisation of any kind. Their names and ranks were registered and they were provided with a new identity document (*bulletin individuel*), on which their personal details and financial aid entitlements were recorded. The military intendant also saw to the allocation of accommodation and supervised their daily sanitation, heating, water, and bedding requirements.[31]

The initial arrangements proved inadequate, however. Only a handful of rank and file soldiers were among the first Poles admitted to the depot. As a result, the barracks were underutilised while the expense of the officer's hotel lodgings was greater than expected. Health precautions were also ineffective. Sensitive to reports that the refugees were 'unkempt and unclean' and were arriving from countries infected with cholera, the intendant of health had recommended their quarantine in Fort Griffon outside the city walls. But his instructions were ignored as the refugees in Besançon – 'as elsewhere', it was note – were allowed to move freely within the city and among the local community.[32]

By February 1832, the depot of Besançon accommodated 968 Polish refugees, who made up a total monthly expenditure of 50,577 francs.[33] It had therefore become uncomfortably crowded itself. The 'inconveniences' this caused for both the refugees and the townsfolk, which were not spelt out in the police reports, prompted the War Ministry to approve the relocation of soldiers and non-commissioned officers into surrounding towns, such as Salins and Lons-le Saunier (Jura), and Vesoul (Haute-Saône). Some other refugees were given special permission to live outside the depot in Dôle (Jura), Luxeuil (Haute-Saône), and Pontarliers, Montbéliard, and Ornans (Doubs).[34]

While going some way towards relieving discomfort within Besançon, these arrangements disrupted the steady administration of the depot. The division of responsibilities between the military and civilian authorities was uncertain. As the refugees spread out into these outlying towns, some at quite a distance from Besançon, civil administrative responsibilities were also spread across departments and communes, while the military garrison of Besançon maintained overall responsibility for discipline and the refugees remained under the authority of the military intendant. Yet the civil authorities of these towns were responsible for the payment of their allowances, the provision of documents of identity, which also authorised and recorded their payments, and the provision of accommodation. Related administrative matters were a further imposition on their civil duties. To receive their allowances, the refugees were required to report each fortnight to the mayor's office of the commune in which they lived, or the prefecture of police if they lived in the *chef-lieu* of the department. Accounting and financial reconciliations therefore followed. The transfer and resettlement of refugees was a particular administrative burden. An exchange of correspondence between the various departments and municipalities in which the refugees were resettled was only the start. Appropriate accommodation had to be found and transport arranged; the transfer of funds, the preparation of documents, including passports and travel authorisations, all created extra work for the various administrative levels concerned.

More importantly, local officials in the communes where refugees first registered their arrival were often the first to determine whether they could properly be considered refugees, and therefore whether the law of April 1832 applied to them. Proper registration was necessary if the refugees were to be paid financial assistance, but to justify the claim they had to provide documentary evidence of their reasons for expatriation and of their former military rank or social position. The first groups of Poles who arrived in late 1831 and early 1832 already possessed these documents as they had been issued by French legations abroad. The refugees who followed later were less organised, and had often made their way under their own initiatives. The local municipal authorities therefore needed to pay them much greater attention. They relied on information and instructions from the Interior Ministry, but in the absence of conclusive documentation from the refugees, the testimony of friends and supporters within France was vital. Their own appraisal of the veracity of the claims put to them were more likely personal judgements made on their impressions and the refugees' need for financial help.[35]

That was the first step to the grant of asylum. The second step was provisional authorisation for the payment of an allowance. The individual's details, and recommendations of a suitable place for residence, were despatched through the prefecture to the Interior Ministry. Once the minister's approval was received definitive arrangements could be made. Refugees who had not requested financial assistance when registering their arrival could move on with much less hesitation, but they could not later claim an allowance. The cities of Paris, Lyon, Grenoble, Marseille, Bordeaux, Nantes, and Rouen were closed to all refugees, both assisted and unassisted, because of civil disturbances they had experienced, the potential for further unrest, and their already large number of foreign inhabitants.[36]

Assisted refugees, to be sure, were free to leave their depots and therefore escape the restrictions imposed on them, but they would surrender their allowances if they did so. As many had no other means of support, this was not a realistic option, and so the depots served their main purpose of containment while providing care through financial aid. Even so, many refugees sought approval to move to other depots, in order to reunite with friends and comrades from whom they had become separated during their emigration, or to seek out better opportunities for employment. Younger refugees often sought permission to take up courses of study, such as law in Dijon, medicine in Paris, and medicine and the sciences in Montpellier.[37] All these requests required further processing through the exchange of documents and recommendations between mayors, prefects, and the Interior Ministry.

Three levels of the state's administration—the local mayors' offices, the departmental prefects, and the central Interior Ministry—therefore mediated the refugee's relationship with the state. At each level, the refugee's personal character and motives were scrutinised, which sometimes made their positions precarious. Only at the local level was there personal contact between the refugees and the state. The local officials were therefore the state's key agents in maintaining the social order, and the potential for disturbances among the refugees made them highly suspicious and even fearful of their activities within the depots. Still, local officials had much discretion in their dealings with the refugees, and certainly through their personal contacts they had the opportunities to respond to them as individuals. They were therefore more inclined to favour the refugees in the provision of assistance and authorisations for travel; indeed, the Interior Ministry frequently complained that passports and travel expenses were being issued with too little circumspection.[38]

The refugee depots therefore served French interests in containing the refugees and placing them under police surveillance. But they conferred an indefinite status on the refugees themselves. They had been cut off from their past, but had not yet gained full admission to their country of exile. Instead they were placed behind temporary boundaries. This sustained their self-identity as victims of military defeat, and the experience of exile in the depots was all the more reason to hold France culpable for that defeat. Yet the depots were nevertheless places of transition. They provided a long moment for the refugees to mull over their futures: whether to hold firm to their revolutionary ideals in the hope of returning to Poland; whether to remain in France and make the best of it; or whether to launch themselves into a new life abroad.[39] Meanwhile, they could look back to Poland and their military ambitions at the same time as they could look forward to France with both anticipation and regret. Their enforced isolation, despair and idleness, discomfort and material deprivation nevertheless made them restless, creating a worrying mood in the depots. The fear of disorder and unrest justified strict policing.

During 1832, most of the Polish refugees remained in the depots to which they had been first assigned, and a degree of stability had been reached after the great rupture of exile and resettlement. Their concentration in large numbers, confined to one particular place under military command, had preserved their military identities and their revolutionary aspirations, but also deepened their sense of defeat and their self-identity as victims. Three states of mind have been identified among them: illusion, suffering, and nostalgia.[40] Many, especially the senior officers, maintained the illusion that they would soon return to Poland in victory, but their physical separation from their homeland and their former lives, and the psychological deprivation of their great national cause, made their suffering and their defeat that much more acute. They coped with this in their nostalgic and ardent desire to see their homeland again and to fulfil their wishes for Poland's future. The refugees' self-identity was therefore preserved in their military formations.

It pervaded all ranks. The common soldiers and subordinate officers tied their loyalties to their commanders, sustaining themselves by their fidelity to their revolutionary struggle and their great national cause.[41]

Nonetheless, idleness, boredom, and homesickness, and not great deeds, filled their daily lives. This often led to bitter personal and ideological quarrels, which sometimes ended in duels.[42] Their despair was offset to some degree by the sympathy with which the French communities received them. It was common for the civil, military, and religious authorities of the townships that housed a refugee depot to celebrate the anniversaries of their November 1830 insurrection.[43] But this barely compensated. They frequently reproached the French government for not sending military support during the insurrection, or for not paying them more financial aid. One frequent complaint was that their allowances were not sufficient for their daily needs.[44]

They could tolerate their circumstances in the belief that they were on the verge of return. Few therefore troubled themselves with settling and making the most of their lives in France. Their allowances, despite their complaints, let them avoid the toils of labour, and by carelessly incurring debts they could go some way towards emulating the kind of lifestyle they had lost in Poland.[45] But this quickly consumed local goodwill. By March 1833, the refugees in Besançon had accumulated debts to local shopkeepers and merchants of 25,525 francs, which were not expected to be honoured.[46]

In contrast to the assisted refugees in the depots, a significant group of unassisted exiles, Polish aristocrats, notables, and former Polish government figures, had settled freely in Paris, having secured their wealth, or a good part of it, and the freedom of their families. They were able to continue their social and political lives in much the same manner as before, and found an effective outlet for their political ideals and nationalist spirits in the circle of Prince Adam Czartoryski at the Hôtel Lambert on the Île Saint-Louis, the centre of a Polish government in exile for much of the nineteenth century.[47]

There were, therefore, two Polish communities in France, divided by wealth and the freedoms they enjoyed. One group had fled defeat and persecution at the hands of the Russians and their allies in Prussia and Austria, and have been described as a radical red community with whom French republicans and revolutionaries could readily form an alliance in spirit if not in deed. The other, a conservative white community, lived amid the centre of French society, enjoying its high bourgeois culture.[48] Some, like Czartoryski, had arrived much later than the radical community, and, like Adam Mickiewicz, the great poet who gave the exiled Poles their national voice, had been absent from Poland during the insurrection.[49]

The vast majority lived at the margins of French society, confined to depots in the provinces and dependent on France's generosity. Although their differences divided them from the Poles of Paris, their national spirit nevertheless united them. They were, it has been observed, not of one party

or one part of the nation, but of a single spirit: the spirit of Polish democracy, which had been 'born among all these immense despairs of the moth-
erland'.[50] Their confinement in large numbers in the four principle depots
of Avignon, Châteauroux, Bourges, and Besançon, sustained their national
spirit, and their military formations. Soldiers and non-commissioned officers remained with their units, and the loyalty of subordinates to their commanders had strengthened rather than diminished in exile. They could all
reminisce about past battles and dream ahead to resuming the campaign.

The centre of the Polish emigration in Paris, however, seems rarely to have
used its influence to aid their compatriots in the depots. One exception was
a petition to the Chamber of Peers protesting the law of April 1832, which
was denounced as an affront to the Polish struggle for liberty and further
proof of their humiliation. 'For twenty months', the petition declared,
'Italian patriots, Spaniards, and Portuguese have enjoyed French hospitality
peacefully; the arrival of the Poles is the single motivation for this overly
severe measure', which left them with two 'deplorable' choices: deportation,
or a residence assigned to them.[51]

## Rupture in Besançon

The political character of the Polish refugees was one cause for French
suspicions. Another, stemming from the impost of financial assistance on
the French budget, was the belief that many refugees had claimed aid to
which they were not entitled. François Guizot expressed his suspicions that
men of lower rank had posed as officers in order to obtain a higher than
entitled allowance.[52] There was a need, he therefore declared, for a general
review of the refugees and their entitlements. Planned for March 1833, the
purpose of the review was to re-examine the refugees' backgrounds, verify
their ranks, and to confirm or change aid entitlements as necessary.[53]

A commission was established in each depot to conduct the review; it
comprised the departmental prefects, the depot commanders, and municipal representatives. All Poles were ordered to appear before it. The review
therefore introduced another administrative barrier between the refugees
and the state, and disturbed whatever good relations the refugees had developed with the local authorities. The commission now, and not the mayor as
before, authorised their identity documents and decided their level of assistance, and even their character as political refugees.[54]

The review was one attempt by the government to assert even firmer control over the Poles. Another was a decision taken towards the end of 1832 to
relocate some refugees from the crowded depots of Avignon, Châteauroux,
Bourges, and Besançon to other localities.

These two developments followed changes in the distribution and administration of refugees towards the end of 1832. An amnesty of the Spanish
government, announced on 23 October 1832, led to the repatriation for the

vast majority of Spanish refugees. The total refugee population in France fell substantially, reducing the burden on state resources and making space available in other depots into which the crowded Polish depots could be redistributed.[55] The first transfer from Besançon was arranged for 7 March 1833, when a detachment of nine officers and 154 non-commissioned officers and soldiers left for Bergerac in the Dordogne. The transfer of another 300 Poles was also planned.[56]

During March 1833, therefore, the Poles of Besançon faced a rupture to the inertia of life in the depot on two fronts, the general review of their ranks and entitlements, and their dispersal to other parts of the country. Both brought upon them the possibility of further loss and humiliation, as well as the break-up of their military units and their bonds of loyalty. Uncertainty about France's plans and intentions was most the troubling, feeding the rumour that the French government wanted to surrender them to the Russian Tsar.[57] The uncertainties unsettled many. At least seven Poles deserted Montbéliard for Switzerland without authorisation, and consequently all the refugees in Montbéliard were ordered back to Besançon. Then, on 31 March, all refugees registered in the Besançon depot, including those in the outlying townships, were summoned to a general assembly for the purpose of the general review.[58]

There were also recent administrative difficulties that further unsettled the refugees. The law of April 1832, which had been adopted for 12 months, had not yet been renewed by the parliament in March 1833 and consequently budgetary credits for future refugee aid had not yet been authorised. Financial pressures from the diminishing budget were most acute in depots for Italian refugees. In Marseille, allowances had not been paid for four months, and in Montbrisson for two months.[59] In Besançon, the War Ministry stepped in to supplement a shortfall in Interior Ministry funding. Although this assured the continuation of the refugees' allowances, the military paymaster had no authority to issue payment outside the boundaries of the garrison. The refugees in the outlying towns were therefore recalled to the central depot, which increased crowding and unsettled the local populace. Barracks of the French garrison had to be cleared to make room for them. The order also heightened the refugees' uncertainties and seemed to suggest the worst of the rumours about France's intentions.[60]

Across France, Polish refugees were unnerved by the developments of March 1833 and the spreading rumours. In Bergerac, some Poles refused to present themselves for the general review of ranks and entitlements, while others who presented themselves refused to answer questions, protesting that they knew the French government wanted to be rid of them and send them to Russia.[61] The most dramatic response was in Besançon. On the night of 31 March–1 April, the dates of the general review, 23 refugees secretly left. Among them were three majors, three captains, five lieutenants, and ten sub-lieutenants, who, the reports noted alarmingly, were armed with sabres and pistols.[62] Within the week, 421 Poles had deserted the depot.[63]

The desertions confirmed French suspicions and anxieties; they also set alight the dormant passions of the Poles elsewhere. Within ten days, Poles had also deserted Dijon and Bourges, alarming other parts of the country where refugees resided.[64] The fear spread with the news of the events in Besançon that the Poles were about to rise up against the local authorities.[65]

A total of 489 Polish refugees deserted Besançon.[66] With no idea of their intentions, suspicion, fear, and rumour quickly spread across France. The worst fear was of insurrection. The gendarmerie of Beaune reported that the refugees planned to unite with insurrectionary French republicans, or possibly even with French royalists.[67] The secrecy in which the desertions had been organised exacerbated French fears. The deserters' wives and friends gave nothing away, and the silence of the remaining refugees nurtured suspicions that the Poles had formed secret societies to plot insurrection.[68] With no other information at hand, the prefect of the Doubs concluded that leaders of the Polish masonic lodge of the *Maison chévrier* had orchestrated the desertions.[69] Refugee support societies, which helped Poles who could not speak French, were also suspected as secret political clubs.[70]

Their destination was not known until days later, when it was learned that they had made for Switzerland with the intention of going to Frankfurt to join a popular insurrection.[71] By the time they arrived in Berne, however, the insurrection had collapsed, and the deserters were left without plans and without aid. Over the next few months they had moved on; a number drifted back into France, some even later seeking the reinstatement of their allowances.[72]

The government responded to the desertions immediately. Admitting the mistake of holding large numbers of refugees in too few depots, Interior Minister Comte d'Argout ordered the closure of the depots of Besançon and Avignon and the dispersal of the refugees into many smaller depots across the interior and the west.[73] In May 1833, the eight non-commissioned officers, eight soldiers, and 137 officers who remained in the Besançon depot, were issued with a travel itinerary and allowance of 25 centimes per league for their expenses. Soldiers and non-commissioned officers were sent to Bergerac, officers were sent to Caen and St. Brieuc in the west.[74] Refugees from Avignon were sent to the central departments of the Corrèze, Creuse, and Cantal. The military depot at Le Puy was dissolved the following June and the refugees were sent to Cahors, Le Mans, Niort, and Angers. Poles from Bourges were sent to the Landes, Manche, Gard, Aveyron, and Allier, and those from Châteauroux to the Manche, Mayenne, and Charente-Inférieure.[75] From being constrained to a small number of localities, within a short period of time Polish refugees could be found across France.

The redistribution and dispersal of the Polish refugees were so comprehensive that many were transferred between depots on more than one occasion, sometimes more than twice, as numbers were balanced across depots, and as more appropriate localities were decided upon for settlement. Effective policing was the most important consideration in deciding where the refugees would be relocated.[76] Suitable barracks or similar accommodation were also required; the new depots furthermore had to be in towns where the their political views would not easily find local sympathies.[77]

By June 1833, only 16 Polish refugees remained in Besançon: five were too ill to travel; one remained after forfeiting financial assistance; 10 sought permission to remain because of marriage or engagement to women of the city. Three others disappeared without trace, and one died in hospital after the evacuations.[78] A small number of Poles outside Besançon sought permission to settle there. Illness was the most common reason, yet formal authorisation was a major hurdle. The transfer of one Polish Major, Okoloski, from Luxeuil to Besançon for reasons of health was authorised on 19 May 1833, but the prefect of the Haute-Saône did not issue final orders until 28 October.[79] Generally, permission was granted to those who had developed close personal ties with the local community, but even marriage to a local resident was not itself a sufficient reason. The order granting Major Lipski permission to remain because he had married stressed more his close ties with his wife's family, who did not want him to leave, than his marriage itself.[80] Close family ties were also decisive for five other Polish officers who had married in Besançon.[81] Suspicions therefore even extended to marriages arranged to avoid resettlement to another part of France.

In other cases, however, evidence of strong local ties could not sway the authorities. A Polish military surgeon, Pierre Kuczynski, had practiced in Besançon after he arrived with his unit in 1832. He then transferred to Montpellier to study for a diploma in medicine, and, in June 1833, he sought permission to return to Besançon to live and practice. He explained that he was assured a 'great number of clients' among the local community with whom he had developed a great rapport. The community supported his return, and a number of well-placed local citizens testified to his good character, the free care that he had given to the poor and sick previously, and his sound political opinions.[82] The prefect of the Doubs, however, did not support their claims, and recommended that the minister refuse his request in order 'to avoid the possibility that his authorisation could serve as a pretext for others of his compatriots' to return to Besançon.[83]

Before the Poles' dispersal, various forms of sociability—cafés, theatre, boarding houses and hotels, where they were warmly welcomed and honoured—had brought the refugees and local residents together, but there were nevertheless clear lines of demarcation, not least of which were language and culture. Even more, their enduring military formations and bonds of loyalty set them apart from the local communities, as had their subordination to French command and the controls imposed on their associations and movements. There were definite boundaries between their asylum within the depots and the wider communities of the towns around the depots, and the social and economic opportunities they offered.

The refugees' dispersal into smaller depots brought them closer to the local communities. The largest depot, with 321 Poles, was in Cahors; La Rochelle was the next largest, with 156 Poles. Most of these depots also accommodated a small number of refugees from Italy and Spain.[84] The dispersal of the Poles, moreover, broke the bonds of loyalty to their military units and freed subordinate soldiers and officers from their commanders. In their place they had the opportunity to form ties with local communities that were not possible in the larger depots. Over time these became deep personal bonds. When refugees took up work they entered into an economic and social relationship with their local communities that they had avoided in the larger depots. Political relationships also developed. The Poles adapted their political spirits to French national celebrations. On the days of 27, 28, and 29 July 1833, the third anniversary of the July Revolution, the Poles made a series of appeals to the French people, uniting Poland's quest for liberty with France's.[85] Each year on 14 July, the anniversary of the fall of the Bastille, Polish nationalist hopes were also celebrated.[86] A memorial service for General Lafayette in June 1834, the great supporter of the Polish cause who had died the month before, coincided with the anniversary of the death in 1832 of their other great supporter, General Lamarque. The names of their other supporters among the political class were also invoked to celebrate the French revolutionary spirit and to advance their cause of national liberation.[87]

French communities were drawn in turn to support the Poles. A series of petitions was made to the Chamber of Deputies in early 1834 attesting to their good behaviour and the honour that their presence had brought to their towns. The mayor of Tulle (Corrèze) testified that the Poles 'had always been wise, honourable, and praiseworthy'. The inhabitants of Saint-Pierre on the Île d'Oléron (Charante-Inférieure) declared that the 'Polish refugees have distinguished themselves by their good conduct', while the mayor of Blois (Loire-et-Cher) declared that the 17 officers and two soldiers in the depot had 'conducted themselves perfectly honourably'.[88]

These petitions anticipated the review of the law of April 1832, the renewal of which was debated in the Chamber of Deputies in April 1934. Local relations with the Poles demonstrated there was no need for the formal constraints on their freedoms. The government was unmoved by these testimonies and the sentiments behind them, however. It moved instead more ruthlessly to put down insurrection when it broke out and to silence dissent when it was expressed.

# 5

## 'A sentence passed in a shadow, by a hidden power'

One petition in support of Poles, dated January 1834, from 'all the most distinguished persons' of Mortain (Manche), is particularly noteworthy for the sympathy it displayed towards the refugees and for the depth of its antipathy against the government. Léonor Joseph Havin, a deputy from the Manche and representative of the Mortainais, spoke to the petition in the Chamber of Deputies:

> Is it not without deep feelings of sadness that we have seen brought to bear against [the Polish refugees] this exorbitant disposition of the law of 21 April 1832, which leaves them without guarantee and without protection from arbitrary ministerial decisions? You know that, in effect, sirs, a sentence passed in a shadow, by a hidden power, both judge and executioner, and dispensed with imagined pretexts can wrench unexpectedly these unfortunate young men from the breast of France, from this France that, in the naïve effusion of their gratefulness, they call their second mother.[1]

During the debates on refugees in 1831 and 1832, many deputies had voiced their concerns about the nature of the power that the interior minister was assuming, firstly through the administrative measures adopted in response to the refugees, and then under law on refugees of April 1832. Able to determine their rights and entitlements, and whether they could even continue to live in France and enjoy its protection, without having to justify his decisions or put them to judicial review, the minister had assumed in the views of some deputies the arbitrary and hidden powers of despotism.

Havin's denunciation of this 'hidden power' indeed came at a time when the government would reveal how readily it could assume the semblance of despotism to put down ruptures to the public peace and challenges to Louis-Philippe's legitimacy. Meanwhile, the popular petitions from the local communities among whom the refugees lived reflected broader concerns about the heavy hand of the power at the government's disposal.

These communities could see for themselves how the restrictive measures sapped the refugees of their dignity, but their pleas seemed only to have toughened the government's resolve.

The government's belief that the refugees continued to hatch political conspiracies, despite the best efforts of containment and surveillance, compelled it to express more forcefully its view that asylum served French interests and recognised no rights. 'The French nation is free to close or open its frontiers to whomsoever seems to it proper, and on such conditions that it judges appropriate', the Foreign Minister, the duc de Broglie, told the chamber in March 1833. 'By admitting and assisting the refugees', he continued, France 'did not intend to consecrate or recognise a right in their person ... This supposed right is nowhere written down, either in positive law, natural law, the Civil Code, or in reason. The French nation is its own master, just as each man who composes the nation is his own master'.[2]

The reassertion of the state's power over the refugees in the course of 1833 was part of a much greater campaign by Louis-Philippe and his government to secure its authority, to police dissent, and to put down the insurrectionary mood that could still from time to time break through the surface of political stability.[3] These years were indeed critical for the July Monarchy. It was especially sensitive to representations from foreign powers about the political activities among refugees. Tsar Nicholas I challenged the French government for its tolerance of the anti-Russian activities of the Comité Polonais. Broglie submitted to the pressure, and disbanded the Comité, accusing it of having published a programme that was not intended to advance Polish interests but to provoke instead a revolt against Russia. The government similarly threatened to dissolve an Italian committee in Marseille that had circulated an inflammatory journal in Lombardy, Savoy, and Sardinia.[4] This was further evidence for the regime's opponents that the government was more responsive to the opinions of foreign powers than to opinion within France.[5]

More worrying was the open insurrectionary militancy among certain groups of the refugees and other resident foreigners. In February 1834, Giuseppe Mazzini and his followers in his 'Young Italy' movement raised an armed contingent among the refugees to march on Savoy and Piedmont.[6] His aide-de-camp, General Romarino, a commander in the exiled Polish army, had already raised suspicions by his frequent visits to Lyon to recruit members to the expedition. An alarming rumour spread: if the expedition succeeded, a republican insurrection would erupt in Lyon. The government therefore despatched troops to the Italian border to prevent Romarino's return.[7] But the expedition failed, floundering in the cold and snow. It was proof nevertheless that political conspiracies among the refugees could engulf France either in insurrection at home or in a foreign war.

The suspicions endured. Poles were suspected of carrying the seeds of insurrection wherever they settled. Reports circulated throughout 1834 and

1835 that refugee organisations were planning a new insurrection in Poland. 'The number of Polish democrats increases each day', the interior minister informed the foreign minister in June 1835. 'Even young aristocrats join the reformers ... Eighteen months ago there were seven Polish democrats in England; today there were close to five hundred ... their emissaries are in the heart of Poland itself. They are in Leipzig, Dresden, Frankfurt and Berlin'. All were supposedly awaiting the signal from Polish democrats in Paris and London to launch their new offensive.[8]

The strict policing of the refugee depots ensured that insurrectionary plots would not be realised. The insurrectionary challenge from among the French people, however, was much more difficult to police. Lyon had become the focus of social and political unrest at the time, and, as the Mazzini expedition had shown, government officials there were nervous of an outbreak of republican violence.[9] Unrest among the silk workers in 1834, who had already been driven to revolt in 1831 by low wages and poor living standards, had led the literate, politicised, and disillusioned workers of other towns and cities, and the republican Society of the Rights of Man to come to stand beside them.[10] Government ministers, consequently, could not distinguish economic grievances from political sedition and passed the repressive law on associations of 10 April 1834 to outlaw organised protest. Specifically aimed at banning the Society of the Rights of Man, it was used to suppress rioting among Lyon's silk workers.[11] On the night of 13 and 14 April 1834 the government also moved forcefully against rioters in Paris.

The bloodshed in Lyon and in Paris in early April suppressed the insurrectionary ferment and political sedition that had festered since the July days of 1830. But to pacify popular dissent the regime assumed autocratic methods reminiscent of the final years of the Bourbon restoration, resistance to which lay at the very foundations of the July Monarchy.[12] By April 1834, therefore, the July Monarchy had reached a significant turning point. It had secured France's internal order by the ruthless suppression of insurrection and dissidence, and it consolidated its victory over it opponents with the adoption of the September laws of 1835, which followed the worst of the eight assassination attempts on Louis-Philippe. These laws curtailed the freedom of the press, prohibited insults levelled at the king, and outlawed any incitement to insurrection.[13] As well as silencing French republicans, they brought an end to utterances of discontent among refugee groups. Poles and their supporters, who were hitherto outspoken against the conditions they endured, were silent hereafter.

When, in April 1834, a bill was introduced into the Chamber of Deputies to extend for a further 12 months the 1832 law on the residence of refugees, ministers expressed a firmer resolve to assert the government's power over them. Although the 1832 law was originally adopted for 12 months—a concession to opponents who rejected the original proposal for a permanent law—it persisted into 1833. The original bill of 1834 asked no more than its further extension for the next 12 months. But it was later amended to include a clause that imposed a mandatory penalty of two to six month's imprisonment on any refugee who did not comply with an expulsion order to quit France, or who had returned without authorisation after being expelled.[14]

Ministers were unsure how they should justify this amendment, however. There had been no concerns expressed about unenforced expulsion orders or unauthorised returns, and indeed Foreign Minister Broglie had reassured the chamber in March 1833 that the government was using the power of expulsion under the April 1832 law wisely. Expulsion orders, he admitted, had been rare and exceptional; there had only been 27 in a refugee population approaching 8000.[15] These expellees were the more troublesome refugees. Among them were prominent figures, such as the Poles Chodzko and Lelewel, who were expelled for signing an anti-Russian proclamation and therefore endangering France's foreign relations.[16] Other restive Poles had left at the time of the desertions from Besançon in April 1833, or of their own accord at other times.[17] The smaller Polish refugee communities in London and Bruxelles included many who had originally settled in France but who resented the constraints imposed upon them. Consequently, the Poles in London were radicalised by the arrival of expellees from Paris.[18] The refugees in France were therefore more quiescent without them.

The Interior Minister Argout, offered little more than Broglie to reassure those deputies who were ambivalent about the need for the penal sanction. A description of the facts on which the government's decision was based, he told them, would consume too much of their time, but he nevertheless suggested that 'many' expelled refugees had returned to France on two or even three occasions and there was no penalty that could be imposed on them other than their expulsion one more time.

The real reason for the amendment, it became clear, was the civil unrest for which refugees could be blamed. Argout accused them of stirring up riots because of their resistance to expulsion; they were in a 'veritable insurrection against the government and against the authority of the law', he concluded.[19] Internal pressures such as these, suggested Gaillard de Kerbertin, the rapporteur of the legislative commission which drafted the final bill, were fragmenting French society. Foreigners who assumed they had unconditional rights put themselves in opposition to French laws and society, and therefore deserved to be punished under these laws. The laws relating to refugees, Kerbertin continued, expressed the state's sovereign authority to close or open its territory on conditions that it determined; this was a power it could not relinquish. 'You have given the government an arbitrary power', he told the chamber, 'but an indispensable arbitrary power'; it was a weapon of the state against the abuse of its laws.[20]

Deputies who had spoken against the law of 1832 were silent during this debate. Earlier advocates of the right of refugees took no part. Jean-Pierre Pagès, who was so critical of Périer's original restrictions on refugees in 1831, made no further contribution to the debates although he remained on the left of the chamber until 1842. He was, however, highly critical of the law on associations, against which he spoke forcefully in April 1834. Still, almost all deputies now seem to have accepted the view that the refugees could enjoy only those rights the government was prepared to allow. One dissenting voice was Salverte, who rose to condemn the government for replacing the 'sacred' rights of justice, humanity, sympathy, and hospitality with only those rights that it could write onto paper.[21]

The amended law was adopted on 1 May 1834. Despite its penal sanctions, the fundamental principle of a refugee protection was unquestioned, so long as the refugees submitted to French law. Financial assistance was not changed. The more extreme elements of the laws relating to refugees, the deputies could be assured, were only intended for the most troublesome and recalcitrant of the refugees whose presence endangered the civil peace.

## Exiles to immigrants

By 1834, therefore, order had been restored. Over the following years there were far fewer reports of disturbances, and indeed fewer police reports on suspicious refugee activities. Dispersal into smaller depots no doubt contributed to this tranquillity, as did the loss of the more militant refugees through expulsion, the desertions of 1833 and the Mazzini expedition of 1834. Repatriation of all but a few high ranking Spanish officials and clergy after a Spanish amnesty of October 1832 also contributed to the greater sense of order. The ban on criticism of Louis-Philippe imposed by the September laws of 1835 brought an end to Polish petitions and other expressions of their grievances. With little active support from the Polish community in Paris, which had access to government ministers and the court, the refugees in the provinces were left at the margins.

The Polish refugees had entered into a period of transition, therefore, between exile as foreign revolutionaries and migration as a settled foreign community. Many of the Polish refugees realised grimly the permanency of their exile. Listlessness and despair were their dominant moods; their daily lives were lived in poverty. Their grievances alienated them from their French hosts, although they could take comfort from the sympathetic responses they received from local communities among whom they had settled.[22] Their loss of personal freedom, their frequent relocations between depots, and their material discomfort, from dissatisfaction with the climate, the wretched state of their clothing, their lack of money to afford anything more than basic subsistence, Kenneth Lewalski concludes, all poorly affected their physical and mental health.[23] Conscious of their foreignness within France, yet also of their inability to return to their homeland, they faced the choice of remaining dependent on the financial assistance the government continued to provide, and therefore maintaining their self-identity as refugees, or of gaining greater self-sufficiency and integrating more completely into their new communities through work. Many still sought permission to change their place of residence either for work or study, or to reunite with friends and relatives.[24] Many were therefore still searching for permanency in their settlement.

Meanwhile, the numbers of Italian refugees had gradually fallen since 1831, from 1542 to 506 by 1840, following amnesties from the various Italian states. The Portuguese refugees had all but vanished from the official registers as they had gradually returned to Portugal.[25] The Spanish refugees, however, remained in flux, and their numbers rose again after each new disturbance in Spain, in 1833, 1836, and 1839. For the Polish refugees, the townships in which they were now settled were less depots as they had previously known them than places of resettlement and integration.

Integration was not only desirable, it was a necessary means of alleviating their grievances and material deprivation. Local communities were at first sensitive to the distress of individual refugees. The ragged state of their clothing was enough to elicit a charitable response.[26] But charity had its limits. Merchants were advised not to grant credits that exceeded the refugees' daily allowances, yet many refugees nevertheless accumulated large debts. Young Poles in particular did what they could to make a good impression on the local women, or simply to maintain a sense of their own well-being. But this merely disguised their status and did nothing to alleviate the genuine poverty in which they lived. Many got by on only one meal a day or by pooling their resources with other refugees.[27]

Barriers nevertheless remained. Even in the smaller depots the Poles were under police surveillance. Official restrictions on their movements and activities persisted and suspicion followed them about. Many of the Poles had settled in depots previously occupied by Spanish refugees, who had antagonised the local inhabitants and overly bothered the local officials. They looked on the arrival of the new refugees with a similar disdain and apprehension. Moreover, they had heard the stories about desertions, clandestine plots, and the threats they posed to the public peace. Instructed to maintain a close surveillance over them in the wake of the desertions of 1833, the police and gendarmerie were alert to any activities and associations that appeared in any way unusual. The commandant of the gendarmerie of Mont-de-Marsan (Landes) spent three days in October 1833 investigating a report from a subordinate that a local newspaper editor regularly visited some Poles and on one occasion had given them money when he departed, with the cry 'long live the republic'.[28]

Reports such as these were less common after 1833. By 1835, the refugees' material circumstances were more a preoccupation than their faded political aspirations. In that year the government decided to reduce their allowances by 10 percent, in order to reduce the general burden of refugee assistance on the public purse while encouraging the refugees to take on work to become self-sufficient. Although many refugees had complained that their allowances were not sufficient for their daily needs, they were nevertheless reluctant to work to earn their own living. The large refugee depots had greatly limited their opportunities, but now the reduction of their allowances and the belated realisation that their exile was not temporary, led many to re-evaluate their circumstances. Of the 6130 Polish refugees who received allowances in 1837, approximately 5000 were occupied in work in some branch of commerce or industry, or the arts and sciences. Among them, 2056 earned a salary from manual labour or gained some other benefit, such as food, clothing, and lodging.[29] They continued to draw their allowances to supplement their low wages therefore.[30] As far as the government was concerned, the refugees were already on the way to self-sufficiency before it decided that more savings could be made from a further 10 percent reduction commencing on 31 January 1837. Projected savings were calculated at 281,870 francs, reducing outlays from 3,068,701 francs in 1835 to 2,786,831 francs in 1837 (from a high of 4,243,439 francs in 1832).[31]

Younger refugees had already responded positively to their circumstances by seeking out opportunities for work and study.[32] For the majority, and especially those less capable of making a new life for themselves, the reductions in allowances were yet further cause for grievance. Three separate petitions were made to the Chamber of Deputies in 1837 stating that the reductions in allowances seriously disadvantaged those thousands of refugees who were still dependent on them. Older refugees were the most seriously disadvantaged. Others simply could not work, or could not find work suitable for their skills and abilities. They all remained dependent on their diminishing levels of support. The lack of practical skills and poor knowledge of the French language were insurmountable barriers, and their futures held little more than the prospect of further misery.[33] The government acknowledged only one problem from these changes. Education and employment brought extraordinary expenses that could not be met immediately—the payment of fees, the cost of books, instruments, and tools. Special funding was therefore made available to meet these costs.[34]

The greatest encumbrance on the refugees' self-sufficiency was the restrictions on their movements outside their designated depots. Many simply could not find employment nearby. Refugees in the Mayenne, an agricultural department with limited employment prospects, sought work in cities in the neighbouring departments, in Rouen, Nantes, and Le Havre, although Rouen and Nantes were effectively closed to them under earlier ministerial directives.[35] The problem of mobility was acknowledged by the Chamber of Peers in its first serious intervention in the refugee debates. It secured the agreement of the Interior Minister, Adolphe Thiers, to lift restrictions on their movements in order to help their search for work.[36] On 24 July 1839, therefore, the Chamber of Deputies adopted a further amendment to the original law of April 1832 on the residence of refugees, to permit those who had been in France for five or more years to leave their depots without having to negotiate the complexities and delays of obtaining formal approval. In all other regards, however, the refugees remained subject to ministerial control.[37]

The voices of the refugees themselves begin to be lost from the historical record at this time, but brief glimpses remain of the dilemmas many faced as they looked ahead to permanent exile. They could choose increased misery from their reliance on diminishing levels of financial aid, or they could choose to work to improve their living standards. They reflected on the nature of the work they could do and whether suitable work was available near where they lived. Their choice might have led them to consider yet another change of residence, with further disruptions and reorientations. Finally, and perhaps most pressing for the former officers, they were left to ponder nostalgically and regretfully the extent to which these choices would complete the loss of their former glories, their social position and status of rank. All the while they confronted a future that did not hold out return to their homeland, but life instead in a foreign country. As their material discomforts adversely affected their physical health, so these choices facing them affected their mental health. Suicide was the final choice. One Pole in the Sarthe who attempted suicide left this message: 'everywhere I go I am the object of disagreeable proposals, and everywhere I hear the word "suicide" attached to my name'.[38] In all, some fourteen officers committed suicide between 1832 and 1838. Deaths from all causes between 1831 and 1842 amounted to almost ten percent of the Polish refugee population.[39]

Younger refugees who had taken courses in French educational institutions adopted the language and culture more quickly and more easily integrated into professional networks. For the officer class and career soldiers, not proficient in the language, untrained for civilian occupations, and dependent on their military loyalties, there were fewer options. One was service in the Foreign Legion in Algeria.[40] By 1839, Kenneth Lewalski calculates, the majority of the Polish refugees were engaged in some form of occupation: 45% in professional or intellectual work (including students); 35% were craftsmen employed in small workshops; 16% were factory workers; and 2.5% worked in agriculture. But another 1970 Poles were still without work because they did not know French or because they were disabled. Although the level of employment was high, the number who continued to receive financial assistance had fallen by less than one-third, from 6822 to 4974.[41] despite official intensions therefore, many refugees were still entirely dependent on their diminishing allowances while others failed to earn sufficient from their work to free themselves from them entirely.

As their voices were lost from the historical record, public attention was no longer fixed on the large contingents of Polish nationalists, and their revolutionary cause fell from the public imagination. Instead, the community of Polish notables and intellectuals in Paris became the public face of the Polish emigration and its cause of national liberation.[42] They worked within the conservative political and diplomatic circles, enjoying the comforts of its notable and bourgeois society. They mixed with the capital's political, intellectual, and artistic elites, discussing politics discretely while sensitive to the conservatism of the July Monarchy and its neutral foreign policy.

## Spanish refugees and the Carlist Wars

Attempts to define the refugee in the context of the April 1832 law were hesitant and unconvincing. Generally, however, a precise definition did not matter as the main characteristic of the refugee—expatriation for reasons of the political events in their homelands—was clear in most cases, especially when the refugees had served in nationalist or insurrectionary armies. The question as to who was a refugee for the purposes of the law came down instead to the need for financial assistance.

There were circumstances, however, when a more precise classification was required in order to determine whether France still had a protection obligation and therefore whether it should continue to pay financial assistance. Amnesties allowing for the return of refugees raised such questions. After the Spanish government announced its amnesty of October 1832, all but a few high officers and clergy could return safely. The French government therefore decided to withdraw financial assistance to those eligible for repatriation under the terms of the amnesty, as they were no longer in need of protection; so long as they remained in France they were considered travellers.[43] But there were serious flaws in the application of the amnesty. The Spanish legation in France often refused to grant passports even to those allowed to return to Spain. A good number of Spanish refugees therefore fell into dire circumstances.[44] A more precise classification of these refugees and their entitlements was consequently required, since the earlier premise on which they had gained asylum—their past political actions, positions, or views—was no longer a sufficient explanation of their need for assistance. Instructions of April 1834 addressed this: 'Financial assistance will only be maintained for those truly proscribed for political reasons', they stated, and then proceeded to detail specific categories for the Spanish refugees' entitlements to asylum and assistance. Those who had been refused passports to return to Spain, those who had been issued passports but were still afraid of retribution on return, and those formally excluded from the amnesty, continued to receive assistance. Those who could return but chose not to were reclassified as travellers and could not receive assistance.[45]

Despite the difficulties in its implementation, the October 1832 amnesty eventually saw the number of assisted Spanish refugees fall from 2805 to 764.[46]

For all but a few of the most compromised, asylum was temporary for Spanish, Italian, and Portuguese refugees, as amnesties assured their repatriation after a short exile. Their proximity to their homeland, their ongoing political and nationalist engagements, and the flux of their numbers throughout the 1830s, made their exile an interruption between the different phases of their struggles than the permanent migration exile had become for the Poles. Nor was theirs a unified emigration; factional differences were evident, especially among the Spanish refugees.

The reduction of financial assistance over the course of the 1830s gradually withdrew one of the key elements of refugee protection under the July Monarchy. The other key element, the promise of inviolable asylum, was itself challenged as France confronted new refugee movements from Spain during the Carlist civil war of the second half of the decade. In much greater numbers, and of a more diverse character than before, the Spanish Carlist refugees presented entirely new problems.

During the second half of the 1830s the French government justified the need to continue the temporary laws relating to refugees first adopted in April 1832 by the volatility of events abroad and the arrival of new refugees. The Carlist war in Spain was further justification for their renewal each year. As early as January 1834, Interior Minister Argout spoke in terms of the 'internment' of Carlist refugees who had come into France and continued their conflict on French territory. They had to be removed from the border so that France did not get drawn into the conflict and damage its good relations with the Spanish monarchy. The new refugees were not given financial assistance although they were in evident distress. The best response France could make to these new Spanish refugees, Argout commented, was to put them in prison where they could share bread with criminals.[47]

The troubles in Spain of the 1820s had followed Ferdinand VII's attempts to reassert absolutism over liberal constitutionalists after his restoration to the throne in 1814. In 1829, after marrying Maria-Christina of Naples, Ferdinand agreed to a liberal constitution in order to secure the succession of their daughter, Isabella, ahead of his reactionary brother Don Carlos. Ferdinand died on 2 October 1833 and Don Carlos claimed the throne in contravention of the new constitution.[48] Over the following years, Don Carlos and his supporters were at war against the infant Queen Isabella II and her regency of liberal reformers. He turned to the countryside for support.

The deepest currents of Carlism, Raymond Carr explains, lay in the hatred of the countryside for the cities. From its base in the Basque provinces and Navarre, where mayors and officials declared their loyalty to Don Carlos, Carlism extended its influence among the peasantry of the mountains of Aragon and Catalonia. By 1835, Don Carlos had built up, equipped, and trained an army of 20,000–30,000 men, which, by 1837, had advanced to within sight of the walls of Madrid. The Carlist army was incapable of sustaining war against the rest of Spain, however, and from the walls of Madrid it was forced back into the mountains.[49]

During 1836, high-ranking supporters of Don Carlos sought asylum in France but were accused of using their asylum for the recruitment of long-settled Spanish refugees into their army. They were arrested and imprisoned as prisoners of war, and then handed over to the Spanish imperial army. There were some protests that this was a clear violation of their asylum, but Adolphe Thiers, then premier, retorted that the Carlists themselves had breached the conditions of their asylum and had therefore absolved France of any protection obligations. They had also breached treaties by bringing their conflict onto French territory, Thiers continued, and they had therefore imperilled French national security; nothing less than firm and decisive intervention would prevent the militarisation of the Franco-Spanish border.[50]

After the Don Carlos' army had been driven back into the mountains, incursions onto the French side of the border were more common. Carlist troops took refuge there to rest, regroup, and rearm before launching new incursions elsewhere along the frontier. Thiers' government therefore declared the border a special security zone where any Spaniards without proper authorisation would be arrested and detained. This was made a specific provision of the amendment to the law relating to the residence of refugees of July 1839. It created an exclusion zone of 160 kilometres along the frontier. Refugees found within it were placed in depots in central and eastern France.[51]

When the Spanish imperial army made its final advance into Carlist territory during April and May 1839, many thousands of civilians whose lands were devastated in the conflict were forced down from the mountains. Thousands of Don Carlos' supporters abandoned him and swore their allegiance to Isabella II as the legitimate monarch, while thousands more fled across the Pyrénées.[52] Don Carlos himself sought asylum in September 1839, settling in Bourges.[53] By 1840, an estimated 30,000 Spaniards had crossed the mountains into France: partisans of Don Carlos, soldiers in his army, officials of the rebellious provinces, civilians of no political persuasion who had been displaced by the fighting, and even soldiers of the imperial army.[54]

This last group, defenders of the legitimate Spanish monarch, were not considered to be in need of asylum and were repatriated.[55] Carlists who faced retaliation for the rebellion were separated by social position and military rank. The French government seemed to have learned from the mistake of the large Polish refugee depots, where their military formations and allegiances were preserved. The Carlist army and its supporters were therefore broken up and widely dispersed. The higher their rank and status, the further from the frontier they were sent. Clergy, magistrates and civil servants were sent to the Doubs, where the depot of Besançon was reinstituted. Senior officers were sent to the eastern departments of the Ain and the Jura. Officers of the rank of captain and below were sent to the central departments of the Corrèze, the Creuse, and the Haute-Loire. Non-commissioned officers and the rank and file soldiers, along with civilian agricultural workers and artisans, were resettled in the Aveyron, Lozère, Tarn, and Tarn-et-Garonne. The higher ranks without independent means were granted financial assistance, but the lower ranks and civilian workers were put to work on public construction projects to earn a salary.[56] Wives, widows, mothers, sisters, and other relations who had followed Carlist partisans into France were ordered to return to Spain, and refused any assistance if they did not.[57]

The Carlists faced a more hostile reception than refugees before them. Prejudices from the memory of marauding and knife-wielding Spanish refugees of 1831–2 made the citizens of Clermont-Ferrand apprehensive about these new Spaniards they were asked to put up with. Nor did they take kindly to their royalist views. The Carlists found respect only among a few local aristocrats. Their lean material circumstances forced them to work, but manual labour was insecure and unstable. Some left to find work elsewhere, only to return again because work was too intermittent to earn a good living.[58]

The number and diversity of refugees from the Carlist war, and particularly the large number of civilians, distinguished them considerably from earlier refugees. The distinction between assisted and unassisted refugees, with the assisted refugees confined to depots and subjected to strict discipline and surveillance, could not be sustained among the Carlists. Even unassisted refugees, a large group that included the lower ranks and the civilians who were obliged to work for a salary, endured measures of surveillance and controls. Rumours that Don Carlos and his follows were plotting an uprising in Navarre made the police sensitive to all Spaniards within their jurisdiction, and obliged the government to order especially strict controls. In the Orne during 1840, an hourly watch was kept over their movements. The refugees in Alençon were required to sign a register daily between midday and one o'clock; if anyone failed to do so, prefects of the neighbouring departments were immediately alerted. Refugees were also required to make a declaration before leaving their depots. If they were invited to dine with a local notable, they had to surrender a written invitation as proof.[59]

For the majority, this state of asylum was temporary. An amnesty of 30 November 1840, allowed the unconditional return of all non-commissioned officers, soldiers, artisans, and agriculturalists. Officers, magistrates, clergy, and civil employees could also return if they swore fidelity to Isabella II as their queen.[60] Some 14,000 refugees returned to Spain over the following 12 months. Still, 7519 were excluded from the terms of the amnesty and the burden of refugee assistance on the French national budget persisted. Savings from a general reduction in personal financial assistance in 1841 (which continued the progressive reduction in aid commenced in 1835) were consumed on a larger refugee population. Total expenditure on refugee assistance for the two years 1841–3 was 4,560,000 francs, on a par with expenditure in the critical years of 1831–2.[61]

Refugee numbers were also in flux over these years. Continued unrest in Spain in 1841 and 1843 saw more refugees arrive, but further amnesties in 1843 and 1846 followed the final pacification of the insurgent regions in northern Spain. All but the clergy and Carlist officers of the rank of colonel and above could return.[62] Nevertheless, almost 7000 Carlists remained in France after the amnesty of 1843, but in 1845 only a few hundred of them received financial assistance. Of the 200 refugees in Besançon in 1845, only 13 received full allowances; another 23 received a modest 'temporary allowance' of five to ten francs a month. The remainder lived off their own resources or from their labour. Some worked during the agricultural season but had no work during the winter. The incapacitated were supported by public charity.[63]

The question in the political debates on France's responses to the Carlist refugees was no longer about the rights of refugees, or France's protection obligations. Since 1834, these questions raised none of the passions they had in 1831 and 1832. The laws of 1832 and 1834 remained nominally temporary, but the annual debates on their renewal after 1834 were little more than an annual review of the refugee situation and a statement of the reasons why they should be renewed. The troubles in Spain were the clearest justification for their retention.[64] As Argout suggested in 1834, and Thiers confirmed in 1836, the Carlist refugees had dramatically changed the political questions facing the French government. Civil war in Spain, the militarisation of the frontier and Spanish incursions onto French territory were matters of national security and affected France's good relations with the Spanish government. The Carlists were armed combatants who could not be dealt with as refugees seeking asylum.

In 1840, the Interior Minister Rémusat also argued that the Carlist refugees were of a distinct nature to other refugees admitted to asylum. France therefore had to be more ruthless towards them because they were 'entirely different'. The circumstances of their arrival were such that the existing laws were inappropriate and special measures were required.[65] The Carlists, he told the Chamber of Deputies, had appeared still armed, and still engaged in conflict; they had come to France not for protection but to rearm and regroup. Rémusat continued: France might be welcoming and hospitable, but the Carlists posed a problem 'entirely different' to the question of whether they should be granted asylum. They were not individuals in need of protection and humanitarian assistance but potentially hostile agents, whose actions threatened to ensnare France in a civil conflict at its border. They did not merit asylum since they had refused to surrender their arms and give up their struggle. Interdiction, detention, and imprisonment were therefore the most appropriate responses.[66]

Rémusat, in other words, denied that they could even be considered refugees. Consequently, he stripped back the promise of inviolable asylum that had underpinned the July Monarchy's responses to foreign refugees since its origins. France's first duty, Rémusat declared, was to the young Spanish queen; it could not offer asylum to insurrectionists who could again take up arms against her. He went further. The power of expulsion, which was France's main weapon against hostile foreigners, was a necessary power in these circumstances. It was, he said, a 'terrible punishment' that would 'return them to their enemies'.[67] Rémusat, therefore, had conflated expulsion with extradition. It was not, as he saw it, a remedy to be used against those refugees who abused France's laws and for abuses of the terms of asylum; it was the very refusal of asylum.

Rémusat was criticised for overreaching his authority. Such arbitrary acts of a minister of state, one deputy dared argue, demonstrated how far the July Monarchy had stepped beyond the principles and ideals that lay at its foundations.[68] Rémusat was twice reminded that if the laws were inadequate, he should ask the parliament to change them, not act despite them.[69] Yet by now voices of opposition were lone figures. Most deputies kept their own council, and were hereafter silent on the laws relating to refugees when called upon to vote for their annual renewal.

During the 1840s, France continued to employ its three temporary laws on the residence of foreign refugees, of 21 April 1832, 1 May 1834, and 24 July 1839. The refugee depot—a term that loosely described a town in which refugees were ordered to reside and where they were subject to surveillance and control, yet where they were not confined behind wire fences and police guards—was the enduring site of asylum. Here the principle of asylum as *bienfaisance* was given practical form through the measures of containment, care, and control. The refugees did not lack basic material needs and financial assistance gave them at least some margin for independent living. Two key principles endured: the provision of financial assistance paid directly to individual refugees and their families to help them meet their daily subsistence needs, and the promise of inviolable asylum, by which the July Monarchy undertook not to surrender refugees to their enemies. Expulsion, enforced moderately and with circumspection, according to the interior ministers' reports across this period, was a power used to rid France of the more disruptive and militant refugees who failed to abide by French law. Expellees were sent to safe third countries, notably Belgium and Britain, not back to their homelands.

\* \* \*

Originally intended as a permanent regime of containment, care, and control, the law of April 1832 on the residence of refugees was adopted as a temporary measure to placate the concerns of many deputies that the interior minister was assuming too much unmoderated power over policing. The annual parliamentary review brought the possibility that the law might be annulled and that the restrictions on refugees might be lifted. Instead, the powers conferred in the law were reinforced with additional powers in the two amendments of 1834 and 1839. Each year the government presented a case that the powers of these laws were still required to meet the needs of the moment. Continued refugee movements during the late 1830s and into the 1840s, mostly from Spain but also from Italy, and in small numbers from the German Confederation, showed that they were still needed.[70] Without them, it was often remarked, France would be 'disarmed' and unable to defend itself against the challenges to its internal civil and political order, and to its peaceful relations with the great European powers.

Because the laws remained temporary, the conceit that they did not constitute a permanent regime endured. The argument that they were extraordinary measures could placate concerns about the use of arbitrary power and the revocation of refugee rights by offering a further review in 12 months time. In truth, however, the chamber's approval of the laws' extension was a formality. During the 1840s the annual reviews prompted little debate and increasingly a more perfunctory statement was made to explain why their renewal was required.

The government therefore praised the effectiveness of these laws while maintaining their necessity to deal with the ongoing threat to national security and the public peace from new refugee movements. In 1846, it claimed that the stability of the refugee situation had been attained through a combination of the laws, the government's good intentions, vigilance and moderation, and the wise conduct of the refugees themselves. Yet ongoing political crises abroad, especially in Spain, required their renewal and the powers they gave.[71]

The absence of debate was in stark contrast to the early 1830s, when the response of Périer's government to the refugees in 1831 and 1832 concentrated opposition to the July Monarchy. Three themes were pursued in the attacks on the government at that time: the revocation of the rights of refugees; the tendency towards arbitrary rule suggested by the measures deployed against the refugees; and the humiliation of the refugees under the restrictions imposed on them. The rights argument pursued ideals to which states should defer. The measures adopted, however, displayed unregulated power that was contrary to the humanitarian gesture of their admission to asylum. The power of expulsion, which was without juridical oversight, best exemplified what many deputies denounced as the regime's vestiges of despotism. The character of the refugees, above all the Polish nationalists, merited just and humane responses, which the laws of 1832 and 1834 failed to guarantee. By 1834, however, there were few prepared to defend the ideal of refugee rights. Most instead accepted the need for strict controls to ensure the civil order. While assertions of the humanity of its actions suggests that the government was still sensitive to ideals and principles, the rights of the refugees were narrowed to particular benefits conferred by the state, on conditions that it determined. When faced with the 'entirely different' character of the Spanish Carlist refugees, the promise of inviolable asylum was itself rescinded. Asylum had become a matter of French interests alone.

By 1840, changes within the regime and the parliament neutralised the refugee question. The great defenders of the Polish cause, Lafayette and Lamarque, were both dead by May 1834. Pagès was silent after his stance against Casimir Périer in 1831 and the law of 1832. Elections in 1834, 1837, and 1839 produced a more centrist chamber, and parliamentary affairs rested less on matters of principle than on factional interests. Divisions were between Orléanists aligned to Guizot and Thiers and a left around Odilon Barrot, as each vied for parliamentary supremacy.[72]

When Rémusat declared in June 1840 that France's first duty was to the young queen of Spain, he revealed precisely what many critics of the July Monarchy had held against the regime since its earliest days, its deference to the views and opinions of foreign powers. In 1833 it had bowed to Russian and Austrian demands to act against inflammatory organisations that sought to stir up trouble against them. In the 1840s, it bowed to more foreign pressure when it was attacked for its tolerance of the conspiracies of refugees and revolutionaries living in France. One of the more famous occasions was the expulsion of Karl Marx in 1845 following pressure from the Prussian government to shut down the radical German journal *Vorwärts* and to expel the journalists who wrote for it.[73] One year later, Austria's Prince Metternich complained that France had abused the principles of asylum by permitting a campaign among Polish exiles against the Austrian occupation of Cracow. The 'right of asylum' as practiced in France, Metternich protested, amounted to the tolerance of the political actions of the refugees it sheltered against the security of sovereign governments. As the right of asylum held those who profited from it to obligations towards their protecting state, Metternich counselled, so it carried obligations on the part of the protecting state to consider the interests of the countries in whose internal affairs the refugees were meddling.[74] Revolutionary activity was increasingly seen to trouble more than the governments against which it was directed; since asylum sheltered revolutionaries, it nurtured grievances and provided opportunities to conspire, and therefore troubled international relations and the national security of the protecting state.

The Austrian occupation of Cracow in 1846 was the background to the final act of the July Monarchy's response to refugees.[75] Across France there were worries that it might rekindle the dormant insurrectionary passions of its now long settled Polish refugees. Instances of unrest were reported in Toulouse, Amiens, and Le Mans. Revolutionary songs such as *La Varsovienne* and the *Marseillaise* were again heard in public places.[76] French obligations to the government of Austria were readily acknowledged. The government asked the prefects to report what they learned of the attitudes of the refugees, and what language they use in expressing these attitudes, in order to gauge whether they were in contact with the insurgents abroad. A census was also ordered to determine any clandestine departures. Passports to leave the country would only be provided after special permission of the interior minister. Such then were the necessary measures to prevent any dramatic but fruitless gestures among the Poles in France to run to Cracow's aid and therefore damage France's good relations with Austria.[77]

# Part III    A Republican Tradition: Asylum, 1848–1920

On 13 December 1848, the Constituent Assembly of the French Second Republic voted, without debate, to extend for a further 12 months the laws of 21 April 1832, 1 May 1834, and 24 July 1839, on the residence of foreign refugees.[1] Again without debate, on 6 November 1849, the newly constituted Legislative Assembly approved the extension of these laws not for a further 12 months, as had been the practice since 1833, but for a further three years.[2]

Many deputies of these republican assemblies had emerged from the conservative political milieu of the July Monarchy; a number of them at one time or another had previously spoken on the refugee question. The names of Odilon Barrot, Garnier-Pagès, Mauguin, Dupin, and Thiers appeared at various times during the 1830s in the debates on these laws in the former Chamber of Deputies. They now reappear in the new republic's assemblies, but none spoke on their renewal. The Second Republic maintained the refugee regime of the July Monarchy, but the pressure of events would again lead to important transitions in the conception of asylum and its practice, and in the state's obligation towards refugees.

While the parliamentary debates on the refugee laws during the July Monarchy are a rich historical source, the absence of debates during the Second Republic present a number of difficulties in understanding the changing currents. Rather than to political debate we must turn instead to police and ministerial reports and instructions between 1848 and 1851, when, amidst a profound social crisis, France confronted a great demand for asylum after the collapse of revolutions in northern Italy, the Austrian Empire, and the German Confederation. These instructions responded to the immediate dilemmas posed by the new waves of refugees. They reveal a republic concerned more about its obligations to the French people. As the mid-century economic crisis and the red spectre of socialism converged, the terms on which asylum would be offered and respected were again refashioned.

Part III : A Republican Tradition.
Asylum, 1848-1920

# 6
# Asylum and the Mid-Century Crisis

After the fall of Louis-Philippe on 23 February 1848 and the proclamation of a provisional republican government, the powers of Europe mobilised. Prussia, Austria, and Russia all readied their troops, anticipating a neo-Jacobin resurgence in France that would seek again to extend its borders and take its radical republicanism into their realms. As Louis-Philippe had found in 1830, the need to assure the European powers of France's peaceful intentions was urgent. The Foreign Minister Alphonse de Lamartine therefore assured them, and the French people, in a manifesto published on 5 March, that the new republic was not a return to the past but a 'step forward'. France, he assured them all, wanted 'to walk with the world towards peace and fraternity'. Still, the new republic encouraged more radical forces, which pressured Lamartine and the provisional government to adopt a more assertive foreign policy that would once and for all abandon the July Monarchy's humility before the powers of Europe. Polish exiles took this opportunity to reassert their national aspirations and attempt to rekindle the spirit of liberation in the new republic. Delegations were organised to petition the government for funds and arms to sustain a new campaign in Poland. To control the Poles' excessive zeal, the French government proclaimed a Polish legion on 11 March and, on terms negotiated with Prussia and under the supervision of its own ministry of war, Lamartine saw them off from Paris on their journey homeward. Stronger in symbolism than it was a substantive gesture towards Polish liberation—from the start the legion was hampered by the refusal of the German states to allow it to cross their territories under arms—it was a gesture that nevertheless spoke much for republican sentiment. The assurances of Lamartine's manifesto moderated this sentiment, however, and separated moderate from radical republicans in the early days of the new revolutionary government.[1]

There was less need for circumspection in domestic policy. In the same flourish of reforms in the spring of 1848 that saw the abolition of slavery in the colonies, the restoration of the freedom of the press, the replacement of the departmental prefects with republican *commissaires*, the creation of national workshops to assist the unemployed, and the introduction of universal manhood suffrage, Interior Minister Ledru-Rollin announced his intention to rescind the July Monarchy's laws on refugees and immediately lifted restrictions on their movement and their places of residence. In announcing his decision he returned to the language of earlier times: the refugees were 'heroes', he declared, who professed and pursued liberal ideals to which France's revolution was sympathetic; they suffered from their misfortunes and it was France's national sentiment that now broke the shackles that had deprived them of their freedoms.[2]

This flourish of republican sentiment did not live long past the national elections for the Constituent Assembly on 23 April 1848, however, and Ledru-Rollin's resolution did not survive the openly conservative turn that the Republic took between May and June. On 3 June 1848, Adrien Recurt, Ledru-Rollin's successor as interior minister, revoked his resolution and reimposed restrictions on the refugees' freedom of movement and residence. Without these controls, he declared, there was no stopping the accumulation of a 'multitude' of mostly indigent refugees in the capital. From this point there were clear continuities of the refugee regime between the July Monarchy and the Second Republic. Social order and the control of refugees and foreigners more generally were again the dominant objectives of policy and administration.

Social and political pressures were magnified amid the acute economic crisis then facing France. Recurt's intent was to keep indigent refugees out of the capital, where poverty, unemployment, and general economic despair merged with radical republicanism and created an uneasy and militant mood. Intrusive policing attempted to keep a handle on the public peace. The occupation of the Constituent Assembly on 15 May 1848 by members of Parisian political clubs rekindled fears of militant popular political agitation that could plunge the Second Republic into the same morass as the most terrible days of the First. A prohibition on street gatherings led to mass arrests, as both socialist and Bonapartist protests challenged the forces of order.[3] After the June insurrection of 1848, all political gatherings seemed suspect and were subject to rigorous police controls.[4]

With some 174,000 foreigners already resident in a socially and politically turbulent Paris, there was ample justification for Recurt's reimposition of controls on the movement of refugees.[5] But he went further. He cancelled the financial allowances paid to any refugee who had arrived to Paris without sufficient reason since Ledru-Rollin's order the previous March.[6] Too many workers, even foreign workers, were drawn there by the prospect of work and a certain salary in the national workshops, creating even greater problems of competition in a terribly overcrowded labour market and overwhelming imposts on public expenditure. The workshops were therefore closed to all workers who did not live in Paris before the February revolution, and workers from other parts of the country or from abroad were ordered to leave.[7]

Recurt went on to impose even more constraints. Because of the strains on the state treasury, on 1 June 1848 he ordered the reduction of allowances paid to all refugees. As new refugees turned to France after the failure of revolutions abroad, further strains on the budget were anticipated, which could only exacerbate the economic crisis and further unsettle French workers who were already suffering acute levels of poverty and unemployment.[8]

Over the space of three months, therefore, as the political character of the Second Republic was strained between competing moderate, radical, and conservative aspirations, there were sharply contradictory views of what France should do for foreign political refugees. After the violent suppression of the social revolution in Paris on June 1848, the reactionary republican government pronounced its victory over anarchism, at the cost of 3000 civilian deaths and 4000 others transported to Algeria.[9] To assure its victory, the government demanded greater vigilance against the spread of socialism. The refugees of most concern subsequently were not so much those from the national revolutions in northern Italy and Hungary, but from the failed social revolutions in Germany and Austria, where socialists envisioned an international brotherhood shoulder to shoulder with radical French socialists.[10] This was a constant source of anxiety for the conservative 'Party of Order' that had taken the republic into its hands. At a time of severe economic stress, poverty and unemployment were much more pressing concerns than assistance for foreign refugees, so much so that refugees from the European revolutions were hesitantly and reluctantly received as France assumed too many unwelcome burdens with them. Entry, the provision of welfare, and even refugee residence, were all brought into question as the Republic reconsidered its obligations for refugees and its responsibilities at home.

To be sure, financial assistance had been steadily cut back since 1835, but there was no question that it was necessary to help foreign refugees meet their immediate needs. Although it was a large impost on public finances, financial aid was considered an essential component of asylum as protection implied also care for the refugees' welfare. Yet fiscal reality set definite limits. Cut backs in the level of assistance, which all but ceased to be paid to Spanish Carlists in the early 1840s, recognised that they were not sustainable at their prior levels when the numbers of refugees seemed to be ever increasing.[11]

The reduction of assistance consequently separated the question of financial relief from the question of asylum. This was not only because of the larger numbers of refugees; their character and composition had also changed. Many civilians had been caught up in the conflicts around them and did not fit neatly within the designation of political refugees. Financial aid and asylum were therefore becoming two distinct issues. This trend was already apparent with the arrival of refugees from northern Italy in October 1847, and 'other foreigners who have migrated to France under the pretext of the dangers to which they would be subjected in their homelands'. They were granted asylum without question, 'whatever the reasons for their expatriation', but they would not be provided financial assistance. 'With the state of things as they presently are', the Interior Ministry advised the departmental prefects, 'it is not possible to accord even provisional assistance, let alone ongoing allowances.[12]

The collapse of the revolutions abroad during 1848 and 1849 raised the further prospect of countless radical refugees penetrating the French borders and demanding asylum. The growing number of refugees all claiming assistance was the main reason for French reluctance to receive them, but there were also serious doubts about the political causes of their migration and therefore of the legitimacy of their claims to asylum. By March 1849, the refusal of financial assistance had become definite republican policy. Interior Minister Léon Faucher instructed the departments that no refugee who had entered France since the beginning of 1848, and no future refugees, would receive it.[13]

It is doubtful how effective this instruction was, however. The personal dealings that the *commissaires* and later, when they were restored, the departmental prefects had with the refugees gave asylum a human character, and the temptation to pay assistance despite orders not to do so were great. Instructions from Paris stressed the need for the *commissaires* and prefects to turn their backs on the human misery with which they were faced and withhold financial assistance.[14] During 1848, *commissaires* of the departments on the Italian border were ordered for reasons of economy to resist their inclination to pay even provisional assistance to refugees from Lombardy. Reasons of economy were also given for not providing financial assistance to refugees from the popular uprising in the Grand-Duchy of Baden in 1848.[15]

The withdrawal of financial aid therefore withdrew the element of care from the policy of containment, care, and control that endured with the April 1832 law on the residence of refugees and its later amendments. Although the Constituent Assembly had renewed these laws in December 1848, ministerial directives in the meantime had made them effectively redundant. Financial aid through the payment of personal *subsides* had been both the legal and administrative basis on which refugees were confined to their designated depots. The possibility of their loss ensured their proper conduct, but as this aid was no longer paid to new refugees, new forms of control would need to be applied. Instructions henceforth directed that refugees be 'interned' (*internés*).

The term had previously been used in relation to the detention without financial assistance of Spanish Carlists in 1834, as punishment for breaches of French law and hospitality.[16] It also appears in correspondence of June 1833, in relation to Poles in the Haut-Rhin whose papers were not in order and who did not seem to be political refugees.[17] On 7 April 1848, the Director of General Security in the Interior Ministry ordered that refugees from the popular insurrection in Freiburg had their weapons removed from them and be 'interned' in depots in the Doubs, Jura, Haute-Saône, and Marne. The policy of containment, care, and control of the July Monarchy was therefore replaced by a policy that refugees be disarmed at the border if they crossed bearing rifles and sabres, interned on arrival, and dispersed into interior departments (*désarmés, internés, disséminés*). They were, however, allowed to select the depots in which they would prefer to be interned.[18]

About 1000 German refugees were the first to encounter this new policy. They had arrived in the Bas-Rhin after the first uprising in Baden in April 1848, and by May they had been dispersed into other departments. Most had chosen to go to the Doubs. They were sent progressively to Besançon by the new railway line to Cernay from where they continued on foot. As no assistance was paid to them, no formal registers were made of their names, ranks, and social position, leaving an uncertain picture of their composition, political character, and social background. Police surveillance was most conscious of German revolutionary leaders, whose internment was specifically ordered after they had set up a revolutionary committee in Strasbourg and had made public appeals for support.[19] Yet internment suffered from the inefficacy of dispersal and local containment measures. The removal of the Germans from Strasbourg began on 4 May, when 175 individuals set out for Besançon (where 100 settled), Châlons-sur-Marne (where 68 settled), and Vesoul (where 8 settled). By the end of June however, as many as 600 still remained in Strasbourg and in the Bas-Rhin. They filled their time with military exercises and parades to maintain their morale and win the support of the Strasbourgeois. They even placed themselves at the disposition of the French government to go to Paris and fight for the republic against the June insurrection.[20]

Despite these measures of containment, republican sympathies between the French and Germans were evident across Alsace. In May, the *commissaire* of the Bas-Rhin described them as 'German patriots' in his correspondence with the mayors through whose communes the Germans would pass. A clear echo of the universal revolutionary patriotism of the First Republic, the term does not appear to have been used again in official documents after the June days of 1848, and the replacement of the *commissaires* by prefects more in tune with the conservative turn of the republic.[21] By the end of August, furthermore, a large number of Italian refugees from conflict in the Austrian Lombardy-Venetia had joined the Germans and further emphasised the urgency of measures for containment while also exacerbating the social impact of the refugee movements of 1848. The Italians were also interned, after being separated into their military and civilian components, in depots in Besançon and Bourges. In Besançon, they were organised into battalions of 1000 men under the command of a lieutenant-colonel and placed under French military discipline. They were accommodated in barracks for 2000 men, were provided linen, shoes and a daily ration of bread, and wood for heating.[22]

The Italian refugees of 1848 were from an exiled nationalist army. Like earlier Italian refugees, they had failed in their struggle against Austrian occupation. Their revolutionary republicanism was therefore clear, and so too was France's obligations to protect them.[23] In contrast, there were doubts about the political character of the German refugees, particularly those from the popular insurrection of April 1848 in the Grand-Duchy of Baden. Forty of them were recognised as members of the Baden Republican Corps (*colonne républicaine Badoise*) who had been captured and maltreated before arriving in Strasbourg.[24] Yet their political migration, the French authorities complained, was also the pretext for the emigration of vagabonds, young German men and others who wanted to take advantage of French hospitality and the benefits that would flow from it: financial aid in the short term, and over the longer term the avoidance of military service at home and an education at the expense of the French.[25]

The frontier between Alsace and Baden was particularly sensitive during these years of insurrection, and became the site of more concentrated policing. There was, first of all, the potential for the passage of refugees to mire France's relations with the German states. The Grand-Duke of Baden, for example, complained about the threat posed by the presence of German refugees in Strasbourg and the Bas-Rhin. They had to be removed from the frontier as quickly as possible therefore.[26] On the other hand, the French feared that unrest in Germany could spill over the Rhine so it was necessary that cross-border movements were more actively monitored. Reports in February 1849 that German refugees were secretly assembling at Mulhouse in preparation for a general uprising in Baden prompted the internment of all German refugees in Alsace. Between February and May 1849, the left bank of the Rhine was closed to German refugees; those already in France and any who arrived and demanded hospitality were immediately dispatched to more central departments. Among these were both rich and poor refugees, and, marking a significant change in the character of the refugees, a substantial number of socialist revolutionaries.[27]

## True political refugees

The provenance of these new groups of refugees was comparable initially to previous groups. Engaged in popular insurrection during 1848, their character and aspirations were little different to the refugees who were of such concern to the July Monarchy. German refugees were called 'German patriots' even in ministerial instructions, while the reception of refugees from the Piedmont—assemblage in military depots and the persistence of their military formations—recalled that of the Polish nationalists in 1831–2.[28] Internment and dispersal however gave their reception a more negative character.

The Spanish Carlist refugees of the late 1830s had been disarmed at the border for security reasons before they were dispersed into the various depots set aside for them, but France's political and social crises of 1848–9 gave greater urgency to the shift in policy towards disarming, internment, and dispersal. The disarming of refugees was a necessary security measure to control the border, to intercept contingents of foreign revolutionaries, and to neutralise their militancy. It was essential therefore to intercept militant socialist republicans even before they entered France. To this end, a military cordon was placed along the frontier with the Palatinate and Baden to intercept any German insurrectionaries the moment they touched French soil.[29] Internment kept the refugees under the state's control, and kept them under surveillance without financial assistance until they were dispersed into the interior departments. Dispersal, finally, continued past practices of removing refugees from frontier regions and restricting their movements to keep them out of crowded urban centres, above all out of Paris. Refugees from the east were sent in small detachments to western departments, the Vendée, Loire-Inférieure, Orne, Morbihan, Finistère, Côtes-du-Nord, Ille-et-Vilaine, Manche, and Calvados. They were specifically excluded from the ports of Brest, Cherbourg, and Caen.[30]

Internment described containment and control without the provision of care. Yet the provision of care through material and financial assistance had hitherto classified political refugees as a distinct subject of public policy and legitimised measures of policing. How then were political refugees now classified? The instructions of Interior Minister Faucher of 18 May 1849 went some way to answering this when he counselled his prefects that their 'duty was to reconcile the demands of humanity and policy by according asylum only to foreigners who were irrefutably (*incontestablement*) political refugees'. The instruction continued: 'others have no particular right to invoke asylum or to enter France and stay here'.[31] This excluded those not from countries immediately neighbouring France, and any foreigner who could be repatriated under the terms of an amnesty. Those who were truly political refugees (*réfugiés veritables*) therefore were specifically excluded from repatriation under the terms of amnesties.[32]

Nationalist revolutions, civil conflict, and liberation struggles against oppressive regimes had readily identified political refugees up to now. Italian refugees of 1847 were welcomed in the same manner as 'all foreigners who sought asylum [whatever] their reasons for expatriation'.[33] Amnesties, furthermore, specifically identified categories of refugees who could not safely return because of their political allegiances or past actions, and therefore had a demonstrable claim to asylum.[34] The identification of the refugee was less clear, however, when civilians had been caught up in events and forced into exile alongside combatants or revolutionaries.

During 1848–9, France declared that it offered asylum to 'proscripts of all causes'. The most identifiable refugees were still those revolutionaries 'who sympathised with our principles and our flag', such as Italian nationalists from Lombardy-Venetia who had risen against the Austrian emperor.[35]

Italians from the Piedmont, who were engaged in conflict against the Kingdom of Sardinia, were not considered to be political refugees in need of asylum as they were favoured by an amnesty that permitted their return without falling foul of the law.[36] The character of refugees changed as the political revolutions of 1848 gave way to social revolutions during 1849. The proper classification of the refugees was then more problematic. Faucher's instructions of March 1849 that only those who were verifiably political refugees would be granted asylum identified two principle changes: many refugees were socialist rather than nationalist revolutionaries and therefore were more likely to be civilian rather than military; among the civilians were many young men who had come to France to better their lives but who could nevertheless return 'without exposing themselves to judicial penalty'.[37] In this category Faucher placed Austrian and German subjects fleeing the reactions to their various insurrections of 1848 and 1849.[38]

He also placed in this same category Lombard, Polish, and Hungarian nationalists, although they had gravely compromised their personal safety and were in need of asylum. Faucher insisted that refugees would only be admitted into France if they were from those countries with which France shared a border (*limitrophe*). Refugees who crossed a third country before arriving in France, such as the Poles, would henceforth be refused asylum. This was the clearest indication of the republic's shift in the conception and application of asylum. Faucher announced in April 1849 that even Poles from Cracow and Posen, who had fled Austrian oppression since its occupation of the two cities in 1846, would not be allowed entry, as France would no longer tolerate Austria's refusal to honour its own obligations to protect refugees on its territory, refugees indeed of its own making. 'Without ceasing to be faithful to such honourable precedents', Faucher wrote apologetically to Foreign Minister Drouyn de Lhuy, 'France ought to refuse access to Poles sent from Cracow and Posen'.[39] It was a signal to all foreign powers, not just Austria, that they also had obligations to grant asylum to refugees; they could not simply force them onto France.[40]

Yet Faucher was well aware that the refusal to admit new Polish refugees contradicted the past spirit of asylum and French respect for Polish nationalists. How France could refuse them admission while still claiming its fidelity to these 'honourable precedents' therefore required a substantial redefinition of asylum and France's obligations to refugees.

## Republican asylum

Policy of the republic therefore sought to separate refugees from others caught up in the broad sweep of the political and social movements of the mid-nineteenth century. Internment, however, implied that asylum was temporary even for those properly considered to be political refugees.

Without the payment of financial assistance, it was assumed that refugees would either become self-supporting through work, or they would move onward to another country; or else, should circumstances permit, they would choose repatriation. In short, the objective was that refugees should disappear in one way or another so they would not be a burden on the state. Military refugees from Italy and Hungary were encouraged to enter the Foreign Legion and therefore serve France in Algeria. Passports were offered to any refugee who desired to go to Britain, Belgium, or North America: they would have to make the journeys at their own expense, but the French government would provide assistance for the cost of their transport to the seaports.[41] Prefects in the eastern departments were instructed to move refugees to western France, while the prefects of western departments were directed to arrange their passage to Le Havre for embarkation to Britain or America.[42] The decision of those who chose not to leave was respected, nevertheless. Even though the interior minister encouraged the repatriation of refugees from northern Italy under the favourable terms of an Austrian amnesty of August 1849, there was no undue pressure on those who chose not to return.[43]

On the other hand, there was a certain degree of pressure to leave placed on those not considered 'irrefutably political refugees'. They were offered passports and travel assistance to encourage their onward migration or repatriation. But repatriation was never forced. Many young Germans who had migrated for reasons other than their political views were compelled to leave the eastern departments and were even offered passports to return to Germany or to go to Switzerland, with the added incentive of 30 centimes for every ten kilometres they travelled until they reached the frontier. But they could decline these offers and remain in France. They were, however, dispersed into to western departments where they would have to provide for themselves by agricultural work.[44]

Internment ceased with their dispersal into the west. No effort seems to have been made to contain them afterwards, or even to trace their onward movements once they had left the eastern departments. In July 1849, French authorities were unable to trace nine Germans whose extradition was sought for their role in assassinations during the troubles in Frankfurt the previous year.[45] Dispersal, in other words, successfully broke apart groups of militant revolutionaries, of whom all trace seems to have been lost as they travelled into the French countryside or migrated elsewhere.

The new terms of asylum therefore addressed the refugee problem by favouring onward migration. Internment was a disincentive to refugee settlement from the moment they arrived in France, while various incentives were offered to encourage their dispersal. Yet measures did not go so far as to refuse residence to refugees who did not choose to move on or to return if the opportunity was available. They sought rather to cut the cost of accommodating and supporting large numbers of political refugees. The true reason for these measures was therefore the state's inability to maintain the cost of refugee welfare, even when not paying direct personal assistance. The refusal of all forms of aid dissuaded refugees from settling. The onward migration of Italian and German refugees was encouraged because the financial burdens they imposed on France could not be sustained. To encourage Hungarians to join the Foreign Legion, they were explicitly told that they would not receive any financial aid if they remained in France and would have to earn their own livings.[46]

Time and again the financial constraints on refugee assistance were explained by the parlous economic conditions. The republic's first priority, it was often remarked, was the welfare of its own citizens. General instructions of April 1849 on the measures for Italian refugees and others from Austrian territory stressed the government's more pressing obligations to the French people. When the prefects might have been inclined to grant what limited welfare they could, they were reminded that 'in the present circumstances a great number of French citizens, mostly of the labouring classes, are exposed or subjected to privations and misery for the want of work and resources'.[47] Not even political refugees warranted special assistance in these circumstances.

In other words, there was no capacity in the national budget to alleviate their conditions. Since the June days of 1848, national workshops for the unemployed had been closed and the government spent no more on social welfare for its people. At the same time as it refused assistance to refugees because of the need to relieve the misery of its own people, the government could provide no relief for poverty among the workers or welfare for the unemployed. It has been estimated that France required additional revenue of 100 million francs to meet its commitments. When in need of funds for unemployment relief, tax receipts had dried up and it was unable to raise loans.[48] In these circumstances, financial relief for foreign refugees could scarcely be countenanced. Their onward migration was a better solution than asylum and residence. It cut the costs of assistance and made sure that the refugees themselves would not fall into poverty if they too had no prospect of work.

Interior Minister Léon Faucher was nevertheless conscious that fiscal reality conflicted with the right of asylum for refugees, an ideal to which, in his own words, the republic held fast.[49] At the same time as economic misery inside France justified withdrawing financial assistance from foreign refugees, the term the 'right of asylum' appears more frequently in ministerial directives. It expressed traditions and ideals to which the republic was heir and to which it should adhere, even if it was incompatible with the circumstances then facing it. Instructions of 31 March 1849 stated that 'France grants asylum and protection to all those suffering misfortune'; those of 15 April 1849 committed the republic to this tradition: 'France has always practiced the right of asylum in the broadest sense of its meaning.

The republican government will remain faithful to the procedures that honour the national character'.[50] And again, on 18 May 1849: 'France, faithful to its antecedents, opens its territory and accords asylum'.[51] Yet these principles were quickly modified by statements why they needed to be set aside. The instructions of 31 March 1849 are typical: the miserable conditions within France prevented it from 'indefinitely supporting all foreigners whom political events drive from their homes'.[52]

The evocation of these principles claimed them for the republic but their negation in the face of the economic and social conditions of the time did not necessarily render them of the past. Rather, the right of asylum was a tradition and ideal to which the republic could aspire; it encapsulated past principles that were meaningful again within republican consciousness. The tension between actuality and ideals attempted to balance the republic's humanitarian obligations with political exigencies. The appearance of German socialists in the east claiming asylum could only imperil the conservative 'Party of Order's' hold on power in the face of the challenge from radical republican socialists. It was even suspected that the insurgents of Bavaria and Baden had planned to hoist the 'red standard of socialism' in Alsace and stir revolution in all the frontier departments, taking it all the way to Lyon.[53] Yet the spirit of French tradition embedded in the ideal of a right of asylum was upheld in their admission. They evoked admiration for the actions that had compelled them to seek asylum, yet the ideal of asylum was moderated by their internment to stymie their revolutionary impulses.[54]

The more interventionist measures of policing from early 1849 to disarm, intern, and disperse refugees, placed a considerable onus on the prefects of the departments on France's eastern frontier to distinguish between those who were and those who were not political refugees. In the confusion of the moment when dealing with new arrivals from failed insurrections across the Rhine, it was not really possible to make an accurate assessment about each individual. To help distinguish those who were political refugees from those who were not, the Interior Ministry required, in the first instance, a complete record of all refugees from Poland, Germany, Hungary, and Spain in each department—a huge task which, for the Prefect of the Bas-Rhin, required a daily census, conducted at 8 p.m., of all lodging houses, hotels, and any private dwellings where foreigners might be staying, in order to tally new arrivals and departures.[55]

It was certain, nevertheless, that foreigners who were not considered to be political refugees had no right to invoke asylum. Their presence was not desired as they could only aggravate the misery of French workers.[56] But distinction between political refugees and others was seldom clear. As noted above, German youths among the refugees from Baden who were accused of entering France 'to avoid military service ... or to obtain a free education' were not forcibly returned if they declined the opportunities for repatriation presented to them. Similarly, refugees from Piedmont who, because of an amnesty were not considered political refugees, could remain in France, not as refugees, to be sure, but as foreign immigrants.[57] Yet as immigrants they were subject to the same measures for internment and dispersal as those classified as political refugees: they were removed from frontier departments and sent to specific locations. This narrow distinction between political refugees and immigrants without political reasons for remaining in France irredeemably changed the status of refugees in public policy, law, and common perceptions.

## The 'undesirable' foreigner

In 1849, socialist revolutionaries presaged a migration of a different kind. A foreign proletariat grew with the international mass migrations that so characterised the second half of the nineteenth century. At this time, Patrick Weil suggests, migration entered history because it had become a 'problem', of much larger numbers, of urbanisation and industrialisation, and consequently of proletarianisation.[58] Already alert to the red spectre of socialism since the June days of 1848, the legislators of the republican assemblies turned to address their fears of the undesirable outcomes of immigration. One of the most troublesome was the arrival of foreign socialists.

Within this context, the Republic drafted a new nationality code, which included specific provisions under the title 'policing foreigners' (*police des étrangers*). The justification for the provisions on policing in a law that codified the acquisition of French nationality by foreign residents lay in concerns about the inadequacy of existing laws to respond to the unwelcome consequences of migration. Vigilance was not a sufficient safeguard against the potential menace of new immigrants, it was stated in the government's report to the assembly on the bill. There were deeper social problems that nurtured both socialism and migration than mere vigilance could identify and isolate. The growth of industry and urban population, 'with the crises these caused', heightened bourgeois anxieties that the conservative and stable political and social order could again be ruptured. 'Population growth after a long peace, the changes brought about by industrial growth, and the demands of general well-being', the report suggested, were all threats that could 'degenerate into a permanent crisis'.[59] To prevent this, the state had to attend to the needs of its own citizens and better control the flow of immigrants who, 'often without consent and always without resources ... paralyse our efforts of reducing poverty'. The enforcement of laws against beggars and vagabonds were too slow to have any impact. Better policing of the frontier was therefore preferable, for example by properly separating those who were 'irrefutably political refugees' from those who were not, or by refusing entry to or expelling from the country 'undesirable' foreigners in order to avoid the growth of 'misery' inside France.

The outcome therefore was the power to expel undesirable foreigners under articles seven and eight of the new naturalisation law of 3 December 1849. This was a direct response to the recent political upheavals and the growth of poverty across Europe, which imposed on France the 'most frequent invasions' of foreigners. Poverty had created a new category of foreigner: the 'undesirable', who made an imposition on French hospitality while providing little in return, and indeed, who even corrupted the social fabric.[60]

The undesirable foreigner was a sufficiently vague figure that could take form as circumstances suited. One form was the revolutionary who hatched conspiracies against the social and political order, working secretly within a 'vast association of agitators': they had 'abdicated the idea of a homeland [to] go wherever there is the possibility of upheaval and reform themselves in foreign states'.[61] As the crisis from social, economic, and political change rounded on the elusive figure of the undesirable foreigner, new measures of intercession and control were deployed against common immigrants as much as against political refugees.

The nationality code of 3 December 1849 also introduced safeguards against a foreigner's accession to citizenship, without which the integrity of popular sovereignty and the expansion of suffrage to all adult males would be compromised. Indeed, the need for a new law was argued on the grounds that the Provisional Government had hurriedly introduced an 'ill-considered' and 'improvised' naturalisation decree on 28 March 1848 that had 'abused the privilege' of French citizenship by granting it to many unworthy of it. Some 2439 foreigners were naturalised under this decree, and all the men gained the right to vote without the least consideration of their merits.[62]

The differences, conceptual as much as legal, between refugees, immigrants, and foreigners broadly speaking, were increasingly narrowed. The republic nevertheless maintained the distinct regime for political refugees. The laws of the July Monarchy on the residence of foreign refugees still formed the basis for the administration of refugee assistance, although the refusal of financial aid to new refugees had replaced the policy of containment, which was framed around the provision of aid, with internment and its sense of detention and penalty. In the mind of Interior Minister Faucher, there was little conceptual difference from the administrative regime instituted under these laws and new republican practices. Of concern to Faucher in late 1851 was the tendency of the departmental prefects to treat refugees as common foreigners. This had allowed refugees to change residence without the government's permission and therefore to move back into the large cities, Paris especially, or into the border regions. He reminded the prefects that many important formalities had been neglected when they were essential in the political climate of that time. The current administrative regime applying to the residence of refugees, Faucher confirmed, was that of the law of 24 July 1839: only those refugees who had lived in France for more than five years had no need for official approval to change their residence, and Paris and the Franco-Spanish frontier remained closed to them.[63]

In reality, the policing of refugees had taken significant new directions since 1848. The refugee depot was no longer the centre of policy as internment and dispersal had scattered refugees around the country. Unlike containment in depots, where refugees were kept very much alive in the consciousness and anxieties of public officials, government ministers, and the general public, the imperative of refugee policy under the Republic was to see the refugees effectively disappear into the French interior or by their onward migration. The refugees were lost into the general foreign population and therefore had fallen under the common measures of policing and public administration applied to foreigners.

The expulsion provisions of the 1849 nationality law also marked a notable change in this direction. They extended to all foreigners the powers set down in the April 1832 law on the residence of refugees. Simply, they gave the interior minister the authority to order the immediate expulsion of any foreigner from French territory for acts prejudicial to the public order, a decision that would be made on an individual basis through normal administrative process.[64]

Previously separated by the laws of 1832, 1834, and 1839, refugees and other foreigners were all now subject to the same sanction of expulsion for a breach of French law or their perceived threat to the public peace. These laws expired in December 1852, at the end of the three-year prolongation voted by the Legislative Assembly in 1849. This special legal regime on the residence of refugees therefore ceased. Expulsion powers had been superseded by the provisions of articles seven and eight of the 1849 nationality law, and other prohibitions on refugees—on their movements and associations, unauthorised entry to Paris and other large metropolitan centres— were police and administrative measures sanctioned under instructions from the interior minister.

## The emperor's *droit de grâce*

On 2 December 1851, the Republic was taken into the hands of the usurper Louis-Napoléon. A new regime of the policing of foreigners had commenced with the suppression of opposition to his coup d'état. Suspects included foreigners 'whose presence appears to be politically dangerous', and on 12 December 1851 an emergency law ordered the prefects to provide their names to the head of national security in the Interior Ministry so that they could be expelled.[65] Still, even in this volatile political climate, asylum for refugees was protected. Some prefects, it was realised, had gone too far in their recommendations for expulsions, as they had recommended refugees whose security could not be assured upon repatriation. The Head of General

Security admonished the prefects for having 'misunderstood in the gravest possible way the right of asylum'. No measures would therefore be taken to expel anyone who would be put at peril.[66] This assured refugees of protection at a time of highly active policing and mass arrests.

This guarantee of asylum coincided with the flight of exiles from Louis-Napoleon's police state. Arrests after the coup, totalling 26,884, drove radical democratic and socialist republicans underground and into exile in Switzerland, Belgium, and England. A community of French political refugees in Geneva, John Merriman writes, were close enough to the French border to 'peer across at the nervous French guards and to think about raising an army with the help of German and Italian revolutionaries.'[67] They were in contact with socialist leaders in France, held political rallies and songfests, political funerals, and even a lottery for their own benefit. Spies were sent to infiltrate them, while a large armed force policed the frontier to keep them at bay.[68] French exiles in London also bided their time. Among them were Ledru-Rollin and others banished during the conservative repression of socialism in 1849, who became integral to the early international socialist movement.[69] Finding the support of other revolutionary exiles from the European upheavals of 1848 and 1849, dreams of the victory of the universal social and democratic republic nurtured new plans for international socialist revolution.[70]

Their banishment had brought them together in opposition to the conservative and imperial powers that ruled the continent, which sustained the political crisis through a period of police repression during the 1850s.[71] About 1000 political refugees from France had joined 2500 Polish and 260 German refugees in London. They lived and met unencumbered by police surveillance, with few controls on their activities and associations. London had now become the centre for international revolutionaries, a role formerly played by Paris.[72] There were also the great nationalists, such as the Italian Mazzini and the Hungarian Kossuth, who had both been banished from Paris after Louis-Napoleon's coup. Or there were the more shadowy figures like those behind the unification of social revolutionaries into the International Working Man's Association in 1855 and First International in 1864, writers and revolutionary theorists like Karl Marx, Michael Bakunin, Alexander Herzen, and others who preached insurrectionary violence against imperial government.

The July Monarchy's laws on the residence of refugees expired in December 1852. They were replaced by police instructions issued on 9 April 1853 by Napoléon III's Minister of General Police, Charles Maupas. Restrictions on refugee movements were lifted; refugee depots were therefore abolished. However, refugees were still barred from Paris, Lyon, and Marseilles and their urban hinterlands. Border regions were also closed to refugees. Spanish refugees were still barred, as before, from residing within 160 kilometres of the Spanish border. Polish and German refugees were barred from residing in the departments on the Swiss and German frontier, and Italian refugees were barred from the departments on the Italian frontier.[73]

The concessions allowed to refugees, however, were granted only by omission from the new instructions. They lacked any statement affirming certain freedoms but instead persist with a language of prohibition. They admitted that the common law would suffice for the regulation of foreigners and no exceptional powers were required to police refugees. It followed that there should be clear rules for the prefects' administration of their responsibilities. But the foreigner, and not the refugee specifically, was the subject of the instructions. The preamble states that the aim of the instructions was to reinforce the regime that applied to the residence of foreigners. New arrivals were called 'migrants' (*nouveaux emigrants*) under the instructions, until an official determination was made about their status. As with earlier measures, they had to be 'disarmed and sent immediately to a town at least 100 kilometres from the border, and placed under the surveillance of the local authorities'. It would then be decided whether there was 'reason to tolerate their residence'.[74] The term 'migrant' had therefore replaced 'refugee', suggesting that the purpose of these instructions was more than simply replacing obsolete laws with new administrative arrangements. There was little that was new in the responses to migrants, whether or not they were refugees, on their arrival. All were classified as 'foreigners' and none had formal constraints placed on them except for the prohibitions against residing near the frontier and in the larger cities. Finally, instruction authorised the local police to refuse admission (*repousser*) to 'any category of foreigner'—now a general designation—'who had found asylum in another country'.[75]

The distinctions between refugees and foreigners were therefore considerably narrowed. The instructions left little to distinguish between them on arrival: all who sought to enter France were removed from the frontier while a judgement was made as to whether they could remain. The instructions do not explain how this would be done, however, but the decisions were devolved to the prefects who did not need to seek formal authorisation from the central ministry in Paris. This left considerable scope for the prefects to judge who should or should not be allowed entry.

The instructions of 1853 consequently reduced the power of policing over political refugees and spread existing powers more broadly over foreigners. They contributed to the conflation of refugees with foreigners in public policy, which, Gérard Noiriel concludes, suggest certain weaknesses of the state in relation to immigration. These weaknesses were evident in the uncertainty of laws, the permeability of frontiers, and the weakness of the police force, which left refugees and other foreigners sufficient margin to manoeuvre so that they were no longer constrained by exile.[76] Indeed, as the character of the refugees changed, they could not be readily distinguished among the new mass migrations across Europe and eventually across the Atlantic. Special measures for the policing of refugees had in fact fallen into disuse, and the anxieties that once arose with the consciousness of refugees had given way to a new awareness of the unwelcome consequences of migration. The narrowing of the distinction between refugees and other foreigners obscured the special status of refugees and nullified principles invested in a notion of their right of asylum. It also obscured France's protection obligations. As they were all subjected to the same regime of policing, little room remained for principle.

Napoléon III's Second Empire refashioned France into a police state to foil revolutionaries whose aim was to destabilise the regimes of Europe.[77] Diplomatic protest, surveillance of the frontier and the Channel coast, and infiltration of the refugee communities in London, Belgium, and Switzerland, to gather intelligence about their operations and pre-empt their conspiracies, were some of the measures taken to nullify the influence of the red spectre abroad after its suppression at home.[78] Foreigners within France were not above suspicion of complicity in these plots. Secret police surveillance continued throughout the 1850s.

The surveillance of foreign revolutionaries was made all the more difficult by the new currents of popular migration. From the east and south, large numbers converged on France, to enter its industries or to reach the Atlantic seaports for passage to America. They came in their largest numbers from Italy, Belgium, Poland, and Spain, traditional source countries of France's immigrants and refugees. Displacement, alienation and exile, the themes of the revolutionary epoch and the burden of refugees, was becoming common experience amidst these demographic upheavals.

Yet in the face of these movements, the fear of a permanent crisis from population growth, industrialisation, and immigration seemed to have passed with the mid-century crisis and Napoleon III's suppression of socialist republicanism. New foreign workers fed France's industrial expansion; free trade agreements among European states in the 1860s opened the doors to the exchange of merchandise and the free circulation of people, and measures for controlling their flow fell into disuse. The freedom to travel made passports obsolete; laws that had made them an obligation were officially suppressed for west European nationals.[79] Capitalism required labour and attracted foreign workers much more quickly than the state could develop mechanisms of border controls to regulate migrant entry. The nation gained from new wealth, but industrial expansion led to the doubling of the number of foreigners to about one million by 1880. It also brought to French cities, Noiriel adds, the immigrant 'ghettos' of the new industrial suburbs.[80] They lived separately from French communities, and the new demographic realities engendered pronounced dichotomies of identity, culture, and ethnicity.

Political refugees, socialist revolutionaries, and foreign anarchists were concealed within these migrant flows. The more militant and dangerous moved between cities and counties as their revolutionary spirit took them, assisted in their passage across poorly policed borders by the new networks of railways and steamships, by the growing popular migrations, and by their access to false documents. While police surveillance was still alert to their potential menace, they could circulate within France like other immigrants, until such time as their actions or police intelligence gave reason for concern. They were also proof that the security of one country often depended on policing in another and that national security required solidarity between states for the regulation and punishment of political crimes.[81]

\* \* \*

What then was the meaning of asylum if the distinction between the refugee and the foreigner had narrowed? The refugees' reasons for expatriation had distinguished them from other foreigners; they could not remain in their homelands because of a danger to their person or liberty. The separate regime for refugees, the special laws relating to their residence, the grant of financial aid, and the promise of inviolable asylum, had previously recognised their distinct status because they were unable to return to their homelands without a threat to their lives of liberties. By the police instructions of 1853, this distinction was no longer made in French law. Instead, all foreigners were loosely bound together under a similar regime of policing, while articles seven and eight of the nationality law of 1849 sanctioned the expulsion of any undesirable foreigner. Financial aid was no longer forthcoming, and inviolable asylum seemed no longer certain. Instead, the opposite of asylum, extradition, would identify the refugee.

Because extradition surrendered an individual to a foreign state that sought to exact punishment for an offence against its law, it recognised the law of that state, its system of justice, and its right to exact the punishment. If these crimes were of a political nature or an act of conscience, then the nature of political crimes and just penalty were brought into question. Extradition could amount to the refusal or annulment of asylum if the protecting state handed over an individual to be punished for a political act or an act of conscience. Conversely, the refusal of extradition was a guarantee of a right of asylum because it protected a refugee from unjust punishment. Asylum was consequently defined by exceptions to extradition. Indeed, asylum and extradition had become so intertwined by the mid-nineteenth century that they seemed synonymous. One text on the legal code relating to foreigners dating from 1853 certainly listed them as one and the same: its index entry, 'Asylum, right of (*Asile, droit de*), contains one reference: 'see Extradition'.[82]

In the context of extradition, asylum moved into the legal domain, in which questions of criminality and proper justice came to the fore. Systems of justice, therefore, had to keep specific boundaries between the domains of the right of asylum, under which political acts and acts of conscience were protected, and criminal justice, under which common crimes could rightly be punished. The French Justice Ministry had reported as much in 1833 when it advised that extradition arrangements were necessary between states that had a common interest in repressing criminal behaviour to maintain order and public security.[83] Only now in the mid-nineteenth century had this become central to the relations between states and the legal status of refugees. The test of which applied in the case of any one individual— whether a refugee was accorded asylum for actions expressing legitimate political conscience, or the refugee was instead a fugitive wanted for criminal acts—was less a political one, which had the potential to strain diplomatic relations, than a legal one. Because extradition law addressed disputes over which applied in any particular case, by defining exemptions it defined a refugee's right of asylum.

The turning point was the identification of political acts—once thought legitimate as one of the fundamental principles of the rights of man, liberty from oppression—as crimes against sovereign government and national security. The Orsini affair of 1858 best illustrated how criminal acts of political violence had become. Felice Orsini, an Italian refugee from London, had travelled secretly to Paris and, on 14 January 1858, attempted to assassinate Napoleon III and Empress Eugenie as they left the Paris opera. Orsini and two co-conspirators hurled three grenades, missing their targets but killing eight bystanders and wounding 150 more.[84] Indignant at this outrage, the French government accused the British of complicity by its tolerance of conspiracies among its refugees. Relations between the two governments were subsequently strained as each argued their views on asylum. Britain held to its liberal principle that the government should not interfere in an individual's life while France asserted that it was both proper and necessary to constrain the activities of refugees when their intent was to take terrorist violence into foreign countries. Asylum as practiced in Britain, the French accused, aided revolutionaries and harboured assassins. 'Ought the right of asylum protect such a state of things? Is hospitality due to assassins?' the French Foreign Minister Colonna-Walewski asked his British counterpart.[85] Despite French pressure that it reconsider its policy of unrestricted and unmoderated asylum, the British government refused to concede to change, furthering anxieties on the continent that it would remain a haven for criminals, conspirators, and assassins.[86]

Among the socialist revolutionaries that Britain harboured, governments on the continent complained, there were terrorists and 'assassins', like Orsini, who launched a campaign of terror across Europe to weaken the foundations of capitalism and imperialism. One French writer asked: 'why are friendly governments powerless to destroy these laboratories of assassins? How are the sacred laws of hospitality to apply to these ferocious beasts?' They were rhetorical questions, of course, but they demonstrate how political terrorism perpetrated by small bands of revolutionaries and exiles had changed the foundations of asylum. Acts against sovereign governments were of such a kind that they could only be classified as 'crimes that cause horror to the entire world' and their perpetrators were unworthy of protection from retribution or justice.[87]

The Orsini affair united the European states in their common interest of political order and national security against this new political terrorism. To this end asylum would henceforth defer to 'treaties, the preservation of tranquillity, or affection for foreign powers'. Governments and sovereigns moreover had the discretion about what measures they should take against refugees, whether to protect them or expel them.[88] International agreement on political crimes marked a fundamental change in the nature of politics and government from the mid-nineteenth century. The offences for which individuals could find protection under a foreign power were not immutable, the Italian jurist Egidio Reale writes, but changed to reflect different perceptions of criminality and justice.[89] Differences of institutions and opinion, the prohibitions made in each state against intervening in the affairs of another, the variability and instability of forms of government and political institutions, the practicalities of political repression, and human sentiments, Reale observes, were all debated and contended during the mid-nineteenth century; so too were the nature of political offences. The profound difference between crimes of common law and politics was incontestable, yet, Reale continues, what was considered an honourable action on one side of the frontier or in one era could be considered criminal on the other side or in another era. The immorality of political offences, in short, varied according to epoch and circumstance.[90]

These then illustrate new directions in the nature of asylum from the mid-nineteenth century. Juridical questions about justice and criminality had replaced political questions about revolutionary causes, rights, and public policy responses. For a while these were dressed in a rhetoric that recalled traditional conceptions of asylum, complete with the assertion of absolute authority in the context of the Orsini affair and the policing of socialist revolutionaries. The essence of monarchical asylum was reaffirmed for the Second Empire, therefore. Asylum rested on both the emperor's humane discretion and his authoritarian firmness. Asylum was a 'grace' (*droit de grâce*), a clemency that the emperor could extend, after reflecting upon issues of national interest, the nature of offences, treaty obligations, diplomatic relations, and the rigours of punishment that would be a refugee's due if repatriated.[91]

'Grace', extradition, and national security, were in fact bound in a web of dependency. One state's security required asylum for refugees in another, for, it was asked, without the clemency of a foreign power how could another expel the politically dangerous? 'If a man cannot flee' and find protection elsewhere, 'he will conspire'. States were therefore bound into a network of mutual security. If asylum was the exercise of clemency by one state, then it was nevertheless beholden to recognise the interests of another, for the preservation of security, the public peace, and the integrity of systems of justice.[92]

# 7
# Socialist Revolutionaries, Mass Migration, War: 1870–1920

The mid-nineteenth century marks a historical rupture between migrations of two distinct natures, the political migrations of the age of revolutions, and the popular industrial migrations of the second half of the century. The point of division between them was as much in the French consciousness of migration as it was in the character and composition of the migrants. The social movements of mid-nineteenth century, the rationale behind the 1849 nationality law suggests, exposed France to the unintended outcomes of migration, the most alarming of which was the undesirable foreigner who benefited from French hospitality but was really a threat to the stability of its social and political order, and, most importantly, over whom France had limited control.

Since the failure of the social revolutions in 1848–9, resistance to the conservative bourgeois order and autocratic monarchies became more violent and desperate, and political migrations assumed more sinister forms. Revolutionaries were no longer the heroes of national liberation as in the past; they were shadowy figures concealed within the new migrations, plotting socialist revolution or anarchist terror against the European regimes.

The new consciousness of foreigners among the French was perhaps the major distinction between the two eras of migration separated by the social, political, and economic crises of the mid-nineteenth century. As Patrick Weil remarks, migration became a problem from this time, and one indicator of this is the greater attention it attracted in both public policy and popular consciousness.[1] But what was this problem? If the state resisted the social tide of massed migration during the economic and political crises of the late 1840s and the early 1850s, it had bent by the 1860s to the forces migration had unleashed and accommodated the free movements of people as it did the free movement of merchandise.[2] The liberalisation of passport controls during the second half of the nineteenth century lifted constraints on the freedom of movement, and at least until the First World War released many millions from their traditional ties to land, community, and nation.[3] The need for the free movement of foreign labour for economic and industrial expansion was greater than the state's need to police its borders and regulate the residence of foreigners. The problem of migration was therefore one of perception. The force of the currents of migration did not so much pose problems for the state; indeed, the state would benefit from the economic growth and industrial expansion from new migrant workers. Rather, it was a problem for the nation, which was exposed to the massed movement of foreign workers who would settle in new communities in the French cities, changing the urban demographics and introducing new and distinct cultures. The dichotomy between the national and the foreigner was all the more pronounced as migrant numbers grew and their cultures were all the more visible in the French streetscapes. The foreign population doubled to about one million by 1880, and continued to rise by 40,000–50,000 each year, a figure higher, Gérard Noiriel observes, than for such renowned countries of immigration as Argentina and Australia.[4]

Against this background, the *droit de grâce* of the Second Empire, if it had any meaning beyond mere imperial rhetoric, was little more than faded fabric of the past. Amid the currents of modern migration and capitalist expansion, asylum leaped beyond imperial toleration after the great national and ideological ruptures of the Franco-Prussian war and the Paris Commune in 1870 and 1871 into new, yet undefined, forms. With the bloodletting of the *semaine sanglante* of 22–9 May 1871, France itself was the oppressor. Thousands sought asylum abroad, fleeing along the traditional paths of French exiles to Bruxelles and London. Even then they were not necessarily free of political vindictiveness of governments sympathetic to the security of others. Most famously, Victor Hugo was expelled from Bruxelles for opening his house as sanctuary to communard refugees.[5] Thousands more were exiled to New Caledonia.[6]

As the Third Republic consolidated its political institutions and republican political culture grew more assured, it set about defining the nation more precisely through a new nationality law adopted in June 1889.[7] During the 1880s the state reimposed itself on immigrants and foreign residents in response to new uncertainties among the French people and parliamentary deputies alike about the benefits of migration.[8] Both extradition and expulsion were key instruments of the state against the undesirable and the troublesome foreigner. In certain ways the practice of both also defined the idea of the nation through questions about the true republican character of hospitality and asylum for political refugees.

The study of asylum and refugee protection in the second half of the nineteenth century is therefore made problematic by the convergence of refugees with the broader streams of popular industrial migrations. The sources are accordingly more scarce; political debate was rare and ministerial interventions rarer still. A scattering of texts in law, politics, and commentary must suffice to piece together how refugees and their asylum were conceived in the new republic. As the same regimes of entry and residence applied to refugees and other immigrants, it is perhaps even problematic to speak of asylum. What distinctions were there then between the two? How was the term 'political refugee' sustained in the vocabulary of migration, and how was asylum sustained as a principle? Extradition law had a vital role to play. Refugees were also defined in the context of expulsion. Socially, they were tainted by the racialist turn against the foreigner at the end of the century.

## Extradition, expulsion, and republican national consciousness

Extradition law was perhaps the major factor that sustained asylum and the classification of the political refugee. During the Second Empire, revolutionary terrorism had given extradition such an importance in matters of foreign relations that treaties and conventions were agreed on common security interests. Political conspiracies and secret plots against state security and the public peace were criminalised, even if the targets were other countries. Once acts of political conscience were outlawed, asylum could be denied legitimately and an individual handed over to his persecutors. Precisely what were legitimate acts of political dissent and what were criminal plots, however, could really only be decided in the consideration of laws on extradition.

In the mid-1870s, the Justice Ministry recognised that extradition, as it had been practiced in France, was imprecise and prone to error. It did not always ensure the surrender of an individual culpable of an offence to face punishment in a foreign country, nor did it protect individuals from punishment for legitimate acts of political dissent.[9] Identified errors included the questionable identity of the subject of a petition for extradition from a foreign government, and the arrest and detention of an individual before a formal order had been authorised and signed. As extradition concerned international arrangements, and the circumstances in which an extradition order was enforced were normally set down in treaties that bound two powers in legal and diplomatic agreements, the French law and administration of extradition were reformed in 1875 so that it conformed more closely to international standards. Dutch and Belgian models of judicial intervention were followed to ensure just and transparent decisions that would leave no room for error or complaint. Ministerial decisions, the terms of extradition petitions, and the particular details of the individual were subsequently reviewed by a *Procureur* of the Republic before an order was finalised.[10] The process adjudicated the nature of the offences for which extradition was sought and the penalties applicable to these offences in order to determine whether the punishment was in proportion to the crime. It also scrutinised the system of justice of the petitioning state in order to determine that it conformed to appropriate standards. These tests went some way towards assuring the right of asylum for refugees when extradition was sought for political offences. The rejection of an extradition petition implied either that the offence was justifiable as a legitimate act of political conscience, or that the penalty for it was excessive or unjust.

During the final quarter of the nineteenth century, when incidents of political violence and terrorist outrages increased alarmingly, the number of extradition treaties into which France entered grew significantly, and more frequent demands were made on it to surrender political refugees, anarchists and others to whom it gave sanctuary. Extradition was also the subject of much critical study. A key theme was the insecurity of states in the face of political violence; the legitimate right, indeed the obligation, of a state to defend itself against those who would strike at its institutions and its peace, was another, even if that meant the pursuit of political criminals into the countries that gave them asylum. Principles of individual rights and the inviolability of the person were readily set aside when the security of the state demanded the use of unrestrained power against its enemies. Thus, one thesis presented to the Faculty of Law in Grenoble in 1894 concluded that asylum had evolved into its 'third phase', the recognition of the dangers that came from the indulgence of political criminals.[11] The first phase of asylum, it suggested, characterised by the repression of political criminals who then turned to other countries for asylum, concluded in 1833. The second phase, from 1833 to 1856, was characterised by the indulgence of political criminals through the right of asylum. Political offences were then excused as the exercise of the right and even the duty of insurrection against tyranny, but their indulgence had produced only crimes against the state. The 'political offence', it was argued, 'is one of the greatest infractions that can be made, as it sacrifices the security of the state and compromises the development of the entire society'.[12] The state's obligation was therefore the punishment of the criminal and not the recognition of rights and the protection of offenders for acts of political dissent. This was the purpose of extradition.

Not all studies admitted that the specific purpose of extradition was to punish political offences, but they nevertheless agreed that extradition was imperative in the modern political context. Political crimes had an impact even beyond the borders of the countries in which they were perpetrated, as asylum in another country gave the offenders the freedom to continue their conspiracies. But this was only one aspect of the broader problems of security. International cooperation and the development of international law united peoples and their nations in treaties to protect their common security interests; all would adopt in common the legitimate and necessary sanctions of penal law.[13]

Extradition for political offences was the denial of asylum, and its justification lay in the violent acts of communist revolutionaries, anarchists, and terrorists during the 1880s and 1890s, which struck directly at national political institutions and European security generally. The wave of anarchist terror in France during 1891–4, which saw the bombing of restaurants, the Paris stock exchange, and the Chamber of Deputies itself, rocked its bourgeois society and its political order. In a cycle of crime, punishment, and retribution, 11 anarchist bomb explosions killed nine people, wounded many more, and spread fear through French society. The terror culminated on 24 June 1894 when an Italian anarchist stabbed and killed the President of the Republic, Sari Carnot, in Lyon.[14] Laws of December 1893 and July 1894 responded to this violence by repression. They allowed the courts to consider the activities of certain political immigrants as anarchist propaganda, which made them guilty of acts of violence and murder.[15] Anarchist violence tainted other foreign revolutionaries and political refugees allowed asylum. Any association with violence or anarchism was sufficient to warrant their expulsion. Between 1894 and 1906, approximately 1600 foreigners, mostly Italian anarchists, were expelled.[16]

Unlike extradition, expulsion orders were not subject to judicial oversight. They remained, as specified in article seven on the policing of foreigners in the 1849 nationality law, an administrative decision confirmed by the interior minister without any obligation to report or justify them. Their intended subjects, undesirable foreigners—the poor, vagabonds, and beggars—were not subsequently its main targets. In practice, expulsion was used as well against any foreigner who troubled the public peace or its security interests. Most orders were made and enforced in obscurity. Only when they were made against highly visible political figures did they raise difficult questions about the interior minister's discretionary powers. One such case was the expulsion of the Russian exile Peter Lavrov in 1882.

Until then, Lavrov had lived largely untroubled among the large Russian émigré community in Paris. He had been smuggled from prison in Russia and eventually made his way to Paris, where he arrived two weeks before the Prussians set siege to it in September 1870. He lived through the siege, and then the Commune and its violent repression; then, in 1872, he left for Zurich before settling in London, where he edited a Russian political journal, *Forward!* He returned to Paris in 1877.

A central figure among Paris' Russian socialists, opposing factions made conflicting demands of Lavrov's time and energies. He set aside his writing and publishing to take a more active role. In 1881 he became an agent of the 'Red Cross of the People's Will', an organisation that raised funds for Russian political prisoners. Since one of its objectives was to incite public opinion against the Tsar, the French government decided that he was a threat to its good relations with Russia. The expulsion order was issued on 10 February 1882; he left France three days later.[17]

His expulsion would probably have passed without controversy had it not been for a young radical deputy, Clovis Hugues, who raised it as a matter of concern in the Chamber of Deputies. Elected as a deputy for Marseille the previous year, Hugues sat on the extreme left of the chamber. He had already acquired some notoriety after spending five years in prison for publishing inflammatory material. This was an opportunity he seized on to make an impact in the capital.[18]

Hugues put the blame for the decision to expel Lavrov squarely on the premier and Foreign Minister Charles de Freycinet, and the previous incumbent Léon Gambetta. He accused them of hounding Lavrov from the country, of violating French hospitality, and in doing so of bringing liberty and 'the very principles of the Republic' into question. How could the expulsion of a 'passer-by caught up in a revolution' be possible, Hugues asked, if the government respected its traditions of liberty? His own neo-Jacobin views of these traditions found little support. He spoke through interjections and ridicule: 'We are among those', he said, 'who think that, for France, there are no foreigners ... those who think that after the French Revolution we have no right to speak of foreigners'.[19] He went on to attack Freycinet and Gambetta for overreaching the authority of the law of expulsion. As arbitrary as it was, he argued, it was nevertheless limited to matters of public order and national security, and Lavrov had been accused of neither. Lavrov's crime, Hugues continued, was to raise money to assist political refugees, 'those who have come to France because of their love of liberty'. And again: Freycinet and Gambetta had exacerbated their actions by failing to explain them to the parliament; they had therefore demonstrated that there were no safeguards against the arbitrary and vengeful surrender of individuals to a foreign power, and they had consequently abused the laws of both expulsion and extradition.[20]

No other deputy was prepared to speak in support of Hugues and the matter quickly faded from public attention. Lavrov returned to France after an absence of three months and resumed his former place among Paris' Russian socialists.[21] Gambetta held his own counsel against Hugue's attack, but Freycinet, quite separately from debate in the chamber, agreed that the arbitrary powers of the laws of expulsion were not consistent with the nature of government in the new republic.[22]

The question subsequently became one of the proper legal basis for expulsion, not so much its use. A legislative commission was established in 1882 to investigate the existing law on expulsion and to consider recommendations for reform. At its first session, the commission agreed that discretionary and arbitrary powers at the disposal of a minister of state, even in matters of public order and security, were no longer in accord with the democratic mores of the republic.[23] Indeed, the commission's investigations found that they were well out of step with the practices among France's neighbours, which expelled foreigners only after judicial review or parliamentary assent. In Britain, the commission heard, the power was invested in the monarch, who acted on the instructions of parliament; in Belgium, another constitutional monarchy, the power was invested in the Council of Ministers; in Switzerland, it was invested in the Federal Council.[24] The need for amendment was therefore clear, but it was much more difficult for the commission to agree how the law should be changed.

Two proposed amendments were discussed. The first suggested applying the power of expulsion only in times of war, but this was not considered sufficiently responsive to other security needs and therefore progressed no further.[25] The second proposition maintained expulsion as a necessary police power, but suggested its moderation by transferring the authorisation of an expulsion order from the interior minister to the Council of Ministers. No other police power would be affected, it was conceded; the borders would remain protected as the police still had the authority to remove a foreigner who sought unauthorised entry or who had been condemned for criminal behaviour. With one dissenter, who claimed that the existing powers were better, the commission adopted this as its preferred option.[26]

Consensus broke down, however, over the very issue that had led to the call for legislative change in the first place, the status of political refugees. The extent to which the preferred proposal would improve the protection of refugees divided the deputies on the commission. It was commented that Britain was much more respectful of the right of asylum than France, and that Lavrov's expulsion was an example of just how this power could contravene the rights of political refugees. There were, the commission heard, flaws in the practice of asylum that needed to be corrected along with reform of the law on expulsion. But there were serious divisions about how this could be done. One group of deputies believed it was inconceivable that political refugees could face expulsion at all, while another insisted that the state had to remain 'alert to and armed against the menace of foreigners' at the borders, who used 'French hospitality to oppose liberal institutions'. Compromise propositions, such as one precluding foreigners with three years uninterrupted residence from expulsion, merely evaded the question.[27]

At this point, Interior Minister René Goblet intervened. Expulsion, he held, was used to protect French interests and was rightly ordered only when a foreigner compromised the state's security. This guaranteed the protection of political refugees, since no foreign government could demand and expect an individual's expulsion from French territory.[28] While this provided some reassurance that the government respected the right of asylum for refugees, the minister did not address the original problem of expulsion orders, that it was a power entirely within his discretion for which there was no judicial review or parliamentary assent.

As the commission tried to resolve the conflicting demands of state security and the guarantees of refugee protection, the issues became more confused. One proposal suggested that the power of expulsion could be exercised differently for a foreigner who, 'by a declaration to the municipality of his residence ... confirmed by two French citizens' claimed to be a political refugee and therefore was formally approved as a person who 'merited the protection of the French authorities'. The proposal was unworkable, the minister replied, because of the difficulty of identifying the distinguishing characteristics of a political refugee in the first place, and then writing them into an amendment to the laws. It was sufficient, he maintained, that political refugees, like other foreigners, could ask for admission to domicile and enjoy the benefits that flowed from it; this would secure their permanent residence and therefore their protection from expulsion.[29]

This was effectively an admission that no distinctions could be made either in law or in public administration between refugees and other immigrants. They both shared common conditions of entry and a common legal status as resident foreigners. Both had equal access to residence and domicile, and were equally subject to expulsion if it were warranted. No distinctions were made between political, economic, or other reasons for migration, and the deputies on the commission held fast to the belief that expulsion was an essential power against undesirable foreigners.

The more protracted process of redrafting the nationality law itself commenced in 1882 and was finally adopted into law on 28 June 1889.[30] Historians find this new nationality law a major reference point in republican political culture because it set out more precisely than previous laws the division between those who belonged to the nation and those who do not, between the French and the foreign.[31] The boundary between the foreigner and the national was delineated by other means as well. Continued high levels of immigration stirred some deputies to condemn immigrant workers as self-serving and privileged because they were not subject to the same obligations as French workers, above all tax and military service. Various initiatives, such as a residence tax, attempted in some small way to redress the privileges of foreign workers.[32]

The state intervened in immigration in the late-nineteenth century, therefore, to moderate the stresses between the French and foreigners. But state intervention also prescribed the place of foreigners within French society, assuring their separation and distinctness from the national. The Third Republic became nationalised as the opposing origins of the national and the foreign came into conflict. The French national was not only challenged by the foreigner, as Noiriel argues; more than this, French nationality was based, Charles Sowerwine concludes, on the identification of the 'other' that was not French.[33] The boundary that separated the foreigner from the national was rationalised as republican rejection of particularism and the privilege of one group over another.[34] The more the republic distinguished the French from the non-French in conceptions of nationalism and republicanism, however, the more pressing seemed to be challenge of the 'other'. This stirred nationalist anxieties, and in the minds of some only expulsion, a demonstration of total state power against foreigners, would suffice to meet it.

While politicians reviewed this power and considered its moderation, one jurist defended its integrity. Arthur Desjardins wrote in the *Revue des deux mondes* in 1882 that refugees and foreigners could not be distinguished in the application of expulsion orders since foreigners and criminality were interrelated realities of modern society. Asylum was valid when it served to protect the vulnerable against abuses of power, but it lost its purpose when it ensured the impunity of criminals. Is it not desirable, Desjardins asked, that 'wrong doers' be found and punished? Rights and duties should not stand in the way of international cooperation on extradition and the prosecution of criminals; the borders could never be safe otherwise.

> Is it not a gross and childish conception of international rights and duties that paralyse the application of the laws necessary for hindering two neighbouring people from reciprocal arrangements for surrendering their wrong-doers? Does this not create a grave public peril on the frontier of each country? Would the frontier departments be habitable if criminals can disrobe themselves of their culpability?[35]

Desjardins continued in a manner that recalled the debates of earlier times: if hospitality placed an obligation on those who gave it, did it not impose a greater obligation on those who received it? This question, asked many times in the years since Casimir Périer posed it in 1831, was still contentious. It divided opinion about the role of government in relation to foreigners and refugees, the validity of its guarantees of protection and rights, and even the principle of asylum itself. Desjardins posed many questions, for which he gave one answer: the role of government was to maintain public order, and therefore its duty was 'to keep all foreigners under surveillance and, at certain moments, to pay particular attention to some of them'.[36]

The depth of anxieties that migration had aroused was rooted in the association of the foreigner with criminality. The jurisprudence on extradition had exposed associations between foreigners, political crimes, and threats to the peace and national security, but Desjardins' anxieties were more deeply rooted in the undesirable consequences of migration. It was particularly urgent for Desjardins in this era of mass migration that the government fulfil its duty to maintain the public order. But the distinction he drew between the French and foreigners was not social or political; it was their different racial origins. Complete assimilation between the national and the foreigner, he contended, was contrary to the nature of things; humanity did not form a single nation: there were separate races, and each had their own 'fatherland'.[37] Attentiveness in policy, policing, and the role of government were therefore essential for the protection of the French race.

Desjardin rounds discussion back to the problematic of political asylum at a time when there was little to distinguish refugees from other immigrants. He also takes the question of the national–foreigner dichotomy to its natural conclusion, that of the racial distinctions between them. The Third Republic was not only nationalised as the opposing origins of the national and the foreign came into conflict, it was also racialised as foreigners were separated from the nation behind the boundaries that the new nationality code had promulgated. At the turn of the century, this racialisation would erupt into the Dreyfus Affair, with all its bitter consequences, when the foreigner was found even among French citizens, and when deep seams of xenophobia and anti-Semitism were revealed within the very fabric of the republic's culture and society.

It is difficult even to speak of political refugees when there was no distinction between their status under French law and the status of other immigrants and foreign residents. Did it matter, then, that there were no expressed protection obligations so long as refugees enjoyed the freedoms and protection of rights that the open migration regime and domicile allowed? The answer must be qualified. Refugees at this time had unrestricted access to the labour market, were unconstrained under the common regime applying to all immigrants in their movements, their places of residence, and their political associations and activities, provided they did not breach French law. This sufficed for the protection of the vast majority of migrants who considered their expatriation involuntary, such as the large Russian émigré community in Paris. This regime offered effective protection to political refugees so long as the republic was able and prepared to admit free migration and guarantee the civil rights for resident foreigners. Problems arose when, under the stress of political circumstances, such as anarchist violence, anti-foreign sentiments found a receptive audience. Or when there was the stress of economic conditions, such as during the depression years of the 1890s, when the government gave in to popular demands for the protection of French workers from the competition of immigrant workers.[38]

## The new refugee movements of the early-twentieth century

New refugee movements appeared soon after the turn of the twentieth century, most notably from the Russian Empire after the 1905 revolution.[39] Police reports of the time were not certain about how to classify these new groups, as their composition, and their political, economic, and religious motives for expatriation were not so clear. These refugees were not actors in political events, but bystanders caught up in revolution and the repressions that followed. There was only a small number of those who could be classified as 'political refugees', as they had been long conceived. They were given a new description, as 'ideological refugees' (*réfugiés idéologiques*). Other new categories described their religious and national composition. Jews were specifically identified; so were Orthodox Christians. Or they were categorised by their ethnicities—Russians (*grands-, petits-, blancs-Russiens*), Lithuanians, Latvians, Finnish, Kirghiz, Georgians, Armenians, Tartars, and again, Jews (*Israélites*).[40]

These classifications highlight the most striking feature of political migrations in the early-twentieth century, their diversity and their nature as popular movements. People were on the move from Europe's east, into the west and across the Atlantic, introducing new and distinct religious and national cultures and forming new ethnic clusters. Previous migrations into France were largely from neighbouring countries, and as a result there were enduring cultural and national continuities. They reflected established settlement patterns, particularly in the border regions, and deep historical and cultural ties. They came mostly from Italy, Spain, Portugal, Switzerland, Belgium, and Poland. They were predominantly Catholic, and most spoke a Latinate language; or they merely continued the long traditions of cross-border movements and settlement. Or, as in the case of the Poles, there were unique historical ties. The new immigrants, however, had new and distinct origins; they were from further to the east, and brought with them new cultural practices.

These new migration currents were also felt well beyond the continent. The years from 1900 to the outbreak of the First World War witnessed the highest levels of transatlantic migrations yet. Economic contraction during the 1890s, which brought immigrant and national workers into more open competition, stirred popular anti-immigrant sentiments. Nationalism had also gained strength within immigrant-receiving countries and higher barriers were put up between their citizens and their immigrants. Under the pressure of numbers and ethnic diversity, therefore, the new migrants had a greater impact on national consciousness than previous migrations. Ethnic clusters in the larger cities soured popular sentiment, and anti-immigrant discourses turned against them for their adverse impact on the dominant national culture. Antipathies to Jewish communities in the East End of London and other British cities led directly to the adoption of the 1905 Aliens Bill to restrict and regulate migrant entry.[41] The appearance of Yiddish newspapers and shop signs on the streets of Paris unsettled French society and contributed to mounting popular intolerance of the recently settled Jews from eastern Europe.[42]

The United States was by far the preferred destination of Europe's emigrants. As numbers peaked between 1901 and 1910, a highly organised and divisive campaign for immigration restriction gained great momentum. A total of 8,056,040 Europeans arrived in these years, more than the total for the two previous decades.[43] Laws in 1892 and 1907 had already restricted migration from China and Japan through the west coast. On the east coast, American nativists divided the old migrations that had settled the country from the racially distinct, new migrations from southern and eastern Europe, whose impact they believed was so detrimental to the vitality of the American race.[44]

These international trends are a reminder that even well before the First World War there was growing reaction to the rise of ethnic and cultural difference in Western societies. From the turn of the century migration was racialised by the reaction in host countries to its new characteristics, to such large numbers and disparate ethnic composition, and to the cultural impact it had.[45] The classification by national origins of the new migrations into France after the 1890s was consistent with a political culture in which nationality had become the key indicator of identity and belonging.

Another's difference was in turn the marker of exclusion. It was mandatory that foreign workers register their residence and employment, carry proof of identity, and report and justify a change of residence. In 1912 their identity documents also recorded anthropometric features such as height, the size of chest, length and size of head, and ethnicity.[46]

Restrictions on the migrations within which refugees moved narrowed their possibilities for sanctuary. They were undistinguished among migration flows, but refugee flows, such as the Jews from the east forced to move by anti-Semitic pogroms in the Russian empire, were also massed popular movements, undistinguished from the common tide of labour and economic migrations. Revolutionaries also remained hidden within these migrations, moving from place to place as their need, their politics, and flight from the police required. But there were also countless victims of political repression, invisible bystanders caught up in great events around them.

## The impact of war, 1914–20

The war emergency of August 1914 emptied French factories and the countryside as men were called to the front, while refugees from the war zones in Belgium and the north and east of France were hastily evacuated to the southwest, where they were put to work in the factories and the fields to serve the war effort.

Just as hastily, arrangements were made for their reception, but aid agencies struggled to keep a firm hand on the allocation of resources. Assistance for the communities to which the war refugees had been evacuated was a priority. Meanwhile, the Chamber of Deputies rushed through laws on requisitioning, aid, and security issues, and orders for the internment of enemy aliens. During September and October, nationals of the German and Austrian empires were ordered to register with the police, even if they were long established residents of France. They were then sent to internment camps out of harm's way on the coast of the Vendée.[47]

The labour market was urgently reorganised to fill the gaps left by the general mobilisation. The Agriculture Ministry brought in rural workers from Italy, Greece, Portugal, and Spain. In October, a joint office of the labour and interior ministries was established to organise the unemployed and war refugees to fill urban labour shortages. The War Ministry later set up the Colonial Workers Service to recruit and deploy labourers from the French colonies of north and west Africa, Indochina, and Madagascar. Their labour was needed urgently, but the terms of their work contracts ensured that they would not be allowed to compete with French workers.[48]

In all, about three-quarters of war refugees were French men, women, and children evacuated from the war zones in the north and east. In 1914, there were also 205,000 foreign war refugees resettled in western and southern France, of whom more than 90 per cent were Belgian. They were later augmented by a small number of Serbs and Montenegrins. The number of foreign war refugees increased slightly by 1918, to 290,000; in comparison, French war refugees rose from 660,000 to 1,580,000 over the course of the war.[49]

Trains from Belgium and northern France brought the war refugees to Bordeaux as the Germans advanced on Paris. They were placed in outlying communes to avoid overcrowding the city and were lodged in requisitioned hotels and put to work in factories.[50] The Belgian government had escaped by ship to Le Havre, and King Albert established his seat at the nearby village of Saint Adresse. This was the centre of the Belgian refugee community for the duration of the war. In its exile the Belgian government maintained autonomy over its displaced citizens but relied on the French administration for statistical and personal data for the purposes of military service orders, refugee welfare, and policing. In Le Havre itself, Belgians were put to work in the outlying fields and in the port, which by then had become a British naval depot and military garrison. As more Belgian refugees arrived by ship at La Rochelle later in 1914, they were placed in accommodation centres hastily prepared in requisitioned orphanages and pensions. Belgian priests were very public in their work for the material and spiritual welfare of the all war refugees, including resettled French men and women, in noticeable contrast, it was remarked, to the indifference of the local population.[51]

The war refugees were perceived locally as an imposition at a time of great stress and anguish. In November 1914, when 1044 refugees arrived in Angoulême, some 400 kilometres from the front, there was considerable demand on the municipality for accommodation and food. Public funds were insufficient for their relief and the public was asked to contribute additional assistance which it could scarcely afford.[52] These same communities in the rear also received the wounded and prisoners of war, which entailed more requisitioning of local resources. This strained local tolerance further, and the war refugees did not help their situation by complaining openly about the conditions they had to put up with. The local communities, suffering through the war in their own ways, resented their ingratitude.[53]

During 1915, as the war ground on in stalemate, more attention was paid to the organisation of assistance to the war refugees. It was most urgent that a proper accounting of their numbers, dispersal, and personal details was made for three critical reasons: to identify and conscript men of military age and assess skills and occupations for labour placement; to identify suspect foreigners, especially nationals of enemy powers; and to reconcile families members who had been separated into different parts of the country during the evacuations. As a consequence, an elaborate bureaucracy was created around the registration and provision of aid for war refugees, and the identification of each individual foreigner residing in each commune.

The task of compiling the monthly registers of war refugees alone illustrates the intense administrative efforts in keeping track of the movements into and out of the departments so as to ensure an accurate record of names, ages, locations, and occupations of refugees who could be called up for military or other war service. Attention also turned to confirming the status of resident foreigners, to ensure that they complied with their conditions of residence, that their identity documents were in order, and that they abided by the conditions of their residence permits. [54] In each commune, therefore, a census was made of resident foreigners. The mayors filed their detailed lists with the departmental prefecture, which were then compiled in a consolidated report for the Interior Ministry. In the Isère, to cite just one example, these records leave a rare snapshot of the population of resident foreigners. Most communes reported only a handful of them; some reported none at all. Most were residents of long standing who performed their occupations as declared, conformed to the specified regulations, and therefore gave no cause for concern.[55]

An elaborate welfare system was also established around the war refugees. Following the adoption of a statute on assistance for war refugees in 1916, mayors and prefects received a vast amount of correspondence expressing personal misfortunes (the separation of families, the state of their welfare, the plight of children, exorbitant rents, unemployment) and requesting allocations of assistance under the statute.[56] On rare instances, foreign refugees complained about their living conditions, but found the prefects less receptive. A young Serb studying in Lyon requested an allocation of aid but was refused because an autonomous *Office Serbe* was responsible for the welfare of Serbs in France.[57] Indeed, foreign refugees and foreign workers who sought financial assistance were accorded little sympathy by public officials left struggling under the weight of their responsibilities. Even hospitals had difficulty reclaiming expenses from the local administrations. A Serb who had been admitted to hospital in Charbonnière near Lyon had no money to pay for treatment; the hospital covered the cost, but could hardly later secure reimbursement from the prefecture. It had similar difficulties obtaining reimbursement for the cost of treating two Greek factory workers.[58] By 1917, the administration of war refugees had been taken out of the hands of the prefectures; it was instead devolved to a network of ad hoc agencies created to serve specific functions: the distribution of funds to the departments, the maintenance of registers for war service and employment, and the policing and punishment of deserters among the war refugees.[59]

As the Belgians were subjects of their government in exile, they made no special claims on French aid, although French authorities cooperated with the Belgian government on registrations and policing. Similarly, Serbs were expected to turn to the autonomous *Office Serbe* for welfare assistance. To be sure, the numbers of Serbian refugees in mainland France was small. The work and service they provided is uncertain, but they had a special place in French consciousness during the war. France had after all entered the war to defend Serbia, and French assistance had ensured the safe evacuation of the

120,000 survivors of the epic 1916 retreat of the Serbian army across the mountains to the Albanian coast.[60] They had been resettled mostly in Corfu, Tunisia, and Corsica, but Serbs also fought alongside the French, and the movements of groups of Serbs can be traced across southeastern France. Some 1462 Serb workers, artisans, students, some soldiers, of all ages, from young children to old men, passed through the Isère in the first half of 1916. Most moved on quickly to a military depot in Toulon, or to other departments to find work.[61] The presence of Serbs in Lyon made such an impression on the local community that the municipality organised a special *Journée Serbe* on 25 June 1916 to raise funds for refugee relief. The sale of special ribbons in Serbian national colours, and medallions with imprints of Prince Alexander and inscriptions, in French and Serbian, to the 'glorious defenders of Serb liberty', raised a total of 29,918.70 francs for Serbian refugee relief. Other municipalities wanted to follow Lyon's lead, but found it difficult to obtain enough metal for minting more medallions.[62]

War had an enduring impact on migration, and in its wake on the status of refugees and the practice of asylum. Restrictive polices became the norm. Essential for reasons of security in time of war, to control the entry and movements of potentially subversive foreign enemies, to detain nationals of enemy powers, and to ensure the sound functioning of the military and the war economy, restrictions remained in place thereafter. Internationally, restrictions on the movement of peoples were the norm. Passport regimes had been reimposed and were rigorously enforced. Nationality and identity were only demonstrable by bearing a passport issued by the government of one's homeland. In order to enter a foreign country it was not sufficient simply to hold a passport; it also had to be stamped with a visa by the diplomatic officials of the country to which entry was sought, and only then after an enquiry into the reasons for travel demonstrated that there would be no danger to the national interest or a breach of the law.[63] The distrust of foreigners that had formed at the turn of the twentieth century therefore took firmer hold during the war. The policing of espionage, enemy infiltration, and military desertion was as essential for national security and the preservation of scarce resources as it was essential for social cohesion.

At war's end the refugees were submerged within the countless displaced and dislocated, demobilised soldiers and the emerging new waves of refugees who would soon impress themselves on European consciousness. The protection of domestic workers was a priority in the post-war labour market, which was bloated by colonial workers, unemployed foreigners, refugees, and political agitators. Even well before the armistice, in February 1918, before victory was assured, the French metallurgist union warned the armaments ministry of working-class anxieties over the preponderance of 'foreigners, Protestants, and the maimed' competing for scarce resources. It also contained the warning that some of these foreigners were from an 'inferior civilisation', a none-too-subtle allusion to colonial workers. France owed it to its soldiers and its dead 'to protect their homes from such a prospect, worse than what they proudly fought against'.[64] The peace, when it came, promised to be divisive, and there was an urgent need to ensure social cohesion and to restructure the labour market so that it could absorb demobilised soldiers.

The impact of war and the war refugees was therefore at its most critical in 1918 and 1919. Both demobilisation and the repatriation of the displaced were slow and tortured. The larger cities had become more crowded with the war refugees who had left the factories and fields where they had served the war effort and were now on their way back to their towns and villages. Indeed, in December 1918, Belgian refugees were specifically ordered to remain behind because the conditions of the Belgian countryside made their return impossible.[65] In January 1919, there were 34,498 war refugees in the Rhône, more than twice the number than at any time during the conflict. Their numbers fell slowly. By October, 28,520 still remained.[66] They were a visible drain on resources as everyone took stock of their personal situation, counted the cost of the war on themselves, their families, and their communities, and worried about scarcities at a time when foreigners and outsiders were holding down jobs that should be vacated for the local men returning from the front. The repatriation of colonial workers was one step towards the restoration of normalcy in the labour force. But the loss of some 1.3 million men left significant gaps in the labour market, which could only be filled by foreign workers.[67]

* * *

What, then, was the impact of war on the broader conceptions of asylum and refugee protection? There is compelling evidence that popular antipathies towards the displaced and those recruited into the French war effort informed anti-immigrant attitudes afterwards. Even the French evacuees well behind the front line met with a surprising degree of antipathy. They experienced underlying popular sentiments that, when under stress and confronted with difference, reacted against outsiders.

In his study of the French people during the Great War, Jean-Jacques Becker observes a fracturing of attitudes to foreigners from the beginning of the war. Many of France's resident foreigners, he writes, tried to enlist to repay a debt they felt they owed their adopted country, but there was no immediate need for their service because the army was overwhelmed with French conscripts, while the nationalist press objected to foreigners joining the national cause. But there were also contrary sentiments, Becker continues. Many French believed that their national cause was so right foreigners would be 'desperate to flock to the colours'. Still, Becker concludes, foreigners could not do enough to rise above French suspicions: Belgians were found to be defeatists and hard to please; other foreigners were accused of refusing to do the work they were offered, of being lazy.[68]

Uncertainties and anxieties, social, economic, and political, which followed the war, heightened these sentiments. This then highlights the force that the voices calling for protection would later have, for the protection of the labour market from foreign workers and for the protection of the state from foreign infiltration. Becker again recalls that the confrontation between French and foreign workers seemed to be long remembered: foreigners were not only accused of stealing French jobs; their presence in the factories had caused French men to be sent back to the front.[69] The war therefore evoked a mix of sentiments towards foreigners: the affinities with foreign refugees, such as for the Serbs, were always brittle, and the suspicions of foreigners turned antipathies on to those with whom the French had few if any affinities. Suspicions even turned against long-settled foreign residents, which would endure into the period of national recovery to follow when France's reliance on foreign workers to compensate for the gaps the war left in its workforce was indicative of a loss of national vitality.

Finally, the war led to dramatic institutional developments. An elaborate administrative apparatus had developed around the war refugees, the management of the labour force, and the provision of welfare. State resources were mobilised to assist war refugees and place foreign workers into vital sectors of the workforce. Refugees and foreigners were therefore drawn more completely into the machinery of state, but the institutional apparatus could also be used against foreigners. This would have profound implications for the responses to refugees over the following years.

# Part IV 'Around the corner from a hostile France, a France more amicable', 1920–39

The twentieth-century problem of refugees began with the restrictions on migrations that followed in the wake of the First World War. This was an era of massed movements of displaced peoples, rendered stateless by the collapse of the old European empires and the emergence in their place of new nation-states, whose national prejudices turned against outsiders, the ideologically impure, the ethnically different, foreigners. All were intrusions, Hannah Arendt writes, as these new states engaged with modernity and set about creating a homogeneous national homeland.[1] The old nation states of Europe looked on hesitantly, overwhelmed by their own difficulties. Meanwhile, the United States withdrew into isolation from Europe and began to close its borders to new migrants.

Yet it is also an era that resisted the full force of the negative currents of post-war politics. The international refugee crises of the post-war years took asylum beyond national governments little able to cope, and little willing to bend to accommodate refugees. This was therefore also an era in which states were caught between the forced displacement of refugees and constraints on asylum. It was an era of emerging conceptions of refugee rights and the need for an international regime to protect these rights, but it was also an era of exclusion and prohibitions, of camps and internment, which, when taken together, marked the end of asylum.

A study of this leap into the modern era of international refugee crises commences from a step into memory: personal, historical, and national memories have shaped responses to this period. It is an era lived by many hundreds of thousands of refugees and their descendents; the marks of it are still seen, although increasingly rarely, in the restaurants and bookshops of France's larger cities, in books and on film.

Writer and filmmaker Henri Verneuil took himself back into his memory of his Armenian family's experience of exile when he retold the story of their arrival in Marseille in 1921. It seems the world was in rupture; thousands of Armenians crammed the port, evacuated from the eastern Mediterranean, waiting their turn for permission to enter France. These are the survivors of the massacres and deportations that had scattered the Armenians to the 'four corners of the world, or by chance to a land of asylum'.[2] Verneuil assumes the voice of the young boy who senses the deep anxieties of his family as they stand before the customs officer, slowly realising the significance of this moment. 'My memory of childhood begins with that stamp; it hung in the air forever. The faces of my mother, my father, and my two aunts, fixed on this object, prove the importance of the stamp on our papers'. Their papers are stamped: 'Stateless' (*Apatrides*).[3] One undetermined status has been exchanged for another: his family was no longer uprooted and displaced, but formally stateless. This simple, anxious, but highly significant rite of passage has given them asylum so that they might leave behind past trauma and reset their roots.

They were, however, foreign, and exposed to daily tensions and hostility, even into their home. They settled quickly. They shared the floor of their apartment building with a French family. One kitchen served both their apartments, but their neighbours had occupied it as their own. They refused to leave after their meal when this new foreign family came to use the oven. Verneuil remembers the shouts and swearing; his father scoffed at the absurdity of having food to eat but having to beg for the use of an oven to cook it. They begged outside. A baker nearby was more welcoming. He recalls: 'around the corner from a hostile France, we discovered a France more amicable at the baker's oven'.[4]

Those who found asylum in these years experienced in their own private ways many contradictory impressions of France at the same time hostile to their foreign origins yet sympathetic to their circumstances. Contact between the French and foreigners multiplied remarkably during the post-war years, Ralph Schor observes. Foreigners appeared as neighbours, as shopkeepers and taxi-drivers, or as a child's companion at school; in the streets, cafés, and sports stadiums foreigners and French mixed daily. This engendered on the part of the French amicability, indifference or hostility at the same time, either aiding the refugees' integration or alienating them from their land of asylum.[5]

Historical memory of twentieth-century migration and asylum in France begins with these years. But it is commonly a history reviewed through a distorting lens. The anti-foreign and anti-refugee antipathies that emerged in the 1920s, and were most raw in the 1930s, are often seen as marking the origins of the Vichy regime's anti-Semitic laws and deportations. This period is therefore remembered as one of 'habituation', to borrow from Michael Marrus, during which the foreigner, particularly the Jew, was perceived to be an enemy of the state. The unique problems of the period, and the causes of the greater crisis of the 1930s, are consequently obscured though this distorting lens.[6]

This historical memory contradicts the national memory of France as the land of liberty and asylum in this era of new refugee migrations. France offered sanctuary, work, and welfare when few other countries were able or willing to admit refugees in similar numbers. In his remarkable 1938 survey of the interwar refugee crisis for the Royal Institute of International Affairs

_N.B_

in London, Sir John Hope Simpson observed that France was the nation *par excellence* of refuge in Western Europe, and that the French people cherished the ideal of the right of asylum for refugees.[7] In his own mind, however, the right of asylum had no substance; it was merely a sentimental phrase, an impressive description of the moral wrong of excluding a helpless person, while devoid of meaning in its actual practice.[8]

The right of asylum is most expressed in memory and traditions, as a past to which present experiences aspired but which, for contingent reasons, could not be put into practice. It described, in this sentimental sense, an idealisation of values of toleration and hospitality for foreign difference and for the protection needs of the oppressed and displaced of other nations. Yet, in the 1920s, Schor writes, the French were not only struck by the number and diversity of the refugees, they were also struck by the national conflicts of other states that they brought with them. France had become more than a place of asylum, it was a crossroad of international rivalries. In the face of the refugee influx therefore, Schor continues, all sides of politics doubted if France could remain true to its tradition of welcome. The political parties of the left and right were split in their views 'less on the principle than on the application of the right of asylum'.[9] The admission of refugees and respect for their misfortunes were generally sure in popular sentiment. Antipathies centred on the practical difficulties of facilitating the arrival of new refugees. On this the political parties diverged. Those on the right demanded a selective approach to the right of asylum in order to exclude agitators, criminals, and the sick and maimed, and on the extreme right the exclusion of any with leftist political views. The left, on the other hand, was more supportive of an unrestricted right of asylum.[10]

The division of principle and practice, the dissociation of assistance and accommodation from broader, principled, humanitarian concern for the protection needs of refugees, reveal a volatile and fluid notion of the right of asylum. Was it then an empty shell to be filled with contingent opinion and argument? Simpson suggested that the notion was no more than a sentiment, a gesture of respect for distressed refugees, which had little to do with the actual circumstances of their arrival and admission. Yet the persistence of the phrase and the values it signified would indeed show that the right of asylum was a live concept that animated debates about principle and practice. It was a phrase that continued to signify principles to which defenders of the rights of refugees returned to reinvest France's policy decisions with the recognition of the refugees' humanity. In this way, then, the memory of asylum, and the national memory of France as a land of liberty and the land of asylum, would shape responses to refugees during the interwar years, when the currents of xenophobia seemed to have swept principle away.

Still, it was a forlorn hope to cling to these ideals. In practice and policy, exclusion, fuelled by xenophobia, led directly to the end of asylum in internment camps and centres of detention as France fell into the dark years of occupation and collaboration.

# 8
# Migration and Asylum After the Great War

Refugees came in greatest numbers from those countries where change was most profound and most violent: from the Soviet Union and its ideological remaking of the old Russian Empire; from the Turkish republic, created out of the Ottoman empire; from the rise of Mussolini's Fascists in Italy; from the violent race policies of Nazi Germany. They were victims of great events, a civil population displaced by ideological ruptures and refused a place in the future of the new and reformed nation-states.

The refugee movements of the 1920s presented a problem of international significance, and national responses were no more than small contributions to a much greater dilemma. The impact on Europe was made worse by the closure of the traditional channel of European migration into the United States and other new world countries. Burdened by the impact of war and the costs of reconstruction, much of Europe had little place for them. France was unique in its demand for foreign workers, and refugees were taken up in the post-war labour migrations upon which its recovery and reconstruction depended. The demand for labour coincided with the humanitarian needs of the refugees and their search for resettlement opportunities. Principles of asylum were seldom argued while the economy was able to absorb them and provide them work; the refugees were classified as foreign workers and subject to the laws and regulations on immigrant labour. The 'refugee problem' was consequently addressed in terms of foreign labour, as the place of refugees depended on good economic conditions and the ability of the labour force to maintain the high level of foreign workers. How then were principles of asylum argued and sustained across changing economic conditions?

## People on the move

As Europe emerged from the war it faced new and unimagined numbers of refugees. They were yet another problem of the post-war settlement, along with the repatriation of prisoners of war and displaced civilians, the placement of demobilised and mutilated soldiers back into their societies, the recovery of the dead and the rehabilitation of the war zones. Refugees from the 1917 Bolshevik Revolution were already a feature of many European cities: former diplomats of the Tsar's government, aristocrats and high bourgeois living outside Russia at the time of the revolution, or travellers caught up in events and unwilling to return and submit themselves to Bolshevism. But there was no Russian refugee problem as such until the collapse of the White Russian Armies that brought an end to the civil war of 1919–21.[1] Soldiers and civilians alike fled the Red Army and soon refugees could be found in all the countries along the Soviet Union's long frontier, from Finland in the northwest to China in the east. Every city of central and eastern Europe, it was claimed, had a colony of Russian émigrés struggling to preserve the remnants of their former culture. They were a 'whole nation in miniature': bishops and monks, army commanders and servicemen, judges, lawyers, professors and students, employers and employees, landowners and peasants, Orthodox, Catholics, Protestants, Jews, Russians proper, Ukrainians, Tartars.[2] Various estimates put their number in 1922 between 1,500,000 and 2,100,000, but later revisions showed these were highly inflated. There were between 60,000 and 70,000 Russian refugees in France at that time according to the revised estimates.[3]

While countries in the European heartland faced tremendous burdens of resettlement and assistance, the real Russian refugee crisis was experienced on the periphery, in Constantinople, then under British and French occupation. By November 1920, evacuations from Odessa had brought to this ancient city about 170,000 White Russians in flight from the victorious Red Army; many more had been scattered elsewhere around the Balkans.[4] They were dependent on the aid of various committees of the Red Cross, the Save the Children Fund, and the governments of the occupying forces.[5] Their resources for relief were soon exhausted, however, and reports of poverty, starvation, and disease, turned international attention to what was quickly developing into a major humanitarian emergency. The European powers, so soon after the Spanish influenza, looked with dread at the outbreak of epidemic disease among the refugees in Constantinople, fearing its spread into Western Europe.[6]

The International Committee of the Red Cross estimated there were some 800,000 Russian refugees in Europe in 1921, a figure that went well beyond its capacity for the provision of humanitarian relief, and the capacity of other private agencies. It was also a figure that posed a problem greater than any one nation could deal with. Gustav Ador, President of the International Red Cross, therefore requested the assistance of newly formed League of Nations to aid in their resettlement. For Ador and the Red Cross, the refugees represented more than an unfolding humanitarian disaster; they represented a failure of the international system that only the League of Nations, with its mandate for negotiating international solutions, could properly address. How was it possible, Ador asked the Secretary General of the League, Sir Eric Drummond, in February 1921, 'that there should be 800,000 men in Europe unprotected by any legal organisation recognised in international law'.[7] The legal position of these refugees alone complicated all other problems. Even if the refugees stranded in Constantinople could afford to buy their passage out, their lack of valid travel documents prohibited their entry into another country.

The League of Nations accepted Ador's request and established a High Commission responsible for refugees. After his success in the repatriation of prisoners of war on behalf of the League, the Norwegian Arctic explorer, scientist, and diplomat, Fritjof Nansen, was appointed to the post and set about coordinating the efforts of private relief organisations and national governments to assist and resettle as many of the Russian refugees as possible. He was charged with three specific tasks: defining the refugees' legal position; coordinating relief; and organising repatriation or, otherwise, resettlement and employment in countries where they could find employment to support themselves.[8]

The Russian refugee problem therefore led to the establishment of an international organisation for the assistance of refugees and the beginnings of an international regime for refugee protection. Its role was limited, however. Resettlement and employment opportunities depended on the willingness of national governments to admit them, but their lack of passports and other formal documents barred their cross-border movements since no country was prepared to admit them without guarantees that they were able to move on at a later time.

Nansen's work soon grew to include other refugee groups, most notably the Armenian survivors of the 1915 genocide and later persecutions. In 1919, there were an estimated 600,000 Armenians dispersed about the French mandated territories of Syria and Cilicia in southeast Turkey, and in the British mandated territories of Palestine, Persia, and Iraq. These were survivors of the forced expulsions from eastern Turkey.[9] While the occupying forces remained, the Armenians were assured protection and many slowly returned to their places of origin, but when France entered into a treaty with Turkey in 1921 to restore to it Cilicia and parts of Syrian territory, Armenians fled into lands that remained under French protection. They were soon scattered about the eastern Mediterranean, from Syria and Palestine, to Greece, Cyprus, and Egypt. A third migration followed the Turkish nationalists' capture of the Greek city of Smyrna (Ismir). One hundred thousand Armenians followed the flight of approximately one million Greeks: many thousands fled to Constantinople and compounded problems there.[10] While the Armenians remained within the mandate territories they were the responsibility of the mandate powers. There were as many as 100,000 Armenian refugees in Syria and Lebanon alone. Of these, about 40,000 were under direct British and French administration in camps in Beirut and the Syrian towns of Aleppo and Alexandretta.[11] Large subscriptions from wealthy Armenians in Constantinople, Egypt, and Romania, and from charities in the United States, raised funds for general relief of the rest.[12]

The initial work of Nansen's High Commission concentrated on repatriation schemes. Nansen himself negotiated arrangements with the Soviet government for the return of Russian refugees once conditions had stabilised in the Soviet Union, and he sponsored a plan for the resettlement of Armenians in uncultivated regions north of Yerivan in Soviet Armenia.[13] Both strategies foundered, however. The Soviet repatriation scheme was abandoned because suspicions on all sides made it inoperable.[14] The plan for settlement in Yerivan collapsed because of the lack of funds. In the meantime still more refugees from the former Ottoman Empire appeared around the Mediterranean: Asyrians in Marseille; Asyro-Chaldean Christians in the Caucasus; Ruthenians, Montenegrins, and Turkish 'Friends of the Allies', among whom was a small group of Kurds.[15]

Without a document of identity or a verifiable juridical nationality, a refugee in interwar Europe was a legal anomaly. This problem was exacerbated by Soviet denationalisation decrees of 1921, and the Turkish denationalisation of Armenians in 1923, which left them all stateless, deprived of any protective legal status, without access to consular services, and unable to provide or obtain documents pertaining to their educational and professional qualifications or civil status which were necessary to re-establish themselves and their families in another country. Critically, they could not obtain passports and therefore could not take up employment opportunities where they were available.[16] The congestion in Constantinople and other places could not be relieved in these circumstances because the refugees could not be resettled.

Nansen's work for refugees is therefore best remembered for the documents of identity adopted for Russian refugees in 1922, which were named after him as the 'Nansen Passport'. The scheme was extended to Armenians in 1924, and in 1928 to other refugee group from the former Ottoman Empire.[17] Nansen's High Commission also established offices in countries of settlement to provide a quasi-consular service. They assisted refugees in their dealings with national governments, helped verify their civil status, arranged for the translation of documents, and received representations from organisations concerned with the interest of refugees. Representatives of the Nansen Office in France were officially appointed by the League's Secretary-General, and received diplomatic recognition from the French Government.[18]

The evacuation of Russian refugees from Constantinople followed quickly once the Nansen Passport arrangements had been put in place. France, which could use their labour, was able to take a large number of them.[19] The refugees, however, had limited choice in where they could go. The international agencies attending to their welfare could achieve only so much, and the measures they could put in place to facilitate their evacuation—the shipping to transport the refugees out of Constantinople, resettlement plans they could reach with governments, and the costs they bore—largely favoured resettlement in France. Indeed, they would have achieved little were it nor for France's willingness to come to their aid. Yet, when given a choice of a destination, personal factors led the refugees themselves to decide on France: the desire to follow relatives and friends, and the opportunities France offered for their children's education. It has been remarked that for many of them France had become a vision in their collective conscience, because of its culture and its tradition as a land of asylum.[20]

This tradition would come to represent so much more for such a large number of the displaced and stateless refugees when they found that the historical outlet for Europe's unwanted, the United States, had turned its back on them. In a general mood of isolation from Europe's old antagonisms, the nativist revival within the United States succeeded in its calls for immigration restrictions. The first restrictive law of 1921 placed quotas on the number and composition of new immigrants. These were based on a percentage of the immigrant nationalities recorded in the 1910 census. A second law in 1924 reduced the quotas further and based numbers and origin on the immigrant nationalities recorded in the 1890 census, which favoured heavily immigrants from the traditional source countries of northern Europe over the new immigrants of darker complexion, odd appearance, and distinct cultural practices from southern and eastern Europe and the Mediterranean. These laws saw the level of immigration into the United States plunge dramatically, from 805,000 in 1921 to around 300,000 in both 1925 and 1926, and to just 97,000 in 1931.[21] Other countries soon followed the United States' restrictionist example. Canada and countries of South America worried that if they did not also restrict immigration, then those unable to enter the United States would inundate them.[22]

The impact of immigration restriction in the Americas was indeed decisive, because the refugee problem of the interwar years began with the loss of these overseas migration opportunities. With the long-time outlet for Europe's displaced and unwanted effectively closed to new migrations, they cluttered the cities of Europe, and found few were prepared to accommodate them.

## Labour migration

France was alone among European societies in the years immediately after the First World War which could admit these stateless refugees in numbers large enough to have a significant impact on their resettlement. Although France itself faced many internal problems and antipathies towards foreigners, its national interests and the needs of refugees converged. The demand for workers was great, to replace the losses from the war and to assist in the task of reconstruction. At the same time France needed new hands, there were so many stateless refugees looking for new opportunities.

Contemporary estimates were of some 400,000 refugees in France in the mid-1920s.[23] Although later calculations showed that these estimates were exaggerations, the exaggerations themselves would suggest the refugees' high visibility within French society.[24] In addition to the refugees, there were also more than one million foreign workers in France between 1921 and 1924.[25] The refugees were therefore absorbed into this large foreign labour force. They consequently assumed a dual status: they were refugees in need of asylum, but they were also foreign workers.

Foreign workers were essential to fill the gaps in the workforce, but they had to be dispersed about the labour market in such a way as to fill those occupations where labour was most needed while giving priority to French workers. The regulation of the entry and placement of foreign workers therefore attempted to balance the divided interests of employer groups and labour organisations. The French government intervened in migration because labour recruitment exposed competing interests between industry and workers. Both turned to the government to protect particular interests. For employers, the recruitment of foreign labour was essential for economic recovery, while French labour organisations resisted competition from immigrant workers and the undercutting of salaries. Employer interests dominated government action, however. In 1919, the Permanent Conference on Foreign Labour (*Conférénce permanente de la main-d'oeuvre étrangère*) was established to prioritise occupations for which labour was required and the nationalities sought to fill them. Italians, Poles, and Czechs were particularly favoured, and treaty arrangements were entered into with the governments of Italy, Poland, and Czechoslovakia to ensure their regular supply. Generally, the government took only a small part in the recruitment of foreign labour, and intervened only so far as was necessary to limit tensions between French and foreign workers. Private consortia, such as the General Immigration Society (*Société Générale de l'Immigration*—SGI) instead undertook the recruitment of workers. The SGI gained a monopoly over east European labour migration and over government policy to the exclusion of labour organisations.[26]

Although most immigrant workers entered France on work contracts, the foreign-labour market was loose, Gary Cross observes. There was a high turnover of workers, with many moving about the country from job to job. A free, informal, and often illegal foreign labour market flourished, rendering government regulation half-hearted and ineffective. Poor housing, poor working conditions, and inferior rates of pay were all factors behind the high turnover.[27] The regulation of immigration, moreover, was politically expedient and strongly biased in favour of business. The government placated French labour, Cross writes, to avoid social unrest by directing foreign labour into employment that French workers shunned. This led to a dual labour market, with the French labour force entrenching itself in a superior employment status with superior levels of pay and conditions.[28]

Government, employer groups, and labour organisations therefore all had different priorities with regard to immigration and the recruitment of foreign labour, but nevertheless concurred in broad objectives. As Cross explains, the recruitment of workers outside France suited the economic needs of the country in three ways: it assisted in reconstruction in the immediate post-war years; it was necessary for economic development; and it provided a supplementary workforce, as beneficial to French labour as to French capital.[29] Although the different interests of each group caused tensions over the purpose, scale, and objectives of immigration, in the short term economic conditions favoured the employment of large numbers of foreign workers while holding these tensions in check.

Refugees were readily absorbed into the labour market as there was a demand for their work. They worked separately, re-establishing themselves and their families socially and economically without unduly antagonising French workers. French employers seized the opportunity to hire as many of them as possible, while the French government willingly came to the assistance of the League of Nations' humanitarian efforts.[30]

## Marseille, gateway between two stages of exile

Marseille in the 1920s has been described as a 'clearing house' (*centre de triage*) for the uprooted and displaced, from across the Mediterranean.[31] The city was more than a place of entry into France; it was a place where transition between the past, present, and future was negotiated. Here many refugees stayed, like Verneuil's family, as disembarkation at the port of Marseille ended their first stage of exile. They could now look ahead to resettlement. They had the good fortune of moving from the port to an apartment, and very shortly thereafter the father moved into employment. Over time, they became acculturated into this most cosmopolitan of French cities. Self-employment, education, and class advancement followed in due course, of which the young son was the beneficiary. In theatre, literature, and film, he expressed the French culture in which he had been educated, while mindful of his origins and the hostilities he had traversed.[32] Others did not have such good fortune, and their passage from exile abroad to exile in France was much more troubled.

Marseille was for them a liminal moment of readjustment between two stages of exile. Far from a place of resettlement, it was a place of redirection and dispersal to another yet uncertain future. From here refugees spread out, to meet up if their fortunes allowed with family or relatives from whom they had been separated during their first traumatic stage of exile, or else to take up offers of employment and therefore find a new place for themselves. They went above all to Paris, or the Côte d'Azure; they went north along the 'traditional axis of the Rhône', to Lyon, Grenoble, and Saint-Étienne.[33]

It was assuredly a political migration into Marseille, but a political migration of a different kind. These refugees had not been actors in great events but were victims, overwhelmed by great events.[34] From 1921, the port of Marseille set down refugees from camps all about the Levant: Russians from Constantinople, Armenians from Syria, Lebanon, and Greece, Asyrians and Asyro-Chaldeans from the Caucasus and Greece. Italians and Spanish refugees would arrive in later years.[35] The numbers of each refugee group are uncertain. Not only were their movements highly fluid, records were imprecise as refugee aid societies often double-counted, or made loose estimates. Contemporary sources put the number of Russian refugees in France in the early 1920s at about 100,000, Armenian refugees at over 60,000, and Assyro-Chaldeans at about 15,000.[36] The American Red Cross estimates for Russian refugees, at 175,000 in France in 1920, were consistently the highest. John Hope Simpson's review of the figures for his 1938 survey concluded that the number was less than half of this, at between 60,000 to 68,000 in 1922.[37] The numbers of Armenians who passed through Marseille in these same years grew during the 1920s as the camps in Beirut, Aleppo, and Alexandretta were slowly cleared, rising to somewhere between 30,000 and 60,000.[38] Later in the decade, Armenians from camps in Greece and Constantinople joined established communities, such as in Nice where they were recruited into employment in an Armenian business enterprise.[39]

The refugees were depersonalised in public-policy responses. Their protecting state stood aloof from them, and deferred assistance and welfare to private aid organisations. The state's role was the regulation of their entry into the labour market. Some arrived with work contracts but most without them, and their transition from refugees to foreign workers was therefore delayed. In the meantime they were almost entirely dependent on the private welfare services. Refugees who arrived without work contracts could not be moved quickly out of Marseille, and because of the growth in refugee numbers, unemployment in Marseille itself grew.[40] Housing was also scarce. Consequently, camps were established to relieve the strains on accommodation in the city and to help the refugees settle before being redirected into employment in the French interior.

Russian refugees were placed in the camp Victor-Hugo, a former military barracks adjacent to the St. Charles railway station, beckoning their onward passage it would seem. The camp was supervised by the Russian Red Cross, which provided water, lighting, and electricity, and free transit into the French interior once employment contracts had been found.[41] In April 1925, the camp housed 350 refugees, but had already served to reorientate many hundreds more whom the French national labour office (*Office de la Main-d'Oeuvre*) had placed in employment.[42] Because of age or infirmity, however, some refugees could not be placed. Although the camp was officially closed in 1929, in 1935 the Save the Children Fund found refugees who had been permanently resident there for as many as 12 years.[43]

Armenian refugees were mostly accommodated in Camp Oddo, where, because of their rapid influx during 1922 and 1923, overcrowding and living conditions were much worse than in Camp Victor-Hugo. Administration of the camp was handed over to Armenian organisations, which were also given 80,000 francs by the French government to aid in refugee resettlement. Funds for the maintenance of the camp and the medical care of the refugees were raised from the broader Armenian community.[44] As the camp quickly filled, these funds were soon exhausted. On 18 September 1923, it housed 780 men, women, and children; two weeks later the number had risen to 1200 and by 26 November to 2327. The best efforts of the agencies that attended to the refugees had little effect. The camp was poorly drained, and hot and dusty in the summer; the accommodation was squalid and hygiene was poor, malnutrition and disease could not be avoided. There was even an outbreak of plague. Overcrowding was such that new refugees were barred from entering the camp and a concerted effort was made to place the refugees in employment away from Marseille.[45]

Local officials became increasingly uneasy with the growth of poverty and declining standards of hygiene in the camp. The mayor of Marseille complained that new arrivals could not be admitted, and called for the repatriation without delay of these 'lamentable human herds' who were a 'great public danger for the entire country'.[46] The government took heed. It decided to close the camp in July 1925, and the foreign minister instructed the diplomatic missions in Constantinople, Salonica, and Athens to limit the number of entry visas they issued. But this was only a temporary interruption, and the refugee migrations resumed again in 1926 at the same level as before.[47]

Immigrant communities stepped forward to aid their distressed compatriots when the French government remained aloof. Their effectiveness in the provision of welfare, and their important mediating role between refugees and the government, were acknowledged by the French Foreign Ministry's recognition of their offices as their communities' official representatives. The *Offices Russes* for Russian refugees succeeded the pre-war Russian diplomatic services in both their personnel and their functions.[48] A further 10 aid organisations were established in Paris, three in Lyon and two in Marseille to assist Russian refugees.[49] Two Armenian offices, the Groupe Pacalian and the Groupe Hadisian, assisted Armenian refugees in their dealings with French officials by granting certificates on various questions of civil status, translating documents, and verifying signatures.[50] Other Armenian aid offices also stepped forward to meet particular needs, three in Paris, two in Lyon, and one in Marseille.[51] But their activities were constrained by their reliance on private funds. Official assistance, it seemed, only went so far as the admission of refugees to the large foreign labour force.

The importance of these migrations to Marseille cannot be underestimated, historians of the city contend. Between the wars it was a city of people in transition, between exile and migration, and between migration, settlement, and naturalisation. It occupied an intermediate place between the more traditional zones of rural and seasonal migration in the southwest and southeast, and the great industrial and urban centres where there was a need for new workers.[52] The city facilitated the transition of this 'human herd' from one phase of exile, as stateless refugees, to another, as workers within France's vast foreign labour force. During the 1920s, many tens of thousands of refugees passed through it. Most, about two-thirds, moved on. But the numbers are only part of the story; the change to France's demography was the enduring legacy of these migrations. Marseille therefore represents the greater changes across France. By 1935, some 21,000 Armenians remained in the department of the Bouches-du-Rhône, and 14,000 in Marseille itself.[53] At that time, France was waking to the realisation that its foreign population numbered about three million, or some seven per cent of the total population.[54]

## Italian anti-fascists

In the mid-1920s, one-fifth of Marseille's population was Italian, augmented and renewed by new migrants from Piedmont and Liguria. If Marseille was a city of transition, then Lyon was a city of settlement. By 1926, some 25,000 Italians who had crossed the mountains to escape the fascists had settled in the industrial suburbs of Villeurbanne and Gerland.[55] This was only a small sample of a new migration from Italy. From an Italian population of some 450,000 in 1921, by the early 1930s France accommodated about one million, or two million if naturalisation and French citizens of Italian descent are included.[56]

The migrations of the 1920s were as much a continuation of the long historical currents of emigration from the peninsula as it was a new migration from the rise of Mussolini's fascists. Historians therefore find it difficult to distinguish specifically the anti-fascist political refugees (the *fuorusciti*) from the larger currents. Yet it must properly be called a political migration because it also comprised workers and peasants from northern and central Italy where the reaction of the fascists and the capitalist class to worker and communist militancy had made their lives intolerable.[57]

As they had come from a culture with a long tradition of migration, there was a powerful sense among these Italians that Italy had no place for them and they needed therefore to start their lives anew elsewhere.

France was their natural destination once the United States had closed its doors to new immigrants. Its proximity, the tradition of Italian migration across the alps, France's tradition of liberty and the economic opportunities it offered, were the tangible and sentimental forces that drove this migration. Work, freedom, and a good living, which France could then provide, was a more powerful motivation in the early 1920s than was the protection of their political opinion they would find there. 'We can no longer live in our homeland', it was stated among Italian socialists. 'We go to France for work and freedom'.[58] But many Italian anti-fascists also found that France offered them the opportunity to continue their political militancy.

They therefore followed the traditional pattern of nineteenth-century migration from Italy, yet they also had much in common with the other nationalities who had been displaced by political circumstances in their homelands. Both the economic and political motives of migration came together in the remarkable example of Italian settlement in the French southwest, a depopulated agricultural region in need of people to resettle the countryside and to provide labour for its growing industry. The migration followed a decision in 1922 to recruit Italian workers into factories in Auch, in the department of the Gers. Work permits were arranged under the terms of the Franco-Italian labour exchange treaty of 1919, and financial grants were made available as incentives for family migration. The success of attracting new immigrants to Auch led to similar arrangements in the departments of the Lot-et-Garonne, the Tarn-et-Garonne, and the Haute-Garonne. By January 1927, a total of 24,289 Italians were officially registered, but as many had arrived without work permits and were therefore not registered, unofficial estimates put the total Italian population in these departments at this time at around 100,000.[59]

Economic factors were therefore significant. Active recruitment in the southwest provided opportunities for families in northern Italy who suffered from poor agricultural production on their small land holdings. With the money they earned from the sale of their property, they could buy a much larger one in these departments. These opportunities were also available to political migrants at the time when they needed to escape Italy. Parliamentarians, bankers, teachers, and university professors who had lost their positions under the fascists bought large estates and set about renovating them; they employed other Italians and therefore encouraged further migration. All the French required of property owners was evidence of their financial means to house and feed their families; all it required of workers was a work contract supported by an employer.[60]

Some historians distinguish the political refugees from the main migration currents by their continued anti-fascist militancy in exile. They find records of the political refugees in the membership lists of Italian political organisations that reformed in France, or in the Italian sections of the French communist and socialist parties, and even the more moderate Radical party and the League for the Rights of Man (*Ligue des Droits de l'Homme*).[61] They appeared mostly from 1926, when organised opposition within Italy had become impossible, but they never numbered more than 2.5 per cent of the total Italian emigrant population.[62]

While a great many Italians had left for France for political reasons after the fascists had assumed government in Rome, the political refugees among them were largely self-defined by their continued political militancy. Party leaders and principles, banned in Italy and fleeing imprisonment or even death, figure highly among the anti-fascist *fuorusciti*. They were the most militant and maintained their ideological commitment and political ambitions, even shaping French public opinion through the media, public rallies, and publications, and political opinion through their influence in the communist and socialist parties.[63] Others held less firmly to their political ideas and actions, or gave them up entirely to aid their resettlement and to assure their personal security, especially as fascist agents were active among the Italian refugees in France. Ideological and political commitments were much less firm among the middle ranks of anti-fascist militants, therefore. Many had gone into exile after banishment, or they had suffered repression at the hands of the fascists, such as the loss of employment or blacklisting, which made exile their only option. Because of fears for their personal safety, the trauma of exile, and the need for financial security for themselves and their families, they put aside their political aspirations and sought instead to integrate themselves more fully into French life. This was all the more imperative in the 1930s when repression at the hands of French police, the possibility of losing a job, and even the threat of expulsion for political militancy, made many break their remaining ties with their parties.[64]

Could their resettlement in France therefore properly be called exile? Unlike other refugee communities, few were formally stateless. Many could, if they so chose, return to Italy, but many could not return without a real threat to their lives or liberty. Many were assuredly refugees in flight from persecution. There was, nevertheless, a clear division between a general popular migration from fascism and the exile of militant political actors, driven out for their anti-fascism; these were rightly called *fuorusciti*. Moreover, the fascist government was as active among the emigrant community to police their activities as it was to promote Italian culture and the sentimental regard for, and the practical benefits of, their Italian nationality. This helped combat anti-fascist propaganda while showing the desire of the government in Rome to stem the loss of Italian nationals by holding the diaspora close to home.[65] One might no less accurately therefore classify this as another stage of Italy's long history of migration that had begun in the mid-nineteenth century and reached its peak in the early twentieth century.

## The problem of migration, the problem of asylum

During the 1920s, France made no distinction in public policy between migration for economic reasons and migration for political reasons. The boundary between the two was truly blurred. Even the admission of the Nansen refugees from the Middle East and the Soviet Union, who had been rendered stateless for political reasons, blurred the boundary between humanitarian and practical responses. The humanitarian gesture of their resettlement was moderated by the practical need for their labour; they were above all a large migrant group upon whom France could call for its own needs.

French responses to these refugee migrations were accordingly practical rather than principled. Refugee protection was channelled into the urgent necessity of resettlement, which was best served by making use of all available foreign labour for the purposes of post-war recovery and economic development. Refugees became foreign workers, and their legal status was thus fixed. Their relationship with their protecting state was negotiated through work contracts, work and residence permits, and the network of employers, government employment services, and officials from the various branches of the Interior Ministry, whose duty it was to certify their permits.

Because France seemed alone in its capacity to absorb refugees in such numbers during the 1920s, Sir John Hope Simpson observed that it was indeed the nation *par excellence* of refuge in western Europe, and that the French people cherished the ideal of the right of asylum.[66] Simpson identified the clear continuities in the admission of the displaced, and commended France for its support for the League of Nation's humanitarian work. The policies that these refugees met with, however, bring his claims into question. The aloofness of the state from the refugees, which saw aid and assistance devolved to private organisations, left them subject to the regime of labour control and employment regulation. Since they were admitted within the streams of foreign workers and their legal status was fixed to their work and residence permits, their asylum was sure only so long as their was a place for them within the labour market.

When economic circumstances changed in the mid-1920s, labour market constraints exposed tensions between the French and France's foreign workers. Gary Cross concludes that three outcomes of labour migration in particular turned public opinion against immigrants. One was the formation of 'alien colonies' in the cities and industrial regions, which led to the perception of foreign workers as the threat to French culture. The second was the creation of a class of floating alien workers who moved between temporary and seasonal work, with rapid mobility and a lack of community ties; this nurtured suspicions of clandestine behaviour among foreign workers and reinforced popular distrust. The third was that immigrant workers had been concentrated at the lower socio-economic levels and were therefore marginalised from French society; it was assumed that this made them susceptible to political radicalism.[67]

As unemployment doubled in 1926–7, from 245,000 to 510,000, public opinion found a ready explanation in the excessive numbers of foreign workers who had been brought in over the previous years.[68] Immediately the government responded and imposed prohibitions on foreign labour to try to solve the unemployment crisis. The arithmetic was simple: with over a half a million unemployed French workers and over one million foreign workers, the removal of even a small number, it was commonly believed, would restore full employment. This justified calls for restrictions on new immigration and the forced removal of foreign workers by the refusal to issue or renew residence and work permits. French consular officials were thereupon instructed to reduce the numbers of work contracts they issued, and inside France existing regulations were applied more forcefully: clandestine employment was clamped down upon, unemployed foreign workers were repatriated, and voluntary departures were facilitated by the payment of their return passage.[69] The terms of existing work contracts were also enforced more rigorously. This provided a means of revoking residence permits, especially of foreign workers in industries with high levels of unemployed French workers. The conditions of residence permits were also tightened. Proof of legal entry into France and guarantees from two French citizens were mandatory. The validity of a residence permit was reduced to two years; upon expiry a new permit was required and the conditions of employment were then reappraised. There were no longer any guarantees that a work or residence permit be renewed.[70]

The turn against foreign workers at a time of economic stress was one manifestation of profound social anxieties about the impact of immigration on France and on the French population. These anxieties also undercut the security of asylum for refugees and the stateless. Because they had been admitted into the foreign labour force, they were subjected to the new exclusionary measures that took hold from 1926 and were a highly vulnerable target of the mounting xenophobia during the years of economic, social, and political crisis that followed.

Economic stress and the realisation, through the daily experience of the French people, of the size of the foreign population, compounded anxieties of demographic stagnation. It seemed to commentators, demographers, and many participants in political debates, that the French nation was in decline and that immigration as it had thus far been conducted had only further harmed it. Immigration was therefore one dimension to a larger problem of national and racial consciousness among the French people, which stemmed from the losses of the First World War. Indeed, immigration was symptomatic of French national weakness and the inability of the French race to recover its former vitality.[71] Historians attentive to the voices of racism within immigration discourses of these years have exposed tendencies towards racial selection behind the façade of civic and republican models of integration, assimilation, and naturalisation. Through these tendencies, the foreigner was recast as a racial 'other' in whom the anxieties of the time were invested.[72] Ideas of racial hygiene also gained a significant following because the grafting of different racial lines within the French population stirred anxieties over its future character. But the real question confronting France was the economic imperative of immigration and therefore how restriction and selection should be applied to manage the risks of foreign penetration.[73]

Immigration, population, and demographic stagnation were three parts of the one problem, which had a much longer history and a more ineluctable hold on French consciousness than the recent disquiet about the large foreign labour force. By the late 1920s, all these issues had gained greater currency through a new literature on the impact of migration that was as remarkable for its approaches to the problems it exposed and the apprehensions it stirred as it was for the speed of its production.[74]

By that time one of the world's leading countries of immigration, France, Marcel Paon observed in 1926, had failed to shape immigration to its national interests. He cited the examples of the United States and Australia to argue that it was better to select immigrants before their arrival in order to determine if they had a minimum standard of health, education, and moral character to adapt to local life.[75] Paon's ideas are noteworthy for the view they give into the opinions on migration among the political class. He served as head of the national labour and agricultural service (*Chef du service de la main-d'oeuvre et de l'immigration agricole*) and on the Interministerial Commission on Immigration, which had been created in 1920 to bring together different ministerial functions on immigration matters. From 1928 he also served as chief of staff to Charles Lambert, a minister of Edouard Herriot's government who had gained a reputation for his expertise on immigration and had been a key sponsor of the new nationality law of 1927.[76]

Selection, Paon held, would facilitate assimilation and serve French interests because it would identify those with the best aptitude for settlement. His aim, therefore, was a policy that sought out the best combination of individual, cultural, and national characteristics among prospective immigrants: youth, health, social background and occupation, religion, language. Most importantly, selection would identify those best suited to settlement on the land. The problem with migration as it had been conducted thus far, Paon insisted, was that it had created an urban–rural demographic imbalance by favouring settlement in the cities; the cities continued to expand with the growth of immigration while the rural population declined. Urban centres all had their own 'islands of foreigners' while the countryside was in desperate need of young and fecund families to repopulate the land. This, in his view, should be the aim of immigration policy.[77]

Yet there was nothing to be feared from migration, Paon insisted, even in this poorly organised form. By his calculations (a comparison of France's population growth with the global population over the course of the nineteenth century, allowing for the losses of First World War), he concluded that France's population had regressed by 2,500,000, while immigration had made up only a fraction, between 885,000 and 1,000,000. This was hardly cause for concern about the longer term dangers to the French nation, he concluded.[78]

When the size of the foreign population was put at more than 3,000,000, however, there was reason to worry. This was the general view after the publication of Georges Mauco's 1932 study on the French population and the impact of immigration, probably the most cited work of its kind from these years. His was a more scientific study in comparison to other, polemical works. With almost 600 pages of data, graphs, charts, and analysis to demonstrate the deep penetration of foreigners, Mauco gave ample reason for French pessimism about the future composition of their population and the demographic surety of their nation. Mauco lamented the cultural distance between the French people and its new immigrants and warned about their impact on the French nation and civilisation. Racial characteristics clearly separated the two. The superior intellectual and cultural qualities of the French were in stark contrast to the inferior, backward, immigrant workers. In comparison to the dynamic French, they were altogether 'unsophisticated' and 'intellectually lazy'.[79] The lingering hold of their own national identity and culture, as well as the influence of their national governments, also divided them from France and the French. They maintained their national cultures and resisted assimilation; their divided loyalties were as troublesome for French national security as it was for the integrity of French culture.[80]

The place of foreigners within the French population had therefore entered into public and political discourse. Serious questions were being asked about the nature of policy and France's national interests. Since the late-nineteenth century immigration had served its economic interests, but under the stress of post-war social, economic, and cultural change, demographic imbalance and change in the composition of the population, the public mood had turned against foreigners and the purpose of immigration.

While the problems were detailed in a number of texts and commentaries, few proposals for reform to immigration policy were put forward, however. Restriction through selection was the most-favoured strategy, since selection would best serve France's economic and demographic needs. New young families to settle the depopulated countryside and fill the void in agricultural labour were preferred ahead of further industrial migration to the cities, and the best families were found in countries of a similar character to France. Charles Lambert, an advocate of selection, considered 'Latins'— Spaniards and Italians—ideal for France's purposes. Other Europeans, Belgians and Dutch, Scandinavians and Slavs—Czechs, Poles, Russians— were also ideal; they were all 'prolific and strong', and would have a beneficial influence on the French race.[81]

Yet there was no interest within the wider political milieu to change migration policy. Certainly, there was general consensus about the problems of migration and the need to regulate more tightly the provision of work and residence permits because of the economic circumstances, but this could be dealt with by administrative measures. There was greater reluctance to legislate the status of foreigners and to set in place a legal regime that prescribed the conditions of entry and residence. One reason for this was the chronic political instability of the interwar years, which disrupted continuity in government and therefore stood in the way of substantial legislative and administrative reform. Indeed, in 1926, Eduoard Herriot's government established a high commission for immigration and naturalisation, headed by Charles Lambert, to implement and oversee immigration policy, but it lasted for only six weeks, failing with the fall of the government.[82] Lambert revived this approach to the administration of migration in 1931 when he presented a draft statute. It failed for lack of support, however.[83]

Even though so much attention was paid to immigration and foreign workers, few distinctions were made between different groups. Foreigners were broadly conceived; they were a distinct social group, set apart from the French, remote and isolated by their class and racial character. They were a foreign proletariat occupying discrete quarters of French cities in relation to whom particular administrative measures needed to be taken. Anxieties about their impact on the French population and even French civilisation blinded observers to their diversity: their origins, to be sure, but also their reasons for migration, their status within France, their expectations for the future and their own forms of sociability, both among themselves and among the French communities in which they lived. Importantly, no distinctions were made in relation to refugees. They had become lost within the mass of the foreign proletariat in the large cities and industrial centres.

The League for the Rights of Man, however, kept the plight of refugees before public consciousness. It claimed a distinct position for political refugees within the migration regime as, it maintained, they were due the right of asylum 'without reserve'.[84] The League maintained a moderate position on migration that recognised the distinct status of refugees, mediating the extremes of restrictionists and a more openly liberal approach of the left. But one wonders how excesses such as this were received: refugees were, in one view, 'ragged, appalling, bearing the stigmata of what they had suffered, having left at each station of their Calvary more of their strength and sometimes a little of their blood'.[85] Far from an emphatic declaration of Christian sympathy for all that refugees had endured, such excess betrayed the antipathies refugees faced in public consciousness. Perhaps this was an exaggeration to stir conscience rather than consciousness when refugees suffered from their status as foreign workers.

The laws on immigration needed changing, Marcel Paon had argued, because immigration was leading France to decay. It was becoming the 'world's dumping ground'.[86] Lambert's proposed legislation would have facilitated the removal of 'the undesirable, the suspect and the useless' while assimilating those best suited to revitalising the nation. However, Paon, Mauco, and Lambert offer no guarantees for the asylum of refugees.

Jean-Charles Bonnet describes the period from the mid-1920s as one of mixed pressures over immigration policy: pressure from individuals and organisations, ideological pressures, and both temporary and permanent pressures.[87] Public policy was most responsive to the economic impact of migrant workers, and under the pressure of economic depression they were increasingly marginalised within the French economy and society. The first steps towards an exclusionary migration regime were taken when foreign workers had their work permits revoked to clear their occupations for unemployed French workers. Public policy was subsequently geared to the removal of unwanted or undesirable foreigners by expulsion, most commonly after breaching French law—which could include a simple matter of working without a valid permit—and refoulement, the refusal to grant a work or residence permit, or the revocation of existing permits. Those facing expulsion or refoulement had neither protection from nor remedy against abuses or errors.

Refugees were as vulnerable as any other foreign worker, and the special protection needs of stateless refugees, who could not be repatriated, or exiles from political persecution, who could not be repatriated without risk to life or liberty, were subsumed within this exclusionary political culture. Few stateless refugees faced expulsion, yet some expulsion orders were nevertheless issued, and they were a threat to others. Armenians made up one per cent of the expellees between 1925 and 1929, Maud Mandel calculates (about 370 out of a total of 34,300 orders).[88] They were made against those who had served a penal sentence for a common crime, but then faced the double penalty of being refused legal residence afterwards. They became exiles over again, fleeing French law by going underground into a clandestine and illegal existence.[89]

The introduction of restrictive quotas on foreign workers in 1932 adversely affected a great many more refugees. Quotas fixed the number of foreign workers in any one enterprise at a maximum of 10 per cent. Consequently, some refugee enterprises ceased to function. Even refugees employed for a decade or more were not immune. Few refugee or immigrant enterprises could continue to function, and unemployment included the risk of the annulment of a residence permit. Even cultural organisations were affected. Orchestras and choirs, arts and crafts workshops, theatres and cinemas, printeries, which had employed from within their refugee communities and served these communities, were forced to close. In 1935, the Save the Children Fund reported that the years since the introduction of the quotas had been the most difficult yet for refugees, as the loss of employment was devastating for the individual, their families, and for their communities, and undermined the certainty of their asylum.[90] Forced into unemployment by these restrictive quotas, they had to contest re-entry to the labour market under an even more restrictive regime of work and residence permits. As unemployed foreign workers, they were then exposed to orders of refoulement or expulsion.[91]

The problem of immigration in these years was therefore how France could accommodate its large foreign population while economic and social circumstances changed. Public opinion turned against them, and in public discourse they were reconceived as a racially and culturally insidious force. Increasingly restrictive administrative measures were taken to remove them from those sectors of the labour force where they were in competition with French workers.

The problem of asylum was how France could respect the protection needs of refugees when they were subjected to the same legal regime that applied to foreign workers. There was no residence permit nor other administrative measures that recognised their distinct status as either stateless refugees who had lost the protection of a national government, or political refugees who faced persecution at the hands of their national governments. The problem of asylum was therefore the refugees' lack of a definite legal status, which left them without protection under French law. The Nansen passport provided no guarantees of protection and was no substitute for protection under domestic law. It had been devised and adopted to facilitate the cross-border movements of refugees left stranded without passports or other documents and who were refused consular services. It provided no other guarantees, and the terms of their asylum were entirely at the discretion of the national governments of the countries that had admitted them.

This lack of protection was subsequently a priority at the League of Nations. At an intergovernmental meeting on refugees in June 1928, it was reported that whatever the good intention of governments in fulfilling their undertakings under the earlier refugee arrangements, the arrangements themselves were no substitute for the protection that only national law could provide.[92] The greatest difficulty for the refugees, it was concluded, was their exposure to restrictive measures protecting national labour markets and the orders of expulsion and refoulement, which were all too frequently made against them.[93]

The French government's view on asylum at this time was perhaps best expressed in its delegation's submission to this meeting. In all respects, it reported, French law protected refugees; they had free access to the courts and legal assistance was available to them just as it was available to French nationals, and the same regulations for employment applied to them as to any other foreigner. But, brushing aside the concerns just expressed in the meeting about the difficulties to which they exposed refugees, the French delegation insisted that they were subject to the same measures of expulsion and refoulement as other foreigners, even though not all could enter another country.[94] Asylum, in short, did not mean that refugees were entitled to a distinct status in law and distinct administrative arrangements. Rather, they enjoyed the freedoms that life in France offered them but they were also held to the same laws and regulations as others.

# 9
# The German Refugee Crisis, 1933–5

Refugees began to flee Germany from the moment of Hitler's assumption of power in January 1933. Their flight intensified after the Nazi consolidation in March. The rush to 'de-judaise' the German arts, civil service, and education, and the 1 April 1933 boycott of Jewish businesses, signalled for many German Jews the urgent need to leave.[1] Others the Nazis would not tolerate also fled, democrats, socialists, pacifists, academics, journalists, Catholic priests, and Protestant pastors—roughly 15 per cent of the total number of refugees in 1933.[2] In response, the French Foreign Ministry instructed its consular officials in Germany to deal urgently with applications for entry visas. The Interior Ministry invited the prefects of the eastern departments to receive without reserve refugees from across the Rhine.[3] These initial instructions were issued in the belief that the flight from Germany was temporary and that special measures were only required to deal with an abnormally high demand for entry visas. Yet demand remained high as the year progressed and, on several occasions, the French government affirmed its traditions of hospitality in the face of this rising human tide.[4]

The refugee crisis of 1933 coincided with a period of political instability and ineffectual government) which witnessed a succession of five governments in 14 months, and of six cabinets in 20 months.[5] Policy continuity was ensured however by an Interministerial Commission for the German refugees. All ministries with an interest in refugee policy were represented to plan a common strategy, Foreign Affairs and the Interior, Labour, Agriculture, Health and the Colonies. Interior Minister Camille Chautemps set out the policy framework at the commission's first session in May 1933. He noted that the number of German nationals in France was still small (54,000 Germans compared very favourably with 490,000 Spaniards and 518,000 Poles). Therefore, he concluded, France was hardly likely to be overrun by the new refugees. Still, it was necessary to consider what measures needed to be taken to regulate their entry as their numbers were surely to rise: a 'permanent hostility' to Jews had been installed in Germany, Chautemps declared, which would oblige many more to leave.[6] Care therefore needed to be taken in deciding for economic and security reasons who was allowed admission. For a start, there was no place in the economy for German intellectuals and merchants; no Germans, furthermore, could remain in departments along the German frontier. Under Chautemps' direction therefore, the first session of the Interministerial Commission adopted the key measure that would shape French policy towards the refugees from Germany during the 1930s, a policy of vetting (*filtrage*) at the border, so that only those who were truly refugees would be admitted.[7]

The refugees from Germany therefore faced mounting barriers to asylum in France: of visas, passports, residence and work permits, and a society that questioned its capacity to admit them into its workforce, economy, and social life. A visa issued by a French diplomatic mission held out the promise of protection but the conditions on residence and employment that followed withheld any guarantee of asylum. Instead, the refugees confronted police and administrative officials who were much less respectful of their circumstances than the consular officials who had issued their entry visas. They found in France an 'uneasy asylum', as Vicki Caron calls it.[8] It was assuredly an uncertain asylum. Their onward migration was favoured at the same time as it became more difficult for them to secure it.[9] After the League of Nations appointed a High Commissioner for the refugees from Germany in October 1933, the French government decided that no new refugees would be allowed to settle; the best it offered was temporary passage to a place of final settlement. The new High Commissioner was henceforth responsible for them, and financial and material assistance and relief for the refugees was left to private aid organisations.[10]

## 'At evident, immediate risk'

The German Jewish refugees therefore suffered from the unfortunate coincidence of their appearance at the same time France realised that it could barely absorb new immigrants into its society and economy. As the refugees from Germany continued to breach the frontier, often by illegal means, French anxieties intensified. The Jew, particularly the eastern Jew, embodied much deeper anxieties than those arising from the current crisis. Prevailing anti-German sentiments deflected anxieties about French national security onto them, and middle-class professionals anxious about their economic position saw them as nothing other than unwelcome competition. But Jews also evoked fears embedded in long-held cultural prejudices last witnessed in the early Third Republic.[11] Paula Hyman writes that French society was ambivalent to any foreigners but above all to Jews, whose concentration in Paris made them particularly visible. The Jew, she argues, was often depicted sympathetically as the victim of persecution but was also the object of vehement anti-Semitic rhetoric.[12] Immigrant Jews also evoked anxieties among France's native Jewish population that this latent anti-Semitism might find new force and they would also be its targets.[13] Immigrant Jews therefore very much embodied French vulnerabilities.

At the very time when refugees turned to France for protection from persecution in Germany, France itself had consolidated its regime of exclusion, for economic reasons, for reasons of security, and because there were deep anti-foreign and anti-Jewish phobias that had risen to the surface under the stress of circumstance. Official directives on what measures should be taken in response to the refugees consequently display mixed sentiments and intentions. In a memorandum of 3 May to the premier, Edouard Daladier, Foreign Minister Joseph Paul-Boncour wrote that faced with the acts of violence perpetrated against the Jews in Germany, 'the Republican government can only remain faithful to its humanitarian traditions and hospitality'.[14] Instructions to the consular officials in Germany, however, stressed two pressing concerns that should determine the grant of entry visas: the dangers arising from economic and social conditions, and national security considerations. 'Serious inconveniences would ensue', Paul-Boncour advised the French ambassador in Berlin, 'from receiving those entirely bereft of resources who ... would inevitably become a charge on the French community. Furthermore, we would run great dangers if we admit those manifestly suspect'.[15] Visas, therefore, were issued only after careful consideration, and were only given to those who had satisfied the consular officials that they could comply with all the guarantees demanded of them: that they had sufficient means to live independently, and that their previous activities in Germany would not prejudice the French public order or its security concerns.[16]

It is open to speculation how rigorously consular officials enforced these instructions when faced with the urgency of the persecutions in Germany and the needs of those crowding the consulate buildings each day trying to get a visa to leave. Departmental prefects complained in 1934 that consular officials were issuing visas to Germans far too readily.[17] Even so, there were rigid conditions on the approval of a visa and the entitlements that came with them. Applicants who could not provide satisfactory evidence were refused without question, and those who were successful in obtaining a visa were allowed only two months residence in France; they were thereafter obliged to apply for a residence permit or leave.[18]

As the queues to obtain a visa grew and the provision of supporting documents delayed departure, those who sought consular visas were not so hard-pressed by their circumstances to quit Germany as those who took immediate flight. Many had gone directly to the French border without visas and even without a passport. Recognising their circumstances, the Interior Ministry instructed officials in the border regions not to refuse admission to anyone who was at 'evident, immediate risk'. These refugees were then removed from the eastern departments and allowed 20 days to apply for a residence permit.[19]

An entry visa assured flight from persecution, but as they allowed only a short, temporary stay in France, they provided little more than passage from one hurdle to another. The challenge of obtaining a residence permit followed. Immigrants and refugees from Germany therefore had moved from the consular officials, who exercised guardianship of French borders, to the formidable protective barriers of the police.

The laws and regulations on the issue and renewal of residence and work permits were subject to frequent amendment during the late 1920s and the 1930s, as the government strove to keep up with changing economic conditions and the shifts in the public mood against foreign workers. Changes had modified the grounds on which permits could be revoked and had tightened conditions relating to the employment of foreigners. Regular procedural changes to deal with contingencies, furthermore, made the regime of residence and work permits often unpredictable, if not arbitrary.[20]

The requirements for obtaining or renewing residence and work permits created at least momentarily a personal relationship between immigrant workers, refugees, and the public officials with whom they came face to face. The officials had it within their powers to profoundly change their life fortunes. Laws and procedures directed them, but their subjective responses no doubt had some influence. Barbara Vormeier comments that decisions regarding the issue of these permits often depended on the officials who made them.[21] When the foreigner was a recently arrived refugee who had not yet settled into the labour market, there must also have been much sympathy as well as mistrust and uncertainty. The possibilities of personal prejudice also shaping these decisions cannot be discounted.[21a]

As refugees had the same legal status as foreigners, the laws pertaining to their eligibility for a residence permit was clear. The rules that applied in 1933 were those of the law of 10 July 1929 on the issue and renewal of identity cards.[22] All foreigners over the age of 15 were required, within eight days of arrival, to submit an application for an identity card at the commissariat of police or mayoral office of their place of residence. The application required proof that proper entry was made. The names of two French citizens attesting to the person's identity and status were also required. A provisional identity card of limited validity was issued which authorised residence while the formal identity card was processed. This could take several months.[23] The identity card was valid for two years, at the end of which the holder had to apply again for its renewal. Renewal was in reality a fresh application for residence. The onus fell on the applicant to provide all the documentation necessary to establish that the conditions required for renewal were satisfied.[24] The identity card would be refused to foreigners who had not conformed to regulations, or it was revoked from those who no longer 'offered desirable guarantees', on either economic or security grounds.[25] In May 1932, this provision was amended to allow for the refusal of an identity card to those 'found in an irregular situation', a provision aimed at unauthorised employment and clandestine entry, and at those whose visas and residence permits had expired and had not been renewed. In these cases, the individual concerned faced refoulement after the revocation of all authority to remain in France.[26]

The lack of a distinct legal status for refugees had particularly telling consequences. The refusal or revocation of residence entitlements denied them asylum, and their refoulement left them vulnerable to forced repatriation. The only working definition of a refugee made during 1933 was contained in the instruction to border officials to admit those at 'evident, immediate risk'. But as far as the issue of visas and residence permits were concerned, the predominating factor was that suitable 'guarantees' were made about their suitability for residence, a requirement unrelated to humanitarian protection.

Most of the refugees who arrived in France in 1933 found work permits almost impossible to obtain.[27] A foreign worker had firstly to obtain a work contract from an employer, which in turn had to be approved by the labour placement office, the *Office Départemental de Placement*, in the department where they were intending to take up residence, after an inquiry into the employment conditions in the proposed occupation.[28] During the period of recruitment of foreign labour in the 1920s, the work contract and the Labour Ministry's authorisation would be obtained before the foreigner had entered France.[29] The regulations in place in 1932, based on Labour Ministry instructions of 7 April 1927 and the law of 1929, related to the recruitment of foreign workers outside France and were vague about the provision of the work permit for new immigrants who had arrived without a contract.[30] Amendments of 23 October 1933 made no attempt to address the urgent situation of refugees unable to obtain a work permit.[31]

These exclusionary trends show that, despite declarations of fidelity to its traditions of hospitality, France actively dissuaded refugees from settling. They were caught up in the general intent of removing unnecessary foreign workers. Although the highest levels of expulsion were reached in 1931–2, the numbers obliged to leave through refoulement because they had been refused residence and work permits or had had them revoked, peaked in 1934, clear evidence of the exclusion of refugees.[32]

Those required to leave had to make their own arrangements for departure, and they could only enter another country after obtaining authority by way of an entry visa. This was impossible for those against whom an expulsion order had been issued.[33] Refoulement, on the other hand, was not a police order, merely the lack of permission to remain. Yet, failure to leave opened the way to a formal expulsion order. Failure to comply with an expulsion could result in imprisonment. The refusal of protection, in short, offered the stark alternatives of a precarious and often illegal existence in France, illegal residence abroad, forced expulsion under police escort, imprisonment or repatriation.[34]

Such direct acts as expulsion or refoulement by the refusal of a residence and work permit were not the only forms of exclusion. Yet even residence itself seemed exclusionary, as refugees were forced to the margins. Old army barracks on the outskirts of Paris served as refugee camps. In these *bastions* large families occupied single rooms. Heating, bedding, and lighting were inadequate. Bereft of possessions left behind in their flight from Germany, they clung to a few valuables, a family portrait, or books of religion.[35]

## Two concurrent strands of policy

As refugees from Germany were subjected to the regulations relating to foreign workers and were denied special recognition as refugees, a paradox was exposed. The ministries represented on the Interministerial Commission were acutely aware of their distinct nature as refugees. The commission, after all, was formed to respond to the refugee crisis. This had significant conceptual consequences. There were in fact two problems to deal with: identifying the refugee, or, in other words, distinguishing them from other foreigners; and assistance when France could no longer absorb them.

One of the barriers to distinguishing refugees from foreigners generally was that the vast majority of the refugees in the interwar years were indeed foreigners and travellers, on the move because they were victims caught up in great events. This was quite different to the idea of the political refugee that persisted in the language about which refugees were still spoken and with which responses were formulated. But this was no longer a sure definition. Jewish refugees from Germany, unlike socialists and communists, for example, could not be properly classified as 'political' refugees since they were victims of Nazi racial persecution. International measures since the end of the First World War had reflected the changes of refugee populations; the problem they addressed, however, was not the persecutions the refugees had suffered but their lack of a clear juridical identity.[36] Their juridical status remained unclear even under the domestic laws of those countries in which they were resettled. Most difficulties arose from attempts to apply the term 'refugee' consistently to the various displaced groups drifting across Europe in the juridical void of statelessness. The League of Nations' arrangements relating to Russian and Armenian refugees adopted the criterion of former juridical nationality to identify those entitled to the Nansen passport. The practical implications of refugee assistance, however, had the most far-reaching consequences: financial aid, resettlement opportunities, employment openings, and housing, for the large numbers of people in distress, all imposed considerable burdens on host countries already suffering economic and social stress.

France could deal with the refugees as foreigners, yet, it was firmly held, exclusionary measures were justified because a solution to the refugee situation was to be found only at the international level. This precedent for refugee assistance had been set by the Nansen refugees of the 1920s; similar arrangements, if properly applied, would help resolve the problem of the refugees from Germany. France fulfilled its obligations for the Nansen refugees by taking in more than any other nation. Now that conditions in France had changed and it could no longer receive refugees, it was beholden on other nations to take on the burden. National assistance for refugees was accordingly deflected into international measures for relief and resettlement. This was the position of the Interministerial Commission during 1933. By mid-1933, France was still alone in bearing the burden of refugee protection, having admitted at least 25,000 of the estimated 60,000 refugees who had left Germany, four times more than any other country.[37] Solutions lay, the commissioners believed, not inside France but outside, through international cooperation and international resettlement measures.

The various dimensions of the refugee problem, national responses and international solutions, the legal issues of the status of refugees, third-country resettlement, and the practical issues of material assistance, were all detailed in a series of briefing notes prepared for the members of the commission for its first session of 27 May 1933.[38] The first note described the meaning of the term 'political refugee' in the context of the present crisis and the international refugee arrangements adopted in the 1920s. These instruments were no more than the 'embryo of a statute', the note states; it was therefore important 'to fill this gap by determining the characteristics of an individual assuming the title of "political refugee", and the advantages that flow from it'. The second note describes one of these advantages: the 'right of asylum'. Stressing the international context of the refugee situation, this note explains that the right of asylum must be shared between all states: 'the exercise of this right carries a charge for all nations that grant it, which should be distributed equally. States neighbouring the refugees' state of origin should not be expected to bear it alone'. The third note recognised that only an international organisation could disperse the refugees fairly among other nations, taking into consideration the economic situations in each of them.

The remaining notes relate to asylum within states. The fourth asserts national rights over the right of asylum, as the grant of asylum did not prohibit the removal of an individual for having abused it; yet it was impossible for France to execute orders of refoulement or expulsion when the frontiers of other states were firmly closed. The fifth addressed the need for a document of identity that assured a refugee's legal status. The sixth recognised the obligation of states to provide assistance, but under current economic conditions there was no spare capacity within national budgets. The need for an international organisation and international funds to provide for refugee assistance was evident, since a state acting alone was unable to fulfil its responsibilities.[39]

The international efforts to assist the Russian and Armenian refugees in the 1920s were therefore a valuable precedent. They offered an example of international cooperation under an organisation dedicated to the redistribution and resettlement of refugees, and from this flowed the advantage of an internationally recognised statute that defined the refugees. The inclination to view the German-refugee problem as analogous to the earlier post-war refugee crises, however, suggests a failure to comprehend the nature of the new dilemma. Past measures had the allure of suggesting ways forward when solutions seemed elusive, but they were elusive because of the new problems the refugees faced. The French Foreign Ministry's representatives in Geneva, its League of Nations' Service (*Service Français de la Société des Nations*), indeed cautioned that the international measures for the Russian refugees in the 1920s offered 'false analogies' to the problems posed by the refugees from Germany. The lack of protection was first of all quite different. The Russian refugees were refused diplomatic protection and legal recognition by the Soviet Government; the German refugees on the other hand had suffered persecution inside Germany but they did not lose their juridical nationality when they left. Many still had valid German passports and could return to Germany if they wished to do so. Moreover, the employment situation at the time of the Russian refugee crisis favoured their rapid integration into the economic and social life of the countries where they found asylum. More urgently, it was considered, an international statute for German refugees was fraught with the danger of encouraging the Nazi government to step up its anti-Jewish campaign to force Jews to leave at an even higher rate, assured that other countries would admit them. The League of Nations Service therefore recommended against an international organisation established under the League of Nations. The refugees from Germany, it believed, would instead be better served by private aid associations.[40]

In October 1933, when the League nevertheless decided to appoint a High Commissioner responsible for international assistance for and the resettlement of the refugees from Germany, it created a non-political organisation independent of the League, but it could not avoid political pressures from concerned national governments. The High Commission's governing body was composed of nominated representatives who asserted their own government's priorities. For France, the priority was to divest itself of the burden on its resources brought upon it by its existing refugees and exclude new refugees for whom it had no place. At the second session of the Interministerial Commission on 16 October 1933, Foreign Ministry representative Blanchet announced that the 'liberalism we displayed at the start has come to an end'. Interior Minister Chautemps supported him, proposing that, as the League of Nations was now addressing the refugee problem, France could decide to prohibit access to German refugees altogether.[41] A thorough revision was subsequently made of the instructions and procedures for the issue of consular visas in Germany for intending travellers, ensuring that none arrived in France with the belief that they would be allowed to establish domicile.[42]

Exclusionary measures now had firmer logic. The disproportionate number of refugees France was expected to accommodate was proof that it bore an undue burden when economic conditions made it unable to absorb them. While France had assumed its responsibilities, other states had erected barriers at their frontiers, preventing France from the free exercise of its sovereign right to control the flow of immigrants or the expulsion of foreigners. International assistance under these conditions would therefore provide a more equitable redistribution of the refugee burden.[43] Senator Henri Bérenger, France's representative on the governing body of the High Commission for the German refugees, put this position to its first session in December 1933. France, he announced, had suspended its instructions regarding the issue of visas and residence permits to German refugees, pending their classification by the High Commission and their redistribution to other countries. 'France and its private organisations have done more than their duty in response to the humanitarian problem posed by events in Germany', he told the governing body. But it could not continue to do so: 'there is the danger of a political problem being added to the social problem', he continued. 'France cannot be hospitable indefinitely ... it will consent to be a clearing house (*voie de triage*) but not a holding centre (*voie de garage*) for all refugees'.[44]

From this moment, refugee policy diverged into two concurrent streams: exclusion, through prohibitions on entry, which were justified by the international measures for assistance and resettlement adopted by the High Commission; and measures relating to German refugees residing in France. Although consular officials ceased to issue entry visas to Germans, a measure that had 'stopped the exodus', the pressure for asylum could not be so simply controlled.[45] Formal prohibitions only encouraged clandestine entry, and clandestine refugees only exacerbated the problems France faced when it turned to dealing with the refugees already inside the country.

The task of providing for the refugees' immediate welfare and material assistance was taken up by private and community organisations, which proliferated in response to the influx of refugees from Germany. The principal national aid association was the National Committee for the Welfare of German Refugees, Victims of Anti-Semitism (*Comité National de Secours aux Réfugiés Allemands, Victimes de l'Antisémitisme*).[46] Constituted in July 1933 from a number of private organisations that sprang up the previous April, the National Committee was financed by donations from French Jewish societies and the general public. By the end of 1933, it had already provided assistance for some 9000 German Jewish refugees who had no independent means.[47] Senior representatives included Jacques Helbronner and Henry Bérenger, who both represented France on the High Commission for German Refugees, and the Jewish financiers Edmond and Robert de Rothschild. In 1933, the National Committee had spent some eight million francs in aid; in October alone, about 3000 refugees had called on its assistance. By then, however, its funds had run down to such an extent that it asked the government to step in to assist its work.[48]

Even internationally, governments hesitated to contribute. Aid and relief agencies were instead dependent on funds raised from private institutions, philanthropic organisations, and public appeals. These contributions could not be sustained at the levels required. The High Commission for the German refugees, on which so many expectations had been placed, was itself entirely dependent on private contributions, which it found were all but exhausted by November 1934.[49]

The burdens of charitable relief further emphasised the need for the international redistribution of the refugees. Helbronner, representing the National Committee at the third session of the Interministerial Commission on 22 October 1933, announced that private organisations could only provide temporary assistance; a solution was to be found in the refugees' 'placement, employment, and the provision of the means to live and to help their families'.[50] Even so, the refugees in France were still refused work permits, and the government was not prepared to change this. Instead, the Interministerial Commission became preoccupied with plans for the dispersal of refugees into the agricultural regions of southern France.

These plans had an immediate appeal. They were a sure means of channelling refugees away from the professions in which they were unwanted competition for the French middle classes, and into occupations for which there was a demand for labour. They would also be removed from the eastern departments where they were regarded as a security risk, and from industrial cities where they could fall under the influence of socialists or communists.[51] Among the plans were barracks set-aside by the War Ministry to house the refugees while working the fields. The Agriculture Ministry was ready to place the refugees in work 'where there is a shortage of labour, or where the land is undeveloped'.[52]

Effective solutions to refugee assistance and settlement were elusive, nevertheless. Little attention was paid to the viability of plans for agricultural resettlement. One plan put to the fourth session of the Interministerial Commission by Marcel Paon, a well-known advocate of rural resettlement and then the head of the labour service in the agriculture ministry, was to send refugees to Corsica. A small number, two or three, would go to the agricultural college in Ajaccio to learn to work the land; more would then follow. Funds for the scheme would have to come from private agencies, however, such as the National Committee, until the resettled refugees had found employment.[53]

Even before these plans were fully developed, private organisations embraced them as a strategy for assisting refugee emigration. Helbronner reported that a German group had already raised seven million marks to buy abandoned lands in the department of the Lot with a view to resettling 200 families. Similar schemes were suggested for the Creuse.[54] But the prospect that plans for agricultural settlement might facilitate further refugee immigration made them immediately suspect. The accumulation of German refugees in the 'recovered territories' of Alsace and Lorraine, for example, was particular cause for concern. Le Hoc, head of the office for Alsatian affairs, reported that a Parisian institution had bought a property in the department of the Moselle to establish a professional agricultural school for refugees without awaiting the approval of the Agriculture Ministry. This, Paon, at the Agriculture Ministry, confirmed, would have been refused, since its objective was to facilitate the entry of new German refugees.[55]

Still, private organisations worked to help the placement of refugees in agriculture as the best means of helping them adapt to life in exile. The Russian organisation, the ORT (in French, the *Société de Propagation du Travail Industriel et Agricole parmi les Juifs*—The Society for the Development of Jewish Industry and Agriculture) included professional education and retraining for the declassed bourgeoisie among its work for Jewish refugees, and promoted the creation of cooperative workshops and agricultural settlements.[56] The Hehaloutz, an organisation based in Jerusalem, set up agricultural and artisanal schools in a number of regions in France.[57] Other organisations, such as the Association for German Refugees in France (*Association des Émigrés d'Allemagne en France*) and the Association for Concord and Progress (*Association Concorde et Progrès*), also recognised the need to develop agricultural resettlement opportunities for the refugees from Germany, which required in turn special attention to their retraining and reorientation.[58] The Association for Alsace-Lorraine in the Saar (*Association des Alsaciens-Lorrains de la Sarre*) persuaded a training centre on the Ile d'Oléron off the coast near La Rochelle, which commonly took in apprentices from Alsace and Lorraine, to take in some young German refugees to train them in oyster farming.[59] But in 1933, any centre that accommodated German refugees was keenly scrutinised. The prefect of the Charente-Inférieur, and both the foreign and interior ministers, inquired into the training centre before the labour minister reassured them of its proper background and intent. Concerns were less about the centre itself and the individuals organising it, than the response of the local inhabitants, who had already complained that there were 'too many foreigners' on the island. The prefect therefore forewarned the interior minister that 'they would scarcely be welcoming to new German workers who can't find a position anywhere else.'[60]

Distinct groups of German refugees in specific localities were a common cause for concern and suspicion. In July 1933, an English Quaker, Edith Pye, proposed the settlement of a group of German refugees on deserted farms in the department of the Pyrénées-Orientales. The ensuing correspondence between the prefecture, the Foreign Ministry, and the Interior Ministry reveals the misgivings with which such propositions were approached. There was little inquiry into the details of the scheme: the numbers involved, the objectives of settlement, the plans for agricultural development, and financial arrangements for putting it in place. The foreign minister was instead more concerned that Pye's proposal would appear to imply the settlement of German refugees who had already found asylum in England.[61] The plan was eventually abandoned after a self-declared 'French Quaker' in Paris denounced Pye as a political agitator and accused her of organising the resettlement of a group of German political agitators in Paris: 'They are not Quakers', the denunciation read, 'although their nefarious action is financed by naïve English and American Quakers'.[62] The response from officials in the Pyrénées-Orientales, however, pointed to serious questions about the viability of this and similar proposals for agricultural settlement in southern France. The lands had been abandoned because they were not sufficiently productive, and plans to develop them would be a poor economic proposition. The unviability of the lands, the Prefect concluded, explained why they had been vacant for years.[63]

The plans for agricultural settlement reveal the contradictions in French responses. While ministerial representatives at various sessions of the Interministerial Commission suggested they were ideal for assisting refugees while also putting them into useful work, suspicion and distrust predominated. The plans warranted attention, but although preliminary discussions occupied much time, little effort was made to developing them further, particularly when it came to the question of finance. Nor would the exclusionary measures relating to refugee settlement and the availability of work permits be relaxed to facilitate these schemes. It was important, however, as much for the representatives of government and private aid organisations as for the refugees themselves, that there were discussions of a positive nature on what to do about those who could not be repatriated, who could not find onward passage, and who could not otherwise find employment. A semblance of progress was maintained while effective solutions were elusive.

Nevertheless, the viability of agricultural settlement schemes remained very much in doubt. The High Commission for the German refugees reviewed the many plans that were put forward to it for resettlement both in Europe and overseas, and concluded that the financial outlays to get them off the ground were far too great for the few refugees who might benefit. The refugees themselves, above all, were mostly from the middle-class professions and were completely inexperienced and untrained in manual or agricultural labour on which these schemes were based.[64] The plans were, in short, a distraction from the real failure of refugee assistance.

## The *Institut Montesson*

Jewish organisations, however, took the possibilities of agricultural settlement very seriously as they suggested a strategy for the immediate settlement of German refugees, and a number of organisations sprang up to provide training and experience in agriculture and artisanal crafts to prepare refugees for manual work. One was the Institut Montesson, which was established at the Château de la Tour in the township of Montesson in the department of the Seine-et-Oise. Its aim was to reorient German-Jewish emigrants so that their chances of finding employment opportunities were improved. It provided shelter to refugees while training them in the kinds of work in which there was a demand for labour, largely in agriculture and manual labour. It declared in a statement of its aims and objectives that acts of charity, although indispensable at the first stage of emigration, were insufficient for the longer term needs of the refugees. The reorientation it offered was driven by the desire to avoid labour competition with French nationals, and to avoid the emigration itself from becoming 'disquietingly proletarianised' in unskilled labouring occupations in the industrial cities. Its purpose first and foremost was to preserve the culture and identity of those uprooted from Germany while sparing them conflict with French workers. Self-sufficiency and self-definition in exile were imperative for sustaining themselves in their place of resettlement. The institute therefore undertook training in the kind of occupations that would give them a place within France. The 'need for agricultural labour and the abandonment of rural properties', often cited in political debates and arguments about the role of immigration, was the niche in which the Jewish refugees could find their place. Young men and women, 'whose existence in Germany has become impossible', would thereafter have reason to dedicate their lives to their new homeland.[65]

The Institut Montesson provided more specific details of its origins and objectives in correspondence with the prefect of the Seine-et-Oise when its activities had come under investigation. It emphasised the refugees' break with their German past and their wish to become integrated into French society.

> We are a group of German refugees, Jews, victims of Nazi intolerance. All the time a latent anti-Semitism has afflicted us in Germany; but the manner in which it has developed in recent times has forced us to destroy definitively all bridges with our country of origin. We have already repudiated our nationality and have decided to find in France, if it allows us, a new homeland. Such is the spirit that moves us.[66]

The institute had come under investigation because the prefect of the Seine-et-Oise, under instructions from the Interior Ministry, made some preliminary inquiries into the activities and personal backgrounds of the refugees accommodated at the Château de la Tour. Indeed, the institute had raised interest at the highest level of government, as the prefect reported to both the premier and the interior minister. His initial report included a list of the 54 resident German refugees, with details of their financial means and their legal status.[67] He reported that there was no reason for the institute to be considered suspect; indeed, its objectives were approved in principle. Nevertheless, the individuals it accommodated were closely examined. In March 1934, the interior minister again instructed the prefect of the Seine-et-Oise to examine the refugees assisted by the institute, this time to provide details of their previous domicile in Germany, and to learn whether they had suffered any 'physical abuse at the hands of the German authorities because of their political opinions or their religion': in other words, to determine whether they could legitimately claim to be political refugees in flight from persecution.[68]

It would appear that the Institut Montesson was brought under suspicion following the request from one of its instructors, Ernst Pietrkowski, to regularise his legal status. Pietrkowski, a 31-year old Polish Jew, formerly resident in Germany, arrived in France on 20 October 1933. He had been arrested by the Nazis and left Germany after obtaining an entry visa from the French consulate in Zurich. Since his arrival in France, he had lived at the Château de la Tour, and, on 2 November 1933, sought permission to remain beyond the expiry of his entry visa.[69] A condition of his entry prohibited him from undertaking paid employment. The prefect of the Seine-et-Oise referred the request to the Interior Ministry because he was unsure whether Pietrkowski was eligible for a residence permit.[70] He provided the following details in his referral:

> Pietrkowski has declared that he has come to France, after having been arrested by the Nazis, to avoid other persecutions. Exercising the profession of agriculturalist, he has settled at Montesson, at a school of reorientation where he desires to learn French and then later work in agriculture. He claims to have personal resources but has provided no evidence of them.[71]

The Interior Minister's response was swift and definitive: 'because of his undertaking not to remain in France beyond the validity of his visa, there are no grounds to authorise the German national Pietrkowski to reside in France'.[72]

This, in effect, was an order of refoulement which required him to leave France before his visa expired on 17 January 1934. Pietrkowski protested this decision on the grounds that his former persecution in Germany made it unsafe for him to return, and because he desired to establish himself in France. He invoked a right of asylum, describing his persecutions in Germany thus:

> Being Jewish I was forced from my occupation in Germany. I was arrested by the Aryan police on 1 July 1933 on the pretext that I expressed a bad opinion about Minister Goering. I was imprisoned for twelve days; I was harshly treated and whipped with a metal rod. I still bear the scars on my body. I was released on condition that I leave Germany.[73]

Pietrkowski went on to claim that he was properly qualified as an agrono-mist and had formerly earned his living in agriculture; he entered the Institut Montesson to learn French while living on his own resources, which were enough for him to purchase a property if he were allowed to settle in France. The general secretary of the National Committee supported his request for a residence permit, but he won no official sympathy. His letter to the interior minister has a note in the margin, 'no further action' (*rien à faire*), a simple bureaucratic dismissal that compelled Pietrkowski to leave the country without any assurance for his future security.[74]

Once Pietrkowski's claims for asylum were dismissed, the students and instructors at the Institut Montesson fell under suspicion. Were they also legally residing in France? Were they also actually victims of Nazi persecutions? This attempt by a refugee to formalize his legal residence thus inadvertently brought about the end of the Institut Montesson's noble attempt to assist and reorient other refugees into their place of resettlement so that they could serve France in their asylum. The rigid enforcement of the regulations restricting the residence and employment of refugees contradicted the stated preference of government officials for their dispersal into agricultural labour. Refugee assistance was effectively discouraged, as it would only encourage their desire to remain and attract even more refugees after them. Asylum was therefore also refused to students and other instructors at the Institut Montesson. By March 1935, most had been ordered to leave France, and the loss of key personnel through their *refoulement* all but closed down the institute. It was transformed from a centre for refugee assistance and retraining into a small commercial enterprise. Under the name of the Ateliers Latour, it turned to the manufacture and sale of metalwork and woodwork.[75]

## 'True political refugees'

Each new wave of refugees during the 1930s accentuated the unfolding cri-sis of asylum. A further rupture was the Saarland plebiscite of 5 January 1935 to restore the Saar to Germany. An industrial region on the Franco-German border, the Saarland had been administered by France since the 1919 peace settlement under a League of Nations mandate. The plebiscite on its future political arrangements—union with France or restoration to Germany—had been scheduled since France took on the mandate. The result now left the French border very exposed to new refugees, among them French sympa-thisers and collaborators, and anti-Nazis who had gone to the Saar to escape persecution. Many therefore fled Nazism a second time.[76]

The French government maintained that the settlement of Saar refugees was a matter for the League of Nations, and that France's responsibility extended only to those whose political attitudes, race, or religion gave them plausible reasons to fear reprisals from the German government; only they were legitimately political refugees and were to be admitted to France.[77]

Yet Interior Minister Régnier was adamant that because the number of those who had come to France immediately after the plebiscite approximated the number of plebiscite votes for integration with France, they were French sympathisers and not political refugees. Only German Jews and the leaders of political parties hostile to Germany could claim the protection of the French government therefore.[78] There followed on 24 January the forced refoulement of 'a thousand' Saarlanders across the German border, and the closure of the border behind them. It was a sight that astounded outside observers for the authoritarian way in which it was conducted, and the fact that the French had let it 'happened under the jeers of the Nazis'.[79]

The French government justified its actions because it needed to police the border and movements across it far more rigorously. Formal regulations prescribed who could cross it: those with personal or business ties were favoured, as were those who could live independently and therefore would not be an encumbrance on the French labour market.[80] Under these conditions, over half of those who sought admission were allowed entry: a total of 4045 from 6753 Saarlanders who had presented themselves at the border by 8 February. Another 467 were subsequently returned after an examination of their papers. By 20 February, the number of admissions had fallen to 4831, from 11,141 who sought entry, with 502 later refoulements.[81]

During the Saar emergency of January 1935, therefore, restrictions on immigration and refugees turned to the frontier itself. As restrictive regulations on residence and foreign workers were strictly enforced, so a concerted effort was made to regulate entry at the vulnerable points on the border. As admission favoured those whose ties with France best assured their integration, and those with the means to support themselves, divisions between refugee groups emerged, with distinct categories identifying those allowed to reside unhindered and those vulnerable to the force of France's restrictive practices. Those who were identified as most exposed to persecutions or retributions for their political backgrounds, race, or religion, were divided from the popular movements. France acknowledged its particular protection obligations for those who had advocated union of the Saar with France and had therefore compromised their security if they remained after the region was returned to Germany. All these groups were properly designated as 'political refugees'. Within the popular movements, those with ties to France, whether familial or business, were divided from those who did not have these ties. Admission favoured the former while the remainder had no place; many disappeared into the growing tide of clandestine refugees, finding illegal passage across the border and an illegal existence inside France.

Others, France insisted, although displaced by events, were the responsibility of the League of Nations and should be brought into its international effort for refugee resettlement. Until the League had decided what it could do for the Saar refugees, a decision it did not reach until July 1935 when the Nansen passport was extended to them, they were returned to the Saarland.[82] Two classes of refugees had therefore been created, one, the 'political refugees', for which France recognised a protection obligation, and the other a popular movement from political ruptures whose welfare and fortunes depended largely on international gestures. Both nevertheless contended with the same restrictive and hostile regime that then characterised asylum.

French responses, to be sure, were confused and driven as much by the fear of the impact of new refugees on the French labour market as by the unexpected emergency that followed the Saar plebiscite. The great uncertainty about what to do was reflected in an Interministerial Commission meeting on the Saar issue in June 1935. Despite concerns for the welfare of the refugees, the Labour Ministry categorically opposed the very suggestion that be allowed to work. In the name of French workers, the Labour Ministry prhibited any further competition between foreign and French workers.[83] A colony in Brazil was mentioned, and the War Ministry stated that it would not oppose the recruitment of qualified individuals into the Foreign Legion. The Interior Ministry, for its part, considered that France could not properly decide its policy without knowing how much it would be reimbursed by the League of Nations for the expenses it had already incurred for its assistance to the Saar refugees. In the meantime, it was caught in a dilemma; it could not expel them, and, the Interministerial Commission was acutely aware, could it not 'purely and simply cast them onto the street'.[84]

The Saarland refugees therefore brought into question once again the most difficult aspect of the refugee problem, a refugee's status within French society. By refusing them permission to work, the government opened up sharp divisions between the left and right in the Chamber of Deputies. Government measures had extended protection to refugees by allowing residence, but stripped asylum of substance by revoking work entitlements. Their residence therefore was highly precarious, as they could easily fall foul of the law by any illegal act on which their bodies and souls depended. Questions about the meaning of asylum and of France's responsibilities were consequently asked in debates in the chamber and other attacks on government measures, in propositions for law reform, and in general critical commentary of policy measures and the conditions of refugees.

The challenge from the left was first taken up by Jean Garchery, a communist deputy from Paris, who argued that the refusal of the right of refugees to work had stripped them of the right of asylum, as protection was meaningful only if refugees could earn a living. In a debate of 29 January 1935 that grew from an expression of grievances to a wide-ranging defence of asylum, in ideological terms by the left and in more practical terms by the right, the critical issue was the government's refusal of work permits. This had forced many refugees into illegal employment and therefore exposed them to the possibility of expulsion for breaching French law. Garchery argued that expulsion and refoulement were not only the cause of great anxieties among refugees but also harmed the French republic because of the secrecy of their execution. Only an inquiry into the practices of expulsion and refoulement, he demanded, along with the abrogation of the law of 3 December 1849 which authorised expulsion, would again demonstrate that France's main concern was the respect for a refugee's right of asylum.[85]

Garchery's attack recalls the instance of Clovis Hugues in 1882, when he accused the government of secrecy and unaccountability in its arbitrary use of these powers. Hugues had also called for the abrogation of the expulsion provisions of the law of 3 December 1849, but a half-century later the same problems persisted, their arbitrary use and the denial of protection. Both Hugues and Garchery stressed the principles of the right of asylum and French republican traditions, which expulsion and refoulement violated. The right of asylum made no distinction as to the nature or character of refugees, Garchery argued; rather it advanced the principle, forgotten in practice, of aiding those in need of protection. He therefore laid at the feet of the government a demand that it give its assurance that hospitality and the right of asylum would continue to be respected as it had been in the past (a demand greeted with loud applause from the left of the chamber).[86]

Edouard Herriot, then minister of state in Pierre Flandin's government, stepped in to fend off Garchery's attack. The right of asylum was not threatened, he assured the chamber; the problem the government was addressing was that of foreign labour. With 400,000 unemployed French workers, and 800,000 foreign workers, Herriot insisted, there could be no guarantees for any foreigner who lived in France. The numbers showed that France could no longer accommodate all foreigners who wanted to live and work here, but despite that, Herriot claimed, the right of asylum was assured for those who were 'truly political refugees'. Garchery had complained, Herriot continued, not about the denial of principle but about security precautions necessary in the face of such a variety of foreigners and such complexity of their circumstances.[87] The government's measures therefore did not conflict with republicanism. It was fitting that 'reason, good sense, justice' and

> the French republican spirit incites us to make the distinction between the true political refugee, who has a right to protection, and those who, under the name of political refugee, give themselves over to certain practices incompatible not only with policy regulation but also with those of common law.[88]

This marks a contrast not only between true and false refugees, but also between good and bad ones. Anything less than the measures the government had taken would open asylum to those who did not merit France's protection, such as subversives, political agitators, foreign infiltrators, and those who broke the law, who all exposed the country to serious dangers.

The 'republican spirit', Herriot concluded, was assured because these measures strengthened republican institutions, especially the right of asylum.[89]

The divergence between the left and right in the Chamber of Deputies on the question of the right of asylum therefore also marked a divergence between them on republicanism. Herriot offered a closed republic, self-protective and rigorous in the implementation of its laws and justice against foreigners, fearing their impact on French society and its national security. The right of asylum as practiced in the face of the foreign influx of the mid-1930s, he could therefore maintain, was at once consistent with republican traditions and a central plank of republican justice. On the political left, the right of asylum was fundamental to an open republic, receptive to foreigners and humanitarian in spirit towards those seeking France's protection from the dangers to their lives and liberties they faced in their own countries. It was also a republic receptive to a past that had informed it with traditions of hospitality and tolerance. Asylum therefore also embraced a nationalist spirit, which the fascist Jacques Doriot, in the year before he established his ultra-nationalist Parti Populaire Français, described as a 'sacred tradition of this country'.[90]

Two questions remained open for argument and assertions of moral probity. How were the distinctions made between true and false refugees? Did the right of asylum have meaning if it could be used to legitimise exclusionary practices? Herriot could assert that the identification of those who were truly political refugees upheld the integrity of the right of asylum, because it assured the protection of those who were at genuine risk because of their political background, race, or religion. This was evidence enough that the government's approach served French interests. The Foreign Ministry made this clear in its dealings with the High Commission for German refugees when pressed about France's restrictive refugee policy in 1934. France was obliged to consider the character and the circumstances of all who sought admission, and as a consequence the right of asylum could not take precedence over the government's sovereign right to make laws in respect to refugees.[91]

Herriot, however, made no defence of the restrictions that even the true refugees faced. If these were considered, socialist leader Léon Blum intervened, then there was no right of asylum in practice. The right of asylum, Blum argued, could not be separated from the right to work, and as residence entitlements largely depended on employment, and therefore on the provision of work permits, the refusal to issue work permits was effectively a denial of asylum. Blum therefore suggested that the distinction between a true and a false refugee was an economic one. Refugees without private means did not find asylum in France because they were barred from the labour market; they instead faced removal from the country if they tried to earn a living.[92] Blum cut to the quick when he identified the fundamental elements of the crisis: the measures employed by the government and its administration forced refugees to break the law, and therefore left them vulnerable to refoulement and expulsion.[93] These had become the central planks of immigration policy, Garchery had complained; they allowed France to refuse admission to refugees it deemed undesirable and to divest itself of unwanted foreigners because of their impositions on the labour market.[94] By separating the right to work and the right of asylum, Blum continued, the government had erected 'a wall of money' between two categories of refugees, those who had no need to work and those who could not live without it.[95]

Ralph Schor comments that the right of asylum was contested between the left and right 'less on the principle than on the application', with rightist parties demanding a selective approach while the left was more supportive of an unrestricted approach.[96] The debate of 29 January 1935 illustrates this divergence at its clearest. The right of asylum framed the terms of public policy on both the right and left. As Flandin's government defended itself from the criticisms railed against it, the left offered a defence of the rights of those suffering under the weight of the exclusionary measures.

The broad distinction between left and right, however, misleadingly simplifies this crisis of asylum. Certainly, as this debate demonstrated, the left was readily identified as the socialist party, the *Section Française d'Internationale Ouvrière* (French Section of the Worker's International—SFIO) and the French Communist Party (PCF). But the right is more elusive. The exclusionary measures of the 1930s had been taken by governments of the Radical Party, which bridged the centre and included a socialist wing that Edouard Herriot himself led, and which would, in 1936, enter into the Popular Front coalition with the SFIO and the PCF. The governments of Pierre Flandin (8 November 1934–1 June 1935) and Pierre Laval (7 June 1935–24 January 1936) are especially criticised for their anti-immigrant and anti-refugee positions. On the extreme right, nationalist sentiment was distinctly xenophobic, but as Jacques Doriot's contribution to the debate of January 1935 shows, nationalist sentiment could also take some comfort from the invocation of the French tradition of asylum.

Across the political spectrum, opinion shifted with each refugee group. By the 1930s, the Russian and Armenian refugees had established themselves and, although vulnerable to the restrictive regulations on foreign workers, they posed few problems for public policy. They had a distinct status of sorts under the Nansen passport scheme, but most importantly they had integrated into France. Most hostility was directed at the latest refugees, the German Jews. They were victims twice over, of French anti-Semitism and of resistance of French professional class to their competition. Associations of lawyers and medical practitioners were instrumental in securing restrictive laws that prohibited the entry of foreigners into their professions. French Jews were especially anxious that foreign Jews might upset their hard-won status by flooding the professions and alienating opinion. Trade unions, acting to defend French workers against foreign competition, displayed similar xenophobic tendencies and pressured governments to bar foreign workers completely from occupations with high levels of unemployment.[97] On the other hand, socialist and communist refugees from Italy and Germany found sympathisers and supporters, and even engaged militants, among French socialists and communists, and because of this French conservatives and nationalists could not suspend their suspicion that they were subversives and a threat to national security.

There was therefore a complex mix of allegiances, sympathies and antipathies that formed, and even reformed, on a shifting political surface. Public opinion, as Schor has measured it in journals, newspapers, and other forms of public discourse, spread across the range, but it was clear nevertheless that France felt itself exposed and vulnerable before an ever-pressing foreign migration. The exclusionist tendencies were profound, and it was extremely difficult to take a stand against it. There was difficulty, first of all, in winning consensus, even within the chamber. Even the most exclusionary measures were incremental in nature; amendments to existing laws responded to protectionist impulses and anxieties in public opinion, while the volatility of government made sweeping reform of the law impossible. France's malaise, furthermore, was the ideological conflict about what was in its own best interests. Politics and society were therefore fractured and at times France turned against itself, such as during the 1934 Paris riots and the 1936 general strike after the election of the Popular Front. As the international situation deteriorated, with Germany adopting a more assertive foreign policy when it reoccupied the Rhineland, and with the outbreak of civil war in Spain, France seemed to drift towards even more restrictive tendencies as it became more sensitive to the threats at its borders and the pressures from still more refugees.

# 10
# Reform, Renewal, and the End of Asylum

Restrictionists had gained the upper hand, but voices advocating reform to take immigration policy away from these restrictionist tendencies could still be heard, most prominently within the socialist and communist parties. They argued for more humanity in public responses, and their contributions to public discourses about migration and asylum suggests that Schor's assessment of the divergence on the question of right of asylum does not go far enough. The political left and right were separated by more than divisions over the function of asylum, that is, the how and when admission should be allowed and to whom it should be allowed. These voices of reform intended a return to the fundamental principles of asylum. The right's negation of asylum went well beyond the exclusionist tendencies of public policy; it also amounted to the negation of the principles asylum had traditionally signified. The neglect of these principles, the advocates of reform insisted, continued the exclusionist drift in policy. Asylum, they argued, was above all invested with ideals that recognised the innate right of refugees to protection from the sources of their troubles, which in turn imposed an obligation on their protecting state to recognise their rights and to respect their humanity in domestic law and public policy. The arguments for the reform of immigration policy first and foremost aimed to reinvigorate asylum with these ideals.

## Reform and renewal

Taking the lead among the advocates of reform was the socialist deputy Marius Moutet. In November 1934, he presented a draft statute on immigration that was a direct response to a further tightening of existing restrictive measures. On 20 November 1934, the government put forward a bill to amend the law of 3 December 1849 on expulsion to impose a mandatory prison term of one to five years for the failure to comply with an order. Its explicit purpose was to equate the breach of an expulsion order with infractions of the Civil Code's prohibitions on the residence of individuals who were recognised as a danger to the public order or national security.[1] Moutet's proposition was listed for 11 December 1934, and was actively promoted by the League for the Rights of Man, which published in full the draft bill and Moutet's exposition to chamber.[2]

A member of the central committee of the League for the Rights of Man and the socialist party's own immigration committee, Moutet had established a reputation in humanitarian causes and assistance for foreign workers through his ties with Russian refugee groups and as a director of the association The Friends of Foreign Workers (*Les Amis des Travailleurs Étrangers, Comité Français pour le Statut et la Défense des Travailleurs Étrangers*), made up of socialists and trade unionists sympathetic to this cause.[3] His proposition centred on the affront the treatment of foreigners caused to the values of the rights of man, 'one hundred and fifty years after their declaration'.[4] Exclusionary policies belittled the nation as much as they abused the rights of the immigrants, Moutet protested, as they rendered their freedoms precarious and subjected them to an arbitrary decision of the interior minister. There was no protection from error, the abuse of power, and even retribution, as expulsion was a decision taken in secret, with no consideration of an individual's circumstances, and with no formal justification. It was therefore, Moutet asserted, analogous to the *lettres de cachet* of the old regime by which the king could arbitrarily condemn a subject. Only the intervention of the League for the Rights of Man and the socialist party itself, Moutet continued, had prevented expulsion from being abused as a means of vengeance against commercial rivals or creditors through false denunciation.[5]

Moutet insisted that this regime, based on a law of 1849 which had not been amended since, failed to reflect modern legal principles and failed to guarantee rights. 'Must we,' he asked, 'keep this totally arbitrary regime ... or should we find one that is more liberal and more just and is yet responsive to the government's preoccupations with civil order and the number of foreigners?' Moutet's proposed statute on immigration would sweep away this antiquated law and renew the immigration regime with statutory provisions that addressed a variety of concerns that migration raised: the moderation, through judicial safeguards, of the ministerial power of expulsion; clarification of the legal status of foreign residents and foreign workers; the regulation of foreign labour; the protection of the rights of refugees; the regulation of migration proper; and even the regulation of the laws on the surveillance of suspect foreigners.[6]

Without going so far as to categorise distinct types of foreign residents, Moutet distinguished two broad classes: those who could be expelled and those who could not. The first class required administrative and legal protections to guarantee their rights from arbitrary power, which only a judicial review of ministerial orders could ensure. The second class comprised refugees and the stateless, who were most vulnerable, as they could not be repatriated or expelled into other countries, and therefore should be protected against expulsion. It is for their protection that the right of asylum had to be reinvigorated with principle. Moutet's proposition was therefore a major statement of both principle and intent that confronted the restrictionist drift of public policy. It identified the reform necessary to redress the worst elements that had become far too evident in the application of policy. Although the proposition made no further progress through the chamber, the League for the Rights of Man continued to advocate it as a statute suitable for the reform of immigration policy, and it remained a model for subsequent reform proposals.

The left's defence of the rights of refugees gave the supporters of reform hope that the Popular Front would adopt a new statute on immigration after it was elected to government in May 1936.[7] Marcel Livian, who also held a position on the socialist party's immigration committee, published his own immigration code at this time, setting out a legal framework on which all aspects of the entry and residence of foreigners, including provisions that legislated for the status of refugees, would be based.[8] But it was a new proposition for a legal statute put forward by a communist deputy from the Rhône—Georges Lévy—in July, that held out the promise of comprehensive reform. Lévy's proposal aimed to do nothing less than reconfigure entirely the legal and moral basis on which foreigners could live and work in France, and on which refugees would be guaranteed asylum.

Lévy reflected the views of a genuine coalition of the left, as he spoke for 70 other deputies who had put their name on the bill.[9] He took Moutet's proposition of December 1934 as his starting point, and even began his exposition of his own statute's intentions by quoting in full the first four paragraphs of Moutet's exposition. This strengthened Lévy's argument that the circumstances confronting foreigners over the year and a half since Moutet had put forward his proposition had indeed worsened. He gave the examples of the fathers of French children having their residence permits revoked, and of husbands and wives being separated by expulsion orders. Refugees and stateless were obliged to leave the country although every frontier was closed to them, and were thereupon imprisoned for failing to leave. France, Lévy asserted, could no longer claim to be the 'land of asylum' it was once believed to be, as it no longer offered guarantees of protection to those most in need of it.[10]

Lévy proposed as much as Moutet in terms of the power of expulsion. He backed Moutet's bid to repeal the 1849 law on expulsion and proposed further juridical safeguards before an order could be enforced. But Lévy's propostion went beyond Moutet's in important ways. It set out a social and labour policy that would apply equally to French and foreign workers. The right to work for foreign workers would be legislated, as were other social rights, such as the right to change occupations and professions, guarantees of salary, pensions and unemployment relief, and the right of membership in political, cultural, and labour organisations. A legislative statute, Lévy declared, would return immigration policy to democratic conceptions inspired by French tradition.[11]

The protections extended to refugees and the stateless were Lévy's major innovation. They were to be exempt from expulsion, refoulement, and extradition altogether. His statute codified rights due to refugees and the stateless and set down a definition of the refugee.[12] It also set down the social and civil rights of resident foreigners, which were protected by law, and it limited state intervention to two prescribed conditions: conspiracy against the security of the state, and a grave breach of the law.[13]

The propositions of Marius Moutet and Georges Lévy addressed more than the absence of a formal statute on migration and the residence of foreigners and refugees. Because their primary concern was the absence of principle from policy, the propositions can be properly considered as the renewal of policy. Their intent was the reinvigoration of policy with principles of justice and the recognition of rights that had been stripped away over the years since the late 1920s, as the measures against foreigners became increasing exclusionary and punitive. By the mid-1930s, as Jean Garchery had protested to the Chamber of Deputies, expulsion and refoulement had become the corner stones of French policy. This had rendered the protection of refugees uncertain, and indeed had negated the principles underpinning asylum. These propositions reset asylum on firmer ground, assured of its protective principles.

Moutet and Lévy worked for a new statute in domestic law. The exclusionary trend in government policy, however, had so disillusioned other advocates of reform that they turned away entirely from statutes of domestic law to seek solutions at the international level. As preparations were being made at the government level for a League of Nations conference on the refugees from Germany, scheduled for Geneva in July 1936, where the terms for new intergovernmental arrangements would be settle upon, these advocates of reform turned their attention to the possibilities of entrenching the principles of asylum in international law. The question they asked was how the new intergovernmental arrangements might compel governments to liberalise their domestic restrictions on the rights of refugees.

To this end, a non-governmental preliminary conference was organised in Paris on 20 and 21 June 1936 to draft a text to put to the forthcoming Geneva conference. Under the title Assembly for the Right of Asylum (*Rassemblement pour le Droit d'Asile*), representatives from political parties, trade unions, and other concerned organisations met to discuss the refugee problem and canvas solutions. It brought important together political figures from European socialist and communist parties with international associations that had taken an active part in refugee assistance, such as the League for the Rights of Man and the International League against Anti-Semitism, various Quaker agencies, the International Union of League of Nations Assocations, and the International Red Cross.[14]

Speakers were united in their belief that the international scope of the refugee problem gave the right of asylum a meaning and purpose greater than national political preoccupations. It followed that the principles it signified should inform an international regime relating to the protection of refugees. The evident failure of national governments to respect the right of asylum influenced the conference's objective therefore, which was to agree to a text that was fit for incorporation into the League's proposed arrangements. This failure also proved the need for an effective international organisation to take on the responsibilities of refugee protection that national governments had abandoned, especially after the failure of the original High Commission for German Refugees established in 1933.

For the purposes of this preliminary conference, refugees were broadly considered to be 'those who are chased from their homelands for having defended liberty and peace'.[15] With this in mind, the principles that underpinned asylum could be more precisely identified. Marcel Cachin, a communist senator from Paris, stated that the objective of the conference was to 'assure political exiles ... of the right to live a dignified existence in the democratic nations where they find refuge'. The failure of governments was demonstrated by this one premise. 'We find ourselves', Cachin continued, 'needing to remind the leaders of the great democracies of their obligations to respect the old right of asylum, a secular right, a right applied in the oldest civilisations'.[16]

Jean Longuet, a delegate of the socialist party, emphasised this notion of an 'old' right of asylum. It was a very ancient and noble French tradition, he said, which the revolution had adopted as its own, which the Second Republic assumed when recalling Karl Marx in 1848, and which Gambetta and Jaurès defended during the Third Republic.[17] Longuet exalted the valued ideals of this right, which could now guide Europe through the problems it faced. It was a right that merited the creation of an independent, international judicial body to protect and defend refugees from the abusive authority of the state.[18]

Expressions of principle, however, could not leverage opinion away from the pragmatic question of effective solutions. Once the question of solutions was asked, therefore, it was apparent that the League of Nations' arrangements had their own failings, because they too could not assure protection. Paul Perrin, secretary of the organising committee of the preliminary conference, believed that the League of Nations' intergovernmental arrangements were not suitable in their current form to serve as a statute on the right of asylum. Perrin explained that they applied to one category of refugees at a time and made no distinction between those who were political refugees and those who were not; they did not uphold the inviolability of the right of asylum; they did not separate the conditions of employment for refugees from arbitrary administrative acts of national governments; and they did not guarantee the free social and cultural activity of refugees. They were nevertheless, he maintained, a starting point for a new understanding of asylum and the rights of refugees. The arrangements relating to Russian, Armenian and other Nansen refugees had normalised their legal status, and had consequently set in place certain principles of refugee rights. Residence entitlements in their countries of asylum extended commensurate rights: the right to work, the right to welfare, and protection from refoulement, expulsion, and extradition. When these rights were not assured, governments failed in their protection obligations. Their failure was sufficient reason for new arrangements, Perrin believed. He therefore suggested a new text that would correct the failings of the existing intergovernmental arrangements and put in place new norms that would hold governments to respect the right of asylum. Above all, a new text would give a definition of the refugee that was more applicable to immediate circumstances than the definitions in the existing arrangements which identified specific classes of refugees based on their national origins. Only this would guide governments, Perrin declared. 'We must try to define the notion and the legal status of the political refugee in a text which, by its nature, can be used in all free countries for their legislative labours'.[19] More directly, the final resolutions of the conference demanded five specific acts of government to redress the difficulties their policies had imposed on refugees: an amnesty for all political refugees; a prohibition on their expulsion; the annulation of all existing expulsion orders; a right in law to work and hold a salaried position; and the recognition of a document of identity which conferred on refugees all their rights.[20]

Reflecting the fact that so many delegates represented labour organisations and European socialist and communist parties, the conference agreed to a definition of a refugee in which the key element was political persecution at the hands of fascism. Speakers referred to 'political refugees', who the final resolutions described as those 'forced to migrate not only because of their political activities, but also for their unionist, pacifist or scientific activities'.[21] Persecution for religious or racial reasons was secondary, relegated to the third article of the final text.[22]

This made possible two quite distinct interpretations of the conference's outcome. One commentary suggested that asylum, because it defended rights from the abuses of government, also resisted the existing political and economic order and was therefore inherently revolutionary. 'No government of a democratic country', it held, 'can bar political immigrants on the pretext that in principle it does not accord the right of asylum to political refugees'.[23] A new revolutionary coalition could therefore form around the right of asylum, since it could combine the heritage of revolution with the misery of the economic depression to become a powerful political weapon. The popular movement and refugees were united against the political and economic order and therefore could provide a means of mobilising the *petite bourgeoisie*, peasants and workers against modern capitalism; their struggle against the giants of industry was the same as the bourgeoisie's revolutionary struggle against tyranny and feudalism.[24]

A more conservative commentary was published by the League for the Rights of Man, condemning the conference for misrepresenting the nature of the refugees then seeking asylum and for misunderstanding the nature of the persecutions they were fleeing. The speakers had in mind only 'political refugees' actively engaged in a struggle against fascism, it stated, whereas in reality the vast majority of refugees were 'non-protagonists' and victims of politics, who had become refugees 'in spite of themselves'.[25] It was in respect to these refugees, it argued, that the right of asylum needed to be reconceptualised and reinvigorated with principles of rights and juridical safeguards.

While international instruments guided national responses to refugees, they failed to address the problem of translating the principles they represented into a coherent and effective regime that guaranteed refugee protection. Only domestic law could address this problem, and therefore the League for the Rights of Man remained concerned about the failure of protection under French law and continued to advocate a new statute on migration and the status of refugees to assure their rights. It once more promoted the 1934 proposition of Marius Moutet because, it claimed, of all the propositions put forward and debated, it was a 'text very ready for enactment in law'. It addressed the concerns that the League for the Rights of Man had expressed over recent years—that expulsion was a penal measure and therefore required judicial authority, and that refugees needed to be protected from it—and did so in the most comprehensive way, by the complete abrogation of the law that authorised it.[26] But there was a sting. Expulsion had become such a major problem because no other country would accept an expelled refugee; they were consequently imprisoned for failing to comply with an expulsion order. Some other means of dealing with refugees facing expulsion orders was therefore required. Exclusionary tendencies had penetrated deeply, and the fear of dangerous elements infiltrating France in the guise of refugees was very strong indeed. In these circumstances, the League advocated internment under police supervision as the most viable alternative.[27]

## The refugee question and the Popular Front

Georges Lévy's proposition for a statute on immigration and the status of refugees was put to the Chamber of Deputies two months after the Popular Front's electoral victory of May 1936. While broadly supported, it made no progress. He put it back to the chamber again on 8 December 1936, insisting that it be given urgent attention because conditions continued to deteriorate and the evidence of xenophobia was all too common.[28] Again, on

17 January 1937, Lévy recalled the bill, and again won the chamber's support that it be adopted as quickly as possible.[29] But at no time was the statute itself put to a vote; it faltered as the Popular Front faltered.

Because it came to power with such promise, the Popular Front suffers from the criticism that it achieved little on immigration reform and the status of refugees in its short term in government. Jean-Charles Bonnet writes that one searches in vain for a text on these issues during Léon Blum's first government. This is a striking failure for Bonnet, as so many on the left had declared support for changes to immigration policy and the reinvigoration of the right of asylum. The draft statutes of Marius Moutet and Georges Lévy were ready for passage into law, and Blum himself had spoken against the punitive tendency of the immigration regime in January 1935. But no progress was made. Bonnet concludes that the Popular Front simply did not have enough time to legislate on such a complex issue.[30] This may be so, but this failure has raised questions about the Popular Front's ability to withstand the great social and economic pressures that had driven the exclusionary policies in the first place.[31]

Responding to this criticism, Marcel Livian, a member of the socialist party's immigration committee during the Popular Front, published a memoir in 1982 to defend its record.[32] The Popular Front's achievements, Livian asserts, are not to be found in a futile search for one major text but in the accumulation of a number of initiatives that in total amounted to a significant departure from former policy. If, however, one were to seek a single measure of significance taken by Blum's government in 1936, Livian argues, it was the signing of the 4 July 1936 League of Nations' provisional arrangements for the refugees from Germany.[33] They committed France to the recognition of a specific legal status for these refugees and to the implementation of international norms of refugee protection. In Livian's view, this was the first step towards the restoration of humanity in refugee policy.

These intergovernmental arrangement followed the trend that had commenced in the 1920s. The attention of Blum's government to them was further demonstrated by its ratification of the convention relating to Russian and Armenian refugees agreed by the League of Nations on 28 October 1933 but which had remained unratified since. By signing up to the convention, Blum's government agreed to adopt in French law the norms of protection it set down and the rights due to refugees that were implicit in them—to residence and work, to full social equality, to protection from expulsion, refoulement, and extradition.[34] The turn from domestic measures responsive to domestic concerns towards international norms was therefore, Livian argues, a major innovation in refugee policy during the short life of the Popular Front.

The 1936 arrangement relating to the refugees from Germany recognised their precarious legal status under domestic law and extended to them certificates of identity akin to those provided earlier to the Nansen refugees.[35] All German nationals who had come to France as refugees from Nazism could now present themselves to claim a certificate of identity under the arrangements, and therefore gain legal residence and secure work permits.[36] The certificates also allowed them to enter another country and return. They were no longer classified as foreign workers or resident foreigners and therefore were no longer subject to the same exclusionary laws on residence and work.

It was indicative of the state of the refugee problem in 1936 that the way forward for Blum's government was not through reform of domestic law but through intergovernmental arrangements. The right of asylum for refugees was assured through their legal classification as refugees recognised by international agreement. This, in Livian's view, best assured the fidelity of the socialist party to 'the right' of asylum, 'the right' to work, and therefore 'the rights of man'.[37]

The implementation of the arrangement brought refugee assistance to the centre of state administration. A consultative commission was established to administer the system of identity certificates for the German refugees. In the process, it became the point of liaison between the League of Nations, the Interior and Foreign ministries, delegates of the High Commission for the German refugees that had been reformed in 1936 under the League of Nations itself, and representatives of such organisations as the League for the Rights of Man, and the International League against Anti-Semitism. German refugees were represented by German organisations.[38] The commission's main objective was to prescribe the criteria under which refugees would qualify for the certificate of identity and to screen them, but it also identified gaps in the arrangement and solutions to fill them.[39] It was therefore instrumental in building a more complete and effective regime. The definition German refugees were given in the arrangement was one matter that the commission thought could be improved upon, because it placed the emphasis on the loss of legal protection of the German government rather than on flight from racial, religious, or political persecution.[40]

Livian's defence is merited, as the consultative commission offered the promise that any German entering France after the adoption of the 1936 arrangements could present a case for recognition as a refugee. It marked in its intent a liberalisation of the responses to refugees because it required the benevolent consideration of individual circumstances.[41] Nevertheless, the border remained firmly closed to new refugees, so it was the intent rather than the practice that suggested the liberalisation of policy. The Foreign Ministry had quite definite views on how France should face the refugee problem from this moment on. The consensus among Foreign Ministry officials at the July 1936 intergovernmental conference in Geneva, Vicki Caron finds, was that a more liberal policy towards refugees could only be possible when the size of the refugee population had stabilised. This amounted to nothing less than a prohibition on the admission of new refugees.[42] The situation, as one official put it in June 1936, was still evolving; 60,000 refugees had left Germany since the Nazis had seized power, but millions of others in the east remained candidates for emigration.[43] The priority of foreign policy, therefore, was to insulate France from these large numbers of potential refugees.

In this, France was echoing the consensus at the intergovernmental conference. No country would extend a liberal policy on refugee admission so long as other countries barred entry. The 1936 arrangement therefore addressed the circumstances of existing refugees but offered no solutions for the continuing problem. The conference indeed had no intention of providing solutions. It was declared in advance that it would 'betray its mission if it made unconsidered promises and encouraged an exodus that could aggravate troubled economies. Its object is to confront the present reality and try to stabilise it with every possible measure'.[44] This meant closing borders to new refugees while existing refugees were settled, or resettled elsewhere, and were therefore much less a burden on the national governments sitting at the Geneva conference.

## Towards the end of asylum

Far from the renewal that some had sought by the reform of the laws and regulation of immigration, or even the liberalisation of policy that seemed to have been promised with the adoption of the 1936 intergovernmental arrangements for the German refugees, a major step was instead taken towards the end of asylum.

Since the League of Nations appointed a High Commissioner for the refugees from Germany in October 1933, French governments insisted that refugees would find only temporary asylum as their protection needs would henceforth be the responsibility of the High Commission through international measures for their assistance and resettlement. This would relieve France of its burden, it was imagined, as these temporary refugees would be redistributed among other nations. Yet because the United States refused to concede any ground on its restrictive immigration quotas to admit refugees from Europe, and other new world countries followed its example by remaining closed to refugee resettlement despite the best efforts of the High Commissioner to negotiate suitable arrangements, no such redistribution was possible. France consequently insisted that it could do no more: it already had admitted the largest numbers of refugees and could not be expected to continue to admit more while the United States and other countries refused to share the burden.[45]

Refugee policy was subsequently fractured, with clear divisions between various refugee populations. The intergovernmental arrangements of July 1936 equated the refugees from Germany with the Nansen refugees of the

1920s, and France recognised its obligations under these arrangements for those admitted prior to 1 Janaury 1937. But asylum was denied to any who arrived thereafter.

It was commonly assumed that not all who had fled Germany were truly refugees. Indeed, the dilemma of these years, Caron demonstrates, was that restrictive policy measures were framed around fears that fifth-columnists and other undesirables, and more unwelcome competitors for French jobs, were hidden among the refugees.[46] These profound suspicions seldom allowed the French to see the genuine character of those in flight from Nazism. Even the definition set down in the intergovernmental arrangements of July 1936 seemed ambiguous when put under scrutiny. It defined a German refugee as an individual who, 'in law or in fact ... does not enjoy the protection of the Government of the Reich'.[47] Derived from the definitions adopted in the earlier intergovernmental arrangements for the Nansen refugees whose statelessness left them without the protection of any government, this definition seemed not to recognise their unique origins as victims of racial, religious, and political persecution whom the Nazi Reich wanted to rid itself of.

Moreover, France could not isolate itself from the refugee movements coming from central and eastern Europe simply by closing its border. Denied legal admission, refugees turned to illegal means. The closure of the border indeed escalated the refugee problem. The question for French domestic policy and law was subsequently how to deal with these illegal refugees.

This is why one final attempt to devise a statute on immigration was made in early 1938 when Philippe Serre prepared a comprehensive reform programme. A deputy from the Meurthe-et-Moselle, Serre served as Under-Secretary of State for Labour in Camille Chautemps' government of June 1937, and was appointed to the new office of Under-Secretary of State for Immigration in February 1938. Within a month of his appointment, Serre presented his plans for both institutional reform, through the creation of a new bureaucratic structure that would coordinate all aspects of migration, and legal reform through a new statute.[48]

His plans called for an immigration and naturalisation service to regulate and enforce the administration of policy and coordinate the functions of all ministries with an interest in immigration matters. Its work would be complemented by two agencies, one responsible for frontier surveillance, and the other dedicated exclusively to the vetting of claims for admission as refugees, a refinement of the consultative commission established in 1936.[49] Unlike earlier draft statutes that had sought to reinvigorate asylum with principle, Serre's statute was almost exclusively concerned with control and policing. It enumerated four categories of foreigners: industrial workers, agricultural workers, artisans, and non-workers (tourists and self-supporting immigrants). There were two groups distinguished within each, temporary entrants, with no authority to settle, and those who were authorised to make their residence in France. Lawful and unlawful residence was determined within these categories, and the statute set down regulations and penalties for infractions of residence laws. There were 19 separate articles on the enforcement of expulsion orders, which allowed for an appeal to a special commission.[50] Importantly, the draft statute contained no provisions relating to entry, and the laws on residence and work permits remained unchanged. The one concession to a statutory guarantee of protection for refugees was their exemption from expulsion orders. Serre's statute proposed instead that refugees who could not be expelled should be interned in labour camps.[51]

It is this point that most strongly marked Serre's draft statute and administrative reforms as a point of transition between earlier proposals for the liberalisation of policy and reactionary policy that reinforced powers of policing and control. Serre's plans reflect new tensions in the refugee question that had arisen since 1936. He formulated his statute amid contradictory pressures. Deputies on the right expected him to reinforce surveillance and repression, while the left expected legal guarantees.[52] Trade unions and professional organisations demanded stronger measures of labour market protection and entry to the professions, while immigrant workers pressed their demands for more effective action against illegal immigration in order to protect their own hard-won gains.[53] Serre himself stated that his objective was to devise complementary institutional and statutory reform, believing that the political dilemmas of the refugee question were too great to be resolved in the enactment of a single law. A range of initiatives was instead required, in his view, in order to achieve all the desired outcomes of sound policy.[54]

These contradictory pressures made consensus on immigration reform and refugee policy impossible. Moreover, a background of political violence shaped the protectionist character of Serre's plans. Outrage at political assassinations, terrorist attacks, and other politically motivated violence—at the centre of which were foreign agitators—turned the notion of France as a place of asylum into an image of France as the 'rubbish dump of Europe'.[55] Laws that strengthened the government's powers of policing foreigners were favoured much more in popular opinion than concessions to the rights of refugees and foreigners. The deteriorating international political climate was also significant. The German occupation of Austria in March 1938 unleashed new refugees and new restrictive impulses.

Serre's proposals seemed to fit well into the mood of the moment, but the response of the Foreign Ministry ensured their failure. It expressed its utmost hostility to the faintest suggestion of liberalisation contained in Serre's plans. Foreign Minister Paul-Boncour indeed stressed how national measures in relation to refugees were now limited only to the provisions of international agreements. The term 'political refugee', he suggested, related to interpretations of international conventions. Discrete national statutes on asylum led the refugee question in new and difficult directions.[56] It suited France's intentions that there were no guarantees of the right of asylum in international convention; rather, Paul-Boncour continued, international conventions lifted the burden on individual states. The work of an international body charged with refugee assistance and resettlement in other parts of the world had absolved individual states of their protection obligations and would therefore help remove refugees from France and divest it of the social and economic distress they had brought with them. A statute on immigration and the status of foreigners would instead hold France to obligations towards refugees that would have 'grave consequences'. Because Serre's draft statute, Paul-Boncourt stressed, would grant guarantees and confer rights, it was as valid for future refugees as it was for existing ones. They were undesirable, and reform would only encourage them and their 'complete lack of scruples'; their 'disingenuousness', the 'fraudulent means' by which they had gained entry to France, Paul-Boncour went on 'condemned to misery and degradation ... [our] ... small businesses, artisans, intellectuals, not to mention the burden they place on housing'.[57] A consultative commission of the kind Serre proposed furthermore would not only encourage this immigration, it would also encourage the formation of refugee associations, which had the potential to compromise France's diplomatic relations, and would turn the loyalties of refugees away from their place of asylum.[58]

Serre's draft statute consequently went no further. From April 1938, following the dissolution of the Popular Front with the fall of the Chautemps government, Jean-Charles Bonnet writes, a government emerged that shared popular anxieties about the 'inassimilable foreigners [who] lived among themselves, married among themselves, had their own religion, their own priests, their own newspapers, their own customs, but asked for and often received unemployment assistance'.[59] Formed by the Radical Party under premier Edouard Daladier, this government was decidedly more reactionary to the political dilemmas posed by refugees, immigrants, and foreigners. This attitude shaped its first measure, a decree-law of 2 May 1938 on the policing of foreigners, which pitted the power of the state against these 'inassimilable' elements.[60]

Each new turn of events in Germany and central and eastern Europe in the late 1930s not only marked a deterioration in the international political climate, it also threatened an escalation of the refugee crisis and spurred a deepening of anti-foreign and anti-Jewish sentiment in France. The political response was to put even more resources into policing foreigners and on restricting refugee entry. The German *Anschluss* of Austria in March 1938 signalled a new round of Jewish persecutions and a dramatic flood of new refugees into Western Europe. The anti-Semitic laws that had been introduced in Germany over the previous five years were introduced immediately in Austria. Before the *Anschluss*, some 25,000 refugees were leaving Germany annually; the number grew considerably afterwards.[61]

The numbers at this time are no more than estimates, however. The League of Nations estimated that no less than 120,000 refugees left the Third Reich in 1938–9.[62] One guess put the number in France at 40,000, with another 1000 to 1500 clandestine arrivals a month, giving a total of some 30,000 German and Austrian Jews illegally in France, when the decree-law of 2 May 1938 was adopted.[63] France's resolve against admission therefore held firm, but it could not police the entire border. Restrictions on entry only nurtured these clandestine movements and French anxieties consequently found a new source of concern in these large numbers of illegal foreigners fighting the tide of exclusionary and repressive policing.

Decree-laws of 14 May and 12 November 1938 consolidated that of 2 May with specific regulations and penalties. Together the three laws constituted a new, punitive regime on entry, residence, and the employment of foreigners, centred on the needs of policing and national security.[64] Sanctions included imprisonment for clandestine entry, for unjustifiable delays in applications for residence permits, and, for those with valid permits, for the failure to advise a change of address. Policing was also extended to French citizens who accommodated them, whether commercially or privately; they faced penalties for failing to declare a foreigner's presence.[65]

Still, amidst a punitive regime, statements of principle were both necessary and expected. Asylum was sustained as an ideal while acts of the government denied it in practice. The ever-growing number of foreigners had compelled the government to act, Daladier declared, for reasons of national security, economic security, and the public order. Yet France's traditions of hospitality and liberalism were protected, he reassured the deputies in the chamber when announcing the decree-law of 2 May. 'The present decree-law does not modify any of the normal conditions of access to our territory', Daladier said, nor did it restrict the 'traditional rules of French hospitality, and its spirit of liberalism and humanity, which is one of the noblest aspects of our national spirit'. This 'spirit of generosity', he continued, extended to those 'whom we regard as foreigners of good faith'. The resolve was firm, on the other hand, to inflict 'severe penalties [on] every foreigner who shows himself unworthy of our hospitality'. Among these were those who had 'illegitimately' assumed the title of political refugee and had abused French trust by doing so. The law, in short, aimed to create 'a purified atmosphere surrounding the foreigner of good faith' that maintained traditional benevolence while applying 'just and necessary vigour' against those considered unworthy of France's hospitality.[66]

This 'purified atmosphere' required a clear distinction between clandestine immigrants who had illegally entered France and political refugees who could demand asylum. The League for the Rights of Man considered article 2 of the decree-law of 2 May an important departure from the general application of laws relating to foreigners that made no concessions for refugees. The article stated: 'political refugees who, at the time of their entry into France, have claimed this status at the first frontier post in forms and conditions that will be determined, will be the object of an administrative inquiry for which the Interior Minister will make statutes'.[67] This, in the view of the League, marked the first recognition in French law of the 'political refugee' as a specific juridical notion and not a description of fact.[68] But other commentators were critical of the classification because it failed to recognise the true nature of a refugee's flight. 'They have hidden at friends' houses; they have wandered in the countryside, in forests, and taken to the roads and have found the frontier [...] Then they have secretly penetrated French territory'. They were clandestine immigrants left unprotected by the 'rigorous and negative' measures of the law.[69]

This article assured an investigation of all foreigners who declared they were political refugees at the moment they entered France, but how this would be conducted was not prescribed in any of the three decree-laws of 1938. The League for the Rights of Man envisaged this as a task most suited to the consultative commission established for the implementation of the July 1936 arrangements, an impartial, juridical body that had given 'the most encouraging results', and which Philippe Serre had suggested could serve precisely this purpose in his proposals of March 1938.[70] Instead, the government conferred this authority onto the police through general instructions that set out the criteria under which a political refugee could be admitted.[71]

These instructions commenced from the entirely negative premise that there had been such 'scandalous abuse' of the classification of the political refugee in the past. How then could a political refugee be identified? It was decided, firstly, to turn back 'without pity' all foreigners, even political refugees, who had previously been expelled or whose name appeared on a circular of 'interdiction'. Secondly, each person presumed to be a political refugee was required to demonstrate a reason, other than an ideological one, for choosing France as a place of asylum. Personal attachments, prior residence, a 'perfect knowledge' of the language, previous services in France, business or intellectual affairs with certain 'honourable' French groups, were demonstrable criteria. Thirdly, admission was refused to foreigners coming from a third country where they could have stayed and requested asylum. Finally, belatedly, it was accepted that in certain circumstances admission had to be granted to any who could demonstrate they were forced to flee from imminent danger to their lives or they faced the complete loss of their possessions.[72] Rather than a degree of freedom in asylum, however, they faced placement in reception centres.[73]

It was also finally recognised that not all expulsion orders could be carried out as few refugees found a country prepared to admit them. It was expected, nevertheless, that the individual facing expulsion should approach the consular authorities of at least three countries where the greatest chance of being admitted were believed to exist. The refusal of these foreign consulates to issue a visa was therefore irrefutable proof of their inability to find asylum elsewhere. Internment followed. The prefects who instigated the expulsion order then recommended where they should be placed, normally a commune where there would be the 'least inconvenience' for the maintenance of public order and the safeguard of national security—that is within easy proximity of the police or gendarmerie. They also had to be placed where there were opportunities for suitable employment or where the internees could live in a milieu where 'moral and financial assistance' from charitable organisations was available. The individual was allowed to circulate freely within the limits of the circumscribed territory but was required to report to the local police or gendarmerie weekly during the first year, and monthly thereafter.[74]

In view of the criticisms throughout the decade of the arbitrary and inhumane use of refoulement and expulsion against refugees, and their imprisonment for failing to leave when ordered, it is not surprising that the new decree-laws seemed to introduce more humane methods for dealing with those whom France wanted to be rid of. It provided a degree of protection when refugees had been previously cast adrift, to be tossed from one border post to another, or from one country's prison to another's.[75] Yet these provisions, it must be remembered, related to those recognised as political refugees and therefore excluded the increasing number of clandestine refugees whose illegal status left them entirely without protection.

Through 1938 and 1939, therefore, French policy was dedicated towards the exclusion of new refugees. The end of asylum is marked, firstly, by Foreign Minister Paul-Boncour's rejection of Serre's proposals and his statement that international measures would help France divest itself of its refugees. It would be marked later by France's turn against these same international measures for refugee assistance. It was marked finally by a relentless trend towards internment.

In June 1938, Daladier's government displayed its good faith in international initiatives when France agreed to host a conference called by President Roosevelt of the United States to form an Intergovernmental Committee on Refugees. Held at the spa resort of Evian-les-Bains between 6 and 15 July 1938, the conference aimed to persuade countries hitherto reluctant to accept refugees to open their borders. Its failure was evident even before it commenced, however, as all of the main powers approached it as an opportunity to further their own exclusionary agendas. In its preparatory meetings prior to the conference, the French government insisted that France was at saturation point and could absorb no more.[76] In this it was as one with Britain and the United States, whose delegates also came to the conference to defend their policies against further refugee entry while asking at the same time other countries to lift their restrictions.[77]

Failure at Evian left the refugees in Europe with little hope. Things grew worse thereafter. The Czech crisis of September 1938, the adoption of anti-Jewish laws in Italy, and various measures against Jews in Romania and Poland, all stressed that the refugee problem was without end. In France, a crackdown on foreigners followed the Czech crisis, to identify and expel any who did not have valid documents. In November, an anti-Jewish backlash followed the murder of an official of the German embassy in Paris, Ernest von Rath, by Herschel Grynszpan, a German-born Polish Jew illegally resident in France. The *Krystallnacht* pogrom of 9 November that von Rath's murder inspired in Germany foreshadowed new clandestine refugee movements. Here was evidence for those so inclined to believe it that Jews were intent on ensnaring France in war against Germany. Asylum, it could be fairly believed, had been exploited by the Germans who had organised illegal migrations of their 'less desirable elements' and 'false refugees' to undermine French security. The crackdown on foreigners was intensified, therefore, as attempts were made to purge Paris of recent Jewish arrivals. But it was not possible to expel them as no other country would admit them. Nor could new refugees arriving illegally from Germany, Austria, or Czechoslovakia be turned back. Internment was the only other option.[78]

## Refugees at two frontiers

When Daladier announced the decree-law of 2 May 1938 and claimed that it was motivated by 'traditional rules of French hospitality, and its spirit of liberalism and humanity', he turned back to an ideal that circumstances and events could not sustain. It was imperative, nevertheless, that the ideal be recalled as it maintained the principled currents of asylum and the place France traditionally accorded to refugees and other foreigners. The ideal stressed that the circumstances of the time were exceptional and required exceptional measures for the protection of the French people and national security. Daladier was therefore compelled by this sentiment of 'national spirit' to sustain the illusion of principle behind the exclusionary and punitive regime his government sanctioned.

The decree-laws of 1938 had singularly failed in their aims of stopping clandestine entry and removing illegal immigrants.[79] There were indeed highly organised clandestine channels, which were even published in German newspapers to encourage Jews to leave. This itself justified French suspicions that the German government was to blame for France's problems because it wanted to offload its Jews.[80] One illegal channel was through Saarbruck and Forbach, and German and Austrian refugees apprehended by the French police carried detailed instructions about how they were to negotiate each separate step of the way: which tram to take through Saarbruck, times of departure and arrival, how to get into Forbach, and at which hotels they could find lodging.[81]

During these difficult years, all Germans and Austrians who sought to enter France were suspect. There was mounting evidence that temporary entry to obtain a migration visa from another country's consulate in Paris had become a ruse to breach French restrictions. Affidavits from respondents in the United States who had undertaken to assist the migration of friends and relatives, presented to obtain an entry visa for France, often proved to be fraudulent. Even those who intended to settle overseas might by chance be left stranded if a migration visa was refused, or there would be such a long delay before departure that all hope of emigration was lost. Temporary visas for the purposes of onward migration were consequently suspended; legitimate entrants therefore were rendered illegal by the force of circumstance.[82]

Many were also ensnared in an 'infernal cycle', imprisoned when an expulsion order could not be enforced because they had been refused entry to another country, or were forced back into France and again imprisoned.[83] When stripped of its principles, asylum had given way to a penal sanctions, clandestinity, and criminality. The absence of principle sapped refugees of their spirit; it also seemed to sap the French republic of it own spirit, and of the very traditions of hospitality, liberty, and humanity that Daladier had extolled. Principle was only evident, Vicki Caron highlights, in the odd act of good conscience by a policeman confronted with personal tragedy, or in the shame of the judges who, powerless under the law, bowed their heads when passing sentence.[84]

The illusion of humanitarian spirit also sustained unrealistic ambitions that the refugee problem could be addressed by agricultural and even colonial settlement schemes. These plans, which had been considered soon after the impact of the refugees from Nazism was first felt, re-emerged in 1939 when all other measures had been exhausted. Plans for resettling refugees in depopulated agricultural regions were revived as a vital measure for refugee assistance, and some historians consider them evidence of liberalising tendencies in French refugee policy.[85] Behind them was the recognition of the failure of restrictive policy and the need for a more humane response that removed refugees from the cycle of clandestinity and criminality. Yet they also maintained the illusion that a solution to the refugee problem was possible without suspending the restrictive and exclusionary regime that protected France from their numbers, their character, their impact on its cultural and political life, and their competition in the overcrowded labour market. It was forgotten in the renewed interest in settlement schemes that they had not progressed earlier because they conflicted with the anxieties that had justified this punitive regime.

A greater illusion was the interest in overseas colonial settlement, which suggested a solution to the international problem but which really only cast a veil over failures to assure the safety and welfare of displaced European Jews. France therefore was not alone in entertaining the possibilities; Britain, the League of Nations, the United States President's Advisory Committee on Refugees, and various Jewish organisations also proposed overseas settlement plans. At various times, consideration was given to Jewish refugee colonies in such diverse parts of the world as Kenya, Northern Rhodesia, Tanganyika (Tanzania), Nyasaland (Malawi), Angola, British Guinea,

204 *Refuge in the Land of Liberty*

Madagascar, Mindanao, New Guinea, North-West Australia, San Domingo, Colombia, Guyana, and Russia.[86] The remoteness of these proposed colonies is clearly significant in the overall conception of the Jewish question at the heart of the refugee question. All these plans confirmed that there was no place for the Jewish refugees of central and eastern Europe. Yet these speculative plans maintained the illusion that something should be done for them, and that something could be done without lifting restrictive barriers.

\* \* \*

While refugee policy throughout the 1930s was fixed firmly on the eastern frontier, events in Spain diverted the government's attention to the southern frontier. New Spanish refugees appeared soon after the proclamation of the Spanish Second Republic on 14 April 1931. Within months, anti-republican propaganda spread false stories of persecution, one consequence of which was the refusal of Spanish travellers to leave France. In this early phase of the Spanish Republic, therefore, the French government made it clear that any Spanish nationals coming to France did so of their own accord and had no justification for claiming persecution of any kind.[87] By March 1932, however, it was forced to admit to persecutions of clergymen and higher church officials and to respect their demands for asylum as political refugees.[88] Although asylum was accorded willingly, in keeping with the expectations of refugees in the past they were reminded that they must submit themselves, 'completely and without reserve', to French law and therefore not to agitate in Spanish affairs. To avoid any potential diplomatic problems they were removed from the border regions to north of the river Loire.[89] Aristocratic Spanish families and members of the upper-middle class, meanwhile, turned their backs on the 'red' revolution and abandoned Spain for the French Basque coast.[90]

A traditional movement of refugees from Spain into France had therefore re-emerged before the nationalist insurrection of July 1936. War and defeat forced its civil and military victims across the Pyrénées. Exile, resettlement, and repatriation were their common experience, as it had been for Spanish refugees from the civil conflicts of the nineteenth century. Forty-eight hours after the civil war had commenced, Léon Blum's government recommended that the reception of Spanish refugees would conform to French tradition and respond to their humanitarian needs. They would be allowed provisional residence until it was possible for them to return.[91]

While Blum's government might have been tardy in response to the refugees from central and eastern Europe, it was nonetheless preoccupied by refugees from Spain. Between July and the end of 1936, it issued some 20 separate ministerial instructions, and another 40 in 1937.[92] The flow of refugees was highly fluid, shifting with the sudden turns in the civil war. French policy responded to each of these turns, insisting that the need of refugees to the protection of France was transitory and that they would return after a short delay.

Immediate repatriation was therefore encouraged; otherwise, the refugees were removed from the frontier departments and placed in reception centres between the Garonne and the Loire rivers. Longer-term arrangements were discouraged, and already by August 1936, a retreat from the declared humanitarian objectives of French responses was evident. With each new wave of refugees came French insistence on repatriation.

The first major refugee movement into France came after the battle of Irùn and the fall of the Basque lands to the nationalists in September 1936. It numbered some 15,000 republican militia and civilians. The second wave, following the final stage of the northern campaign and the nationalist offensive against Bilbao from May to October 1937, constituted about 120,000 militia and civilians. The third wave, of some 25,000, followed the nationalist occupation of the Alto Aragón in the spring of 1938. Women, children, and the elderly left in large numbers and as many as could be repatriated were returned to their places of origin; militia were returned to safe republican zones by Perpignan. By the end of 1938, about 40,000 Spanish refugees remained in France, many of them children.[93]

From the start of the emergency in late 1936, ministers spoke in terms of temporary refugee movements and of the need to restrict the charge on public funds. The policy objective was therefore refuge in the short term with a view to prompt repatriation. In order to contain the impact of these refugees, therefore, it was inappropriate to authorise refugee settlement and to issue work permits.[94]

The same pressures that had poisoned responses to German refugees poisoned responses to the Spanish refugees. Public opinion and the mood among the parties in the Chamber of Deputies were divided along ideological lines. Fears of the dangers of infiltration and of laying France bare before an even greater foreign penetration marked the position of the right, while the left asserted its sympathies with the Spanish Popular Front.[95] Economic considerations largely determined the status of Spanish refugees in France. Those of independent financial means were classified as tourists and could remain in the frontier departments, as could those for whom a French resident provided accommodation.[96] Following questions from various departments about work entitlements (the Department of the Landes, for example, suggested it could put the Spanish refugees to work because it had a need for forestry workers after a damaging fire in August 1937), the interior and labour ministers did not object in principle to the grant work permits if the refugees 'could obtain an employment contract'. They could then remain not as refugees but as foreign workers.[97]

By December 1937, the war emergency had stabilised, and a general repatriation of all Spanish nationals who had no authority to remain was begun.[98] But none of the measures taken till then prepared France for the sudden influx that followed the republican retreat from Barcelona in late January 1939, and again after the final nationalist victory in March. By April, possibly as many as 500,000 refugees had crossed the Pyrénées.[99]

Because France was unprepared for this new emergency, Louis Stein writes, it refused to see the problem in its true dimensions; the refugees could not be received and dispersed in a controlled way, and as a result there was chaos on a grand scale.[100] Arrangements were hastily improvised, and the brutality of France's reception stripped asylum of any remaining vestige of principle.

Geneviève Dreyfus-Armand puts the best light on France's admission of the Spanish republicans by asserting its respect for the republican obligation of asylum in the face of mounting xenophobia.[101] Other historians agree that admission of the Spanish evacuees marked respect for the 'French tradition of asylum', but their assessments are qualified by the weight of the ambiguities in policy after admission.[102] Patrick Weil writes that despite the conditions of reception and the intention of even forced repatriation, 'the principle of the right of asylum was not called into question'. Republican values, he writes, allowed measures to 'resist the strains on politics and growing xenophobia', and, although grudgingly, France realised its humanitarian responsibilities.[103] Certainly, no deputy in the chamber would dare have suggested that the refugees be left to face the nationalists' machine guns as they advanced north to the border, and so the best protection France could offer was safe passage across. But there were nevertheless those who believed that France could not bear the added burden of another half a million foreigners, and even Interior Minister Albert Sarraut, into whose care the Spanish republicans fell, insisted that security and economic issues took precedence over humanitarian concerns.[104] Consequently, Denis Peschanski observes, the government made three decisions that aggravated the situation: for reasons of national security it refused to place the evacuees in military camps, which were equipped and able to harbour them; it refused to accept the wounded and sick into French hospitals, again for reasons for security; and, again because of security concerns, it refused to allow the republican militia to maintain their units, which could have greatly aided organisation and distribution, and allowed chaos to take hold instead.[105]

Protestations of principle and the defence of asylum only hold for admission; it reduces the question of humanity in French actions to one of either allowing them to cross into France or of leaving them at the mercy of the vengeful nationalists, and puts too fine a gloss on the failure of humanity in asylum afterwards. One seeks in vain a humanitarian impulse in the manner in which they were received and accorded asylum while under French protection. Instead, the gesture displayed in the admission of the Spanish republicans pales next to the overwhelming economic and security preoccupations of French officials as a result of which asylum was accorded with the utmost reticence and assumed a starkly inhumane character.

The republican militia were greeted by gendarmes and mobile guards of Senegalese cavalry and infantrymen who lined the roads across the frontier to contain, disarm, and direct them to hastily improvised internment camps on the beaches of the Pyrénées-Orientales. Families were separated at the frontier, and women, children, the elderly, and infirm were transferred to accommodation centres in the interior.[106] Official attitudes hardened considerably during the evacuations between January and March 1939. Worst was the attack from the extreme right, who denounced the republicans as a horde of dangerous radicals unloosed upon France, who would rob, rape, pillage, and destroy homes and fields, and even join with French communists in an armed insurrection.[107]

Such opinion found comfort in the internment centres and concentration camps that became the Spanish republicans' experience of exile. At the frontier they were held at triage centres, in Pras-de-Mollo, La Tour-de-Carol, Boulou, Bourg-Madame, Arles-sur-Tech, and Saint Laurent-de-Cerdans, where they rested briefly before their separation and redirection to internment centres.[108] Men of sound health and military age were placed in camps on the beaches of Argelès-sur-Mer, Saint-Cyprien and Le Barcarès. Women, children, the elderly and infirm were placed in internment centres north of the Garonne.[109]

The first camp, at Argelès-sur-Mer, was no more than a fenced-off section of deserted beach. The commandant placed in charge lacked precise orders and was told simply to make a camp urgently. As a result, barbed wire was laid out to confine the Spanish militiamen before barracks and latrines were constructed. While safely under military guard, the internees were exposed to the wind, rain, and cold at the height of winter. They found shelter from storms by digging into the sand, but the sand itself was soon polluted because of the lack of latrines. Voluntary agencies were relied upon to supplement the meagre government food rations. Conditions in Saint-Cyprien were scarcely better. A few kilometres to the north of Argelès, it was also a strip of fenced off beach. The first internees were placed there on 7 February, and reduced the crowding in Argelès to between 65,000 and 75,000 republicans, but it was itself quickly filled beyond capacity within one week to as many as 95,000 internees. The camp at Le Barcarès, a little further north still, opened on 11 February. It was better equipped because it was intended for the use of Spaniards in the course of repatriation, but with barracks sufficient to accommodate only 3000 refugees, as many as 60,000 were still left to find meagre shelter on the beach.[110] More camps were clearly required and over the next few months they were built at Bram in the Aude, Agde in the Hérault, and Vernet-les-Bains and Rivesaltes in the Pyrénées-Orientales. The camp at Gurs in the Basses-Pyrénées was built specifically to accommodate Basques, aviators, and veterans of the international brigade.[111] By 10 March, numbers in Argelès and Barcarès had been reduced to between 40,000 and 50,000 each.[112]

Albert Sarraut had himself called them concentration camps because they were intended only as temporary internment centres to keep the refugees together until they were repatriated. There was little imperative therefore to better equip them and to improve the living conditions of the internees.

Mismanagement and ill-preparedness suited the government's intention of not letting the refugees settle and recover before their massed repatriation could be arranged with the Spanish nationalists. On 18 February, then, it announced that it would accelerate repatriation.[113]

Further north, in the accommodation centres of the central departments, convoys of women, children, and the elderly and infirm were received; some were dispatched again to northern departments. Within a short period of time, they numbered about 170,000, spread across some 77 departments.[114] Medical examinations and anti-viral vaccinations were mandatory, and those who had come into contact with the sick were placed in isolation. Under the provisions of article 25 of the decree-law of 12 November 1938, all refugees were required to live in departments, *arrondissements*, or cantons assigned to them, and any found outside these limits or who otherwise failed to conform to injunctions would be treated firmly.[115]

The accommodation centres were very diverse. In some departments, all available locations were put to use: schools, holiday camps, sanatoriums, barracks, uninhabited houses, old factories, mills, halls, disused churches and prisons, farm houses, and stables. Although they had shelter, unlike the militiamen exposed to the elements on the beaches of the Pyrénées-Orientales, their general living conditions were nevertheless poor and neglected. There was often only one stove in the poorly heated dormitories, and in the winter of 1939–40 water froze in the taps. In some places they had no beds and slept on straw spread on the ground.[116]

The civilians were subject to as much surveillance and policing as the internees in the camps. Discipline was intrusive and strict, to assure the French public as much as to intimidate the refugees. The police presence was increased in the departments that housed refugees, and periodic sweeps of the towns and countryside rounded-up any who had slipped the net.[117] In the camps themselves, the internees were subjected to frequent roll calls and confinement. For a breach of rules or disturbance, they faced a form of solitary confinement on an exposed piece of beach with no blankets or other protection from the cold and rain.[118] There was also little protection from the abuses of guards, such as beatings, theft, and bastardisation.[119]

Four distinct permits were devised to distinguish various classes of refugees and to limit their status before French law. A provisional identity card of variable duration was issued to those whose personal situation and 'honour' would normally have entitled them to a residence permit in other circumstances. A provisional passport was issued to refugees who were not considered dangerous, but who were nevertheless not allowed to travel freely; their concentration in one locality provided more effective control. Most of the Spanish refugees received this passport. It was renewable each month, and was valid for residence in only one designated department, commune, or municipality. The final two forms of permits were a means of keeping particular individuals under close surveillance. They were effectively detention orders under article 11 of the law of 2 May 1938. One order was that they remain in a designated place; the other, an order confining them to a special detention centre, was used against individuals considered to be a danger to national security and the public peace.[120]

This last order effectively created a class of political prisoners. Spaniards and international brigaders identified as communists and anarchists, and other refugees considered troublemakers in the camps, were incarcerated at the ancient Templar fort of Collioure (Pyrénées-Orientales), where conditions were especially repressive and deplorable, or in Le Vernet (Ariège).[121]

The Spanish evacuations of 1939 therefore had left significant marks across southern and central France. A growing network of camps and internment centres had become the face of asylum, in which political refugees, defeated militia, and civilians were held until their repatriation. Even before the numbers of Spanish republicans had assumed such proportions, however, France had no place for them. French responses were necessarily limited by the unforeseen dimension of the evacuations from Spain and the strains it placed on already overstretched resources. But when asylum was stripped of principle, as it had been progressively stripped through the course of the 1930s, all that remained were hastily prepared camps, strict, harsh and often deplorably repressive reactions, and a policy of swift repatriation.

The deliberately harsh conditions the refugees faced intimidated them into accepting the inevitability of repatriation. It began slowly, but numbers fell progressively. The camps emptied from 173,000 in mid-June 1939, to 84,688 by 15 August, to 53,000 on 15 November, and, a figure calculated with much less certainty, to somewhere between 35,000 and 80,000 at the end of December 1939.[122] Emigration to other countries was one part of the gradual fall in numbers.

Repatriation did not have the impact that the French government had desired, however. Interior Minister Sarraut insisted that repatriation would be a voluntary decision of the refugees themselves and there would be no forced returns. 'These men', he announced, 'so long as we are unsure whether they will suffer reprisals, will not be returned by force ... France will not put them before the firing squad'.[123] To this end, the government had sought guarantees from the nationalists in Spain that no reprisals would be taken against repatriated republicans. Despite these assurances, repatriation broke down. The indirect pressures on the Spaniards to leave France were great. No plans were made to improve their living conditions and Spanish nationalist propaganda was encouraged in the camps to convince them that they were assured of a safe return. There were also more direct pressures. Reports of the forced return of children, which in turn forced the parents to return, periodic raids to round-up refugees and send them back, particular instances of refugees being handed over to Spanish nationalists, all dissuaded the republicans from cooperating with the French police. The Spanish government also delayed repatriations, processing no more than 200 or 300 a day, and insisting that only one border crossing be used, through Hendaye in the Basses-Pyrénées, when the bulk of the refugees were on the other side of the country. This would seem to leave little doubt that the nationalists did not want the Catalan evacuees in the Pyrénées-Orientales to return to Catalonia. Furthermore, assurances of non-retribution were soon forgotten as stories came back about sentences passed on republican militia. Rumours of the summary execution of returning communists and anarchists nullified propaganda within the camps and stirred even greater resistance to repatriation.[124] With the start of the Second World War in September 1939, many republicans decided that it was better to dare return to Spain than fight on the side of the French who had treated them so harshly over the past months. Others put aside their grievances and enlisted in the French army to continue their fight against fascism.[125] At the time of the armistice, June 1940, some 125,000 Spanish refugees remained in France.

The Spanish refugees of 1939 profoundly unsettled the mood in France. Louis Stein describes an unnamed but potent force that had taken hold, which erupted in panic, as these 'hordes of dangerous radicals' were unleashed. This 'Great Fear of 1939', as Stein calls it, was in part a phobic obsession with Marxism that was situated in the Spanish republicans, and in part an insidious anxiety about French vulnerability before all foreigners.[126] This great fear was yet another manifestation of xenophobia and raw anxieties that had become exposed piece by piece through the escalating domestic and international crises of the 1930s and as France faced the ceaseless waves of foreigners breaking on its frontiers. Indeed, France's ill-preparedness and reticence before the retreating Spanish republicans were the final signs of the end of asylum.

The end of asylum had come amid these profound anxieties about the place of foreigners in France. Under the stress of economic depression, political instability, and demographic fears, the urgent need for control and containment overwhelmed humanitarianism. Existing laws and administrative measures could not respond to the humanitarian needs of refugees, and, under pressures from deep within French society, no government could reform migration policy to secure the status of refugees. Asylum was stripped of principle in an ever extending system of restrictive and exclusionary measures and finally by punitive laws. By the end of the decade asylum had given way to confinement: imprisonment under the decree-law of 2 May 1938 for failing to comply with an expulsion order; internment in designated locations also under this law when an expulsion order could not be executed; internment in concentration camps; and finally the beginning of a system that made certain refugees political prisoners. The concentration camps on the Mediterranean beaches of the Pyrénées-Orientales were the consequence of France's belief that it no longer had a place for foreigners and could no longer extend asylum to refugees.

It was a belief nurtured by the right wing and poorly resisted by the left. In 1936, the ultra-right journal *Gringoire* represented France as the rubbish dump of Europe, into which surrounding countries cast their unwanted: German Jews and communists; Italian anti-fascists; Spanish anarchists, socialists, and communists.[127] These were not just the unwanted of other countries that were dumped onto France, they were Jews and leftists, who inundated France with their insidious ways. Therefore, as the Spanish republicans poured into the Pyrénées-Orientales, deputies of the right denounced in the chamber these 'galloping, endemic hordes' who would strike at the very heart and health of the French nation.[128] This 'phobic obsession with Marxism', to use Stein's apt phrase, was cause for a second great fear in 1939, after news broke in August of the Nazi–Soviet non-aggression pact. Hysteria amplified suspicion not only of the Spanish republicans because of the strong support the Soviet Union had given them during the civil war, but of all foreign communists.[129] The outbreak of war in September 1939 further amplified these suspicions amid the general public anxieties and phobias. The French Communist Party was itself dissolved on 26 September and its deputies removed from the chamber.[130]

The network of camps hastily put into service during 1939 to accommodate the Spanish republicans now had another purpose. First foreign communists were rounded up and detained under the powers of the decree-laws of May and November 1938. On 4 September 1939, nationals of the German Reich—Germans, Austrians, Czechs, and Saarlanders—whether or not they were refugees, were ordered to report to the police and to register for new identity documents. On 9 September, it was decreed that even naturalised foreigners could be stripped of citizenship on suspicion of a threat to national security; on 17 September, the arrest of all politically suspect foreigners was decreed. Even stateless communists were swept up in these orders to find and arrest enemies of the state. By the end of September, some 18,000 detainees were dispersed about internment camps across the country.[131]

\* \* \*

The fall of France and the armistice of June 1940 stand at a crossroad of this historical narrative. One narrative is of an inexorable continuity witnessed through the history of asylum and the reception of refugees during the interwar years. Increasingly exclusionary measures ended in internment, and from internment the process towards the confinement and detention of any suspect foreigner seems a logical progression. To this might also be added the reclassification of French Jews as foreign, and their round up and internment in concentration camps. Another narrative begins from the rupture of armistice and German occupation, from which the history of French collaboration, the Vichy race laws, and complicity in the Jewish Holocaust begins.

# Conclusion
## The Right of Asylum—A Site of Memory

The reconstitution of the Fourth Republic after the war set down a number of foundation principles to re-establish republican consciousness of human rights and liberties first prescribed in the 1789 Declaration of the Right of Man and the Citizen. Among these were 'all who are persecuted for the cause of liberty have a right of asylum in the territories of the Republic'. This redressed the failure of asylum in the late 1930s, as did the following paragraph, which assured the right to employment without discrimination 'on grounds of origin, opinion, or belief'.[1] The failure of asylum in the 1930s was a failure of its practice as much as its principles. By withholding a right to work no assurance was given for personal welfare, security, and lawful residence. It can be concluded therefore that the Fourth Republic began from the recognition of wrongs perpetrated against refugees and foreigners, and against French traditions of rights, at the end of the Third Republic. The constitutional guarantees of rights and liberty recalled into French memory the 'right of asylum' and made it a fundamental principle of republicanism.

The failure of asylum in the 1930s was also an international failure, which was redressed after the war through the development of an international refugee regime on much surer legal and institutional grounds under the United Nations. The development of this regime can be broken down into three phases. One was the practical solution to post-war problem of refugees and displaced persons, which the United Nations took on through its Relief and Rehabilitation Agency (UNRRA) and the International Refugee Organisation (IRO). The second was a principled statement of the right of asylum, set down in the article 14 of the 1948 Universal Declaration of Human Rights: 'everyone has the right to seek and to enjoy in other countries asylum from persecution'. Finally, institutional developments gave international legal protection to these universal human rights. The United Nations High Commission for Refugees (UNHCR) was established in 1950 to take over the temporary work of UNRRA and the IRO. In 1951, it set about the task of drafting an international convention on the status of refugees, to prescribe legal definition of the refugee and the obligations of states under the convention: to hear and consider claims for refugee status, to ensure fair and equitable living conditions and access to the law, to provide protection from the sources of their persecution.[2]

The recognition of the legal rights of refugees in France, as it was for other signatories, was therefore assured by the adoption in French law of the United Nations' convention relating to refugees. This became effective on 25 July 1952 with the passage of the 'Law Relating to the Right of Asylum' (*Loi relative au droit d'asile*).[3] The law constituted the French Office for the Protection of Refugees and the Stateless (*Office français de Protection des Réfugiés et Apatrides*—OFPRA), which determined whether the application of an individual for refugee status met with the meaning of the convention. The right of asylum was made a technical process that brought a refugee— or now more properly an individual who claimed to be a refugee—before the state bureaucracy and the law.

A separate history begins from this point, which it is not the intention here to recount. The interrelationships of law and society, refugees and the post-war state, international politics, the cold war, third-world development, and post-colonialism, all take this history in entirely new directions.[4]

\* \* \*

Boundaries were drawn around refugees upon their admission to France. They were commonly removed from the cities and placed in specific localities under the scrutiny of the local police. The refugee depot was the recurring element of asylum in France throughout much of the nineteenth century. These were designated centres into which refugees were gathered and special disciplines placed on them. The first refugees considered in this study, Dutch Patriots from their democratic rebellion in the United Provinces of the Netherlands in 1787, were placed in depots in the towns of northern France. Under the July Monarchy, refugee depots were located all about France. They had fallen into disuse by the 1850s, as refugees largely moved into the shadows of the larger popular migrations. Designated centres for the placement of refugees re-emerged in the early twentieth century, as centres of internment and concentration camps. The boundaries drawn around the refugees were now of barbed wire and armed guards.

The refugee depot was not a concentration camp, it must be stressed, certainly not as they are conceived today. It was both figuratively and literally an asylum for the refugees: here refugees were contained and placed under surveillance, but their material and personal welfare was also attended to. France willingly bore the cost of providing for their assistance and, although suspicious of them, recognised its obligations to provide them protection. The depots confined refugees to specific localities but they could mix freely with the local communities. The Polish refugee depots of the 1830s were especially noted for the ways in which the Poles shared their social and commercial activities with the French: they lived in their hotels and boarding houses, ate at their restaurants, met and drank in their cafés, and attended the theatre; when they worked it was with local businesses. This habituated the French to the refugees, while it also integrated the refugees into French society. Different groups found a different reception, however. The warm hospitality for the Poles was in marked contrast to the antipathies of local communities to boisterous, marauding and dangerous Spanish refugees known for their vendettas and political frictions.

The refugee depot effectively disappeared by the end of the 1830s as the refugees merged into local societies. Afterwards it was less precisely named, describing any locality where a contingent of refugees was located and registered for financial aid. When they were reconstituted to accommodate refugees from the Spanish Carlist wars in the 1840s, and from the revolutionary turmoil in Germany, Italy, and Austria between 1848 and 1852, they were spoken of as places of internment. By then, financial aid was withheld from foreign refugees, and without this lure to hold them to a designated locality more forceful policing was required. The nature of internment was undeveloped, however. There was no overt, oppressive policing that the twentieth-century experience of internment calls to mind. Rather, it described temporary assistance, provided with the expectation that the refugees would shortly move on, either by returning to their countries of origin, or migrating onward to other countries. In 1939, internment was defined behind the barbed-wire fences of concentration camps; the last vestiges of an asylum were lost in the aspect of prison camps.

The refugee depot and the concentration camp mark the opposing ends of the path of the principles of the right of asylum across the years since the French Revolution. By 1939, the state exercised its full sovereign authority over refugees to such an extent that they were allowed to reside only on condition of their confinement under armed military guard. It seems appropriate to mark this down as the end of asylum because the responses to the Spanish republican refugees of 1939 showed how devoid of principle asylum had become. The respect for their human dignity was negated in the concentration camps on the beaches of the Pyrénées-Orientales. Their repatriation under duress, above all, withdrew their protection from the sources of their persecution and oppression.

The confinement of refugees in designated depot and later into camps responded to French anxieties, which the refugees both exposed and exacerbated. Each refugee movement was a sign of French vulnerabilities. The international ruptures that caused the refugee movements unsettled it. The national and social revolutions of 1830 and 1848 brought foreign revolutionaries and with them came the fear of revolutionary ruptures, or the fear of France being embroiled in a new foreign war. French anxieties were displaced onto refugees, who were seen as agents of revolution and social turmoil and who needed to be constrained, by their physical confinement to depots and their compliance to French law and the will of the French people.

The meaning and ideals of asylum were therefore reformulated as the French state balanced its protection obligations, the humanitarian needs of refugees, and its own political preoccupations, in response to each successive refugee movement. Since the monarchy received the Dutch Patriots in 1787 and conferred asylum on them as an act of the king's grace, successive French regimes, which had inherited the principles of the natural rights of man and defined national identity in the context of national traditions, all repositioned themselves before their refugee protection obligations because of the demands of contingent political conditions. This narrowed humanitarian responses. To legitimise the break with tradition, ideals were themselves redefined; the right of asylum was reconceptualised either in a new sense, as *bienfaisance* under the July Monarchy, for example, or within new legal and political paradigms, as when the right of asylum was defined by exemptions to expulsion or extradition. The weakness of asylum in the interwar years was a consequence of the diminution in public and political consciousness of the ideals of rights invested in the person of the refugee. By equating refugees with foreign workers and therefore holding them to the same regulatory regime as applied to all other foreigners, their distinct moral status as persons in flight from oppression or persecution was diminished, to such an extent that when the Spanish republicans evacuated Catalonia they were denied the moral status from which protection obligations flow.

Yet this assumes that there was some overreaching principle embedded in the notion of asylum which was, and remains, its hidden conscience. Indeed, this sustained the tensions between the principles of refugee rights and the measures for accommodating and controlling refugee populations. Through this tension, fundamental principles of the right of asylum as an individual human right were preserved. As the state redefined its protection obligations, the principles signified by the right of asylum were acknowledged because the reasons why they could not be honoured had to be explained and justified. The diminution of humanitarian principles in public refugee policy in the 1930s deflected these principles into other spheres, most importantly into the spheres of private aid and international assistance. International refugee law emerged from the failure of states to maintain their refugee protection obligations. The principles adopted in international agreements during the interwar years set norms to mediate the behaviour of states and to ensure recognition of refugee protection needs. The internationalisation of refugee assistance, however, was a significant departure from the traditional values attributed to the right of asylum.

On this basis international law refutes the notion of a right of asylum as an imprescriptible human right, since international law concerns states and is implemented by states. Yet international refugee law also concerns refugees, and, by extending certain guarantees of protection and asylum, certain principles signified by the term, the right of asylum, have endured, among them are respect for the person, humanitarian aid, and protection from the sources of persecution.

The French state's appropriation of power over individuals and its determination of the terms of the admission of refugees were challenged by the principles with which the notion of the right of asylum was invested. The right of asylum signified traditions and law created by custom; it was invested with principles derived from antiquity, and was invoked to demonstrate the decadence of modernity, its antipathy to custom, and its hostility to individual rights. During the French Revolution, the defence of refugees was predicated on the political affinities between the refugees and the French. The natural right expressed here was the right to resist oppression, which was the fundament project of the liberal revolutions of the late eighteenth century. In the 1830s, the defence of refugee rights was still centred on the evocation of ideals of natural rights, and the right of asylum was considered to be an imprescriptible right of the individual, derived from nature. But already the state had assumed the authority to determine what rights refugees could enjoy; these were not rights derived from nature, but those rights that the state deemed proper to confer. Asylum was reconceived as *bienfaisance* and therefore likened to charity: refugees enjoyed France's hospitality, as France's guests, so long as they respected those who offered them asylum. The state continued to assert this authority during the nineteenth century, progressively legislating the conditions of residence and the place of foreigners in French society. Central to its authority over foreigners was the power of expulsion, already present in the law pertaining to refugees made in 1832, but legislated in 1849 as the main sanction of the state against undesirable foreigners.

The antiquity of the right of asylum and the traditions upon which it was founded continued to invest the protection of refugees with principles of rights. In 1831, Jean-Pierre Pagès attacked the July Monarchy's 'abuses' of refugee rights by reminding it of the antiquity of the principles of asylum. It was custom in antiquity, Pagès claimed, that the sacred refuges in the very hearts of cities were venerated, and that those in flight from oppression or violence could find sanctuary in them.[5] In 1939, these antique traditions were still powerfully evocative for some. The deputy Joseph Rous reminded the government of its responsibility to respect the sacred right of refugees to asylum: 'if France had done its duty, as in the past, in according the right of asylum [it would have] respected a great tradition'.[6] France's responsibilities were the same as those of the churches and convents of the middle ages, Rous continued; this was nothing less than to give asylum to those in flight.

This duty was evident even in times of barbarism, he said, when the right of asylum existed even for debtors and murderers. 'Today', he declared, 'as in other times, the man who benefits from the right of asylum is a sacred creature'.[7]

The evocative power of its implied principles is why the term 'the right of asylum' endured while asylum itself was reformulated and given new meaning to meet the political contingencies of successive regimes. Its evocative power is also why it was important that it be stated in refugee debates. The traditions it invoked were conceived as both French and republican. The 1793 constitution had proclaimed France as an asylum for those fighting for their liberty against tyranny. The Second Republic also frequently invoked France's tradition as a place of asylum. On 15 April 1849, Interior Minister Faucher committed the Republic to this tradition: 'France has always practiced the right of asylum in the broadest sense of its meaning. The republican government will remain faithful to the procedures that honour the national character'.[8] And again, on 18 May 1849: 'France, faithful to its antecedents, opens its territory and accords asylum'.[9] But this was a very ambiguous tradition. The 1793 Constitution was never adopted, and its promise of asylum had not been proved in practice. In 1795, republicans turned their backs on the Jacobin legacy and even moved away from the ideals of the natural rights of man to rights prescribed by a man's place in society and the duties he fulfils. Even during the Second Republic, statements of fidelity to traditions were quickly modified by other statements that justified why these traditions needed to be set aside. Especially after May 1848, the Second Republic upheld the principles of the right of asylum while denying it in practice. References to traditions secured the right of asylum as an expression of national character and republican ideals, but, like the 1793 Constitution, they had to be set aside for reasons of political contingency. By 1882, Clovis Hugues could be much more resolute in his proclamation of asylum as a republican ideal, recalling Jacobin principles of the First Republic: 'We are among those who think that, for France, there are no foreigners ... those who think that after the French Revolution we have no right to speak of foreigners'.[10] Later still, in 1935, asylum was synonymous with the Republic, an ideal founded in its principles, its laws, and the institutions of the state. Garchery, on the left, and Herriot from the centre, and Doriot of the right, all claimed that the right of asylum was consistent with their notions of the Republic, although their ideas of the Republic and asylum were quite different.[11]

These declared traditions of the right of asylum, as both French and republican articulate a memory of principles and ideals that were believed to have once been attributed to it. The memory of the right of asylum contrasted with policy objectives that pursued their own contingent ends. There was no contradiction, for example, between the Second Republic's memory of the traditions of asylum and the tendencies of its actual measures for refugee assistance because it evoked the sentiment of past ideals and declared itself their heir. Both Garchery and Herriot could also sustain opposed views of republicanism and asylum because, again, the evocation of tradition restored principles and ideals to this memory. But this was much more than an act of remembering. The restoration to memory of the principles and ideals attributed to the right of asylum was also an act of constructing memory, of re-imagining a past: the tradition was created by its very evocation. Asylum was made into a republican tradition; by mythopoesis, it was made into a manifestation of the spirit of the French people, because it was remade in memory as a site invested with principles and ideals that were not evident in the application of policy.

The right of asylum, therefore, was very much a site of memory in the sense in which Pierre Nora explains the term.[12] It was a symbolic site of memory as it evoked a tradition in which an ideal of history was invested; it was a functional site of memory as practice was tied to tradition and therefore legitimised the reconceptualisation of asylum. In its continuing practice, and through the redefinition of state obligations with each new refugee crisis that France faced during the nineteenth and twentieth centuries, the right of asylum also moved beyond memory and into the mainstream of public consciousness. Political exigencies removed from it the sense of these principles and ideals, while its older memory sought to restore them. In its practice, the right of asylum was dissociated from history at the same time as a veil of tradition and memory was thrown over it.

# Abbreviations

| | |
|---|---|
| AD | Archives départementales |
| AN | Archives nationales de France |
| *AP* | *Archives parlementaires* |
| *Bibliothèque polonaise* | *Société historique et littéraire polonaise, Paris* |
| Dumont-Pigalle | Archives Dumont-Pigalle, Archief Nationaal of the Netherlands, The Hague |
| *Gazette* | *Gazette nationale. Réimpression de l'ancien moniteur. Seule histoire authentique et inaltérée de la Révolution française depuis la reúnion des états-généraux jusqu'au Consulat* (*Mai, 1789–Novembre, 1799* (Paris : Henri Plon, 1858–63). |
| *JO* | *Journal officiel de la République française* |
| LNA | League of Nations Archives, Geneva |
| LND | League of Nations Documents |
| MAE | Archives diplomatique, Ministère des Affaires Étrangères, Paris |
| *Moniteur* | *Le moniteur universel* |
| *Recueil Dalloz* | *Recueil périodique et critique de jurisprudence, de législation, et de doctrine en matière civile, commerciale, criminelle, administrative et de droit public,* éd. M. Dalloz. |

# Notes

## Introduction   Refugees and Asylum

1. Hugo Grotius, *De Jure Belli ac Pacis*, vol. 2, trans. Francis W. Kelsey (Washington: Carnegie Endownment for International Law, 1925), p. 201.
2. Emmanuel de Vattel, *Le droit des gens ou principes de la loi naturelle*, vol. 3, trans. Charles G. Fenwick (Washington: Carnegie Endowment for International Law, 1916), p. 92.
3. Christian Wolff, *Jus Gentium Methodico Scientifica Pertractatum*, vol. 2, trans. Joseph H. Drake (Washington: Carnegie Endowment for International Law, 1934), p. 80.
4. Atle Grahl-Madsen, *The Status Of Refugees In International Law*, vol. 2, *Asylum, Entry and Sojourn* (Leyden: A. W. Sijthoff, 1972), p. 6.
5. Jeremy Harding, *The Uninvited: Refugees at the Rich Man's Gate* (London: Profile Books and the London Review of Books, 2000), p. 5.
6. Grahl-Madsen, *Status of Refugees*, vol. 2, p. 3.
7. Atle Grahl-Madsen, *Territorial Asylum* (Stockholm: Almquist & Wiksell International, 1980) describes the failed efforts of the United Nations in 1960s and 1970s to draft a convention on territorial asylum. Despite numerous efforts, attempts to define the meaning of asylum and codify its application failed.
8. Catherine Wihtol de Wenden, 'Réfugié politique: une notion en crise?' in *Esprit* (mai 1990), pp. 73–6, comments that four per cent of France's immigrant population in 1990 were originally asylum-seekers.
9. Gérard Noiriel, *La tyrannie du national: Le droit d'asile en Europe, 1793 à 1993* (Paris: Calman Levy, 1991), pp. 32–4; Mario Bettati, *L'asile politique en question: un statut pour les réfugies* (Paris: Presses Universitaires de France, 1985), p. 28.
10. Gérard Noiriel, 'Difficulties in French Historical Research on Immigration', in *Immigrants in Two Democracies: French and American Experience*, ed. Donald L. Horowitz and Gérard Noiriel (New York and London: New York University Press, 1992), p. 66.
11. Noiriel, *La tyrannie du national*, suggests a study of the right of asylum, but as its interest is the fractures between foreigners and French nationals, it could not explain the hold of the ideal, a refugee's 'right' of asylum, in the face of circumstances that constrained its practice. Perhaps for this reason the book was later republished under a different title, reflecting more France's current concerns about immigration. Gérad Noiriel, *Réfugiés et sans-papiers: la République face au droit d'asile, XIXe-XXe siècle* (Paris: Hachette, 1999).

## Part I   Asylum and the French Revolution

1. *Gazette*, 14 July 1790, p. 250; Albert Goodwin, *The Friends of Liberty: The English Democratic Movement in the Age of the French Revolution* (London: Hutchinson, 1979), p. 122.
2. *Gazette*, 14 July 1790, p. 114.

3. Ibid., 16 July 1789, pp. 129–31; *Le Patriote Français*, 17 July 1790; *Révolutions de Paris*, 14 July 1790.
4. *Gazette*, 21 June 1790, p. 676; Anacharisis Cloots, *Écrits revolutionaries, 1790–1794*, ed. Michèle Duval (Paris: Éditions Champs Libre, 1979), pp. 28–9.
5. Jules Michelet, *Historical View of the French Revolution, from its Earliest Indication to the Flight of the King in 1791*, trans. C. Cocks (London: George Bell and Sons, 1883), pp. 409–10; John Goldworth Alger, *Paris in 1789–94: Farewell Letters of Victims of the Guillotine* (London: George Allen, 1902), pp. 58–9. My thanks to Barrie Rose for this reference.
6. *Gazette*, 21 June 1790, p. 676; Alger, *Paris*, p. 58; Michelet, *Historical View*, p. 410.
7. *La députation étrangère au Champs de Mars aux Confédérés français* (n.d.).
8. Michelet, *Historical View*, pp. 409–10.
9. *Gazette*, 21 June 1790, p. 676.
10. Georges Lefebvre, *The French Revolution. From its Origins to 1793*, trans. Elizabeth Moss Evanson (London and New York: Routledge, 1962), p. 176.
11. Alger, *Paris*, p. 55.
12. *Gazette*, 16 July 1790, p. 136.
13. This is worth noting as Simon Schama gives a public role to the Dutch Patriots in the festival, without citing a source. Simon Schama, *Patriots and Liberators: Revolution in the Netherlands, 1780–1813* (New York: Vintage Books, 1977), p. 149.
14. Ibid., pp. 149–50.
15. Lefebvre, *The French Revolution*, p. 177.
16. The seminal work is Albert Mathiez, *La révolution et les étrangers: cosmopolitisme et défense nationale* (Paris: La Renaissance du Livre, 1918). More recent additions to the historiography include Sophie Wahnich, *L'Impossible citoyen: L'étranger dans le discours de la Révolution française* (Paris: Albin Michel, 1997); Michael Rapport, *Nationality and Citizenship in Revolutionary France: The Treatment of Foreigners 1789–1799* (Oxford: Clarendon Press, 2000); Peter Sahlins, *Unnaturally French: Foreign Citizens in the Old Regime and After* (Ithaca and London: Cornel University Press, 2004).
17. Lefebvre, *The French Revolution*, p. 177.
18. Jacques Godechot, *La grande nation. L'expansion révolutionnaire de la France dans le monde de 1789 à 1799*, 2nd ed. (Paris: Aubier, 1983).
19. Rapport, *Nationality*, pp. 135f & *passim*; Peter Sahlins, 'The Eighteenth-Century Citizenship Revolution in France', in *Migration Control in the North Atlantic World. The Evolution of State Practices in Europe and the United States from the French Revolution to the Inter-War Period*, ed. Andreas Fahrmeir, Olivier Faron and Patrick Weil (New York and Oxford: Berghahn Books, 2003), pp. 269f.
20. Rapport, *Nationality*, *passim*.
21. Bettati, *L'asile politique en question*, p. 28; Noiriel, *Tyrannie*, pp. 32–4.
22. Ibid., p. 38.

# 1 Exiles and Patriots

1. R. R. Palmer, *The Age of the Democratic Revolution: A Political History of Europe and America, 1760–1800* (Princeton: Princeton University Press, 1959), pp. 324–38.
2. Schama, *Patriots*, p. 146; Joost Rosendaal, 'La liberté est une garce! Les Bataves à Paris (1787–1795)', in *Remous révolutionnaires: République batave, armée française*, ed. Annie Jourdan and Joep Leerssen (Amsterdam: Amsterdam University Press, 1996), pp. 59–60; Joost Rosendaal, '"Parce que j'aime la liberté, je retourne en

France": Les réfugiés bataves en voyage', in *Le voyage révolutionnaire*. *Actes du colloque franco-néerlandais du Bicentenaire de la Révolution française, Amsterdam, 12–13 octobre 1989*, ed. Willem Frijhoff and Rudolf Dekker (Hilversum: Verloren, 1991).

3. Palmer, *Democratic Revolution*, p. 327.
4. Willem Frijhoff, 'La société idéale des patriotes bataves', in *Le voyage révolutionnaire*. *Actes du colloque franco-néerlandais du Bicentenaire de la Révolution française, Amsterdam, 12–13 octobre 1989*, ed. Willem Frijhoff and Rudolf Dekker (Hilversum: Verloren, 1991); Rosendaal, 'La liberté est une garce', pp. 60–1; Rosendaal, 'Parce que j'aime la liberté', *passim*.
5. AN, F15 3504. Report to King, 5 April 1789.
6. Ibid.
7. On Dumont-Pigalle, Jacques Godechot, *La grande nation: L'expansion révolutionnaire de la France dans le monde de 1789 à 1799*, vol. 1 (Paris: Aubier, 1956), p. 258; Schama, *Patriots*, p. 148.
8. Dumont-Pigalle 11. Ordre pour la police, avis aux Hollandois Réfugiés, 16 February 1789.
9. AN, F15 3504. Report to King, 5 April 1789.
10. Dumont-Pigalle 11. Declaration of the King's Intentions, March 1789.
11. Ibid., Public notice, 1789.
12. AN, F15 3504. *Mémoire*, March 1789.
13. Ibid., Report to King, 5 April 1789.
14. Dumont-Pigalle 11. 'Mémoire des principaux Hollandois Réfugiés en France, remis au Comité des Pensions de l'Assemblée Nationales'. This *mémoire* was presented to the National Assembly on 19 November 1790 to argue for continued assistance. Three separate drafts exist. The figure of 2000 subsidised Dutch refugees is included in the second draft, but was marked for deletion and was not included in the final version.
15. Ibid.
16. AN, F15 3504, *passim*.
17. Dumont-Pigalle 8. 20 September 1789.
18. Ibid.
19. Ibid., Huber, 17 October 1789.
20. Schama, *Patriots*, p. 146.
21. Ibid., pp. 145–7.
22. Rosendaal, 'La liberté est une garce', pp. 64–5.
23. Dumont-Pigalle 8. Lambert, 6 December 1789; Schama, *Patriots*, pp. 146–7.
24. Dumont-Pigalle 8. Huber, 17 October 1789; Lambert, 6 December 1789. Cf. Schama, *Patriots*, p. 146.
25. Dumont-Pigalle 8. Van Hoey, 8 December 1789. Schama, *Patriots*, p. 146–7.
26. Dumont-Pigalle 8. Chardon, 19 December 1789.
27. Dumont-Pigalle 11. April 1790.
28. *AP*, vol. 19, 18 September 1790, pp. 63–6.
29. Ibid., p. 66; Philippe Raxhon, 'Les réfugiés Liégeois à Paris. Un état de la question', in *Paris et la Révolution*, ed. Michel Vovelle (Paris: Publications de la Sorbonne, 1989), p. 215.
30. Janet L. Polasky, *Revolution in Brussels 1787–1793* (Bruxelles: Palais des Académies, 1982), chap. 3.
31. Ibid., pp. 94–5.
32. Raxhon, 'Réfugiés Liégeois', p. 214.
33. Ibid.

34. Polasky, *Revolution in Brussels*, pp. 180–2.
35. Ibid., p. 12; Godechot, *La grande nation*, pp. 212–4.
36. Raxhon, 'Réfugiés Liégeois', p. 215.
37. Schama, *Patriots*, p. 149.
38. Dumont-Pigalle 11. Mémoire des principaux Hollandois Réfugiés en France, 19 November 1790.
39. Ibid.
40. Armand-Gaston Camus, *Code des pensions, ou Recueil des décrets de l'Assemblée naionale constituante* (Paris: Chez Boudouin, 1792), Art. XIV, p. 13.
41. *AP*, vol. 50, 17 September 1792, pp. 96–7.
42. *AP*, vol. 36, 29 December 1791, p. 618.
43. John Torpey, *The Invention of the Passport: Surveillance, Citizenship and the State* (Cambridge: Cambridge University Press, 2000), p. 31; Wahnich, *L'impossible citoyen*, pp. 107–8.
44. *AP*, vol. 36, 29 December 1791, p. 618.
45. *AP*, vol. 50, 17 September 1792, p. 97.
46. Ibid., 'Projet de décret sur les pensions à accorder aux Hollandais réfugiés en France', pp. 98–103.
47. Schama, *Patriots*, pp. 143f.
48. Rosendaal, 'La liberté est une garce', p. 60.
49. Dumont-Pigalle 11. Mémoire des principaux Hollandois Réfugiés en France, 19 November 1790.
50. AN, F15 3506, Resumé, an II (1793).
51. Peter McPhee, *The French Revolution, 1789–1799* (Oxford: Oxford University Press, 2002) pp. 93–4; Wahnich, *L'impossible citoyen*, p. 159.
52. AN, F15 3505, Réfugiés hollandais. (n.d. 1792–3).
53. Ibid.
54. AN, F15 3504, Report, 9 Germinal III.
55. Polasky, *Revolution in Brussels*, pp. 204–5; Raxhon, 'Réfugiés Liégeois', p. 217.
56. Rapport, *Nationality*, p. 225; Schama, *Patriots*, pp. 10 & 150–1.
57. Mathiez, *La révolution et les étrangers*, p. 125.
58. Joseph Daris, *Histoire du diocèse et de la Principauté de Liége (1724–1852)*, vol. 2 (Bruxelles: Editions Culture et Civilisations, 1974), pp. 89f; Wayne P. Te Brake, 'Popular Politics in the Dutch Patriot Revolution', *Theory and Society* 14, 2 (March 1985), p. 203.
59. Polasky, *Revolution in Brussels*, pp. 204–5; Raxhon, 'Réfugiés Liégeois', p. 217.
60. Godechot, *La grande nation*, p. 213.
61. Raxhon, 'Réfugiés Liégeois', p. 219, observes that this stage of their exile is studied and understood much less than the first stage since its radicalisation exposed tendencies that nineteenth-century liberal and Catholic historians rejected.
62. Rapport, *Nationality*, p. 225.
63. Mathiez, *La révolution et les étrangers*, chaps 8 & 9; Rapport, *Nationality*, p. 145f; Wahnich, *L'impossible citoyen*, pp. 127f.
64. Mathiez, *La révolution et les étrangers*, p. 92; Rapport, *Nationality*, p. 137.
65. Wahnich, *L'impossible citoyen*, pp. 134–5.
66. *Gazette*, 21 June 1793, p. 688.
67. AN, F15 3499, Administrator of the Department of the Nord, 9 Floreal II.
68. Ibid.
69. Ibid., 4 Ventôse II.
70. AN, F15 3505. Colonistes; Corsicains; AN, F15 3507. Déportés français.
71. Rapport, *Nationality*, p. 227.

72. AN, F15 3499. Committee of Public Welfare, 18 Germinal II; Department of the Ardennes, 6 Fructidor II.
73. Ibid., 25 Thermidor II.
74. AN, F7 4420, Committee of General Security. Register of Belgians in Paris, 1793/an II.
75. AN, F15 3499, Nissette (n.d.).
76. Ibid., 'Ta concitoyenne', 4 Germinal II.
77. AN, F15 3511, Réfugiés Italiens, Frimaire III.
78. Ibid., Committee of Public Safety, 29 Frimaire III.
79. AN, F15 3499, Committee of Public Safety, 14 Prairial II.
80. AN, F7 4420, General Assembly of Belgian Refugees, 7–24 Nivôse II.
81. Ibid., 28 Pluviôse II.
82. Ibid., 17 Ventôse II.
83. Rapport, *Nationality*, pp. 192–6.
84. Ibid., p. 205.
85. AN, AFII 61, 452–3; Sahlins, *Unnaturally French*, pp. 288–9.
86. Rapport, *Nationality*, pp. 195–6.
87. AN, AFII 61, 453, Report.
88. AN, AFII 61, 448, Decree of the National Convention, 13 April 1793.
89. R. R. Palmer, 'The World Revolution of the West: 1763–1801', *Political Science Quarterly*, 69, 1 (March 1954), p. 2.
90. AN, F15 3508, Réfugiés Irlandais; AN, F15 3511; Rapport, *Nationality*, p. 301.
91. Peter McPhee, *A Social History of France, 1780–1880* (London and New York: Routledge, 1992), pp. 73–4.
92. Godechot, *La grande nation*, pp. 244–55.
93. Anna Maria Rao, 'Paris et les exiles italiens en 1799', in *Paris et la Révolution*, ed. Michel Vovelle (Paris: Publisations de la Sorbonne, 1989), pp. 225–6; AN, F15 3511, Report to the Welfare Commission, 23 Frimaire IX.
94. Rao, 'Paris et les exiles italiens', pp. 227–8.
95. Marianne Elliott, *Partners in Revolution: The United Irishmen and France* (New Haven and London: Yale University Press, 1982), pp. 77f.
96. Ibid., pp. 267–71.
97. Thomas Bartlett, 'Miles Byrne: United Irishman, Irish Exile and *Beau Sabreur*', in *The Mighty Wave: The 1798 Rebellion in Wexford*, ed. Dáire Keogh and Nicholas Furlong (Dublin: Four Courts Press, 1996); Michael Durey, 'The Fate of the Rebels after 1798', *History Today*, 48, 6 (June 1998), pp. 21–7.
98. AN, F15 3511, Report to Interior Minister, 28 Ventôse VIII.
99. Ibid.; Elliott, *Partners in Revolution*, pp. 269–70.
100. Rao's major work on this subject is *Esuli: l'emigrazione politica italiana in Francia (1792–1802)* (Napoli: Guida, 1992). See also Anna Maria Rao, 'Les exilés italiens et Brumaire', *Annales historiques de la Révolution française*, 4 (1999); and Anna Maria Rao, 'Les républicains démocrates italiens et le Directoire', *La République directoriales, Clermont-Ferrand* (1997). My thanks to Anna Maria Rao for providing these articles.
101. Rao, 'Paris et les exiles italiens', pp. 226–8.
102. Ibid., p. 226.
103. Ibid., p. 229.
104. Ibid., pp. 229–32.
105. AN, F15 3511. Réfugiés néapolitains et romains. 18 Frimaire IX.
106. Ibid., 23 Frimaire, IX.
107. Ibid.

## 2 Asylum, Empire, and Restoration

1. AN, F15 3513, Réfugiés des colonies.
2. Ian Coller, 'Arab Paris: Arab Lives and Arab Identities in France, 1801–1831' PhD (University of Melbourne, 2006), pp. 57–8.
3. Ibid., pp. 65–7.
4. Ian Coller, 'Egypte-sur-Seine: The Making of an Arabic Community in Paris, 1800–1830', *French History and Civilisation: Papers from the George Rudé Seminar*, 1 (2005), pp. 210–5. See also Ian Coller, 'Arab France: mobility and Community in Early-Nineteenth Century Paris and Marseille', *French Historical Studies*, 29, 3 (Summer 2006), pp. 433–56.
5. Ibid.
6. Coller, 'Arab Paris', p. 87.
7. Ibid., p. 72.
8. Pierre Echinard and Emile Témime, *Migrance: Histoire de l'immigration marseillaise*, vol. 1, *La préhistoire de la migration*, ed. Emile Temime (Marseille: Edisud, 1989), pp. 106–7; Coller, 'Egypte-sur-Seine', p. 215.
9. Emmanuel Monasse, 'L'accueil et l'admission au titre de réfugié politique (1814–1848). Étude dans le département de l'Hérault', in *Pratiques et cultures politiques dans la France contemporaine. Hommage à Raymond Huard* (Montpellier: Centre d'histoire contemporaine du Languedoc méditerranéen-Roussillon, Université Paul Valéry-Montpellier III, 1995), p. 197.
10. Ibid., p. 198.
11. Rafael Sanchez Mantero, 'L'émigration politique en France pendant le règne de Ferdinand VII', in *Exil politique et migration économique. Espagnols et Français aux XIXe–XXe siècles* (Paris: Éditions du Centre National de la Recherche Scientifique, 1991), pp. 17–9.
12. Monasse, 'L'accueil et l'admission', pp. 198f; Peter Sahlins, *Boundaries. The Making of France and Spain in the Pyrenees* (Berkeley: University of California Press, 1989); Sanchez Mantero, 'L'émigration politique', pp. 22–8.
13. Raymond Carr, *Spain, 1808–1939* (Oxford: Clarendon Press, 1966), pp. 121–54; Joseph Pérez, *Histoire de l'Espagne* (Paris: Fayard, 1996), pp. 527–31.
14. Sanchez Mantero, 'L'émigration politique', pp. 22–3.
15. Monasse, 'L'accueil et l'admission', pp. 199–200.
16. Ibid.
17. Echinard and Témime, *Migrance*, vol. 1, p. 138.
18. Sanchez Mantero, 'L'émigration politique', pp. 24–5.
19. Pierre Gerbet, *Auvergne, terre d'accueil. La vie des réfugiés politiques à Clermont-Ferrand de 1815 à 1870* (Clermont-Ferrand: J. de Bussac, 1943), pp. 6–8.
20. Ibid., pp. 8 & 18.
21. AD Loire, 4 M 540, Prefect of the Loire, 10 July 1824, 1 April 1828, 11 April 1828.
22. Gerbet, *Auvergne*, pp. 8 & 18.
23. Renée Lopez and Emile Témime, *Migrance: Histoire de l'immigration marseillaise*, vol. 2, *L'Expansion marseillaise et 'l'immigrtion italienne (1830–1918)* (Marseille: Edisud, 1990), pp. 105–7.
24. AN, C 749. Dossier 42.
25. John Merriman, *Police Stories. Building the French State, 1815–1851* (Oxford and New York: Oxford University Press, 2006), pp. 76f.
26. Sanchez Mantero, 'L'émigration politique', p. 24.
27. AN, F7 12102, Dossier 1746.

28. Emmanuel Monasse, 'Les réfugiés politiques dans l'Hérault de 1814 à 1848: approche méthodologique', *Annales du Midi, Revue archéologique, historique et philologique de la France méridionale*, 108 (1996), p. 209; Sahlins, *Boundaries*, p. 205.

29. AN, F7 11984, 10 June 1822; J. Mathorez, *Les réfugiés politiques espagnols dans l'Orne au XIXe siècle* (Bordeaux: Feret et Fils, 1915), p. 3.

30. AN, F7 11984, Basses-Pyrénées, Interior Minister, 5 February 1822.

31. Ibid., Pyrénées-Orientales, Duc de Montmorency, 2 February 1822.

32. AN, inventory to F7 series Réfugiés espagnols, general introduction.

33. AD Loire, 4 M 540. Prefect of the Loire, 16 April 1821.

34. AD Doubs, M 812, French ambassador at Berne, June 1822.

35. AD Loire, 4 M 540. Mayor of Rive-de-Gier, 25 April 1821.

36. Torpey, *Invention of the Passport*, chap. 2; Rapport, *Nationality*, pp. 135f.

37. AD Isère, 69 M 1, instructions relating to Passports, 20 August 1816. Gérard Noiriel, 'Surveiller les déplacements ou identifier les personnes? Contribution à l'historie du passeport en France de la 1re à la IIIe République', *Genèses* 30 (mars 1998), pp. 77–100.

38. Reports on the policing of travellers for passport infringements appear in the various dossiers in AD Rhône, 4 M 402, February–December 1823; Merriman, *Police Stories*, pp. 120–2.

39. AD Rhône, 4 M 17, Director of Police, Interior Ministry, 2 March 1822.

40. Ibid.

41. AD Rhône, 4 M 402, February–December 1823.

42. AD Isère, 52 M 25; AD Rhône, 4 M 402, 1820–3.

43. Neill Macaulay, *Dom Pedro: The Struggle for Liberty in Brazil and Portugal, 1798–1834* (Durham: Duke University Press, 1986), chap. 8; Luis A. de Oliveira Ramos, 'Le Portugal et la Révolution française (1777–1834)', in *Les révolutions dans le monde ibérique (1776–1834). Soulèvement national et révolution libérale: état des questions*, ed. Christian Hermann (Bordeaux: Presses Universitaires de Bordeaux, 1989), pp. 183–260.

44. AN, F15 3513, Prefect of the Finistère, 18 April 1829; Interior Minister, 12 May 1829.

45. Ibid., 1 May 1829.

46. AD Ille-et-Vilaine, 4 M 430, Interior Minister, 26 March 1829; 2 April 1829.

47. Ibid., Interior Minister, 10 April 1829.

48. AN, F15 3513, Prefect of the Mayenne, 24 August 1829.

49. Ibid., Interior Minister, 27 September 1829.

50. Ibid., AD Ille-et-Vilaine, 4 M 430, Interior Minister, 1 October 1829.

51. AN, F15 3513, Interior Minister, 26 September 1829; Prefect of Mayenne, 12 October 1829, 15 October 1829, 19 October 1829.

52. AD Ille-et-Vilaine, 4 M 430, Interior Minister, 1 October 1829.

53. Ibid., Interior Minister, 28 June 1830.

54. Ibid., Sub-prefect of Fougères, 7 November 1829.

55. Ibid., Mayor of Dol, 11 January 1830.

56. Ibid., Sub-prefect of St. Malo, 26 January 1830.

57. Ibid., Interior Minister, 25 June 1830.

## Part II   Revolutionary Exiles and the July Monarchy, 1830–48

1. Clive H. Church, *Europe in 1830* (London: George Allen and Unwin, 1983), pp. 5–7.

2. Philip Mansel, *Paris Between Empires, 1814–1852: Monarchy and Revolution* (London: Phoenix Press, 2001), p. 255.

3. Ibid., p. 259.

4. J. P. T Bury, *France 1814–1940*, 6th ed. (London and New York: Routledge, 2003), p. 49; A. Jardin and A. -J. Tudesq, *La France des notables*, vol. 1, *L'évolution générale, 1815–1848* (Paris: Seuil, 1973), p. 125.

5. Ibid., p. 126.

6. Irene Collins, ed., *Government and Society in France, 1814–1848* (London: Edward Arnold, 1970).

7. Bury, *France*, p. 54.

8. Philippe Darriulat, *Les patriotes: La gauche républicaine et la nation 1830–1870* (Paris: Seuil, 2001), p. 22; David H. Pinkney, *The French Revolution of 1830* (New Jersey: Princeton University Press, 1972), pp. 42–3; J. Lucas-Dubreton, *La royauté bourgeoise, 1830* (Paris: Hachette, 1930), pp. 74–9.

9. Darriulat, *Les patriotes*, p. 14.

10. *Moniteur*, 27 October 1831, Lafayette, pp. 1973–4.

11. François Guizot, *Mémoires*, vol. 3, *La Révolution du 1830* (Paris: Paleo, 2003), p. 66.

12. *Moniteur*, 1 October 1831, Périer, p. 1718.

13. *Moniteur*, 27 October 1831, Lafayette, p. 1973.

14. Guizot, *Mémoires*, vol. 3, p. 72.

15. The phrase is not found in the 5th edition of the Dictionnaire de l'Académie française (1798) but is found in its 6th edition of 1835, in the example 'Autrefois les ambassadeurs avaient droit d'asile', signifying legal entitlements and state protection. www.lib.uchicago.edu/efts/ARTFL/projects/dicos/ACADEMIE

## 3   The Limits of Tolerance

1. *Moniteur*, 27 October 1831, Périer, p. 1972.

2. Ibid.

3. *Moniteur*, 1 October 1831, Garde des Sceaux, p. 1718. AN, C 749, Dossier 32; Cécile Mondonico, 'L'asile sous la Monarchie de juillet: Les réfugiés étrangers en France de 1830 à 1848' (École des Hautes Études en Science Sociales), 14 September 1995, p. 17; Emmanuel Monasse, 'Les réfugiés politiques dans l'Hérault de 1814 à 1848: approche méthodologique', *Annales du Midi, Revue archéologique, historique et philologique de la France méridionale*, 108 (1996), pp. 201–18.

4. J. Mathorez, *Notes sur les réfugiés polonais dans la Sarthe et le Maine-et-Loire (1833–1873)* (Angers: G. Grassin, 1920), p. 3.

5. Pierre Gerbet, *Auvergne, terre d'accueil. La vie des réfugiés politiques à Clermont-Ferrand de 1815 à 1870* (Clermont-Ferrand: J. de Bussac, 1943), p. 9.

6. MAE, Mémoires et documents, France. Vol. 724; *Moniteur*, 1 October 1831, p. 1718. On the various aspects of assistance, *Moniteur*, 30 March 1832, p. 992. On the separate supplementary credits, *Moniteur*, 1 October 1831, p. 1718; 27 October 1831, pp. 1970f; 2 December 1831, p. 2277.

7. *Moniteur*, 1 October 1831, Périer, p. 1718.

8. Lloyd S. Kramer, *Threshold of a New World: Intellectuals and the Exile Experience in Paris, 1830–1848* (Ithaca and London: Cornell University Press, 1988), p. 527; Daniel Beauvois, 'Le nord de la France et les polonais entre 1831 et 1833', in *Pologne: L'insurrection de 1830–1831. Sa réception en Europe. Actes de colloque organisé les 14 et 15 mai 1981 par le Centre d'Etude de la Culture Polonaise de l'Université de Lille III*, ed. Daniel Beauvois (Lille: Université de Lille III, 1982), p. 43.

9. AN, F7 6780, Isère. 14 March 1831.

10. AN, F7 12329, 10 March 1831; 12 March 1831.
11. Ibid., 14 April 1831.
12. Laurent Louessard, *La révolution de juillet 1830* (Paris: Spartacus, 1990), pp. 218–9; Lucas-Dubreton, *La royauté bourgeoise*, pp. 77–9.
13. *Moniteur*, 1 October 1831, Périer, p. 1718.
14. Ibid.
15. *Moniteur*, 6 April 1832, Guizot, p. 1006.
16. Ibid.
17. Ibid., Parant, p. 1005.
18. *Moniteur*, 30 March 1832, Garde des Sceaux, p. 923.
19. *Moniteur*, 1 October 1831, Périer, p. 1718.
20. *Moniteur*, 10 April 1832, Guizot, p. 1022.
21. *Moniteur*, 27 October 1831, Lafayette, pp. 1973–4.
22. Ibid., Salverte, p. 1975.
23. Ibid.
24. Ibid., Joly, pp. 1970 & 1973.
25. *Moniteur*, 27 October 1831, Pagès, p. 1976. Anne-Joseph Salverte was forced into hiding and was sentenced to death in his absence following the Vendémiaire insurrection of 1794 (but was acquitted in 1796). Under the Restoration, Joly had been an ardent supporter of the democratic movement and spent one year in prison when implicated in a political scandal. Pagès' background was much less eventful, although he was interned after Waterloo for his service as Procureur Imperial of Saint-Girons. He moved to Paris in 1816 where he forged associations with Lafayette and Lafitte, producing a number of literary and political works, and collaborating on liberal newspapers. Among their supporters was Jean-Baptiste Teste, who did not speak during this debate. Teste had twice been forced into exile, first with his republican father after the Thermidorian reaction of 1794, and then for the duration of the Restoration for having served as Napoleon's police commissioner in Lyon during the One Hundred Days. Teste, however, was a moderate in the Chamber, associating himself with Dupin. It must also be remembered that Louis-Philippe himself experienced exile after the 1789 Revolution.
26. Ibid.
27. H.A.C. Collingham, *The July Monarchy: A Political History of France, 1830–1848* (London and New York: Longman, 1988), p. 63.
28. *Moniteur*, 27 April 1832, p. 1129. *Loi relative aux étrangers réfugiés qui résideront en France*, 21 April 1832. 'Art. 1. Le Gouvernement est autorisé à réunir dans une ou plusieurs villes qu'il désignera, les étrangers réfugiés qui résideront en France. 2. Le Gouvernement pourra les astreindre à se rendre dans celle de ces villes qui leur sera indiquée; il pourra leur enjoindre de sortir du royaume, s'ils ne se rendent pas à cette destination, ou s'ils jugent leur présence susceptible de troubler l'ordre et la tranquillité publique. 3. La présente loi ne pourra être appliqué aux étrangers réfugiés qu'en vertu d'un ordre signé par un ministre. 4. La présente loi ne sera en vigueur que pendant une année, à compter du jour de sa promulgation.'
29. *Moniteur*, 6 April 1832, Parant, p. 1005.
30. *Moniteur*, 30 March 1832, Parant, p. 924.
31. Ibid., Barthe.
32. *Moniteur*, 10 April 1832, Lafayette, p. 1020.
33. Ibid., Lamarque, p. 1022.
34. *Moniteur*, 6 April 1832, Parant, p. 1005.
35. *Moniteur*, 30 March 1832, Garde des Sceaux, p. 924.
36. *Moniteur*, 6 April 1832, Parant, p. 1005.

37. *Moniteur*, 10 April 1832, Laurence, p. 1025. Cf. Noiriel, *Tyrannie*, pp. 42–3.
38. *Moniteur*, 10 April 1832, Ministre de la Justice, p. 1025.
39. Ibid., Bavoux.
40. Ibid., Fiot and Lamarque.
41. Ibid., Dupin.
42. Mondonico, 'L'asile sous la Monarchie de juillet', p. 248.
43. *Moniteur*, 10 April 1832, Pagès, p. 1021. The proposed amendment read: 'Art 2. La répartition [de secours] sera faite par une commission présidée par un ministre du Roi et composée de trois pairs et de trois députés. Cette commission fera chaque année un rapport aux chambres sur le nombre et la résidence des réfugiés et sur la somme et la répartition des secours accordés. 3. Chaque réfugié recevra sa part des secours dans la ville où il voudra fixer sa résidence; toutefois le Gouvernement pourra lui interdire d'habiter à moins de 20 lieues des frontières'.
44. *Moniteur*, 10 April 1832, pp. 1022–8.
45. *Moniteur*, 27 October 1831, Périer, p. 1972.
46. Catherine J. Kudlick, 'Giving is Deceiving: Cholera, Charity, and the Quest for Authority in 1832', *French Historical Studies* 18, 2 (1993), p. 462; Louis Chevalier, *Labouring Classes and Dangerous Classes In Paris During the First Half of the Nineteenth Century*, trans. Frank Jellinek (London: Routledge and Kegan Paul, 1973), pp. 188–99.
47. François Delaporte, *Disease and Civilization*, trans. Arthur Goldhammer (Cambridge, Massachusetts and London, England: MIT Press, 1986), p. 10.
48. Catherine J. Kudlick, *Cholera in Post-Revolutionary Paris: A Cultural History* (Los Angeles and London: University of California Press, 1996), p. 38.
49. Ibid., pp. 41f.
50. Beauvois, 'Le nord', p. 63.
51. Kudlick, *Cholera*, p. 49.
52. Chevalier, *Labouring Classes*, p. 15.
53. Delaporte, *Disease*, pp. 54–65.
54. Catherine Duprat, *'Pour l'amour de l'humanité'. Le temps des philanthropes. La philantropie parisienne des Lumières à la Monarchie de juillet* (Paris: C.T.H.S., 1993), p. 33.
55. As, for example, in Sébastien Mercier's *Tableau de Paris*, quoted in Ibid., p. 41.
56. Catherine Duprat, *Usage et pratiques de la philanthropie. Pauvreté, action sociale et lien social à Paris, au cours du premier XIXe siècle*, vol. 1 (Paris: Association pour l'étude de l'hisotoire de la sécurité sociale, 1996), p. 305.
57. Jan Goldstein, *Console and Classify: The French Psychiatric Profession in the Nineteenth Century* (Cambridge: Cambridge University Press, 1987), pp. 44–5.
58. Robert A. Nye, *Crime, Madness and Politics in Modern France: The Medical Concept of National Decline* (Princeton: Princeton University Press, 1984), p. 43.
59. Gérard Bleandonu and Guy Le Gaufey, 'The Creation of the Insane Asylums of Auxerre and Paris', in *Deviants and the Abandoned in French Society: Selections from the Annales Economies, Sociétés, Civilisations*, ed. Robert Forster and Orest Ranum (Baltimore and London: John Hopkins University Press, 1978), pp. 183f.
60. Chevalier, *Labouring Classes*, pp. 137–8.
61. Henri Wallon, *Du droit d'asyle* (Paris: E.-J. Bailly, 1837), pp. 16–28 & 65.
62. Ibid., p. 107.
63. *Moniteur*, 27 October 1831; Pagès, p. 1976.
64. Ibid.
65. Ibid., Guizot, pp. 1971–2.
66. Florence Gauthier, *Triomphe et mort du droit naturel en Révolution, 1789–1795–1802* (Paris: Presses universitaires de France, 1992), p. 252.

67. Rights, Article 6. 'Declaration of the Rights and Duties of Citizens' (22 August 1795). Laura Mason and Tracey Rizzo, eds., *The French Revolution: A Document Collection* (Boston: Houghton Mifflin, 1999), p. 288.
68. Gauthier, *Triomphe et mort*, p. 253.
69. Duties, Articles 3, 5, 6, and 7. 'Declaration of the Rights and Duties of Citizens' (22 August 1795). Mason and Rizzo, eds., *The French Revolution*, p. 291.
70. Jean-Étienne-Marie Portalis, 'Discours préliminaire au Code civil', in *Les droits de l'homme* (Imprimerie nationale, 1801), p. 587.
71. Ibid., p. 592.
72. Articles 7 and 13. 'Titre 1: des Personnes. Code civil des français.' Bibliothèque Nationale de France, http://gallica.bnf.fr/scripts/ConsultationTout.exe?O= N087199.
73. Articles 1 and 4. 'Chartes constitutionnelles du 4 juin 1814 et du 14 août 1830'. Stéphane Rials, *Textes constitutionnels français. Que sais-je?* (Paris: Presses universitaires françaises, 1982), pp. 49–50.

## 4   The Practice of Asylum

1. *Moniteur*, 1 October 1831, Garde des Sceaux, p. 1718; AN, C 749, Dossier 32.
2. Comte Sanislas Araminski, *Histoire de la révolution polonaise depuis son origine jusqu'à nos jours (1772 à 1864)* (Paris: A. Fayard, 1864); Lucas-Dubreton, *La royauté bourgeoise*, p. 79; Michel Sokolnicki, *Les origines de l'émigration polonaise en France (1831–32)* (Paris: Alea, 1910), pp. 97–8.
3. Sokolnicki, *Les origines*, pp. 97–9 & 143–5.
4. R. F. Leslie, *Polish Politics and the Revolution of November 1830* (London: Athlone Press, 1956), pp. 259–60.
5. MAE, Mémoires et Documents, Pologne, vol. 33, 'Rapport sur l'acheminement vers la France des français et polonais, faisant partis des corps de Ramorino et de Rozicky, réfugiés en Galicie', Vienna, 11 Jan. 1832, fos. 25–38.
6. Sokolnicki, *Les origines*, pp. 97–8.
7. *Moniteur*, 30 March 1832, Périer, p. 922.
8. MAE, Mémoires et Documents, Pologne, vol. 33, Vienna, 11 January 1832, fos. 25–38.
9. A. P. Coleman, 'The Great Emigration', in *The Cambridge History of Poland, From Augustus II to Pilsudski (1697–1935)*, ed. W. F. Reddaway (Cambridge: Cambridge University Press, 1941), p. 312.
10. Ibid., p. 311.
11. Thadée Piotrowski, 'Les réfugiés polonais en France sous la monarchie de Juillet', in *Documents sur l'immigration*, ed. L. Chevalier (Paris: Presses universitaires de France, 1947), p. 49; Sokolnicki, *Les origines*, p. 98.
12. Piotrowski, 'Réfugiés polonais', p. 48; Sokolnicki, *Les origines*, p. 144.
13. Leslie, *Polish Politics*, pp. 259–60.
14. *Moniteur*, 30 March 1832, p. 923; MAE, Mémoires et Documents, Pologne, vol. 33, Foreign Minister, January 1833, fos. 122–3.
15. Peter Brock, 'Polish Democrats and English Radicals, 1832–1862: A Chapter in the History of Anglo-Polish Relations', *Journal of Modern History*, 25 (March-December 1953), p. 140 note 10.
16. Mondonico, 'L'asile sous la Monarchie de juillet', pp. 57–65; MAE, Mémoires et Documents, Pologne, vol. 33, Foreign Ministry, January 1833, fos. 78–84.

17. Ibid., Interior Minister, 22 November 1831, fo.47.
18. AD Doubs, M 819, Prefect of the Haut-Rhin, 29 January 1832.
19. AN, F7 6779, Côte d'Or, Commander of the Gendarmerie, 14 February 1832.
20. Beauvois, 'Le nord', p. 48.
21. J.-C. Gouy, 'Les réfugiés polonais au Puy après l'insurrection de 1830', *Cahiers d'histoire*, 3 (1979), p. 84.
22. Maria Straszewska, '"La cause polonaise" de 1830 dans la poésie et le théâtre français', in *Pologne, l'insurrection de 1830–1831, sa réception en Europe* (*Actes du colloque organisé les 14 et 15 mai 1981 par le Centre d'Etude de la Culture Polonaise de l'Université de Lille III*), ed. Daniel Beauvois (Lille: Université de Lille III, 1982), pp. 67–84.
23. 'Les Polonais. *Événemens historiques en quatre actes et en douze tableaux*, par M. Prosper, Cirque Olympique, 22 December 1831' (Bibliothèque polonaise, 30136).
24. AD Bas-Rhin, 3M 48, Commissaire of Police, 29 January 1832; Prefect, 28 January 1832.
25. Collingham, *The July Monarchy*, p. 63.
26. AN, F7 6784, Rapports de Gendarmerie, Vaucluse. 3 August 1832.
27. AD Bas-Rhin, 3M 48, Prefect of the Bas-Rhin, 25 February 1832.
28. Piotrowski, 'Réfugiés polonais', pp. 54–5. By April 1832, Avignon accommodated 1500 Polish military refugees; the majority were officers, with 300 rank-and-file soldiers. Châteauroux accommodated 1000 Polish civilian refugees.
29. Ibid., pp. 51–2; Mondonico, 'L'asile sous la Monarchie de juillet', pp. 191–9; AD Doubs, M 819, Mayor of Besançon, 3 December 1831.
30. AD Doubs, M 820; AD Doubs, M 814.
31. AD Doubs, M 819, Mayor of Besançon, 3 December 1831.
32. Ibid., Intendance sanitaire, 29 November 1831.
33. Ibid., Polonais militaires, 7 February 1833.
34. AD Doubs, M 813, 19–21 March 1833.
35. Mondonico, 'L'asile sous la Monarchie de juillet', p. 250.
36. AD Doubs, M 813, Interior Minister, 19 March 1833.
37. J. Mathorez, *Notes sur les réfugiés polonais dans la Mayenne* (*1833–1860*) (Angers: G. Grassin, 1918), p. 11; *Moniteur*, 12 April 1833, Interior Minister, p. 1028.
38. AN, F1a 38, Interior Minister, 2 March 1831; 17 May 1833; 28 May 1833.
39. Mathorez, *Réfugiés polonais dans la Sarthe*, p. 4.
40. Sokolnicki, *Les origines*, p. 70f.
41. Kenneth F. Lewalski, 'Heroes and Aliens: Everyday Life of Polish Refugees in France during the July Monarchy', *East European Monographs*, 2 (1993), p. 53.
42. Ibid., p. 60.
43. Gouy, 'Les réfugiés polonais au Puy', p. 84. Bibliothèque polonaise, dossiers 30136–30139 & 30147, *passim*.
44. Mathorez, *Réfugiés polonais dans la Mayenne*, p. 4; Mathorez, *Réfugiés polonais dans la Sarthe*, p. 4.
45. Gerbet, *Auvergne*, p. 15.
46. AD Doubs, M 826 (n.d., 1834).
47. W. H. Zawadzki, *A Man of Honour: Adam Czartoryski as a Statesman of Russia and Poland, 1795–1831* (Oxford and New York: Clarendon Press, 1993); Barbara Jelavich, 'The Polish Emigration, 1831–1871: The Challenge to Russia', in *L'Émigration politique en Europe aux XIXe et XXe siècles, actes du colloque organisé par l'École française de Rome, 3–5 mars 1988.* (Rome: École française de Rome, 1991), p. 235 & *passim*.

48. Jelavich, 'The Polish Emigration', p. 235; Brock, 'Polish Democrats', p. 139.
49. Kramer, *Threshold of a New World*, p. 179.
50. Sokolnicki, *Les origines*, p. 70.
51. *À la Chambre des Pairs de France*, 17 April 1832 (Bibliothèque polonaise, 30139); AN, BB17 A 79, 'Pétition des réfugiés polonais à la Chambre des Pairs au sujet de la loi votée par la Chambre des Députés', 17 April 1832.
52. *Moniteur*, Guizot, 6 April 1832, p. 1006.
53. AD Doubs, M 813, 7 February 1833; Commandant du camp, 13 March 1833.
54. MAE, Mémoires et documents, France, vol. 724, 19 March 1833, fos. 340f. The findings of these commissions were examined by a committee in the Interior Ministry, which then advised the Minister on his final decision.
55. AN, F7 12107, Interior Ministry, 15 October 1832; 14 April 1833; 18 November 1833.
56. AD Doubs, M 813, 17 March 1833; Géraud Lavergne, 'Le dépôt des réfugiés militaires polonais de Bergerac (1833)', in *Notices, inventaires et documents: Vol. XX, Études et documents divers*, ed. Ministère de l'Instruction publique et des Beaux-arts, Comité des Travaux historiques et scientifiques, Section d'Histoire moderne et d'Histoire contemporaine (Paris: Les Éditions Rieder, 1933), p. 88.
57. Ibid., p. 92.
58. AD Doubs, M 813, 13 March 1833.
59. *Moniteur*, 31 March 1833, Lafayette, p. 905.
60. AD Doubs, M 813, 2 March 1833; 13 March 1833; 14 March; 19–21 March 1833.
61. Lavergne, 'Le dépôt des réfugiés', p. 92.
62. AD Doubs, M 817, 1 April 1833.
63. AD Doubs, M 813, États nominatifs, 13 April 1833.
64. Ibid., Prefecture of Côte d'Or, 10 April 1833; 23 April 1833.
65. Ibid., Sub-Prefect of Pontarlier, 27 April 1833.
66. Ibid.
67. Ibid., Lieutenant of the Gendarmerie, Beaune, 8 April 1833.
68. Ibid., Prefect of Besançon, 9 April 1833; Sub-Prefect of Pontarlier, 27 April 1833.
69. Ibid., Prefect of Besançon, 9 April 1833.
70. MAE, Mémoires et documents, Pologne, vol. 35, fos. 5–6.
71. AD Doubs, M 817, 11 April 1833.
72. M. A. Kubalski, *Mémoires sur l'expedition des réfugiés polonais en Suisse et en Savoie* (Paris: Merklein, 1836); AD Doubs, M 826, Interior Minister, 20 September 1833; 28 February 1834; 13 May 1834.
73. *Moniteur*, 12 April 1833, Interior Minister, p. 1028.
74. AD Doubs, M 817, Interior Minister, 3 May 1833.
75. Mondonico, 'L'asile sous la Monarchie de juillet', pp. 198–9; Marie-Flora Hubert, 'La Pologne en France au XIXè siècle (1830–1865)' (Université des Sciences humaines, Strasbourg II, 1975), pp. 125–6.
76. Noiriel, *Tyrannie*, p. 54.
77. Mondonico, 'L'asile sous la Monarchie de juillet', pp. 206–11.
78. AD Doubs. M 817, Prefect of the Doubs, 4 June 1833.
79. AD Doubs, M 818, Interior Ministry, 19 May 1833; Prefect of the Haute-Saône, 28 October 1833.
80. AD Doubs, M 817, Interior Minister, 20 May 1833.
81. Ibid., Interior Minister, 24 May 1833.
82. AD Doubs, M 826, 16 December 1833.
83. AD Doubs, M 818, 21 June 1833.

84. MAE, Mémoires et documents, Pologne, vol. 33.
85. *Appel du peuple polonais au peuple français*, 27, 28 & 29 July 1833 (Bibliothèque polonaise, 30147).
86. *Aux réfugiés polonais*, 14 July 1835 (Bibliothèque polonaise, 30147).
87. 'Discours en mémoire de Lafayette du dépôt de Poitiers', June 1834 (Bibliothèque polonaise, 30147).
88. Respectively, 31 January 1834, 1 February 1834 and 6 February 1834 (Bibliothèque polonaise, 30147). Similar petitions were made by the inhabitants or mayors of Nevers, Château-Chinon, Decize (Nièvre), Bourges (Cher), Guéret (Creuse), Saint-Calais, La Flèche (Sarthe), Brive-la-Gaillarde (Corrèze), Fanjeaux, Peyriac-Minervois, Montréal (Aude), Angoulême (Charente) and Tonnerre (Yonne).

## 5 'A sentence passed in a shadow, by a hidden power'

1. *Moniteur*, 26 January 1834, Havin, p. 161.
2. *Moniteur*, 31 March 1833, Foreign Minister, p. 906.
3. Jill Harsin, *Barricades: The War of the Streets in Revolutionary Paris, 1830–1848* (New York: Palgrave Macmillan, 2002), *passim*.
4. *Moniteur*, 31 March 1833, Foreign Minister, p. 906.
5. Ibid., Tracy.
6. Robert J. Bezucha, *The Lyon Uprising of 1834: Social and Political Conflict in the Early July Monarchy* (Cambridge, Massachsetts: Harvard University Press, 1974), p. 122.
7. Ibid., p. 123. AN, F7 6779, Ain, 2 February 1834.
8. MAE Mémoires et documents, Pologne, vol. 33, Interior Ministry, 20 June 1835, fo.273.
9. Pamela M. Pilbeam, *Republicanism in Nineteenth-Century France, 1814–1871* (London: Macmillan, 1995), p. 124.
10. Collingham, *The July Monarchy*, pp. 157f; Robert Tombs, *France 1814–1914* (London and New York: Longman, 1996), p. 362.
11. Bezucha, *Lyon Uprising*, p. 135; Tombs, *France 1814–1914*, p. 362; Peter McPhee, *Social History*, p. 139.
12. Collingham, *The July Monarchy*, p. 160; Harsin, *Barricades*, *passim*.
13. Collingham, *The July Monarchy*, pp. 166–71, *passim*; Tombs, *France 1814–1914*, p. 363; Harsin, *Barricades*, chap. 5.
14. AN, C 762, Dossier 37; *Moniteur*, 3 April 1834, pp. 772–8.
15. *Moniteur*, 31 March 1833, Foreign Minister, p. 906.
16. Lloyd S. Kramer, 'The Rights of Man: Lafayette and the Polish National Revolution, 1830–1834', *French Historical Studies*, 14 (1985), p. 537.
17. AD Doubs, M 826, Interior Minister, 28 February 1834; 13 May 1834; 20 September 1833.
18. Brock, 'Polish Democrats', p. 139.
19. *Moniteur*, 3 April 1834, Interior Minister, p. 776.
20. Ibid., Kerbertin, p. 773.
21. Ibid., Salverte, p. 774.
22. Lewalski, 'Heroes and Aliens', pp. 55f; Simone Waquet, 'Les Polonais de l'exil dans la Nièvre (1832–1880)' *Actes de 54ème congrès de l'Association Bourguignonne des Société savantes* (10–12 juin 1983), (1985), p. 122.
23. Lewalski, 'Heroes and Aliens', pp. 55–8.
24. Mathorez, *Réfugiés polonais dans la Sarthe*, p. 8; Mathorez, *Réfugiés polonais dans la Mayenne*, p. 11.

25. *Moniteur*, 19 February 1834, Interior Minister, p. 354; Mondonico, 'L'asile sous la Monarchie de juillet', pp. 91–2.
26. Gouy, 'Les réfugiés polonais au Puy', p. 84.
27. Lewalski, 'Heroes and Aliens', p. 57; Mathorez, *Réfugiés polonais dans la Sarthe*, p. 4; Mathorez, *Réfugiés polonais dans la Mayenne*, p. 14.
28. AN, F7 6781, Landes, 30 September 1833; 1 October 1833; 3 October 1833.
29. *Moniteur*, 19 May 1837, Interior Minister, p. 1237.
30. MAE, Mémoires et documents, Pologne, vol. 31, 26 January 1837; 6 February 1837, fos. 256–61.
31. Ibid.
32. *Moniteur*, 12 April 1833, Interior Minister, p. 1028.
33. Ibid.
34. *Moniteur*, 19 May 1837, Interior Minister, p. 1237.
35. Mathorez, *Réfugiés polonais dans la Mayenne*, p. 18.
36. *Moniteur*, 6 May 1838, Montalembert and Harcourt, pp. 1133–4.
37. *Moniteur*, 9 June 1839, Interior Minister, p. 926.
38. Mathorez, *Réfugiés polonais dans la Sarthe*, p. 7.
39. Lewalski, 'Heroes and Aliens', pp. 58–9.
40. Ibid., pp. 66–7.
41. Ibid.
42. Jelavich, 'The Polish Emigration'; Zawadzki, *A Man of Honour*, pp. 329f; Kramer, *Threshold of a New World*, chap 4; Joanna Nowak, 'The Elitism of Polish 1831 Émigrés', *Polish Western Affairs*, 34, 2 (1993), p. 81.
43. AN, F7 12107, Interior Minister, 8 November 1833; Préfecture de Police, 22 February 1834. Amnesty was granted to all but a few Spanish constitutionalists compromised by their past political positions. Further concessions in February 1834 extended the amnesty to former deputies forced to leave Spain because of their political views.
44. Ibid., War Minister, 7 November 1833.
45. Ibid. Interior Minister, 14 April 1834.
46. MAE, Mémoires et documents, France, vol. 724.
47. *Moniteur*, 26 January 1834, Interior Minister, p. 160.
48. Pérez, *Histoire de l'Espagne*, pp. 528–33.
49. Raymond Carr, *Spain, 1808–1975*, 2nd ed. (Oxford: Clarendon Press, 1982), pp. 184–91.
50. *Moniteur*, 17 March 1836, Dugabé & Thiers, p. 485.
51. *Moniteur*, 9 June 1839, p. 926.
52. Carr, *Spain, 1808–1975*, pp. 184–91.
53. AN, BB17 A 110, 'Conduite à tenir à l'égard de Don Carlos pendant son séjour à Bourges'.
54. Pérez, *Espagne*, p. 587.
55. *Moniteur*, 17 March 1836, Vatout, p. 485.
56. AN, F1a 43, Interior Minister, 12 June 1840; AD Doubs, M 829, 30 June 1840; 1 September 1840.
57. Ibid., 16 September 1840.
58. Gerbet, *Auvergne*, p. 13.
59. J. Mathorez, *Les réfugiés politiques espagnols dans l'Orne au XIXe siècle* (Bordeaux: Feret et Fils, 1915), pp. 10–2.
60. AD Doubs, M 829, 31 October 1840; 19 December 1840.
61. *Moniteur*, 29 April 1841, Duprat, p. 1157.
62. AD Doubs, M 829, 23 August 1843; 24 November 1846.

63. AD Doubs, M 830, 22 October 1845.
64. *Moniteur*, 17 March 1836, Vatout, p. 485.
65. *Moniteur*, 19 June 1840, Interior Minister, p. 1486.
66. Ibid.
67. Ibid., p. 1487.
68. Ibid., Dugabé.
69. Ibid., Larcy.
70. In 1843, 333 German refugees were recorded in a total refugee population (assisted and unassisted) of 16,443. In 1845, 179 unassisted German refugees were recorded. *Moniteur*, 25 May 1843, Daguenet, p. 1261; *Moniteur*, 18 April 1846, Haussenville, p. 985.
71. Ibid., p. 985; *Moniteur*, 19 April 1846, p. 1004.
72. Collingham, *The July Monarchy*, chap. 16; Tombs, *France 1814–1914*, pp. 363–6.
73. Kramer, *Threshold of a New World*, p. 171.
74. MAE, Mémoires et documents, Pologne, vol. 31, Metternich, 18 March 1846, fos. 314–24.
75. Ibid., fos. 101–9.
76. AD Vaucluse, 4M 201, Interior Minister, 10 March 1846; 21 March 1846.
77. Ibid., 10 March 1846.

## Part III  A Republican Tradition: Asylum 1848–1920

1. *Moniteur*, 14 December 1848, p. 3555. AN, C 924, 459, 13 December 1848.
2. *Moniteur*, 7 November 1849, p. 3540. AN, C 1002, 1177, October 1849.

## 6  Asylum and the Mid-Century Crisis

1. Lawrence C. Jennings, *France and Europe in 1848: A Study of French Foreign Affairs in Time of Crisis* (Oxford: Clarendon Press, 1973), pp. 1–12 & 46–8.
2. AD Doubs, M 1192, 18 March 1848.
3. McPhee, *Social History*, p. 178; Maurice Agulhon, *The Republican Experiement, 1848–1852*, trans. Janet Lloyd (Cambridge: Cambridge University Press, 1983), pp. 51–5.
4. John M. Merriman, *The Agony of the Republic* (New Haven and London: Yale University Press, 1978), p. 54.
5. Philip Mansel, *Paris Between Empires, 1814–1852: Monarchy and Revolution* (London: Phoenix Press, 2001), p. 361.
6. AD Doubs, M 1192, 3 June 1848.
7. AD Rhône, 1 M 112, Interior Ministry, 14 & 19 March 1848, 4 April 1848.
8. AD Doubs, M 1192, 1 June 1848.
9. Mansel, *Paris Between Empires*, p. 412
10. Axel Körner, 'Ideas and Memories of 1848 in France: Nationalism, République universelle and Internationalism in the Goguette between 1848 and 1890', in *International Ideas and National Memories of 1848*, ed. Axel Körner (London: Macmillan, 2000), pp. 85–105.
11. AN, F1a 43, Interior Minister, 11 April 1841.
12. AD Doubs, M 812, 12 October 1847.
13. AD Doubs, M 849, Interior Minister, 31 March 1849.
14. AD Doubs, M 812, Interior Minister, 26 August 1848; Noiriel, *Tyrannie*, p. 60.
15. AD Doubs, M 812, Interior Minister, 26 August 1848; AD Doubs, M 849, Interior Minister, 29 May 1848.

16. *Moniteur*, 26 January 1834, Interior Minister, p. 160.
17. AD Haut-Rhin, 4 M 180, Interior Minister, 14 June 1833.
18. AD Bas-Rhin, 3 M 419, Director of General Security, 27 April 1848. AD Haut-Rhin, 4 M 174, Mayor of Huningue, 27 September 1848.
19. AD Bas-Rhin, 3 M 419, Commaissaire of the Bas-Rhin, 4 May 1848.
20. Ibid., 30 June 1848.
21. Ibid., 4 May 1848; Körner, 'Ideas and Memories of 1848'.
22. AD Doubs, M 812, War Ministry, 24 August 1948.
23. Ibid., War Ministry, 28 August 1948.
24. AD Bas-Rhin, 3 M 419, Commissaire of the Bas-Rhin, 28 April 1848.
25. Ibid., 15 June 1848; AD Doubs, M 849, Interior Minister, 31 March 1849.
26. AD Bas-Rhin, 3 M 419, Interior Minister, 13 July 1848.
27. AD Bas-Rhin, 3 M 420, Interior Minister, 21 May 1949.
28. AD Doubs, M 812, War Ministry, 24 August 1948.
29. AD Bas-Rhin, 3 M 420, Prefect of the Bas-Rhin, 5 June 1849.
30. Ibid., Interior Minister, 23 June 1849.
31. AD Doubs, M 849, 18 May 1849; AD Bas-Rhin, 3 M 415, Interior Minister, 18 May 1849.
32. Ibid.
33. AD Doubs, M 812. Interior Minister, 12 October 1847.
34. AD Bas-Rhin, 3 M 524, Interior Minister, 6 September 1849; AD Doubs, M 829, Interior Minister, 24 November 1846.
35. AD Doubs, M 812, Interior Minister, 26 August 1848, 28 August 1848.
36. Ibid., Interior Minister, [n.d. 1849].
37. Ibid., Interior Minister, 15 April 1849; AD Bas-Rhin, 3 M 415, Interior Minister, 22 May 1849.
38. AD Doubs, M 812, Interior Minister, 15 April 1849.
39. MAE, Mémoires et documents, Pologne, vol. 35, Interior Minister, 28 April 1849, fo. 150.
40. AD Doubs, M 849, Interior Minister, 18 May 1849; AD Doubs, M 1192, Interior Minister, 4 April 1849.
41. AD Doubs, M 812, Interior Minister [n.d. 1849].
42. AD Doubs, M 849, *passim*, 1849–50.
43. AD Bas-Rhin, 3 M 524, Interior Minister, 6 September 1849.
44. AD Doubs, M 849, Interior Minister, 29 May 1848.
45. AD Ille-et-Vilaine, 4 M 408, Interior Minister, 12 July 1849, 17 July 1848; AD Côtes-d'Armor, 4 M 264, Réfugiés allemands, 1848–51.
46. AD Doubs, M 812, Interior Minister [n.d. 1849].
47. Ibid., Interior Minister, 15 April 1849.
48. Tombs, *France 1814–1914*, p. 379.
49. AD Doubs, M 849, Interior Minister, 18 May 1849.
50. Ibid., Interior Minister, 31 March 1849; AD Doubs, M 812, Interior Minister, 15 April 1849.
51. AD Doubs, M 849, Interior Minister, 18 May 1849.
52. Ibid., 31 March 1849.
53. AD Bas-Rhin, 3 M 420, Interior Minister, 3 June 1849.
54. Ibid., Prefect of the Bas-Rhin, 1 June 1849.
55. AD Bas-Rhin, 3 M 415, Interior Minster, 22 May 1849, Prefect of the Bas-Rhin, 19 June 1849.
56. AD Doubs, M 812, Interior Minister, 15 April 1849.

57. AD Doubs, M 849, Interior Minister, 31 March 1849.
58. Patrick Weil, *La France et ses étrangers* (Paris: Gallimard, 1991), p. 27.
59. 'Loi sur la naturalisation et le séjour des étrangers en France', 3–11 December 1848, *Recueil Dalloz*, 1849 (4ème partie), pp. 171–5.
60. Ibid.
61. Ibid.
62. Ibid.
63. AD Rhône, 4 M 406, Interior Minister, 27 August 1851.
64. 'Loi sur la naturalisation', Article 7: Le Ministre de l'Intérieur pourra, par mesure de police, enjoindre à tout étranger voyageant en France de sortir immédiatement du territoire français et le faire conduire à la frontière. Article 8: Tout étranger qui se serait soustrait à l'exécution des mesures énoncées dans l'Article précédent, ou qui, après être sorti de France par suite de ces mesures, y serait rentré sans permission du Gouvernement sera traduit devant les tribunaux et condamné à un emprisonnement d'un mois à six mois. Après l'expiration de sa peine, il sera conduit à la frontière.
65. Howard C. Payne, *The Police State of Louis Napoleon Bonaparte, 1851–1860* (Seattle: University of Washington Press, 1966), p. 48.
66. AD Rhône, 4 M 17, Head of General Security, 22 January 1852.
67. Merriman, *Agony*, p. 129.
68. Ibid., p. 130.
69. Arthur Lehning, *From Buonarroti to Bakunin* (Leiden: E. J. Brill, 1970), pp. 150f; Woodford McClellan, *Revolutionary Exiles: The Russians in the First International and the Paris Commune* (London: Frank Cass, 1979), pp. 2–9; Payne, *Police State*, pp. 28 & 43–6.
70. Ibid., p. 46.
71. Körner, 'Ideas and Memories of 1848', pp. 85–105.
72. Lehning, *From Buonarroti to Bakunin*, p. 169; Bernard Porter, *The Refugee Question in Mid-Victorian Politics* (Cambridge University Press, 1979), chap. 5.
73. Circulaire du ministre de la police générale sur le séjour en France des réfugiés politiques. *Recueil Dalloz*, 1853 (3ème partie), pp. 28–9, Articles 1–4.
74. Ibid., Article 5.
75. Ibid., Article 6.
76. Noiriel, *Tyrannie*, p. 78.
77. Payne, *Police State*, p. 47.
78. Ibid., pp. 47 & 364; Merriman, *Agony*, p. 130.
79. Noiriel, *Tyrannie*, p. 79; Gérard Noiriel, *Le creuset français. Histoire de l'immigration, XIXe–XXe siècles* (Paris: Seuil, 1988), p. 74.
80. Ibid., p. 171; Gérard Noiriel, 'Français et étrangers', in *Les lieux de mémoire*, ed. Pierre Nora, *Français et étrangers* (Paris: Gallimard, 1992), pp. 276 & 285.
81. J. Michaud, *Le droit d'asile en Europe et en Angleterre* (Paris: Amyot, 1858).
82. M. Gand, *Code des Étrangers, ou état civil et politique, en France, des souverains, souveraines, princes, princesses, légations, consulats et simples particuliers étrangers.* (Paris: Chez l'auteur,1853).
83. AN, BB30 1175, 'Examen des exceptions aux principes généraux du droit naturel et du droit des gens universel concernant la juridiction et le droit d'asile' (1833).
84. Payne, *Police State*, p. 274.
85. Porter, *Refugee Question*, p. 62.
86. Ibid., chap. 6.
87. Michaud, *Droit d'asile*, pp. 3–4.

238 *Notes*

88. Ibid., pp. 8–11.
89. Egidio Reale, 'Le droit d'asile', in *Recueil des Cours de l'Academie de Droit International* (Paris: Sirey, 1938), chap. 1.
90. Ibid., p. 553.
91. D'Hector de Rochefontaine, *Procès-Verbal de l'audience solennelle de rentrée de la Cours Impériale de Grenoble, 4 novembre 1861. Étude historique sur le droit d'asile* (Grenoble: A. Baratier, 1861), p. 7.
92. Ibid., p. 40.

## 7 Socialist Revolutionaries, Mass Migration, War, 1870–1920

1. Weil, *La France et ses étrangers*, p. 27.
2. Noiriel, *Creuset*, p. 74.
3. Ibid; Noiriel, *Tyrannie*, p. 79.
4. Noiriel, 'Français et étrangers', pp. 276 & 285.
5. Yves Gohin, 'Préface', in *Victor Hugo, L'Année terrible* (Paris: Gallimard, 1985), p. 14.
6. Alistair Horn, *The Fall of Paris: The Siege and the Commune, 1870–71* (London: Papermac, 1990), p. 423.
7. 'Loi sur la nationalité', *Recueil Dalloz*, 1889 (4ème partie) pp. 59–72. Also, AN, C 3325, Dossiers 1373–1379; C 3384, Dossiers 1649–1651; & C 5410, Dossiers 1513–1515.
8. AN, C 5486, Dossier 1568, 'Proposition de loi tendant à régler la condition des étrangers en France'.
9. AD Rhône, 4 M 17, Justice Minister, 12 October 1875.
10. Ibid.
11. Francisque Grivaz, *L'extradition et les délits politiques*. (Paris: Librairie Nouvelle de Droit et de Jurisprudence, 1894).
12. Ibid., p. 114.
13. Paul Bernard, *Traité théorique et pratique de l'extradition. Commentaire des lois et traités*, vol. 2 (Paris: Librarie nouvelle de Droit et de Jurispridence, 1883), p. 659. See also Heinrich Lammasch, *Le droit d'extradition appliqué aux délits politiques*, trans. A Weiss and P Louis-Lucas (Paris: E. Thorin, 1885); Charles Soldan, *L'Extradition des criminels politiques* (Paris: E. Thorin, 1882).
14. George Woodcock, *Anarchism: A History of Libertarian Ideas and Movements* (Harmondsworth: Penguin Books, 1962), pp. 287–94; Peter Marshall, *Demanding the Impossible: A History of Anarchism* (London: Fontana, 1993), pp. 437–9.
15. Pierre Guillen, 'L'évolution du statut des migrants en France aux XIXe—XXe siècles', in *L'Émigration politique en Europe aux XIXe et XXe siècles. Actes du colloque organisé per l'École française de Rome, 3–5 mars 1988* (Rome: École française du Rome, 1991), p. 37. 'Lois ayant pour objet de réprimer les menées anarchistes', 28–9 juillet 1894, *Recueil Dalloz*, 1894 (4ème partie), pp. 81–7.
16. Michael Marrus, *The Unwanted: European Refugees in the Twentieth Century* (New York and Oxford: Oxford University Press, 1985), p. 26.
17. Philip Pomper, *Peter Lavrov and the Russian Revolutionary Movement* (Chicago and London: University of Chicago Press, 1972), pp. 204–5.
18. A Bitard, *Dictionnaire de biographie contemporaine* (1887).
19. Hugues, *JO, Débats parlementaires*, 24 February 1882, p. 165.
20. Ibid., p. 166.
21. Pomper, *Lavrov*, p. 205.

22. AN, C 3325, Dossier 1374. 'Proposition de loi tendant à rendre applicable seulement en temps de guerre les articles 7, 8 et 9 de la loi du 11 décembre 1849, sur la naturalisation et le séjour des étrangers en France'.
23. Ibid.
24. Porter, *Refugee Question*, p. 3, comments that because of the constitutional issues involved in making an expulsion order, Britain did not order the expulsion of any refugees during the nineteenth century.
25. AN, C 3325, Dossier 1374.
26. Ibid.
27. Ibid.
28. Ibid., 13 March 1882.
29. Ibid.
30. 'Loi sur la nationalité', *Recueil Dalloz*, 1889 (4ème partie), pp. 59–72; AN, C 3325; C 3384 & C 5410.
31. Rogers Brubaker, *Citizenship and Nationhood in France and Germany* (Cambridge, MA and London: Harvard University Press, 1992), chap 5; Patrick Weil, *Qu'est qu'un Français: Histoire de la nationalité française depuis la Révolution* (Paris: Grasset, 2002).
32. AN, C 5486, Dossiers 1568 & 1569. Cf. Brubaker, *Citizenship and Nationhood*, pp. 104–5; James R Lehning, *To be a Citizen: The Political Culture of the Early French Third Republic* (Ithaca and London: Cornel University Press, 2001), pp. 118–9.
33. Noiriel, *Creuset*, pp. 82–3; Charles Sowerwine, *France since 1870: Culture, Politics and Society* (New York: Palgrave Macmillan, 2001), p. 57.
34. Brubaker, *Citizenship and Nationhood*, chap. 5.
35. Arthur Desjardins, 'La loi de 1849 et l'expulsion des étrangers', *Revue des deux mondes* 50 (1882), p. 659.
36. Ibid., p. 664.
37. Ibid., p. 660.
38. Noiriel, *Creuset*, p. 88.
39. Michel Lesure, 'Les Réfugiés révolutionnaires russes à Paris. Rapport du Préfect de Police au Président du Conseil 16 décembre 1907', *Cahiers du Monde russe et sovietique*, 6, 3 (1965), p. 422; Wiktoria Sliwowska, 'Naissance de l'émigration politique russe', *Acta Poloniae Historica*, 25 (1972), pp. 33–56. On the Russian Jewish immigration to France in these years, Paula Hyman, *From Dreyfus to Vichy: The Remaking of French Jewry, 1906–1939* (New York: Columbia University Press, 1979), chap. 5; and Paula E. Hyman, *The Jews of Modern France* (Los Angeles and London: University of California Press, 1998), chap. 7.
40. Lesure, 'Les Réfugiés révolutionnaires', pp. 422–3.
41. Bernard Gainer, *The Alien Invasion: The Origins of the Aliens Act of 1905* (London: Heineman, 1972).
42. Hyman, *The Jews of Modern France*, p. 126.
43. U.S. Citizenship and Immigration Services. http://uscis.gov/graphics/shared/aboutus/statistics/IMM99tables.pdf.
44. John Higham, *Strangers in the Land: Patterns of American Nativism 1860–1925* (New Brunswick: Rutgers University Press, 1988).
45. Lehning, *To be a Citizen*, pp. 113–25.
46. Noiriel, *Creuset*, pp. 88–9.
47. Jean-Claude Farcy, *Les camps de concentration français de la première guerre mondiale (1914–1920)* (Paris: Anthropos, 1995), pp. 20–4.
48. Vincent Viet, *La France immigrée. Construction d'une politique, 1914–1997* (Paris: Fayard, 1998), pp. 33–4. Viet (p. 34, note 3) lists 78,500 Algerians, 18,000

Tunisians, 35,500 Moroccans, 4500 Madagascans, 49,000 Indochinese, and (note 6) 5500 Italians, 25,000 Greeks, 20,000 Portuguese and Spanish labourers, recruited to work in France during the Great War. See also Ralph Schor, *Histoire de l'immigration en France de la fin du XIXe siècle à nos jours* (Paris: Armand Colin, 1996), pp. 40–1; Jean Vidalenc, 'La main-d'oeuvre étrangère en France et la première guerre mondiale (1901–1926)', in *Francia. Forschungen zur westeuropeäischen Gerschichte* (München: Artemis Verlag Zürich und München, 1975), p. 535.

49. Schor, *Histoire de l'immigration*, pp. 38–9.
50. Philippe Chassaigne, 'War, Delinquency, and Society in Bordeaux, 1914–1918', in *Criminal Justice History: An International Annual* (Westport and London: Greenwood Press, 1994), pp. 200–1.
51. Jean-Philippe Bon, 'L'engagement des Catholiques du diocèse de La Rochelle-Saintes dans le premier conflit mondial', *Guerres mondiales et conflits contemporains*, 197 (2000), p. 78.
52. Paul Lévy, 'Les angoumoisins pendant la Grande Guerre', *Guerres mondiales et conflits contemporains*, 182 (1996), pp. 140–1.
53. Schor, *Histoire de l'immigration*, p. 40.
54. AD Rhône, R 1614, Statistics for the Rhône (1914–19); AD Isère, 61 M 16, August 1915.
55. Ibid.
56. AD Rhône, R 1608, *Instructions portant fixation du Régime des Réfugiés* (1916).
57. Ibid., Prefect of the Rhône, 20 & 27 September 1917.
58. AD Rhône, R 1608, Prefect of the Rhône, 12 March 1918.
59. AD Isère, 13 R 222.
60. Tim Judah, *The Serbs: History, Myth, and the Destruction of Yugoslavia* (New Haven, CT: Yale University Press, 1997), pp. 100–1.
61. AD Isère, 13 R 209.
62. AD Rhône, 1 M 154, Prefect of the Rhône, 12 June 1916 & 12 August 1916; Secretary General of the Comité du Secours National, 20 June 1916.
63. Egidio Reale, 'Le problème des passeports', in *Recueil des Cours de l'Academie de Droit International* (Paris: Sirey, 1934), p. 110–2; Torpey, *Invention of the Passport*, pp. 111–21.
64. Quoted in Vidalenc, 'La main-d'oeuvre étrangère', p. 540.
65. AD Rhône, R 1614. Affaires militaires. Réfugiés, renseignement, statistiques pour le département du Rhône (1914 à 1919). État des réfugiés en residence dans le Rhône en 1919.
66. AD Isère, 13 R 222, December 1918.
67. Gary S. Cross, *Immigrant Workers in Industrial France: The Making of a New Laboring Class* (Philadelphia: Temple University Press, 1983), p. 53.
68. Jean-Jacques Becker, *The Great War and the French People*, trans. Arnold Pomerans, (Providence and Oxford: Berg, 1985), p. 136.
69. Ibid., p. 142. See also *Philippe. Nivet, Les refugiés français de la grande guerre. Les 'boches du nord'* (Paris: Economica, 2004).

## Part IV  'Around the corner from a hostile France, a France more amicable', 1920–39

1. Hannah Arendt, *The Origins of Totalitarianism* (San Diego: Harcourt Brace Jovanovich, 1973), chap. 2.
2. Henri Verneuil, 'Mayrig' (France: TF1, 1991).

3. Henri Verneuil, *Mayrig* (Paris: Robert Laffont, 1985), p. 18.
4. Ibid, pp. 29–32.
5. Ralph Schor, *L'opinion française et les étrangers, 1919–1939* (Paris, publication de la Sorbonne, 1985), pp. 95 & 102–33.
6. Michael R. Marrus, 'Vichy Before Vichy: Antisemitic Currents in France during the 1930s', *Weiner Library Bulletin*, 33 (1980), pp. 13–9; Michael R. Marrus and Robert O. Paxton, *Vichy France and the Jews* (Stanford: Stanford University Press, 1981), chap. 2; Vicki Caron, 'The Antisemitic Revival in France in the 1930s: The Socioeconomic Dimension Reconsidered', *Journal of Modern History*, 70, 1, March (1998), pp. 26–7; Vicki Caron, *Uneasy Asylum: France and the Jewish Refugee Crisis, 1933–1942* (Stanford, CA: Stanford University Press, 1999); Richard Millman, *La question juive entre les deux guerres. Ligues de droite et antisémitisme en France, Collection l'ancien et le nouveau* (Paris: Armand Colin, 1992), p. 145; Noiriel, *Creuset*, pp. 337–8; Ralph Schor, *L'Antisémitisme en France pendant les années trente* (Paris: Éditions Complexe, 1992), pp. 309–10; Pierre Birnbaum, 'La France aux Français'. *Histoire des haines nationalistes* (Paris: Seuil, 1993). See Greg Burgess, 'France and the German Refugee Crisis of 1933', *French History*, 16 (2002), pp. 203–29 for a discussion of the historiographical question raised here.
7. Sir John Hope Simpson, *The Refugee Problem: Report of a Survey* (London: Oxford University Press, 1939), pp. 297–8.
8. Ibid., pp. 230–1.
9. Schor, *Opinion française et les étrangers*, p. 313.
10. Ibid., pp. 313–6.

## 8 Migration and Asylum After the Great War

1. C. A. Macartney, *Refugees: The Work of the League* (London: The League of Nations Union, 1930), pp. 8–9.
2. J. L. Rubinstein, 'The Refugee Problem', *International Affairs*, XV, 5 (Sept.–Oct. 1936), p. 716.
3. Macartney, *Refugees*, p. 21; Isabelle Repiton, *L'opinion française et les émigrés russes, à travers la litterature française de l'entre-deux-guerres* (Paris: Institute d'Études Politiques, 1986), p. 11, compares the figure of one million Russian expatriates between 1919 and 1925 counted by the Russian émigré Pierre Kovalevsky with the League of Nations' estimates of 1,160,000, and the figure of 1.5 million adopted by the Conference of Russian Organisations. Michael Marrus, *The Unwanted*, p. 52, accepts the figure of two million Russian and Ukrainian refugees by 1926. Simpson, *Refugee Problem*, p. 82, notes the American Red Cross figure was 1,963,500 refugees in November 1920. His own review of the 1922 figures concluded that the total was more accurately somewhere between 653,600 and 755,200.
4. Macartney, *Refugees*, p. 13. LND A.30.1923.XIII, 4 September 1923, p. 1.
5. Ibid., pp. 12–9.
6. LNA File 12/10311/8822, *Russian Refugees from the Crimea*, Geneva, 14 February 1921; LNA File 11/11690/10598, *Letter from the International Committee of the Red Cross*, 30 March 1921.
7. LND C.M.21/41/32, 20 February 1921.
8. Ibid.
9. Macartney, *Refugees*, p. 50; Christopher J. Walker, 'Armenian Refugees: Accidents of Diplomacy or Victims of Ideology?' in *Refugees in the Age of Total War*, ed. Anna C. Bramwell (London: Unwin Hyman, 1988), pp. 38–50.

242 *Notes*

10. Macartney, *Refugees*, pp. 51–3.
11. LND A.33.1928.XIII, 22 August 1928, p. 5.
12. Macartney, *Refugees*, p. 55.
13. Claudena Skran, *Refugees in Interwar Europe: The Emergence of a Regime* (Oxford: Oxford University Press, 1995), pp. 171–2; Madeleine de Bryas, *Les peuples en marche: les migrations politique et économique depuis la guerre mondiale* (Paris: A. Pedone, 1926), p. 63; André N. Mandelstam, 'La protection international des droits de l'homme', *Recueil des Cours de l'Academie de Droit International*, 38 (1934), p. 153.
14. LND A.30.1923.XIII, 4 September 1923, pp. 14–7; Elena Chinyaeva, 'Russian Émigrés: Czechoslovak Refugee Policy and the Development of the International Refugee Regime between the Two World Wars', *Journal of Refugee Studies*, 8, 2 (1995), p. 147.
15. LND, A.48.1927.VIII (XIII), 5 September 1927, Annex V; Greg Burgess, 'Into the Protecting Arms: The League of Nations and the Extension of International Assistance to Unprotected Persons in the Middle East and Europe, 1926–1928', *Eras*, 1 (2001).
16. Simpson, *Refugee Problem*, p. 64; Fu-Yung Hsu, *La protection des réfugiés par la Société des Nations* (Lyon: Bosc Frères, 1935), pp. 70f.
17. Ibid., pp. 74–5.
18. Simpson, *Refugee Problem*, p. 299.
19. Bryas, *Peuples en marche*, p. 68.
20. Repiton, *L'opinion française*, pp. 24–5.
21. U.S. Citizenship and Immigration Services, http://uscis.gov/graphics/shared/aboutus/statistics/IMM99tables.pdf.
22. Egidio Reale, 'Passeports', pp. 113–4.
23. Bryas, *Peuples en marche*, p. 76; Jean-Charles Bonnet, *Les pouvoirs publics français et l'immigration dans l'entre-deux-guerres* (Lyon: CNRS; Centre d'Histoire économique et social de la Région lyonnaise, 1976), p. 24.
24. Paul Lawrence, '"Un flot d'agitateurs politiques, de fauteurs de désordre et de criminels": Adverse Perceptions of Immigrants in France Between the Wars', *French History*, 14, 2 (2000), pp. 201–21; Donald N. Baker, 'The Surveillance of Subversion in Interwar France: The Carnet B in the Seine, 1922–1940', *French Historical Studies*, 3 (1978), pp. 486–516.
25. Gary S. Cross, *Immigrant Workers in Industrial France: The Making of a New Laboring Class* (Philadelphia: Temple University Press, 1983), p. 55.
26. Ibid., pp. 52–5. Louis Pasquet, *Immigration et main d'oeuvre étrangère en France* (Paris: Éditions Rieder, 1927), chaps. 1–4
27. Cross, *Immigrant Workers*, pp. 137–8
28. Ibid., p. 149.
29. Ibid., pp. 46f.
30. Gary Cross, 'Towards Peace and Social Prosperity: The Politics of Immigration in France during the Era of World War One,' *French Historical Studies* 11, 4 (1980), p. 610; Repiton, *L'opinion française*, p. 27.
31. Marie-Françoise Attard-Maraninchi and Emile Témime, *Migrance: Histoire de l'immigration marseillaise*, vol. 3, *Le cosmopolitisme de l'entre-deux-guerres (1919–1945)* (Marseille: Edisud, 1990), p. 45.
32. See especially his sequel to *Mayrig*, the film of his childhood. Henri Verneuil, '588 Rue Paradis' (France: TF1, 1991).
33. Attard-Maraninchi and Témime, *Migrance*, vol. 3, pp. 45 & 56; 'Refugees: Report on Russian, Armenian, German and Saar Refugees in France' (London: Save the Children Fund, 1935), p. 11.

34. Attard-Maraninchi and Témime, *Migrance*, vol. 3, p. 43.
35. LND, A.48.1927.XIII. 5 September 1927, Annexure V.
36. Ibid.
37. Simpson, *Refugee Problem*, pp. 43, 82 & 297f. On the estimates for Armenian refugees, see especially Appendix IV, p. 558. The details of the smaller refugee groups at this time were outlined in League of Nations Document, A.48.1927.XIII, 5 September 1927. See Burgess, 'Protecting Arms'.
38. Simpson, *Refugee Problem*, Appendix IV, p. 558; LND, A.33.1928.XIII, 22 August 1928; Walker, 'Armenian Refugees: Accidents of Diplomacy or Victims of Ideology?'
39. M. Rozzi, 'La Communauté arménienne à Nice entre 1919 et 1939', *Recherches régionales*, 4 (1987), p. 237.
40. Attard-Maraninchi and Témime, *Migrance*, vol. 3, p. 48; Maud S. Mandel, *In the Aftermath of Genocide: Armenians and Jews in Twentieth-Century France* (Durham and London: Duke University Press, 2003), pp. 31–3.
41. 'Refugees', p. 3.
42. Attard-Maraninchi and Témime, *Migrance*, vol. 3, p. 46.
43. 'Refugees', p. 3.
44. Mandel, *Aftermath of Genocide*, p. 33.
45. Attard-Maraninchi and Témime, *Migrance*, vol. 3, pp. 47–9.
46. Ibid., p. 48; Mandel, *Aftermath of Genocide*, pp. 34–5.
47. Attard-Maraninchi and Témime, *Migrance*, vol. 3, p. 55.
48. Simpson, *Refugee Problem*, p. 299.
49. 'Refugees', p. 1.
50. Simpson, *Refugee Problem*, p. 300.
51. 'Refugees', p. 11.
52. Pierre George, 'L'immigration italienne en France de 1920 à 1939 aspects démographiques et sociaux', in *Les italiens en France de 1914 à 1940*, ed. Pierre Milza (Rome: École française de Rome, 1986), p. 50.
53. Attard-Maraninchi and Témime, *Migrance*, vol. 3, pp. 55–6.
54. Raymond Millet, *Trois millions d'étrangers en France: Les indésirables, les bienvenus* (Paris: Librairie de Médicis, 1938).
55. George, 'L'immigration italienne', p. 50.
56. Pierre Guillen, 'Le rôle politique de l'immigration italienne en France dans l'entre-deux-guerres', in *Les italiens en France de 1914 à 1940*, ed. Pierre Milza (Rome: École française de Rome, 1986), p. 323.
57. Ibid.; Pierre Milza, 'L'immigration italienne en France d'une guerre à l'autre: interrogations, directions de recherche et premier bilan', in *Les italiens en France de 1914 à 1940*, ed. Pierre Milza (Rome: École française de Rome, 1986), p. 28.
58. Pierre Guillen, 'Le rôle politique de l'immigration italienne', in *Les italiens en France de 1914 à 1940*, ed. Pierre Milza (Rome: École française de Rome, 1986), p. 323; G. Marcel-Rémond, *L'immigration italienne dans le sud-ouest de la France* (Paris: Librairie Dalloz, 1928), p. 34.
59. Ibid., pp. 23–9.
60. Ibid., pp. 34–6.
61. Milza, 'L'immigration italienne', p. 29; Guillen, 'Le rôle politique de l'immigration', p. 329.
62. Milza, 'L'immigration italienne', p. 31.
63. Guillen, 'Le rôle politique de l'immigration', pp. 329f; Loris Castellani, 'Un aspect de l'émigration communiste italienne en France: les groupes de lange italiene au sein du PCF (1921–1928)', in *Les italiens en France de 1914 à 1940*, ed. Pierre Milza

(Rome: École française de Rome, 1986), pp. 195–221; Gaetano Manfredonia, 'Les anarchistes italiens en France dans la lutte antifasciste', in *Les italiens en France de 1914 à 1940*, ed. Pierre Milza (Rome: École française de Rome, 1986), pp. 223–55.

64. Castellani, 'Un aspect de l'émigration communiste', p. 201.
65. Milza, 'L'immigration italienne', p. 32; Simpson, *Refugee Problem*, pp. 121–2.
66. Ibid., pp. 297–8.
67. Cross, *Immigrant Workers*, p. 167.
68. Schor, *Opinion française et les étrangers*, p. 455; Bonnet, *Pouvoirs publics*, pp. 15 & 65–70.
69. Schor, *Opinion française et les étrangers*, p. 455.
70. Guillen, 'L'évolution du statut des migrants en France', pp. 35–55.
71. A major theme of this period was natality and, metaphorically, the 'rebirth' of the French race through population growth, motherhood and the family. Karen Offen, 'Depopulation, Nationalism and Feminism in Fin-de-Siecle France', *American Historical Review*, 89, 3 (June 1984); Siân Reynolds, *France Between the Wars: Gender and Politics* (London and New York: Routledge, 1996), chap. 1; Elisa Camiscioli, 'Producing Citizens, Reproducing the "French Race": Immigration, Demography, and Pronatalism in Early Twentieth-Century France', *Gender and History*, 13, 3 (November 2001); Andres Horacio Reggiani, 'Procreating France: The Politics of Demography, 1919–1945', *French Historical Studies*, 19, 3 (Spring 1996).
72. Gérard Noiriel, *Les origines républicaines de Vichy* (Paris: Hachette, 1999), chap. 3; Paul Lawrence, 'Naturalization, Ethnicity and National Identity in France between the Wars', *Immigrants and Minorities*, 20, 3 (2001); Patrick Weil, 'Racisme et discrimination dans la politique française de l'immigration, 1938–1945/1974–1995', *Vingtième siècle* 47, (July–September 1995); Weil, *Qu'est qu'un Français*, pp. 81f; Clifford Rosenberg, 'Albert Sarraut and Republican Racial Thought', *French Politics, Culture and Society*, 20, 3 (2002); Pierre-André Taguieff, 'Face à l'immigration: mixophobie, xénophobie ou sélection. Un débat français dans l'entre-deux-guerres.' *Vingtième siècle*, 47, (July–September 1995).
73. William H. Schneider, *Quality and Quantity: The Quest for Biological Regeneration in Twentieth-Century France* (Cambridge: Cambridge University Press, 1990), chap. 9.
74. Bonnet, *Pouvoirs publics*, pp. 65–6 identifies some 19 texts on immigration published between 1925 and 1927. He lists the following as the most important contributions: Marcel Paon, *L'immigration en France* (1926); André Pairault, *L'immigration organisée* (1926); Charles Lambert, *La France et les étrangers* (1927); William Oualid, *L'immigration ouvrière en France* (1927); and Louis Pasquet, *Immigration et main-d'oeuvre étrangère en France* (1927).
75. Marcel Paon, *l'Immigration en France* (Paris: Payot, 1926), p. 127.
76. Bonnet, *Pouvoirs publics*, pp. 57–9 & 81.
77. Paon, *Immigration*, pp. 181f.
78. Ibid., p. 174.
79. Georges Mauco, *Les étrangers en France. Leur rôle dans l'activité économique* (Paris: Armand Colin, 1932), pp. 557f.
80. Ibid., pp. 510f.
81. Charles Lambert, *La France et les étrangers. Dépopulation, immigration, naturalisation* (Paris: Librarie Delagrave, 1928), p. 75.
82. Cross, *Immigrant Workers*, p. 173.
83. Greg Burgess, 'Selection, Exclusion and Assimilation. The *Projet Lambert* of 1931 on the Reform of French Immigration Policy', In *French History and Civilisation: Papers from the George Rudé Seminar* 1 (2005), pp. 190–207.

84. Bonnet, *Pouvoirs publics*, p. 76.
85. Ibid.
86. Ibid., p. 74.
87. Ibid., pp. 61f.
88. Mandel, *In the Aftermath of Genocide*, p. 40.
89. Ibid., pp. 38–41.
90. 'Refugees', p. 8.
91. Ibid., p. 5. On the quota system, Cross, *Immigrant Workers*, pp. 193–4.
92. LND Réfugiés, 1930.XIII.L, p. 16.
93. Ibid., pp. 23–4.
94. Ibid., pp. 49–50.

## 9 The German Refugee Crisis, 1933–5

1. Saul Friedländer, *Nazi Germany and the Jews: The Years of Persecution, 1933–1939* (London: Weidenfeld and Nicolson, 1997), chap. 1.
2. From the total of 59,300 refugees who fled Germany by the end of 1933, 51,065 where Jewish, and 8235 non-Jewish. LNA C.1612, Opening Session of the Governing Body, 5 December 1933; C.1613, Third Session of the Governing Body, 1 November 1934.
3. AN, F7 16079. Foreign Ministry, 28 September 1933.
4. MAE, Europe 1930–1940, 710, Allemagne. Note, 31 March 1933, fos. 9–12.
5. Sowerwine, *France since 1870*, p. 141; Gordon Wright, *France in Modern Times. From the Enlightenment to the Present*, 4th ed. (New York: Norton, 1987), p. 361.
6. AN, F7 16079, Interministerial Commission, First Session, 27 May 1933.
7. Ibid.
8. Caron, *Uneasy Asylum*.
9. Reale, 'Passeports', pp. 91–188.
10. AN, F7 16079, Interministerial Commission, Third Session, 22 October 1933.
11. Michel Winock, *Nationalism, Anti-Semitism, and Fascism in France*, trans. Jane Marie Todd (Stanford, CA: Stanford University Press, 1998), chap. 7.
12. Hyman, *The Jews of Modern France*, p. 120.
13. Ibid., p. 122; Hyman, *From Dreyfus to Vichy*, pp. 199f; Vicki Caron, 'Loyalties in Conflict: French Jewry and the Refugee Crisis, 1933–35', in *Leo Baeck Institute Yearbook 1991* (New York: Secker and Warburg, 1991), pp. 305–38; David H. Weinberg, *A Community on Trial: The Jews of Paris in the 1930s* (Chicago and London: University of Chicago Press, 1977), chaps 5 & 6.
14. MAE, Europe 1930–1940, 710. Foreign Minister, 3 May 1933, fos. 96–7.
15. Ibid., Note, 31 March 1933, fos. 9–12.
16. Ibid., Consul General, Cologne, fos. 117–21.
17. AN, F7 16079, French Consul, Ostend, 19 February 1934.
18. MAE, Europe 1930–1940, 710, Note, 31 March 1933, fos. 9–12; Consul General, Cologne, fos. 117–21.
19. Ibid., Note, 31 March 1933, fos. 9–12.
20. AN, F7 16054.
21. Hanna Schramm and Barbara Vormeier, *Vivre à Gurs. Un camp de concentration français, 1940–1941* (Paris: Éditions François Maspero, 1979), p. 213.
21a. On this question, see for example Clifford Rosenberg, *Policing Paris. The Origins of Modern Immigration Control between the Wars* (Ithaca and London: Cornell University Press, 2006), chap. 3, which discusses the personnel of the immigration service of the Paris Prefecture of Police and their function in the policing of foreigners.

22. 'Décret réglementant la délivrance des cartes d'identité destinées aux étrangers, 10 juillet 1929', *Recueil Dalloz*, 1929 (4ème partie), p. 271.
23. Schramm and Vormeier, *Vivre à Gurs*, p. 202.
24. AN, F7 16054, 2 June 1932.
25. Article 3. 'Décret réglementant la délivrance des cartes d'identité destinées aux étrangers, 10 juillet 1929', *Recueil Dalloz*, 1929 (4ème partie), p. 271.
26. Article 1. 'Décret modifiant l'art. 3 du décret du 10 juill. 1929 concernant le régime des cartes d'identité d'étrangers, 21 mai 1932', *Recueil Dalloz*, 1932 (4ème partie), p. 125.
27. 'Refugees', p. 17.
28. AN, F7 16054, 20 March 1931.
29. Article 7, 'Décret réglementant la délivrance des cartes d'identité destinées aux étrangers, 10 juillet 1929', *Recueil Dalloz*, 1929 (4ème partie), pp. 271–2.
30. AN, F7 16054, 8 March 1932.
31. Caron, *Uneasy Asylum*, pp. 21–2. Caron notes that despite a promise he would issue work permits to refugees with few restrictions, the labour minister could report that only 200 work permits had been issued up to October 1933.
32. Marcel Livian, *Le régime juridique des étrangers en France* (Paris: Librairie générale de droit et de jurisprudence, 1936), pp. 207–8. Refoulements rose from 5401 in 1932 to 6982 in 1934, while expulsions declined from 9280 in 1931 to 6565 in 1934.
33. Ibid.; Schramm and Vormeier, *Vivre à Gurs*, p. 217.
34. Ibid., p. 218.
35. Richard Breitman, Barbara McDonald Steward, and Severin Hochberg, eds. *Advocate for the Doomed: The Diaries and Papers of James G. McDonald, 1932–1935* (Bloomington and Washington: Indiana University Press and the United States Holocaust Memorial Museum, 2007), p. 219 & p. 256 n24.
36. Livian, *Le régime juridique des étrangers en France*, pp. 177–8.
37. AN, F7 16079, note 2 (n.d., 1933).
38. Ibid.
39. Ibid.
40. MAE, Europe 1930–1940, 710, Service française de la Société des Nations, 24 August 1933, fos. 249–53.
41. AN, F7 16079, Interministerial Commission, Second Session,16 October 1933.
42. MAE, Europe 1930–1940, 711. Contrôle des Étrangers et Visa Consulaire, 18 December 1933, fos. 143–8.
43. Ibid., Interministerial Commission, Fourth Session, 13 November 1933.
44. Leo Baeck Institute, HCR Minutes, P.V. 5. Henri Bérenger. Procès-verbaux du Haut commissariat des réfugiés provenant d'Allemagne, cinquième séance, première session du Conseil d'administration, Lausanne, 7 December 1933.
45. AN, F7 16079, Interministerial Commission, Third Session, 22 October 1933.
46. MAE, Minorités, 448, Aide-Memoire, Réfugiés allemands en France, 22 November 1933, fos. 76–84.
47. Ibid.
48. AN, F7 16079, Interministerial Commission, Second Session, 16 October 1933.
49. LNA, C.1613, Third Session of the Governing Body, 1 November 1934.
50. AN, F7 16079, Interministerial Commission, Third Session, 22 October 1933.
51. Ibid.
52. Ibid.
53. Ibid., Interministerial Commission, Fourth Session, 13 November 1933.
54. Ibid.

55. Ibid.
56. AN, F7 16080, Société ORT.
57. Ibid., Hehaloutz (le Pionnier).
58. Ibid., Association Concorde et Progrès, 10 April 1934 & 15 May 1934.
59. Ibid., Labour Minister, 4 November 1933.
60. Ibid., Prefect of the Charente-Inférieur, 2 November 1933.
61. Ibid., Edith Pye, 21 July 1933.
62. AN, F7 16080, Prefect of the Pyrénées-Orientales, 14 October 1933.
63. AN, F7 16080, Soursac, Main d'Oeuvre Etrangère, 5 August 1933.
64. LNA, C.1613. Summary of the Meeting of Special Committee on Emigration Possibilities, 19 July 1934.
65. AN, F7 16080, Institut Montesson, 1933.
66. Ibid., 28 November 1933.
67. Ibid., Prefect of the Seine-et-Oise, 4 December 1933 & 19 December 1933.
68. Ibid., Interior Minister, 10 March 1934.
69. Ibid., Pietrkowski, 2 November 1933.
70. Ibid., Prefect of the Seine-et-Oise, 6 November 1933.
71. Ibid.
72. Ibid., Interior Minister, 23 November 1933.
73. Ibid., Pietrkowski, 4 December 1933.
74. Ibid.
75. Ibid., Prefect of the Seine-et-Oise, 28 March 1935.
76. Caron, *Uneasy Asylum*, pp. 51–8; MAE, Questions Sociales, 1811, *passim*.
77. MAE, Questions sociales. 1810, fos. 28.
78. Ibid., fos. 5–7 & 28.
79. Ibid., Note, 24 January 1935, fos. 32–3; M. Knox, 24 January 1935, fo. 40.
80. Ibid., Interministerial Commission, 31 January 1935, fo. 94.
81. Ibid., fos. 94–8.
82. Ibid., fos. 272–4.
83. Ibid., fos. 191–3; Procès-verbal, 21 June 1935, fos. 198–200.
84. Ibid.
85. *JO, Débats parlementaires, Chambre des Députés*, 29 January 1935, Garchery, pp. 256–7.
86. Ibid.
87. Ibid., Herriot. See also Bonnet, *Pouvoirs publics*, p. 299, and Caron, *Uneasy Asylum*, pp.49–51.
88. *JO, Débats parlementaires, Chambre des Députés*, 29 January 1935, Herriot, p. 258.
89. Ibid.
90. Ibid., Doriot, p. 259.
91. LNA, C.1609, Ministère des Affaires Étrangères, 19 June 1934.
92. *JO, Débats parlementaires, Chambre des Députés*, 29 January 1935, Blum, p. 258.
93. Ibid., pp. 258–9.
94. Ibid., Garchery, p. 258.
95. Ibid., Blum, pp. 258–9.
96. Schor, *Opinion française et les étrangers*, pp. 313–6.
97. Caron, *Uneasy Asylum*, pp. 21f; Vicki Caron, 'The Politics of Frustration: French Jewry and the Refugee Crisis of the 1930s', *Journal of Modern History* 65 (June 1993); Vicki Caron, 'Prelude to Vichy: France and the Jewish Refugees in the Era of Appeasement', *Journal of Contemporary History* 20, 1, January (1985).

## 10 Reform, Renewal, and the End of Asylum

1. *JO, Documents parlementaires*, Annexe 4144, 20 November 1934, p. 129.
2. 'La propostion de loi Moutet sur le statut des étrangers', *Cahiers des Droits de l'Homme*, 10 March 1935, pp. 157–66.
3. Jean Maitron, ed., *Dictionnaire biographique du mouvement ouvrier français, 1871–1914*, vol. 14 (Paris: Les Éditions ouvrières, 1976), pp. 155–6 & vol. 37 (Paris: Les Éditions ouvrières, 1990), pp. 166–7; Denis Peschanski, *La France des camps. L'Internement, 1938–1946* (Paris: Gallimard, 2002), p. 81.
4. 'Proposition de loi Moutet'.
5. Ibid.
6. Ibid.
7. Bonnet, *Pouvoirs publics*, pp. 314–5.
8. Livian, *Le Régime juridique des étrangers en France*, pp. 222–6.
9. *JO, Documents parlementaires*, Annexe 1417, pp. 940–1; Annexe 937, pp. 1581–2.
10. Ibid., Annexe 1417, pp. 940–1.
11. Ibid., Annexe 937, pp. 1581–2.
12. Ibid. Article 3 of the draft statute defined a refugee as 'a national of a nation whose government has suspended in whole or in part liberties and rights, and is punished by the government for his beliefs and political, religious or philosophical opinions'.
13. Ibid., Annexe 1417, pp. 940–1.
14. 'Rassemblement pour le droit d'asile. Conférence international de 20 et 21 juin 1936, à Paris' (Paris: Bureau international per le respect du droit d'asile et l'aide aux réfugiés, 1937), pp. 3–4.
15. Ibid., p. 6.
16. Ibid., p. 7.
17. Ibid., pp. 8–9.
18. Ibid., p. 9.
19. Ibid., pp. 16–7.
20. Ibid., p. 111.
21. Ibid., p. 118.
22. Ibid.
23. Harry Olten, *Rassemblement pour le droit d'asile* (Paris: Éditions universelles, 1936), p. 20.
24. Ibid., pp. 23–4.
25. J. Rubinstein, 'Le statut des réfugiés politiques', *Cahiers des Droits de l'Homme*, 15 April 1937, p. 233.
26. Ibid., p. 232.
27. Ibid., p. 234.
28. *JO, Débats parlementaires, Chambre des Députés*, 8 December 1936, p. 3397.
29. Ibid., 21 janvier 1937, Item 15, p. 100. When the numbers are known, they reveal that the urgency of the problem was more in the perception than in the imposition of migrant or refugee groups on the French state. By the second half of 1935, the numbers of German refugees in France are believed to have fallen to 10,000. (LNA C.1614.) The official number of German residents in December 1936 was just under 50,000, small in comparison to the more integrated and considerably larger populations of Italians, Spanish, and Belgians (AN, F7 16072, Interior Minister to Foreign Minister, 27 June 1938).

Main Groups of Foreigners Resident in France, by
Nationality, on 31 December 1936

| | |
|---|---|
| Germany | 49,786 |
| North America | 11,467 |
| Armenia | 51,149 |
| Austria | 7,603 |
| Belgium | 211,484 |
| Britain | 34,912 |
| Spain | 410,183 |
| Greece | 21,272 |
| Holland | 8,276 |
| Hungary | 12,240 |
| Italy | 897,732 |
| Luxembourg | 15,303 |
| Morocco | 26,966 |
| Turkey (Ottoman Empire) | 18,086 |
| Poland | 463,143 |
| Portugal | 38,472 |
| Romania | 13,452 |
| Russia (refugees) | 63,349 |
| Soviet Union | 2,527 |
| Yugoslavia | 25,668 |
| Switzerland | 88,880 |
| Czechoslovakia | 41,474 |
| Total | 2,563,531 |

30. Bonnet, *Pouvoirs publics*, pp. 315–8.
31. Rita Thalmann, 'L'immigration allemande et l'opinion publique en France de 1933 à 1936', in *La France et l'Allemagne, 1932–1936. Communications présentées au Colloque Franco-Allemand tenu à Paris du 10 au 12 mars 1977* (Paris: Éditions du Centre National de la Recherche Scientific, 1980), p. 171; Rita Thalmann, 'L'immigration de IIIe Reich en France, 1933–1939', *Le monde juif* (octobre 1979), p. 138; Caron, *Uneasy Asylum*, p. 119.
32. Marcel Livian, *Le parti socialiste et l'immigration. Le gouvernement Léon Blum, la main-d'oeuvre immigrée et les réfugiés politiques (1920–1940)* (Paris: Éditions Anthropos, 1982).
33. Ibid., p. 89f.
34. Bonnet, *Pouvoirs publics*, p. 315. On the 1933 Convention, see Simpson, *Refugee Problem*, Appendix VII, pp. 565–95.
35. 'Arrangement provisoire concernant le statut des réfugiés provenant d'Allemagne, signé à Genève le 4 juillet 1936', *League of Nations Treaty Series*, CLXXI, 1936–7, no. 3952.
36. Livian, *Le parti socialiste*, pp. 98 & 102–3. The date of commencement was scheduled for 5 August 1936, but delays in implementation saw it postponed to 31 January 1937.
37. Ibid., p. 107.
38. Ibid., pp. 95–9.
39. Ibid., pp. 102–3; Caron, *Uneasy Asylum*, p. 125.

40. Livian, *Le parti socialiste*, p. 101. The Provisional Arrangement defined a 'Refugee Coming From Germany' as 'any person who was settled in [Germany], who does not possess any nationality other than German nationality, and in respect of whom it is established that in law or in fact he or she does not enjoy the protection of the Government of the Reich'. Article 1 reads: 'Arrangement provisoire concernant le statut des réfugiés provenant d'Allemagne, signé à Genève le 4 juillet 1936', *League of Nations Treaty Series*, CLXXI, 1936–7, No. 3952. On the organisation and activities of the consultative commission, MAE, Questions sociales, 1805 & 1806.

41. MAE, Minorités, 452. Consultative Commission, 26 October 1936, fos. 36–40.

42. Caron, *Uneasy Asylum*, p. 139.

43. MAE, Minorités, 452. Consultative Commission, 26 October 1936, fos. 36–40.

44. Ibid., Projet de Déclaration, 1 July 1936, fo. 15.

45. Timothy Maga, *America, France and the European Refugee Problem (1933–1947)* (New York: Gerland Publications, 1985).

46. Caron, *Uneasy Asylum*, passim.

47. Article 1. 'Arrangement provisoire concernant le statut des réfugiés provenant d'Allemagne, signé à Genève le 4 juillet 1936', *League of Nations Treaty Series*, CLXXI, 1936–7, no. 3952.

48. Pierre Racine, 'Une expérience adminstrative à reprendre: Le Sous-secrétariat d'état à l'immigraiton et les projets Philippe Serre', *Esprit* 82 (July 1939), p. 610; Bonnet, *Pouvoirs publics*, p. 333; Rahma Harouni, 'Le débat autour du statut des étrangers dans les années 1930', *Le mouvement social*, 188 (July–September 1999), pp. 69–71.

49. Racine, 'Une expérience adminstrative', pp. 611–12; Bonnet, *Pouvoirs publics*, pp. 334–9; Caron, *Uneasy Asylum*, pp. 164–8; Schor, *Opinion française et les étrangers*, p. 646.

50. MAE, Questions sociales, 1819, Statute, fos. 315–27.

51. Ibid., Statute, Article 11.

52. Schor, *Opinion française et les étrangers*, p. 645.

53. Caron, *Uneasy Asylum*, p. 165.

54. 'Une interview avec M. Philippe Serre. Statut des étrangers en France', *Vendredi*, 6 May 1938.

55. Schor, *Opinion française et les étrangers*, pp. 653–5; Schor, *Histoire de l'immigration*, p. 154; Lawrence, 'Un flot d'agitateurs', passim.

56. MAE, Questions sociales, 1819. Foreign Minister, 5 March 1938. fo. 311.

57. Ibid., fo. 308.

58. Ibid., fo. 310; Racine, 'Une expérience adminstrative', p. 614.

59. Bonnet, *Pouvoirs publics*, p. 341; Millet, *Trois millions d'etrangers*, p. 9.

60. 'Décret sur la police des étrangers, 2 mai 1938', *Recueil Dalloz*, 1938 (4ème partie), pp. 235–6.

61. Sir John Hope Simpson, *Refugees: A Review of the Situation since September 1938* (Londong: Oxford University Press, 1939), p. 1.

62. Ibid., p. 25.

63. Ibid., p. 52. Marrus, *The Unwanted*, p. 149.

64. 'Décret réglementant les conditions de séjour des étrangers en France, 14 mai 1938', *Recueil Dalloz*, 1938 (4ème partie), pp. 237–8; 'Décret relatif à la situation et la police des étrangers, 12 novembre 1938', *Recueil Dalloz*, 1938 (4ème partie), p. 163. These laws were passed as decrees by the Council of Ministers,

which was authorised under a law of 13 April 1938 to make decrees necessary for national defence and the economy (see preamble to the law of 2 May 1938).
65. Ibid., p. 236. Respectively, Articles 2, 3, 6 and 7.
66. Ibid., p. 235.
67. Ibid.
68. Andrée Mosse, 'Où en est la question des réfugiés politiques? Ce qu'a donné l'application des décret-lois', *Cahier des droits de l'homme*, 1 June 1939.
69. Maurice Milhaud, 'La question des réfugiés politiques. Pourquoi nous devons les accueillir', *Cahiers des Droits de l'Homme*, 15 August 1938.
70. 'Ligue française pour la Défense des Droits de l'Homme et du Citoyen', *Cahiers des Droits de l'Homme*, 15 August 1938.
71. AN, F7 16072, Note on the application of Article 2 of the decree of 2 May 1938.
72. Ibid.
73. Caron, *Uneasy Asylum*, pp. 192–4.
74. AN, F7 16072, Note to Interior Minister on the application of Article 2 of the decree-law of 2 May 1938 [undated].
75. Ibid., Comité pour la Défense des Droits des Israélites en Europe Centrale et Orientale to Edouard Daladier, 16 May 1938; S Lawford Childs, 'Refugees—A Permanent Problem in International Organisation', in *War is not Inevitable* (London: International Labor Office, 1938), p. 216.
76. F7 16072, Interministerial meeting, 11 June 1938.
77. On the Evian Conference, MAE, Questions sociales, 1815, 1816, 1817; MAE, Allemagne, 712; Minorités, 451; AN, F7 16072. S. Adler-Rudel, 'The Evian Conference on the Refugee Question', in *Leo Baeck Institute Yearbook* (New York: Leo Baeck Institute, 1968); Eric Estorick, 'The Evian Conference and the Intergovernmental Committee', *Annals of the American Academy of Political and Social Sciences*, 203 (May, 1939); Tommie Sjöberg, *The Powers and the Persecuted: The Refugee Problem and the Intergovernmental Committee for Refugees (IGCR), 1938–1947* (Lund: Lund University Press, 1991); Maga, *America, France and the European Refugee Problem*, p. 92; Haim Genizi, *American Apathy: The Plight of Christian Refugees from Nazism* (Jerusalem: Bar-Ilan University Press, 1983), p. 76; Yehuda Bauer, *My Brother's Keeper* (Philadelphia: The Jewish Publication Society of America, 1974), pp. 213–6; Marrus, *The Unwanted*, pp. 170–2; Noiriel, *Tyrannie*, pp. 105–6; Skran, *Refugees in Interwar Europe*, pp. 209–14.
78. Caron, *Uneasy Asylum*, pp. 192–3.
79. Ibid., pp. 206f.
80. AN, F7 15169, Interior Minister, 14 December 1938.
81. Ibid., Interior Minister, 26 December 1938; Divisional Commissaire, Forbach, 21 August 1938.
82. AN, F7 16080, Consul General, Cologne, 1 February 1939.
83. Caron, *Uneasy Asylum*, pp. 210–11; S Lawford Childs, 'Refugees—A Permanent Problem in International Organisation', in *War is not Inevitable* (London: International Labor Office, 1938); Milhaud, 'Réfugiés politiques'; Erich Maria Remarque, *Flotsam*, trans. Denver Lindley, (Boston: Little, Brown and Company, 1941).
84. Caron, *Uneasy Asylum*, pp. 211–13.
85. For example Ibid., pp. 215f.
86. Simpson, *Refugees: A Review*, pp. 2–16; Dorothy Thompson, *Refugees: Anarchy or Organisation* (New York: New York Times, 1938), p. 80.
87. AN, F7 15171, Note for Divisional Commissaire, 3 November 1931.

88. AN, F7 15172, Interior Minister, March 1932.
89. Ibid.
90. Louis Stein, *Beyond Death and Exile: The Spanish Republicans in France, 1939–1955* (Cambridge, MA: Harvard University Press, 1979), pp. 6–7.
91. Geneviève Dreyfus-Armand, *L'exil des Républicains espagnols en France, de la Guerre civile à la mort de Franco* (Paris: Albin Michel, 1999), p. 36.
92. Ibid.
93. Ibid., pp. 34–5; Stein, *Beyond Death*, pp. 6–9.
94. AN, F7 15172, Labour Ministry, 5 November 1936; Dreyfus-Armand, *L'exil*, p. 37.
95. Ibid., pp. 30–1 & 37.
96. AN, F7 15172, Interior Minister, 19 January 1937 & 15 November 1937.
97. Ibid., Interior Minister, 24 June 1937 & 18 October 1937.
98. Ibid., Instructions, 24 May 1938; Under-secretary of State, 13 December 1937.
99. The precise number is in question, and 500,000 is a higher estimate. A figure between 400,000 and 500,000, however, is generally accepted.
100. Stein, *Beyond Death*, p. 18.
101. Dreyfus-Armand, *L'exil*, p. 54.
102. Anne Grynberg and Anne Charaudeau, 'Les camps d'internement', in *Exils et migration. Italiens et Espagnols en France, 1938–1946*, ed. Pierre Milza and Denis Peschanski (Paris: Harmatton, 1994), p. 139; Patrick Weil, 'Espagnols et Italiens en France: la politique de la France', in *Exils et migration. Italiens et Espagnols en France, 1938–1946*, ed. Pierre Milza and Denis Peschanski (Paris: Harmatton, 1994), p. 92.
103. Weil, 'Espagnols et Italiens', p. 92.
104. Dreyfus-Armand, *L'exil*, pp. 46 & 49.
105. Peschanski, *La France des camps*, pp. 37–8.
106. Dreyfus-Armand, *L'exil*, pp. 52–4.
107. Stein, *Beyond Death*, p. 39.
108. Emmanuelle Salgas-Candoret, 'Une population face à l'exil espagnol', in *Exils et migration. Italiens et Espagnols en France, 1938–1946*, ed. Pierre Milza and Denis Peschanski (Paris: Harmatton, 1994), p. 314.
109. Stein, *Beyond Death*, chap. 2; Dreyfus-Armand, *L'exil*, pp. 52f.
110. Marrus, *The Unwanted*, p. 192; Geneviève Dreyfus-Armand and Emile Témime, *Les camps sur la plage, un exile espagnol* (Paris: Éditions autrement, 1995), pp. 20–7; Dreyfus-Armand, *L'exil*, pp. 61–4; Stein, *Beyond Death*, pp. 55–9; Peschanski, *La France des camps*, pp. 98–102.
111. Dreyfus-Armand, *L'exil*, p. 64; Grynberg and Charaudeau, 'Les camps', p. 142.
112. Stein, *Beyond Death*, p. 64; Peschanski, *La France des camps*, pp. 41–3.
113. Dreyfus-Armand, *L'exil*, p. 61; Stein, *Beyond Death*, pp. 60–3; Peschanski, *La France des camps*, pp. 39–40.
114. Dreyfus-Armand, *L'exil*, p. 82.
115. AN, F7 15172, Interior Minister, 14 February 1939.
116. Dreyfus-Armand, *L'exil*, pp. 84–6.
117. Stein, *Beyond Death*, p. 46.
118. Ibid., p. 70.
119. Grynberg and Charaudeau, 'Les camps', p. 141.
120. AN, F7 15172, Interior Minister, 14 February 1939. 'Régimes applicables aux étrangers provenant d'Espagne', 11 February 1939.
121. Stein, *Beyond Death*, pp. 72–3; Dreyfus-Armand and Témime, *Les camps sur la plage*, pp. 41–5.

122. Dreyfus-Armand, *L'exil*, p. 72.
123. Dreyfus-Armand and Témime, *Les camps sur la plage*, pp. 30–8; Dreyfus-Armand, *L'exil*, p. 73.
124. Stein, *Beyond Death*, pp. 84–5.
125. Ibid.; Stein, *Beyond Death*, pp. 86 & 99.
126. Ibid., p. 39.
127. Schor, *Histoire de l'immigration*, p. 154.
128. Stein, *Beyond Death*, p. 39.
129. Ibid., p. 98.
130. Caron, *Uneasy Asylum*, p. 247.
131. Ibid., p. 243; Peschanski, *La France des camps*, pp. 77–80 & *passim*.

## Conclusion    The Right of Asylum—A Site of Memory

1. 'Tout homme persecuté en raison de son action en faveur de la liberté a droit d'asile sur les territories de la République'. Préambule, Constitution de la IVe République. Stéphane Rials, *Textes constitutionnels français. Que sais-je?* (Paris: Presses universitaires françaises, 1982), p. 80.
2. Louise Holborn, *Refugees, a Problem of our Time. The Work of the United Nations High Commissioner for Refugees, 1951–1972*, vol. 1 (Metuchen: Scarecrow Press, 1975); John George Stoessinger, *The Refugee and the World Community*, (Minneapolis: University of Minnesota Press, 1956).
3. Loi 52–893 du 25 juillet 1952 relative au droit d'asile. *Entrée et séjour des étrangers en France. Droit d'asile* (Paris: Les editions des Journaux officials, 22 September 1998), pp. 39f.
4. There is assuredly a vast literature. The works listed here are a sample. François Crepeau, *Droit d'asile, de l'hospitalité aux contrôles migratoires* (Bruxelles: Université de Bruxelles, 1995); Gérard Dhôtel, *Réfugiés: le droit d'asile menacé* (Paris: Syros, 1995); Luc Legoux, *La crise de l'asile politique en France* (Paris: Centre Français sur la Population et le Développement, 1995); Didier Fassin, Alain Morice, and Catherine Quiminal, *Les lois de l'inhospitalité. Les politiques de l'immigration à l'épreuve des sans-papiers* (Paris: La Découverte, 1997); Catherine Wihtol de Wenden, 'Réfugié politique: une notion en crise?" in *Esprit* (mai 1990), 73–86; and Société française pour le Droit international, éd. *Droit d'asile et des réfugiés. Colloque de Caen* (Paris: A. Pedone, 1997).
5. *Moniteur*, 27 October 1831, Pagès, p. 1976.
6. *JO, Débats parlementaires, Chambre des Députés*, Joseph Rous, 10 March 1939, p. 900.
7. Ibid., p. 901.
8. AD Doubs, M 812, Réfugiés italiens et piémontais, 1822–1849, 15 April 1849.
9. AD Doubs, M 849, Réfugiés allemands, 1848–1851, 18 May 1849.
10. *JO, Débats parlementaires, Chambre des Députés*, 24 February 1882, p. 165.
11. Ibid., 29 January 1935, pp. 256–7.
12. Pierre Nora, 'General Introduction: Between History and Memory', in *Realms of Memory*, vol. 1, *Conflicts and Division*, ed. Pierre Nora, trans. Arthur Goldhammer (New York: Columbia University Press, 1996).

# Bibliography

## (1) Archival and primary sources

### Archives Nationales de France

*Ministère de la Justice*

BB17A 79. BB17 A 110. BB30 1175.

*Ministère de l'Intérieur*

F1a 38. F1a 43.

*Police générale*

F7 3884–3893. F7 4420. F7 6779–6784. F7 11976–11980. F7 11984. F7 11994. F7 12016–12017. F7 12060. F7 12102. F7 12107. F7 12110. F7 12329. F7 12585–12586. F7 12838–12839. F7 14823. F7 15166–15169. F7 15171–15172. F7 16029–16031. F7 16051–16052. F7 16054. F7 16072. F7 16079–16080.

*Hospice et Secours*

F15 3499. F15 3504–3508. F15 3511–3513. F15 3881.

*Exécutif*

AFII 61. 448–453.

*Législature*

C 749. C 762. C 924. C 1002. C 3325. C 3384. C 5410. C 5486.

### Archives Diplomatique, Ministère des Affaires étrangères

*Mémoires et documents.*

France. 724. Pologne. 29. 31. 33. 35.

*Europe 1930–1940. Allemagne*

710–12.

*Société des Nations. Minorités. Allemagne*

446–52.

*Société des Nations. Questions Sociales*

1805–6. 1810–11. 1815–17. 1819.

## Archives Départementales

Bas-Rhin:

*Police générale.*
3M 48. 3M 50. 3M 415. 3M 419–22. 3M 445. 3M 524–25.

Côtes-d'Armor:
4M 264–65.

Doubs:

*Police politique. Réfugiés politiques*
M 812–14. M 817–820. M 826. M 829–830. M 849. M 1192.

Haut-Rhin:

*Police*
4M 140. 4M 159. 4M 173–5. 4M 180–1.

*Ille-et-Villaine:*
4M 406. 4M 408–9. 4M 425. 4M 430–2.

Isère:

*Événements militaires:*
13R 209. 13R 222.

*Sûreté Générale*
58M 1. 61M 1. 61M 16. 61M 27. 67M 4. 67M 11–12. 69M 1.

*Police Générale*
52M 4–5. 52M 25.

Loire:
4M 540.

Rhône:
1M 112. 1M 154. 4M 17. 4M 288. 4M 401–7. 4M 413.

*Population.*
6MP 1001.

*Affaires militaires*
R 1608. R 1614.

Vaucluse:
1M 870. 4M 199–204.

## Société Historique et Littéraire Polonaise, Bibliothèque Polonaise, Paris

Dossiers 30136–30139, 30147.
*À la Chambre des Pairs de France*, 17 avril 1832.
*A messieurs les membres de la Chambre des Députés*, 23 janvier 1835.
*Adresse du Comité polonais à la Chambre des Députés*, 9 février 1834.
*Appel du peuple polonais au peuple français*, 27, 28 et 29 juillet 1833.
*Aux réfugiés polonais*, 14 juillet 1835.
*Coup d'œil sur la révolution de Pologne en 1830 et 1831*. Avignon: Pierre Cahillot, 1832.
*Discours en mémoire de Lafayette du dépôt de Poitiers*, juin 1834.
*La Nymphe de la Vistule aux Français*.
*Les Polonais. Événemens historiques en quatre acts et en douze tableaux*, par M. Prosper, Cirque Olympique, 22 décembre 1831. Paris: Librairie Palais Royale, 1832.
*Les Réfugiés polonais aux Chambres françaises*, 1834.
*Manifesto of the Polish Nation to Europe, and Address of the Polish Refugees in France to the British House Commons*, 29 May 1832.
Petitions and declarations from the mayors, officials and inhabitants of various communes, in anticipation of the prorogation of the law of April 1832, 1834.
*Report of the Debate in the House of Commons, 18 April 1832*, London, 1832.

## League of Nations

*Documents*

A.30.1923.XIII, 4 September 1923. C.M.21/41/32, 20 February 1921. A.30.1923.XIII, 4 September 1923. A.33.1928.XIII. 22 August 1928. A.48.1927.XIII. 5 September 1927.

*Archives*

1930.XIII.L. 12/10311/8822, 14 February 1921. 11/11690/10598, 30 March 1921.
*James G. McDonald, High Commissioner for Refugees (Jewish and Other) Coming from Germany*. C.1609, C.1612, C.1613.
Leo Baeck Institute: High Commission for Refugees (Jewish and Other) Coming from Germany, Minutes, P.V. 5.

## Periodicals and publications

*Archives Parlementaires, 1790–5.*
*Bulletin d'histoire éconmique de la Révolution.* Paris: Imprimerie nationale, 1916.
*Cahiers des Droits de l'Homme, 1932–9.*
*Gazette Nationale, ou Réimpression de l'ancien moniteur. Seule histoire authentique et inaltérée de la Révolution française depuis la reúnion des états-généraux jusqu'au Consulat (Mai, 1789–Novembre, 1799)* Paris: Henri Plon, 1858–63.
*Journal officiel de la République française*, 1933–9.
*Le Corsaire, 1832–3.*
*L'Humanité, 1936–8.*
*Le Matin, 1933–8.*
*Le Moniteur universel, 1830–82.*
*Le Patriote Français, 1790–1.*
*Le Populaire, 1936–8.*
*League of Nations Treaty Series.*
*Rassemblement pour le droit d'asile. Conférence international de 20 et 21 juin 1936, à Paris.* Paris: Bureau international per le respect du droit d'asile et l'aide aux réfugiés, 1937.

*Recueil périodique et critique de jurisprudence, de législation, et de doctrine en matière civile, commerciale, criminelle, administrative et de droit public*, éd. M. Dalloz.

*Révolutions de Paris*, 1790–1.

*Refugees. Report on Russian, Armenian, German and Saar Refugees in France.* London: Save the Children Fund, 1935.

*Vendredi*, 1936–8.

## (2) Secondary sources

Adler-Rudel, S. 'The Evian Conference on the Refugee Question.' In *Leo Baeck Institute Yearbook.* New York: Leo Baeck Institute, 1968: 235–73.

Agulhon, Maurice. *The Republican Experiement, 1848–1852.* Translated by Janet Lloyd. Cambridge: Cambridge University Press, 1983.

Alger, John Goldworth. *Paris in 1789–94: Farewell Letters of Victims of the Guillotine.* London: George Allen, 1902.

Anceau, Eric, and Jean-Louis Debré, eds. *Les grands discours parlementaires du XIXe siècle: de Benjamin Constant à Adolphe Thiers, 1800–1870.* Paris: Broché, 2005.

Araminski, Comte Sanislas. *Histoire de la Révolution polonaise depuis son origine jusqu' à nos jours (1772 à 1864).* Paris: A. Fayard, 1864.

Arendt, Hannah. *The Origins of Totalitarianism.* San Diego: Harcourt Brace Jovanovich, 1973.

Attard-Maraninchi, Marie-Françoise and Emile Témime. *Migrance. Histoire de l'immigration marseillaise.* 4 vols. Vol. 3, *Le cosmopolitisme de l'entre-deux-guerres (1919–1945).* Marseille: Edisud, 1990.

Aulard, Alphonse. *The French Revolution: A Political History 1789–1804.* Translated by Bernard Miall. 4 vols. Vol. 1, *The Revolution under the Monachy, 1789–1792.* New York: Russell and Russell, 1965.

Baker, Donald N. 'The Surveillance of Subversion in Interwar France: The Carnet B in the Seine, 1922–1940.' *French Historical Studies* 10, no. 3 (1978): 486–516.

Bartlett, Thomas. 'Miles Byrne: United Irishman, Irish Exile and *Beau Sabreur*.' In *The Mightly Wave: The 1798 Rebellion in Wexford.* Edited by Dáire Keogh and Nicholas Furlong. Dublin: Four Courts Press, 1996: 118–38.

Bauer, Yehuda. *My Brother's Keeper.* Philadelphia: The Jewish Publication Society of America, 1974.

Beauvois, Daniel. 'Le nord de la France et les polonais entre 1831 et 1833.' In *Pologne: L'insurrection de 1830–1831. Sa réception en Europe. Actes de colloque organisé les 14 et 15 mai 1981 par le Centre d'etude de la Culture Polonaise de l'Université de Lille III.* Edited by Daniel Beauvois. Lille: Université de Lille III, 1982: 41–66.

Becker, Jean-Jacques. *The Great War and the French People.* Translated by Arnold Pomerans. Berg: Providence and Oxford, 1985.

Bernard, Paul. *Traité théorique et pratique de l'extradition. Commentaire des lois et traités.* 2 vols. Paris: Librarie nouvelle de Droit et de Jurispridence, 1883.

Bettati, Mario. *L'asile politique en question: un statut pour les réfugies.* Paris: Presses Universitaires de France, 1985.

Bezucha, Robert J. *The Lyon Uprising of 1834: Social and Political Conflict in the Early July Monarchy.* Cambridge, MA: Harvard University Press, 1974.

Birnbaum, Pierre. *'La France aux Français'. Histoire des haines nationalistes.* Paris: Seuil, 1993.

———. *Un mythe politique: 'La République juive' de Léon Blum à Mendès France, Nouvelles études historiques.* Paris: Fayard, 1988.

Bitard, A. *Dictionnaire de biographie contemporaine,* 1887.

Blanning, T. C. W. *The Origins of the French Revolutionary Wars*. London and New York: Longmans, 1986.

Bleandonu, Gérard, and Guy Le Gaufey. 'The Creation of the Insane Asylums of Auxerre and Paris.' In *Deviants and the Abandoned in French Society. Selections from the Annales. Economies, Sociétés, Civilisations*. Edited by Robert Forster and Orest Ranum. Baltimore and London: John Hopkins University Press, 1978: 180–212.

Bon, Jean-Philippe. 'L'engagement des Catholiques du diocèse de La Rochelle-Saintes dans le premier conflit mondial.' *Guerres mondiales et conflits contemporains* 197 (2000): 73–82.

Bonnet, Jean-Charles. *Les pouvoirs publics français et l'immigration dans l'entre-deux-guerres*. Lyon: CNRS; Centre d'Histoire économique et social de la Région lyonnaise, 1976.

Breitman Richard, Barbara McDonald Steward, and Severin Hochberg, eds. *Advocate for the Doomed. The Diaries and Papers of James G. McDonald, 1932-1935*. Bloomington and Washington: Indiana University Press and the United States Holocaust Memorial Museum, 2007.

Brock, Peter. 'Polish Democrats and English Radicals, 1832–1862: A Chapter in the History of Anglo-Polish Relations.' *The Journal of Modern History* 25 (March–December 1953): 139–56.

Brubaker, Rogers. *Citizenship and Nationhood in France and Germany*. Cambridge, MA and London: Harvard University Press, 1992.

Bryas, Madeleine de. *Les peuples en marche: les migrations politique et économique depuis la guerre mondiale*. Paris: A. Pedone, 1926.

Burgess, Greg. 'France and the German Refugee Crisis of 1933.' *French History* 16, no. 2 (2002): 203–29.

——. 'Into the Protecting Arms: The League of Nations and the Extension of International Assistance to Unprotected Persons in the Middle East and Europe, 1926–1928.' *Eras* 1 (2001): http://www.arts.monash.edu.au/eras.

——. 'Selection, Exclusion and Assimilation. The *Projet Lambert* of 1931 on the Reform of French Immigration Policy.' *French History and Civilisation. Papers from the George Rudé Seminar* 1 (2005): 190–207.

Bury, J. P. T. *France 1814–1940*. Sixth ed. London and New York: Routledge, 2003.

Camiscioli, Elisa. 'Producing Citizens, Reproducing the "French Race": Immigration, Demography, and Pronatalism in Early Twentieth-Century France.' *Gender and History* 13, no. 3 (November 2001): 559–621.

Caron, Vicki. 'The Antisemitic Revival in France in the 1930s: The Socioeconomic Dimension Reconsidered.' *Journal of Modern History* 70, no. 1 (March 1998): 24–73.

——. 'Loyalties in Conflict: French Jewry and the Refugee Crisis, 1933–35.' In *Leo Baeck Institute Yearbook 1991*. New York: Secker and Warburg, 1991: 305–38.

——. 'The Politics of Frustration: French Jewry and the Refugee Crisis of the 1930s.' *Journal of Modern History* 65 (June 1993): 311–56.

——. 'Prelude to Vichy: France and the Jewish Refugees in the Era of Appeasement.' *Journal of Contemporary History* 20, no. 1 (January 1985): 157–76.

——. *Uneasy Asylum. France and the Jewish Refugee Crisis, 1933–1942*. Stanford, California: Stanford University Press, 1999.

Carr, Raymond. *Spain, 1808–1939*. Oxford: Clarendon Press, 1966.

——. *Spain, 1808–1975*. 2nd ed. Oxford: Clarendon Press, 1982.

Castellani, Loris. 'Un aspect de l'émigration communist italienne en France: les groupes de lange italienne au sein du PCF (1921–1928).' In *Les italiens en France de 1914 à 1940*. Edited by Pierre Milza. Rome: École française de Rome, 1986: 195–221.

Chassaigne, Philippe. 'War, Delinquency, and Society in Bordeaux, 1914–1918.' In *Criminal Justice History. An International Annual*. Westport and London: Greenwood Press, 1994: 189–208.

Chevalier, Louis. *Classes laborieuses et classes dangereuses à Paris pendant la première moitié du XIXe slècle*. 1958 ed. Paris: Perrin, 2002.

———. *Labouring Classes and Dangerous Classes in Paris During the First Half of the Nineteenth Century*. Translated by Frank Jellinek. London: Routledge and Kegan Paul, 1973.

Childs, S Lawford. 'Refugees—A Permanent Problem in International Organisation.' In *War is not Inevitable*. London: International Labor Office, 1938: 196–224.

Chinyaeva, Elena. 'Russian Émigrés: Czechoslovak Refugee Policy and the Development of the International Refugee Regime between the Two World Wars.' *Journal of Refugee Studies* 8, no. 2 (1995): 142–63.

Church, Clive. H. *Europe in 1830*. London: George Allen and Unwin, 1983.

Cloots, Anacharisis. *Écrits revolutionaries, 1790–1794*. Edited by Michèle Duval. Paris: Éditions Champs Libre, 1979.

Coleman, A. P. 'The Great Emigration.' In *The Cambridge History of Poland, From Augustus II to Pilsudski (1697–1935)*. Edited by W. F. Reddaway. Cambridge: Cambridge University Press, 1941: 311–23.

Coller, Ian. 'Arab Paris. Arab Lives and Arab Identities in France, 1801–1831.' University of Melbourne, 2006.

———. 'Egypte-sur-Seine: The Making of an Arabic Community in Paris, 1800–1830.' *French History and Civilisation. Papers from the George Rudé Seminar* 1 (2005): 208–16.

———. 'Arab France: Mobility and Community in Early-Nineteenth Century Paris and Marseille'. *French Historical Studies*, 29, 3 (Summer 2006): 433–56.

Collingham, H. A. C. *The July Monarchy. A Political History of France, 1830–1848*. London and New York: Longman, 1988.

Collins, Irene, ed. *Government and Society in France, 1814–1848*. London: Edward Arnold, 1970.

Courtois, Stéphane. 'Le PCF et la question de l'immigration, 1936–1948.' In *Exils et migration. Italiens et Espagnols en France, 1938–1946*. Edited by Pierre Milza and Denis Peschanski. Paris: Harmatton, 1994: 163–74.

Cross, Gary. 'Towards Peace and Social Prosperity. The Politics of Immigration in France during the Era of World War One.' *French Historical Studies* 11, no. 4 (1980): 610–32.

———. *Immigrant Workers in Industrial France: The Making of a New Laboring Class*. Philadelphia: Temple University Press, 1983.

Daris, Joseph. *Histoire du diocèse et de la Principauté de Liége (1724–1852)*. 5 vols. Vol. 2. Bruxelles: Editions Culture et Civilisations, 1974.

Darriulat, Philippe. *Les patriotes. La gauche républicaine et la nation 1830–1870*. Paris: Seuil, 2001.

Delaporte, François. *Disease and Civilization*. Translated by Arthur Goldhammer. Cambridge, Massachusetts and London: MIT Press, 1986.

Desjardins, Arthur. 'La loi de 1849 et l'expulsion des étrangers.' *Revue des deux mondes* 50 (1882): 657–80.

Dreyfus-Armand, Geneviève. *L'exil des Républicains espagnols en France, de la Guerre civile à la mort de Franco*. Paris: Albin Michel, 1999.

Dreyfus-Armand, Geneviève and Emile Témime. *Les camps sur la plage, un exile espagnol*. Paris: Éditions autrement, 1995.

Duprat, Catherine. *'Pour l'amour de l'humanité'. Le temps des philanthropes. La philantropie parisienne des Lumières à la monarchie de Juillet*. Paris: C.T.H.S., 1993.

——. *Usage et pratiques de la philanthropie. Pauvreté, action sociale et lien social à Paris, au cours du premier XIXe siècle.* 2 vols. Vol. 1. Paris: Association pour l'étude de l'histoire de la sécurité sociale, 1996.

Durey, Michael. 'The Fate of the Rebels after 1798.' *History Today* 48, no. 6 (June 1998): 21–7.

Echinard, Pierre, and Emile Témime. *Migrance. Histoire de l'immigration marseillaise.* 4 vols. Vol. 1. *La préhistoire de la migration.* Marseille: Edisud, 1989.

Elliott, Marianne. *Partners in Revolution: The United Irishmen and France.* New Haven and London: Yale University Press, 1982.

Estorick, Eric. 'The Evian Conference and the Intergovernmental Committee.' *Annals of the American Academy of Political and Social Sciences* 203 (May, 1939): 136–41.

Farcy, Jean-Claude. *Les camps de concentration français de la première guerre mondiale (1914–1920).* Paris: Anthropos, 1995.

Friedländer, Saul. *Nazi Germany and the Jews: The Years of Persecution, 1933–1939.* London: Weidenfeld and Nicolson, 1997.

Frijhoff, Willem. 'La société idéale des patriotes bataves.' In *Le voyage révolutionnaire. Actes du colloque franco-néerlandais du Bicentenaire de la Révolution française, Amsterdam, 12–13 october 1989.* Edited by Willem Frijhoff and Rudolf Dekker. Hilversum: Verloren, 1991: 137–51.

Gainer, Bernard. *The Alien Invasion: The Origins of the Aliens Act of 1905.* London: Heineman, 1972.

Gand, M. *Code des Étrangers, ou état civil et politique, en France, des souverains, souveraines, princes, princesses, légations, consulats et simples particuliers étrangers.* Paris: Chez l'auteur, 1853.

Gauthier, Florence. *Triomphe et mort du droit naturel en Révolution, 1789–1795–1802.* Paris: Presses universitaires de France, 1992.

Genizi, Haim. *American Apathy: The Plight of Christian Refugees from Nazism.* Jerusalem: Bar-Ilan University Press, 1983.

George, Pierre. 'L'immigration italienne en France de 1920 à 1939. Aspects démographiques et sociaux.' In *Les italiens en France de 1914 à 1940.* Edited by Pierre Milza. Rome: École française de Rome, 1986: 45–67.

Gerbet, Pierre. *Auvergne, terre d'accueil. La vie des réfugiés politiques à Clermont-Ferrand de 1815 à 1870.* Clermont-Ferrand: J. de Bussac, 1943.

Godechot, Jacques. *La grande nation. L'expansion révolutinnaire de la France dans le monde de 1789 à 1799.* 2nd ed. Paris: Aubier, 1983.

——. *La grande nation. L'expansion révolutionnaire de la France dans le mond de 1789 à 1799.* 2 vols. Paris: Aubier, 1956.

Gohin, Yves. 'Préface.' In *Victor Hugo, L'Année terrible.* Paris: Gallimard, 1985.

Goldstein, Jan. *Console and Classify. The French Psychiatric Profession in the Nineteenth Century.* Cambridge: Cambridge University Press, 1987.

Goodwin, Albert. *The Friends of Liberty: The English Democratic Movement in the Age of the French Revolution.* London: Hutchinson, 1979.

Gottschalk, Louis, and Margaret Maddox. *Lafayette in the French Revolution.* 2 vols. Chicago: University of Chicago Press, 1969 & 1973.

Gouy, J. -C. 'Les réfugiés polonais au Puy après l'Insurrection de 1830.' *Cahiers d'histoire* 3 (1979): 83–7.

Grahl-Madsen, Atle. *The Status Of Refugees In International Law.* 2 vols. Leyden: A. W. Sijthoff, 1966 & 1972.

——. *Territorial Asylum.* Edited by Swedish Institute of International Law, *Studies in International Law.* Stockholm: Almquist & Wiksell International, 1980.

Grandjonc, Jacques. 'Mémoires d'un artisan allemand à Paris (1830–1834). Contribution à l'histoire de l'Association patriotique allemande et de la Ligue des Bannis.' *Cahiers d'histoire.* Lyon-Grenoble-Clermont-Saint-Étienne-Chambéry XV (1970): 243–57.

Grivaz, Francisque. *L'extradition et les délits politiques.* Paris: Librairie Nouvelle de Droit et de Jurisprudence, 1894.

Grynberg, Anne, and Anne Charaudeau. 'Les camps d'internement.' In *Exils et migration. Italiens et Espagnols en France, 1938–1946.* Edited by Pierre Milza and Denis Peschanski. Paris: Harmatton, 1994: 139–62.

Guggenheim, Paul. 'Contribution à l'histoire des sources du droit des gens.' In *Recueil des Cours de l'Académie de Droit International.* Leyde: A. W. Sijthoff, 1958: 1–84.

Guillen, Pierre. 'L'évolution du statut des migrants en France aux XIXe—XXe siècles.' In *L'émigration politique en Europe aux XIXe et XXe siècles. Actes du colloque organisé per l'École française de Rome, 3–5 mars 1988.* Rome: École française du Rome, 1991: 35–55.

——. 'Le rôle politique de l'immigration italienne en France dans l'entre-deux-guerres.' In *Les italiens en France de 1914 à 1940.* Edited by Pierre. Rome: École française de Rome, 1986: 323–41.

Guizot, François. *Mémoires.* 4 vols. Paris: Paleo, 2003.

Harding, Jeremy. *The Uninvited. Refugees at the Rich Man's Gate.* London: Profile Books and the London Review of Books, 2000.

Harouni, Rahma. 'Le débat autour du statut des étrangers dans les années 1930.' *Le mouvement social* 188 (July–September 1999): 61–75.

Harsin, Jill. *Barricades. The War of the Streets in Revolutionary Paris, 1830–1848.* New York: Palgrave Macmillan, 2002.

Higham, John. *Strangers in the Land: Patterns of American Nativism 1860–1925.* New Brunswick: Rutgers University Press, 1988.

Holborn, Louise. *Refugees, a Problem of our Time: The Work of the United Nations High Commissioner for Refugees, 1951–1972.* 2 vols. Metuchen: Scarecrow Press, 1975.

Horn, Alistair. *The Fall of Paris: The Siege and the Commune, 1870–71.* London: Papermac, 1990.

Hsu, Fu-Yung. *La Protection des réfugiés par la Société des Nations.* Lyon: Bosc Frères, 1935.

Hubert, Marie-Flora. 'La Pologne en France au XIXè siècle (1830–1865).' Université des Sciences humaines, Strasbourg II, 1975.

Hyman, Paula. *From Dreyfus to Vichy: The Remaking of French Jewry, 1906–1939.* New York: Columbia University Press, 1979.

——. *The Jews of Modern France.* Los Angeles and London: University of California Press, 1998.

Jardin, A., and A. -J. Tudesq. *La France des notables.* 2 vols. Paris: Seuil, 1973.

Jelavich, Barbara. 'The Polish Emigration, 1831–1871: The Challenge to Russia.' In *L'émigration politique en Europe aux XIXe et XXe siècles, actes du colloque organisé par l'École française de Rome, 3–5 mars 1988.* Rome: École française de Rome, 1991: 235–45.

Jennings, Lawrence C. *France and Europe in 1848: A Study of French Foreign Affairs in Time of Crisis.* Oxford: Clarendon Press, 1973.

Jourdan, Annie. *La Révolution, une exception française?* Paris: Flammarion, 2004.

Judah, Tim. *The Serbs: History, Myth, and the Destruction of Yugoslavia.* New Haven: Yale University Press, 1997.

Körner, Axel. 'Ideas and Memories of 1848 in France: Nationalism, République universelle and Internationalism in the Goguette between 1848 and 1890.' In *International Ideas and National Memories of 1848.* Edited by Axel Körner. London: Macmillan, 2000: 85–105.

Kramer, Lloyd S. 'The Rights of Man: Lafayette and the Polish National Revolution, 1830–1834.' *French Historical Studies* 14 (1985): 521–46.

——. *Threshold of a New World: Intellectuals and the Exile Experience in Paris, 1830–1848.* Ithaca and London: Cornell University Press, 1988.

Kubalski, M. A. *Mémoires sur l'expedition des réfugiés polonais en Suisse et en Savoie.* Paris: Merklein, 1836.

Kudlick, Catherine J. *Cholera in Post-Revolutionary Paris. A Cultural History.* Los Angeles and London: University of California Press, 1996.

——. 'Giving is Deceiving: Cholera, Charity, and the Quest for Authority in 1832.' *French Historical Studies* 18, no. 2 (1993): 457–81.

Laborie, Pierre. 'Les Espagnols et les Italiens dans l'imaginaire social.' In *Exils et migration. Italiens et Espagnols en France, 1938–1946.* Edited by Pierre Milza and Denis Peschanski. Paris: Harmatton, 1994: 273–86.

Lambert, Charles. *La France et les étrangers. Dépopulation, immigration, naturalisation.* Paris: Librarie Delagrave, 1928.

Lammasch, Heinrich. *Le droit d'extradition appliqué aux délits politiques.* Paris: E. Thorin, 1885.

Lavergne, Géraud. 'Le dépôt des réfugiés militaires polonais de Bergerac (1833).' In *Notices, inventaires et documents.* Vol. XX. *Études et documents divers.* Edited by Ministère de l'Instruction publique et des Beaux-arts Comité des Travaux historiques et scientifiques, Section d'Histoire moderne et d'Histoire contemporaine. Paris: Les Éditions Rieder, 1933: 86–109.

Lawrence, Paul. 'Naturalization, Ethnicity and National Identity in France between the Wars.' *Immigrants and Minorities* 20, no. 3 (2001): 1–24.

——. '"Un flot d'agitateurs politiques, de fauteurs de désordre et de criminels": Adverse Perceptions of Immigrants in France Between the Wars.' *French History* 14, no. 2 (2000): 201–21.

Lefebvre, Georges. *The French Revolution. From its Origins to 1793.* Translated by Elizabeth Moss Evanson. London and New York: Routledge, 1962.

Lehning, Arthur. *From Buonarroti to Bakunin.* Leiden: E. J. Brill, 1970.

Lehning, James R. *To be a Citizen: The Political Culture of the Early French Third Republic.* Ithaca and London: Cornel University Press, 2001.

Leslie, R. F. *Polish Politics and the Revolution of November 1830.* London: University of London, Athlone Press, 1956.

Lesure, Michel. 'Les réfugiés révolutionnaires russes à Paris. Rapport du Préfect de Police au Président de Conseil 16 décembre 1907.' *Cahiers du Monde russe et sovietique* 6, no. 3 (1965): 419–36.

Lévy, Paul. 'Les angoumoisins pendant la Grande Guerre.' *Guerres mondiales et conflits contemporains* 182 (1996): 139–48.

Lewalski, Kenneth F. 'Heroes and Aliens: Everyday Life of Polish Refugees in France During the July Monarchy.' *East European Monographs* 2 (1993): 47–68.

Lewis, Mary Dewhurst. 'The Strangeness of Foreigners: Policing Migration and Nation in Interwar Marseille.' *French Politics, Culture and Society* 20, no. 3 (2002): 65–96.

Livermore, H. V. *A New History of Portugal.* Cambridge: Cambridge University Press, 1966.

——. *Portugal. A Short History.* Edinburgh: Edinburgh University Press, 1973.

Livian, Marcel. *Le parti socialiste et l'immigration. Le gouvernement Léon Blum, la main-d'oeuvre immigrée et les réfugiés politiques (1920–1940).* Paris: Éditions Anthropos, 1982.

——. *Le régime juridique des étrangers en France.* Paris: Librairie générale de droit et de jurisprudence, 1936.

Lopez, Renée and Emile Témime. *Migrance. Histoire de l'immigration marseillaise.* 4 vols. Vol. 2. *L'expansion marseillaise et 'l'immigration italienne' (1830–1918).* Marseille: Edisud, 1990.

Lorette, J., P. Lefevre, and P. de Gryse, eds. *Actes du Colloque sur la Révolution brabançonne 13–14 octobre 1983.* Bruxelles: Musée Royal de l'Armée, 1984.

Louessard, Laurent. *La Révolution de juillet 1830.* Paris: Spartacus, 1990.

Lucas-Dubreton, J. *La royauté bourgeoise, 1830.* Paris: Hachette, 1930.

Macartney, C. A. *Refugees: The Work of the League.* London: The League of Nations Union, 1930.

Macaulay, Neill. *Dom Pedro: The Struggle for Liberty in Brazil and Portugal, 1798–1834.* Durham: Duke University Press, 1986.

Machin, Howard. 'The Prefects and Political Repression: February 1848 to December 1851.' In *Revolution and Reaction: 1848 and the Second French Republic.* Edited by Roger Price. London: Croom Helm, 1975: 280–302.

Maga, Timothy. *America, France and the European Refugee Problem (1933–1947).* New York: Gerland Publications, 1985.

——. 'Closing the Door: The French Government and Refugee Policy.' *French Historical Studies* 12 (Spring 1982): 424–42.

Mandel, Maud S. *In the Aftermath of Genocide: Armenians and Jews in Twentieth-Century France.* Durham and London: Duke University Press, 2003.

Mandelstam, André N. 'La protection international des droits de l'homme.' *Recueil des Cours de l'Académie de Droit International* 38 (1934): 125–232.

Manfredonia, Gaetano. 'Les anarchistes italiens en France dans la lutte antifasciste.' In *Les italiens en France de 1914 à 1940.* Edited by Pierre Milza. Rome: École française de Rome, 1986: 223–55.

Mansel, Philip. *Paris Between Empires, 1814–1852. Monarchy and Revolution.* London: Phoenix Press, 2001.

Marcel-Rémond, G. *L'immigration italienne dans le sud-ouest de la France.* Paris: Librairie Dalloz, 1928.

Marrus, Michael. *The Unwanted: European Refugees in the Twentieth Century.* New York and Oxford: Oxford University Press, 1985.

Marrus, Michael R. 'Vichy Before Vichy: Antisemitic Currents in France During the 1930s.' *Weiner Library Bulletin* 33 (1980): 13–19.

Marrus, Michael R. and Robert O. Paxton. *Vichy France and the Jews.* Stanford: Stanford University Press, 1981.

Marshall, Peter. *Demanding the Impossible: A History of Anarchism.* London: Fontana, 1993.

Mason, Laura, and Tracey Rizzo, eds. *The French Revolution: A Document Collection.* Boston: Houghton Mifflin, 1999.

Mathiez, Albert. *La révolution et les étrangers: cosmopolitisme et défense nationale.* Paris: La Renaissance du Livre, 1918.

Mathorez, J. *Les réfugiés politiques espagnols dans l'Orne au XIXe siècle.* Bordeaux: Feret et Fils, 1915.

——. *Notes sur les réfugiés polonais dans la Mayenne (1833–1860).* Angers: G. Grassin, 1918.

——. *Notes sur les réfugiés polonais dans la Sarthe et le Maine-et-Loire (1833–1873).* Angers: G. Grassin, 1920.

Mauco, Georges. *Les étrangers en France: Leur rôle dans l'activité économique.* Paris: Armand Colin, 1932.

McClellan, Woodford. *Revolutionary Exiles: The Russians in the First International and the Paris Commune.* London: Frank Cass, 1979.

McPhee, Peter. *The French Revolution, 1789–1799.* Oxford: Oxford University Press, 2002.

——. *A Social History of France, 1780–1880.* London and New York: Routledge, 1992.

Merriman, John. *The Margins of City Life. Explorations on the French Urban Frontier, 1815–1851.* New York and Oxford: Oxford University Press, 1991.

264   Bibliography

——. *Police Stories: Building the French State, 1815–1851*. Oxford and New York: Oxford University Press, 2006.

——. *The Agony of the Republic*. New Haven and London: Yale University Press, 1978.

Michaud, J. *Le droit d'asile en Europe et en Angleterre*. Paris: Amyot, 1858.

Michelet, Jules. *Historical View of the French Revolution, from its Earlierst Indication to the Flight of the King in 1791*. Translated by C. Cocks. London: George Bell and Sons, 1883.

Milhaud, Maurice. 'La question des réfugiés politiques. Pourquoi nous devons les accueillir.' *Cahiers des Droits de l'Homme*, 15 August 1938, 510–13.

Millet, Raymond. *Trois millions d'étrangers en France. Les indésirables, les bienvenus*. Paris: Librairie de Médicis, 1938.

Millman, Richard. *La question juive entre les deux guerres. Ligues de droite et antisémitisme en France, Collection l'ancien et le nouveau*. Paris: Armand Colin, 1992.

Milza, Olivier. 'Les Italiens dans l'économie française (1919–1939).' In *Les italiens en France de 1914 à 1940*. Edited by Pierre Milza. Rome: École française de Rome, 1986: 69–88.

Milza, Pierre. 'L'immigration italienne en France d'une guerre à l'autre: interrogations, directions de recherche et premier bilan.' In *Les italiens en France de 1914 à 1940*. Edited by Pierre Milza. Rome: École française de Rome, 1986: 1–42.

Monasse, Emmanuel. 'L'accueil et l'admission au titre de réfugié politique (1814–1848). Étude dans le département de l'Hérault.' In *Pratiques et cultures politiques dans la France contemporaine. Hommage a Raymond Huard*. Montpellier: Centre d'histoire contemporaine du Languedoc méditerranéen-Roussillon, Université Paul Valéry-Montpellier III, 1995: 197–210.

——. 'Les réfugies polonais dans la société héraultaise sous la Monarchie de juillet.' *Bulletin Centre d'Histoire contemporaine du Languedoc méditerranéen-Roussillon* 53 (1993): 3–25.

——. 'Les réfugiés politiques dans l'Hérault de 1814 à 1848: approche méthodologique.' *Annales du Midi, Revue archéologique, historique et philologique de la France méridionale* 108 (1996): 201–18.

Mondonico, Cécile. 'L'asile sous la Monarchie de juillet: Les réfugiés étrangers en France de 1830 à 1848.' École des Hautes Études en Science Sociales, 14 septembre 1995.

Mosse, Andrée. 'Où en est la question des réfugiés politiques? Ce qu'a donné l'application des décret-lois.' *Cahier des Droits de l'Homme*, 1 June 1939, 324–9.

Nivet, Philippe. *Les réfugiés français de la grande guerre. Les 'boches du nord'*. Paris: Economic, 2004.

Noiriel, Gérard. 'Difficulties in French Historical Research on Immigration.' In *Immigrants in Two Democracies: French and American Experience*. Edited by Donald L. Horowitz and Gérard Noiriel. New York and London: New York University Press, 1992: 66–79.

——. 'Français et étrangers.' In *Les lieux de mémoire*, vol.3, *Les France, 1. Conflits et partages*. Edited by Pierre Nora. Paris: Gallimard, 1992: 276–319.

——. 'Immigration: le fin mot de l'histoire.' *Vingtième Siècle: Revue d'Histoire* 5, no. ( Jan–Mar 1985): 141–50.

——. *La tyrannie du national: Le droit d'asile en Europe, 1793 à 1993*. Paris: Calman Levy, 1991.

——. *Le creuset français. Histoire de l'immigration, XIXe—XXe siècles*. Paris: Seuil, 1988.

——. *Les origines républicaines de Vichy*. Paris: Hachette, 1999.

——. 'L'identification des personnes.' In *Du papier à la biométrie. Identifier les individus*. Edited by Xavier Crettiez and Pierre Piazza. Paris: Presses de la Fondation nationale des Sicences Politiques, 2006: 29–37.

——. *Réfugiés et sans-papiers: la République face au droit d'asile, XIXe–XXe siècle*. Paris: Hachette, 1999.

——. 'Surveiller les déplacements ou identifier les personnes? Contribution à l'historie du passeport en France de la 1re à la IIIe République.' *Genèses* 30 (mars 1998): 77–100.

Nora, Pierre. 'General Introduction: Between History and Memory.' Translated by Arthur Goldhammer. In *Realms of Memory*, vol. 1. Edited by Pierre Nora. New York: Columbia University Press, 1996: 1–20.

Nowak, Joanna. 'The Elitism of Polish 1831 Émigrés.' *Polish Western Affairs* 34, no. 2 (1993): 81–91.

Nowell, Charles E. *A History of Portugal*. Princeton, NJ: D. Van Nostrand, 1952.

Nye, Robert A. *Crime, Madness and Politics in Modern France: The Medical Concept of National Decline*. Princeton: Princeton University Press, 1984.

Offen, Karen. 'Depopulation, Nationalism and Feminism in Fin-de-Siecle France.' *American Historical Review* 89, no. 3 (June 1984): 648–77.

Oliveira Ramos, Luis A. de. 'Le Portugal et la Révolution française (1777–1834).' In *Les révolutions dans le monde ibérique (1776–1834). Soulèvement national et révolution libérale: état des questions*. Edited by Christian Hermann. Bordeaux: Presses Universitaires de Bordeaux, 1989: 183–260.

Olten, Harry. *Rassemblement pour le droit d'asile*. Paris: Éditions universelles, 1936.

Oualid, William. *L'immigration ouvrière en France*. Paris: Editions de la S.A.P.E. 1927.

Ozouf, Mona. *Festivals and the French Revolution*. Trans Alan Sheridan. Cambridge MA: Harvard University Press, 1988.

Palmer, R. R. *The Age of the Democratic Revolution: A Political History of Europe and America, 1760–1800*. Princeton: Princeton University Press, 1959.

——. 'The World Revolution of the West: 1763–1801.' *Political Science Quarterly* 69, no. 1 (March 1954): 1–14.

Paon, Marcel. *l'immigration en France*. Paris: Payot, 1926.

Pasquet, Louis. *Immigration et main d'oeuvre étrangère en France*. Paris: Éditions Rieder, 1927.

Payne, Howard C. *The Police State of Louis Napoleon Bonaparte, 1851–1860*. Seattle: University of Washington Press, 1966.

Pérez, Joseph. *Histoire de l'Espagne*. Paris: Fayard, 1996.

Peschanski, Denis. *La France des camps. L'internement, 1938–1946*. Paris: Gallimard, 2002.

Phillips, Roderick. *Society, State, and Nation in Twentieth-Century Europe*. New Jersey: Prentice Hall, 1996.

Pilbeam, Pamela M. *The 1830 Revolution in France*. London: Macmillan, 1991.

——. *Republicanism in Nineteenth-Century France, 1814–1871*. London: Macmillan, 1995.

Pinkney, David H. *The French Revolution of 1830*. New Jersey: Princeton University Press, 1972.

Piotrowski, Thadée. 'Les réfugiés polonais en France sous la monarchie de Juillet.' In *Documents sur l'immigration*. Edited by L. Chevalier. Paris: Presses universitaires de France, 1947: 43–75.

Pirenne, H. *Histoire de Belgique*. Vol. 5. Bruxelles: Maurice Lamertin, 1926.

Polasky, Janet L. *Revolution in Brussels 1787–1793*. Bruxelles: Palais des Académies, 1982.

Pomper, Philip. *Peter Lavrov and the Russian Revolutionary Movement*. Chicago and London: University of Chicago Press, 1972.

Portalis, Jean-Étienne-Marie. 'Discours préliminaire au Code civil.' In *Les droits de l'homme*. Paris: Imprimerie nationale, 1801: 584–94.

Porter, Bernard. *The Refugee Question in Mid-Victorian Politics*: Cambridge University Press, 1979.

Racine, Pierre. 'Une expérience adminstrative à reprendre: Le sous-secrétariat d'état à l'immigraiton et les projets Philippe Serre.' *Esprit* 82 (July 1939): 609–19.

Rao, Anna Maria. 'Les exilés italiens et Brumaire.' *Annales historiques de la Révolution française*, no. 4 (1999): 713–25.

——. *Esuli: l'emigrazione politica italiana in Francia (1792–1802)*. Napoli: Guida, 1992.

——. 'Les républicains démocrates italiens et le Directoire.' *La République directoriales, Clermont-Ferrand* (1997): 1057–90.

——. 'Paris et les exiles italiens en 1799.' In *Paris et la Révolution*. Edited by Michel Vovelle. Paris: Publisations de la Sorbonne, 1989: 225–35.

Rapport, Michael. *Nationality and Citizenship in Revolutionary France. The Treatment of Foreigners 1789–1799*. Oxford: Clarendon Press, 2000.

Raxhon, Philippe. 'Les réfugiés Liégeois à Paris. Un état de la question.' In *Paris et la Révolution*. Edited by Michel Vovelle. Paris: Publications de la Sorbonne, 1989: 213–24.

Reale, Egidio. 'Le droit d'asile.' In *Recueil des cours de l'Académie de Droit International*. Paris: Sirey, 1938: 470–601.

——. 'Le problème des passeports.' In *Recueil des Cours de l'Académie de Droit international*. Paris: Sirey, 1934: 91–188.

Reggiani, Andres Horacio. 'Procreating France: The Politics of Demography, 1919–1945.' *French Historical Studies* 19, no. 3 (Spring 1996): 725–54.

Remarque, Erich Maria. *Flotsam*. Translated by Denver Lindley. Boston: Little, Brown and Company, 1941.

Repiton, Isabelle. *L'opinion française et les émigrés russes, à travers la litterature française de l'entre-deux-guerres*. Paris: Institute d'Études Politiques, 1986.

Reynolds, Siân. *France Between the Wars: Gender and Politics*. London and New York: Routledge, 1996.

Rials, Stéphane. *Textes constitutionnels français. Que sais-je?* Paris: Presses universitaires françaises, 1982.

Rochefontaine, D'Hector de. *Procès-verbal de l'audience solennelle de rentrée de la Cours impériale de Grenoble, 4 novembre 1861. Étude historique sur le droit d'asile*. Grenoble: A. Baratier, 1861.

Rolland, Denis. 'Extradition ou réémigration? Les vases communicants de la gestion xénophobe de réfugiés espagnols en France.' In *Exils et migration. Italiens et Espagnols en France, 1938–1946*. Edited by Pierre Milza and Denis Peschanski. Paris: Harmatton, 1994: 47–70.

Rosenberg, Clifford. 'Albert Sarraut and Republican Racial Thought.' *French Politics, Culture and Society* 20, no. 3 (2002): 97–114.

——. *Policing Paris. The Origins of Modern Immigration Control between the Wars*. Ithaca and London: Cornell University Press, 2006.

Rosendaal, Joost. 'La liberté est une garce! Les Bataves à Paris (1787–1795).' In *Remous révolutionnaires: République batave, armée française*. Edited by Annie Jourdan and Joep Leerssen. Amsterdam: Amsterdam University Press, 1996: 58–68.

——. '"Parce que j'aime la liberté, je retourne en France". Les réfugiés bataves en voyage.' In *Le voyage révolutionnaire. Actes du colloque franco-néerlandais du Bicentenaire de la Révolution française, Amsterdam, 12–13 october 1989*. Edited by Willem Frijhoff and Rudolf Dekker. Hilversum: Verloren, 1991: 37–47.

Rozzi, M. 'La Communauté arménienne à Nice entre 1919 et 1939.' *Recherches régionales*, 4 (1987): 235–49.

Rubinstein, J. L. 'The Refugee Problem.' *International Affairs* XV, no. 5 (Sept.–Oct. 1936): 716–34.

Ruddy, Francis Stephen. *International Law in the Enlightenment: The Background of Emmerich de Vattel's Le Droit des Gens*. New York: Oceana Publications, 1975.

Rule, James and Charles Tilly. 'Political Process in Revolutionary France, 1830–1832.' In *1830 in France*. Edited by John M. Merriman. New York and London: New Viewpoints, 1975: 41–85.

Sahlins, Peter. *Boundaries: The Making of France and Spain in the Pyrenees*. Berkeley: University of California Press, 1989.

——. 'The Eighteenth-Century Citizenship Revolution in France.' In *Migation Control in the North Atlantic World. The Evolution of State Practices in Europe and the United States from the French Revolution to the Inter-War Period*. Edited by Andreas Fahrmeir, Olivier Faron and Patrick Weil. New York and Oxford: Berghahn Books, 2003: 12–24.

——. *Unnaturally French: Foreign Citizens in the Old Regime and After*. Ithaca and London: Cornel University Press, 2004.

Salgas-Candoret, Emmanuelle. 'Une population face à l'exil espagnol.' In *Exils et migration. Italiens et Espagnols en France, 1938–1946*. Edited by Pierre Milza and Denis Peschanski. Paris: Harmatton, 1994: 313–20.

Sanchez Mantero, Rafael. 'L'émigration politique en France pendant le règne de Ferdinand VII.' In *Exil politique et migration économique. Espagnols et Français aux XIXe–XXe siècles*. Paris: Éditions du Centre National de la Recherche Scientifique, 1991: 17–29.

Schama, Simon. *Patriots and Liberators. Revolution in the Netherlands, 1780–1813*. New York: Vintage Books, 1977.

——. *Citizens. A Chronicle of the French Revolution*. New York: Knopf, 1989.

Schneider, William H. *Quality and Quantity. The Quest for Biological Regeneration in Twentieth-Century France*. Cambridge: Cambridge University Press, 1990.

Schor, Ralph. *Histoire de l'immigration en France de la fin du XIXe siècle à nos jours*. Paris: Armand Colin, 1996.

——. *L'antisémitisme en France pendant les années trente*. Paris: Éditions Complexe, 1992.

——. 'L'image de l'italien dans la France de l'entre-deux-guerres.' In *Les italiens en France de 1914 à 1940*. Edited by Pierre Milza. Rome: École française de Rome, 1986: 89–109.

——. 'L'opinion française et les réfugiés d'europe centrale (1933–1939).' In *De l'exile à la résistance. Réfugiés et immigrés d'europe Centrale en France, 1933–1945. Colloque international, Centre de recherche de l'Université de Paris VIII*. Paris: Presses Universitaires de Vincennes, 1986: 27–41.

——. *L'opinion française et les étrangers, 1919–1939*. Paris: Publication de la Sorbonne, 1985.

——. 'Le parti communiste et les immigrés.' *L'histoire* 35 (juin 1981): 84–6.

——. 'Les parties politiques français et le droit d'asile (1919–1939).' *Revue historique* 540 (1981): 445–59.

Schramm, Hanna and Barbara Vormeier. *Vivre à Gurs. Un camp de concentration français, 1940–1941*. Paris: Éditions François Maspero, 1979.

Simpson, Sir John Hope. *The Refugee Problem: Report of a Survey*. London: Oxford University Press, 1939.

——. *Refugees: A Review of the Situation since September 1938*. London: Oxford University Press, 1939.

Sjöberg, Tommie. *The Powers and the Persecuted: The Refugee Problem and the Intergovernmental Committee for Refugees (IGCR), 1938–1947*. Lund: Lund University Press, 1991.

Skran, Claudena. *Refugees in Interwar Europe: The Emergence of a Regime*. Oxford: Oxford University Press, 1995.

Sliwowska, Wiktoria. 'Naissance de l'émigration politique russe.' *Acta Poloniae Historica* 25 (1972): 33–56.

Soboul, Albert. *The French Revolution, 1787–1799: From the Storming of the Bastille to Napoleon.* Translated by Alan Forrest and Colin Jones. New York: Vintage Books, 1975.

Sokolnicki, Michel. *Les origines de l'émigration polonaise en France (1831–32).* Paris: Alea, 1910.

Soldan, Charles. *L'extradition des criminels politiques.* Paris: E. Thorin, 1882.

Sowerwine, Charles. *France since 1870: Culture, Politics and Society.* New York: Palgrave Macmillan, 2001.

Stein, Louis. *Beyond Death and Exile: The Spanish Republicans in France, 1939–1955.* Cambridge, MA: Harvard University Press, 1979.

Stoessinger, John George. *The Refugee and the World Community.* Minneapolis: University of Minnesota Press, 1956.

Straszewska, Maria. '"La cause polonaise" de 1830 dans la poésie et le théâtre français.' In *Pologne, l'Insurrection de 1830–1831, sa réception en Europe (Actes du colloque organisé les 14 et 15 mai 1981 par le Centre d'etude de la Culture Polonaise de l'Université de Lille III)*, edited by Daniel Beauvois. Lille: Université de Lille III, 1982: 67–84.

Taguieff, Pierre-André. 'Face à l'immigration: mixophobie, xénophobie ou sélection. Un débat français dans l'entre-deux-guerres.' *Vingtième siècle* 47 (July–September 1995): 103–31.

Te Brake, Wayne P. 'Popular Politics in the Dutch Patriot Revolution.' *Theory and Society* 14, no. 2 (March 1985): 199–222.

——. 'Provincial Histories and National Revolution in the Dutch Republic.' In *The Dutch Republic in the Eighteenth Century: Decline, Enlightenment, and Revolution.* Edited by Margaret C. Jacob and Wijnand W. Mijnhardt. Ithaca and London: Cornell University Press, 1992: 60–90.

Témime, Emile. 'Espagnols et Italiens en France.' In *Exils et migration. Italiens et Espagnols en France, 1938–1946.* Edited by Pierre Milza and Denis Peschanski. Paris: Harmattan, 1994: 19–34.

Thalmann, Rita. 'L'immigration allemande et l'opinion publique en France de 1933 à 1936.' In *La France et l'Allemagne, 1932–1936. Communications présentée au Colloque Franco-Allemand tenu à Paris du 10 au 12 mars 1977.* Paris: Éditions du Centre National de la Recherche Scientific, 1980: 149–72.

——. 'L'immigration de IIIe Reich en France, 1933–1939.' *Le monde juif* (octobre 1979): 127–39.

Thompson, Dorothy. *Refugees: Anarchy or Organisation.* New York: New York Times, 1938.

Tombs, Robert. *France 1814–1914.* London and New York: Longman, 1996.

Torpey, John. *The Invention of the Passport: Surveillance, Citizenship and the State.* Cambridge: Cambridge University Press, 2000.

Unger, Harlow Giles. *Lafayette.* Hoboken, NJ: Wiley, 2002.

Urrutia, Louis. 'Les Espagnols carlistes ou isabelinos au Pays Basque français.' In *Exil politique et migration économique. Espagnols et Français aux XIXe—XXe siècles.* Paris: Éditions du Centre National de la Recherche Scientifique, 1991: 53–9.

Van Sas, Nicolaas C. F. 'The Patriot Revolution: New Perspectives.' In *The Dutch Republic in the Eighteenth Century: Decline, Enlightenment, and Revolution.* Edited by Margaret C. Jacob and Wijnand W. Mijnhardt. Ithaca and London: Cornell University Press, 1992: 91–122.

Vauchelle-Haquet, Aline, and Gérard Dufour. 'Les Espagnols naturalisés français et les Espagnols ayant obtenu l'autorisation de fixer leur domicile en France de 1814 à 1831.' In *Exil politique et migration économique. Espagnols et Français aux XIXe—XXe siècles.* Paris: Éditions du Centre National de la Recherche Scientifique, 1991: 31–51.

Verneuil, Henri. '588 Rue Paradis.' France: TF1, 1991.

——. 'Mayrig.' France: TF1, 1991.

——. *Mayrig.* Paris: Robert Laffont, 1985.

Vial, Éric. 'Le casellario politico centrale. Source pour l'histoire de l'émigration politique.' In *Les italiens en France de 1914 à 1940.* Edited by Pierre Milza. Rome: École française de Rome, 1986: 155–67.

Vidalenc, Jean. 'La main-d'oeuvre étrangère en France et la première guerre mondiale (1901–1926).' In *Francia. Forschungen zur westeuropeäischen Gerschichte.* München: Artemis Verlag Zürich und München, 1975: 524–50.

Viet, Vincent. *La France immigrée. Construction d'une politique, 1914–1997.* Paris: Fayard, 1998.

Wahnich, Sophie. *L'impossible citoyen. L'étranger dans le discours de la Révolution française.* Paris: Albin Michel, 1997.

Walker, Christopher J. 'Armenian Refugees: Accidents of Diplomacy or Victims of Ideology?' In *Refugees in the Age of Total War.* Edited by Anna C. Bramwell. London: Unwin Hyman, 1988: 38–50.

Wallon, Henri. *Du droit d'asyle.* Paris: E.-J. Bailly, 1837.

Waquet, Simone. 'Les polonais de l'exil dans la Nièvre (1832–1880).' *Actes de 54ème congrès de l'Association Bourguignonne des Société savantes, 10–12 juin 1983* (1985).

Weil, Patrick. 'Espagnols et Italiens en France: la politique de la France.' In *Exils et migration. Italiens et Espagnols en France, 1938–1946.* Edited by Pierre Milza and Denis Peschanski. Paris: Harmatton, 1994: 87–110.

——. *La France et ses étrangers.* Paris: Gallimard, 1991.

——. *Qu'est qu'un Français. Histoire de la nationalité française depuis la Révolution.* Paris: Grasset, 2002.

——. 'Racisme et discrimination dans la politique française de l'immigration, 1938–1945/1974–1995.' *Vingtième siècle* 47 ( July–September 1995): 77–102.

Weinberg, David H. *A Community on Trial: The Jews of Paris in the 1930s.* Chicago and London: University of Chicago Press, 1977.

Wenden, Catherine Wihtol de. 'Réfugié politique: une notion en crise?' *Esprit* (mai 1990): 73–86.

Winock, Michel. *Nationalism, Anti-Semitism, and Fascism in France.* Translated by Jane Marie Todd. Stanford, CA: Stanford University Press, 1998.

Woodcock, George. *Anarchism: A History of Libertarian Ideas and Movements.* Harmondsworth: Penguin Books, 1962.

Wright, Gordon. *France in Modern Times: From the Enlightenment to the Present.* 4th ed. New York: Norton, 1987.

Zamoyski, Adam. *Holy Madness: Romantics, Patriots and Revolutionaries, 1776–1871.* London: Weidenfeld and Nicholson, 1999.

Zawadzki, W. H. *A Man of Honour: Adam Czartoryski as a Statesman of Russia and Poland, 1795–1831.* Oxford and New York: Clarendon Press, 1993.

# Index